teach yourself...

PowerPoint for Windows 95

Tom Badgett

A subsidiary of
Henry Holt and Company, Inc.

a subsidiary of Henry Holt and Company, Inc.
115 West 18th Street
New York, New York 10011

First Edition—1995

Author:	Badgett, Tom.
Title:	Teach yourself-- PowerPoint for Windows 95 / by Tom Badgett.
Published:	New York : MIS:Press, 1995.
Description:	p. cm.
LC Call No.:	T385 .B28 1995
Dewey No.:	006.6/869 20
ISBN:	1-55828-442-7
Subjects:	Microsoft PowerPoint for Windows. Computer graphics.
Control No.:	95038337

Associate Publisher: *Paul Farrel*

Managing Editor: *Cary Sullivan*

Development Editor: *Debra Williams-Cauley*

Copy Edit Manager: *Shari Chappell*

Technical Editor: *Bud Paulding*

Copy Editor: *Annette Develin*

Acknowledgments

My name is on the front of this book, but I couldn't have written this book alone.

I'd like to thank my patient and flexible editor, Debra Williams-Cauley, who managed short deadlines and beta software with apparent ease.

The technical and copy editors and page layout people take my raw text and turn it into something you can read. Thanks for these chores go to Bud Paulding, Annette Devlin, and Patty Wallenburg. And, thanks to MIS:Press for publishing the book and getting it to you.

I hope you'll study the color section of this book carefully. These images come from a variety of creative and talented people whose companies include:

Projections
8044 Ray Mears Boulevard, #110
Knoxville, TN 37919
615-691-1698

JP Hogan and Company
109 W. Fifth Avenue
Knoxville, TN 37917
615-546-7661

Economic Development Group
PO Box 121613
Nashville, TN 37212

Ackerman Public Relations Slide
Ackerman Public Relations and Marketing
1111 Northshore Drive
Knoxville, TN 379
615-584-0550

Finally, thank you, the readers of this book, for buying it. Your comments and suggestions are welcome at:

Internet:	tbadgett@usit.net
CompuServe:	74777,112
MCI Mail:	tbadgett

TABLE OF CONTENTS

Chapter 4—Using PowerPoint Templates, Clip Art, and Wizards 91

INTRODUCTION

Microsoft PowerPoint for Windows 95 is either a powerful standalone presentation application or one of many powerful tools contained in the Microsoft Office for Windows 95 suite. However you view PowerPoint, if your software needs include the ability to construct graphics and text slides for screen presentation or projection, PowerPoint for Windows 95 is a good choice for getting the job done.

What is PowerPoint?

PowerPoint helps you create a variety of presentation tools, from relatively simple on-screen (using the computer) slide shows, to a full portfolio of materials including overhead projection slides, audience handouts, speaker outlines or notes, 35mm slides, and more. You could also use PowerPoint to construct accent sheets for a printed company report—title pages, graphs, text charts and lists, scanned images, and photographs—but the program's forte is presentation materials.

PowerPoint for Windows 95 is also designated PowerPoint version 7, perhaps to match with Microsoft Word 7, the version of Word that ships with Office 95. Throughout this book when I mention PowerPoint, I mean the current version—PowerPoint for Windows 95 or PowerPoint version 7. From here on, I will refer to this product as simply PowerPoint. This version of PowerPoint maintains the Office tradition of offering the look and feel of other Office applications, especially the word processor Microsoft Word. From the menu to the toolbar to the pop-up Tip of the Day, PowerPoint is very Word-like in appearance and function. Indeed, this latest version of PowerPoint is an even more integral part of the Office suite than its predecessor. You'll see more of this as we go along.

There are some obvious differences between PowerPoint and Word. One difference is the way PowerPoint handles graphics files. Because PowerPoint is designed from the start as a presentation package, there is strong support for clip art (a significant resource supplied with the program), graphics files, text charting, and more. But as a Word user you will find a lot of familiar ground to travel with this program. If you're not a Word user, you still will find PowerPoint easy to learn and use. I'll show you more in this chapter and in the next one that should convince you of that idea, so read on.

The Highlights of PowerPoint for Windows 95

PowerPoint for Windows 95 has several enhancements over version 4.0, but it also remains read-compatible with previous versions all the way back to 2.x. Beginning with Version 4.0, PowerPoint added a number of features to enhance functionality and to make the program easier to learn and to use. Some of these features are very obvious—such as the Tip of the Day, part of the online Help system that displays every time you start PowerPoint—and some are more subtle. While a number of smaller enhancements, changes, and improvements are included in this version, I will discuss them later in the book. The features that I've listed below are highlights of the current PowerPoint release.

General Office 95 Features

This version of Office offers a number of general enhancements that improve the way individual components operate, and that also improve the way the members of the Office suite work together.

AutoCorrect

AutoCorrect corrects misspellings automatically. It also can be configured to serve as a shortcut to inserting repetitive information—such as a company name or logo. You can insert virtually anything into the AutoCorrect lookup table. A simple icon click inserts the data you want.

Spell It

Spell It is an enhancement that corrects misspellings on the fly. Unlike the standard spell check or AutoCorrect that require you to choose a menu item or click an icon to start them up, Spell It is live while you type. This utility identifies misspellings with an underline as soon as the word is typed. You can stop immediately and look up the correct spelling, or you can wait until you have finished a section or the entire presentation before clicking the right mouse button over the flagged word to look up the spelling.

Office Binders

Binders let you merge data from multiple Office applications into a single file. Once the documents are in the Binder, you can edit, store, print, or distribute them as a single file. You can place a PowerPoint file in the Binder with Word and Excel data, for example, then share it all with other users or edit it as a group.

New Templates

When you create a new presentation file you are given the option of using one of PowerPoint's professional templates as a starting point. Templates let you start with a creative design, then add your own ideas to build the final presentation.

Find Fast

Especially in a networking environment with multiple users, it can be difficult to keep track of all of the files you need to use or edit. The Find Fast utility uses high performance indexing tools to manage and organize files. When you type a word or phrase into the File Finder, all files that contain this data are quickly listed.

Auto Clip Art

Creative clip art can enhance your PowerPoint presentation. Now the Auto Clip Art feature can help you choose what clip art to use. After the presentation is complete, you can call up this automatic feature to scan the file and suggest appropriate clip art from the PowerPoint gallery.

Click here...

PowerPoint includes a number of preconfigured templates and slide designs. When you select them from a graphics window, PowerPoint presents a dummy design on the screen. With most of these dummy slides the sections reserved for text have a simple prompt that reads, "Click here to add text." When you position the mouse pointer over this prompt and press the left mouse button once, the prompt text is removed. Now the insertion point is positioned inside the text field so that you can type your own text for this section of the slide. PowerPoint will automatically adjust the font and text attributes according to the design of the screen.

Other text prompts ask for specific information: "Click to add title," for example. And, when the slide includes a place for clip art, you're prompted to "Double-click here to add clip art." A small clip art image accompanies this prompt to make sure you understand. This simple concept can help you create a whole series of slides very quickly, especially if you have done a little design work on your presentation before you start creating the illustrations with PowerPoint.

Clip Art Selector and Viewer

This version of PowerPoint is supplied with a large and varied collection of clip art images. In early versions, to choose a clip art image you had to scan an on-screen list of file names and pick the one you wanted from the list. That works, but even when the names are fairly descriptive, with thousands of choices it can be difficult to locate what you want.

Beginning with PowerPoint 4.0 you can select clip art images from a ClipArt Gallery display. Images are organized into categories, such as Academic, Backgrounds, Cartoons, and so on. When you choose the category, postage stamp-sized images from that group are displayed on the screen. You can scroll through this visual list to find the clip art that you want to use. Figure I.1 shows what this screen looks like.

Customizable Toolbars

Toolbars help you conduct many PowerPoint operations. The program is configured with nine toolbars (some common to Office and other Office applications) that contain common tasks, but you can use the Customize Toolbars dialog box to add, move, or delete the toolbar buttons. Again, if you are familiar with Word, the toolbars supplied with PowerPoint will be easy to learn. Many of the buttons you use in Word are also used in PowerPoint. The Customize Toolbars dialog box groups buttons by task (File, Edit, View, and so on) and displays buttons for each of the menu choices under these main headings. You can use the mouse to drag and drop buttons where you want them.

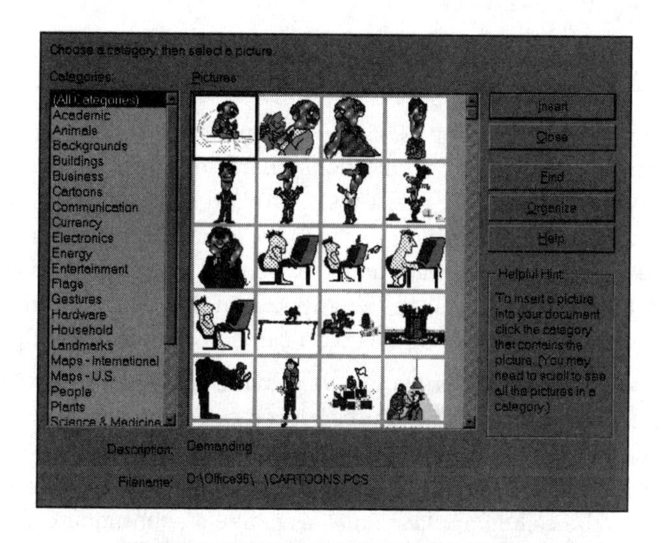

Figure I.1 *ClipArt Gallery main screen.*

Direct Mail

Computing today has come full circle. When I first started working with computers in the mid 1970s, each user connected to a central machine through a serial terminal. We shared disk space, printers, programs, memory, and mail. Then along came the PC. Users sought the power, speed, and privacy of their own personal machine. Now we're getting back together. Products such as Windows for Workgroups, a Microsoft Windows environment that networks machines, let individual users share disk and printer resources and exchange mail.

PowerPoint includes a link to network mail so you can stick an electronic routing slip onto a PowerPoint presentation and send it across the network to one or more addresses. This lets you show other people what you're working on, send interesting mail with clip art or text charts, or ship works in progress around the company for help from different people.

Graph Generator

You can use a separate graphing application within PowerPoint to enter data and draw graphs. This application also is available in Word. While this utility won't replace a full-featured spreadsheet, it works well for simple graph data for visual comparisons, and it removes the requirement that you have Excel installed to use graphs with PowerPoint.

OLE 2.0 Support

Object inking and embedding (OLE) is an important feature in the Windows environment. It lets different applications share information through real-time, "live" links. With OLE 2.0, the latest OLE standard, it is easier to share information among applications, and you can use the current application (PowerPoint, in this case) as the user interface into the remote program. With the previous version of OLE you had to launch the application that contained the linked data before you could edit it. With OLE 2.0 you can edit remote data in place.

PowerPoint also uses this feature to provide another interesting capability: linking. With a PowerPoint link you can insert special icons on your slides that are linked to another presentation or presentation segment. If you click on a HyperLink icon, the linked presentation is launched. When it is completed, you are returned to the calling application. This is like a subroutine call (for you programmers) that can make it easier to create presentation modules for use across a wide range of presentations. For example, you could create a short sequence of slides that illustrates the current sales activity for a specific product. Then you could call this sequence from within a sales promotion presentation, an annual report, a sales strategy session, or wherever this data is applicable.

Report It Word Link

As mentioned earlier, PowerPoint is well-integrated with Microsoft Word and other Office applications. Right on the PowerPoint toolbar is a Report It icon that launches Word automatically and inserts the outline from the current presentation as a Word document. This is done by converting the outline to an RTF (rich text format) document before it is loaded into Word. You can use the full features of Word to edit and format the outline, then return it to PowerPoint.

Tip of the Day

An addition to the PowerPoint Help system, the Tip of the Day dialog box pops up when you first launch the program. The random tips offer suggestions on how to do various PowerPoint tasks. You can disable the automatic Tip of the Day, or you can use the Help menu to display the Tip dialog box at any time.

Once the dialog box is on the screen, you can step through a series of tip screens if you wish.

ToolTips

Icon-based toolbars are nice, but the newer applications are so complex that it can be difficult to remember what the little pictures mean. And, if you are using a high resolution screen (say, 1,024 x 768 resolution) and you're already myopic from years of sitting in front of glowing screens, you can't always see the pictures anyway.

That's where ToolTips comes in. In PowerPoint, when you place the mouse pointer over one of the toolbar icons, a pop-up yellow note bar tells you what the tool does. If you already know the tool you're about to use, the ToolTips display won't bother you because there is a slight delay between the time you point to the icon and when the ToolTips text pops up. That way, you can step through tools without any interference from the pop-up text if you wish. On the other hand, if you need a little help remembering what a specific tool does, simply place the pointer over the icon and wait about a second.

Wizards

A *Wizard* is Microsoft's buzzword for a built-in, interactive macro that helps you conduct software operations. For example, the Pack & Go Wizard helps you put together a package of PowerPoint data for copying to your laptop. The illustration in Figure I.2 shows how this Wizard looks.

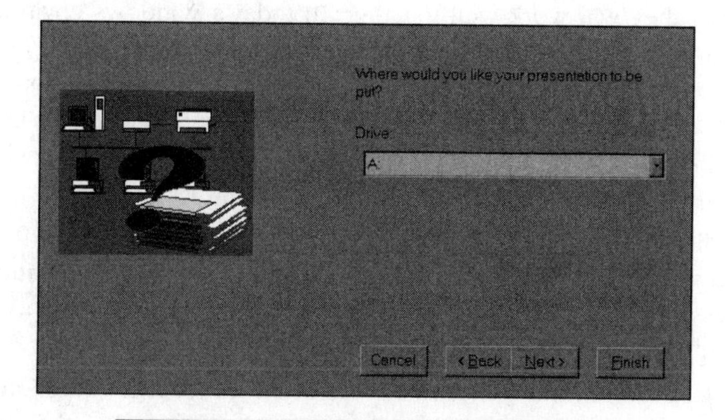

Figure I.2 *Typical Wizard interactive screen.*

In general, however, this version of PowerPoint contains built-in design and operational features that don't need Wizards. The automatic configuration features of PowerPoint appear more a part of the program itself instead of add-on Wizards.

Why Use PowerPoint?

The question "Why use PowerPoint?" involves two issues. The first is, What is the application for PowerPoint, how will it help you in your business or personal life, what jobs can it make easier or more professional? The second is, Why use PowerPoint instead of Lotus Freelance, Harvard Graphics, or other graphics and presentation applications?

Let's look at the second question first. There are many similarities among the top presentation programs on the market today. I don't want to get into a blow-by-blow dissection of each package or a strength vs. limitations argument here. Depending on your perspective, each of the current offerings can be the best for different applications. There are some obvious reasons to choose PowerPoint over another application, however.

The main argument in favor of PowerPoint is that if you are already using Microsoft Word or another of the Office applications, you are familiar with Microsoft's approach to software design and user interface. You can move into PowerPoint from Word very easily. The screens look quite similar and, in fact, some of the utilities and features from Word are also a part of PowerPoint.

By sticking with the products of a single vendor you can be reasonably assured that they will work well together. In today's Windows environment it is increasingly important to be able to share information among different programs. Besides, if you bought Microsoft's Office suite of software so you could use Word and Excel, for example, you already have PowerPoint as part of the package. It is like getting another application free. Why buy another package when you have this one?

In addition, this latest Office—designed to work with Windows 95—is better integrated with the operating environment than earlier products written for previous versions of Windows. This is a strong argument in favor of the PowerPoint/Windows 95 combination package.

Now let's look at the "What can PowerPoint do for me?" question. If you've read the first part of this introduction you can see some of the applications already. This is a presentation package that is designed to support you in preparing stand-up presentations or moderated slide shows as an aid in conveying information to an audience. I suppose you could use it for a user-conducted, interactive presentation with the HyperLink feature, but this is not what PowerPoint is designed to do. It doesn't include enough checks and branching features to make it a strong player in this application area.

You shouldn't look at PowerPoint as only a formal presentation builder. Anytime you are presenting information to someone else, whether it is to a large group or one-on-one to your boss or coworker, this software can help you organize your own thoughts and present ideas in a professional manner. It is much easier to generate simple comparison graphs with PowerPoint than with Excel or 1-2-3, for example. So if you want to sit down to discuss sales figures or cost projections with someone, you can key the figures into the PowerPoint graph generator quickly and easily to produce a professional graph of this information.

The predesigned screens and Wizards help you step through a presentation design so you can make sure you have thought of all the components you need; then PowerPoint helps you build a presentation with professional-looking slides or illustrations. PowerPoint isn't for everybody, but an awful lot of us have it as part of the Microsoft Office suite. Don't automatically write it off because you never give stand-up presentations in the board room. It is equally useful for less formal, short presentations from office planning discussions to homework assignments.

About This Book

This is just one of a whole series of books in the *Teach Yourself...* line from MIS:Press. The intent is for this book to do just what the title implies. It will help you teach yourself how to use PowerPoint. You can approach this task from a number of perspectives. One that will get you up and running with PowerPoint very fast is to take the Weekend Tour that begins in Chapter 2, either as the first thing you do after reading this introduction or after you at least browse Getting Started (Chapter 1). There is enough information in these two chapters alone to help you achieve a fairly high degree of expertise with PowerPoint in a relatively short period of time.

In addition, there is a chapter on designing presentations that should help you get the most out of PowerPoint, and there is plenty of information on using the program and its features. For a quick look at what else is in the book, look at the section What's in this Book later in the introduction.

Conventions We Use

Before we get started, let's agree on some terms and ways of doing things. I'll try to keep the format of this book as simple and as straightforward as possible while, at the same time, making clear the various commands, files, and structures we need to discuss.

First of all, in addition to plain text, throughout this book you'll find icons (small pictures) designed to draw your attention to certain sections. When you see the Note icon, you know we have special information that applies to the main text in that area, and that we feel is important enough to point out.

Beyond that, we have other ways of presenting data in this book that can guide you toward understanding:

- New terms are italicized. These are words we are introducing for the first time and likely will use later in the book. You probably also will find them described in the glossary.
- Keystrokes, file names, commands, and specific options are presented in boldface. Information you enter from the keyboard is shown in boldface, but you won't enter everything you see in boldface. We'll tell you specifically when to type something on the keyboard.
- The individual PowerPoint presentation elements are called slides in this book, even if you may use these elements in ways other than for a slide show. This is a good, general term that describes the screens you design with the software.

In addition, I assume you are reasonably familiar with Microsoft Windows and that you are at least conversant with the major features of Windows 95. I may offer some hints to show you better or easier ways to do some Windows 95–specific tasks, but in general I assume you are familiar with the Windows 95 user interface so that, for example, if I say click on something you know what that means. You should also know the difference between click and double-click, and you should know how to pull down menus and how to manipulate dialog boxes. (However, I will give you a short Windows 95 refresher in Chapter 1, mainly so we can agree on terms and procedures.)

What's in this Book

I've already hinted at some of the things I'll cover in this book. Here is more detail on what you will find.

In **Chapter 1**, I'll help you get started with PowerPoint by showing you the major features of the PowerPoint screen and the user interface.

Chapter 2 gives you a Weekend Tour of PowerPoint. This is a way to read about and try most of the major features of PowerPoint in a relatively short period of time (you don't have to work on PowerPoint over the weekend if you don't want to!). If you study this chapter and try the exercises I suggest, you'll come away with a fairly firm grasp on what PowerPoint can do and how to do it. After that, you can use the other areas of the book for reference and to refine the skills you learned in this chapter.

As I mentioned earlier in this introduction, using PowerPoint to create presentation support slides is relatively easy. The harder part may be learning how to design presentations in the first place. The object of this book is to teach you PowerPoint, but in **Chapter 3** I'll also give you some hints on designing presentations for PowerPoint.

PowerPoint is full of preformed templates and slides, Wizards, and other sub-applications to help you build presentations. In **Chapter 4**, you will learn how to use PowerPoint templates, clip art, and Wizards. You will use some of these features whenever you use PowerPoint, even as part of the exercises in the Weekend Tour and in the Getting Started section, but this chapter gives you additional detail.

One useful and fairly easy application for PowerPoint is to design a speech or other presentation around slides you can show from your computer. You can use the standard computer screen if the group is small, or you can project the images for a large group presentation. **Chapter 5** shows you how to use PowerPoint to create computer slide shows.

Chapter 6, Printing from PowerPoint, offers some hints on producing printed output from PowerPoint. Your printer can produce outlines, speaker notes, audience handouts, or presentation samples. You'll learn how to configure your printer and how to print these portions of a PowerPoint presentation in this chapter.

In addition to straight printing, you may want to create other types of presentation material with PowerPoint. In **Chapter 7**, I'll show you about creating presentation output with PowerPoint. This might include 35mm slides, overhead projector foils, or video.

Among the strong features of PowerPoint is its high level of integration with other Microsoft products. In **Chapter 8**, I'll show you how PowerPoint fits in with other products in the Microsoft Office suite of applications.

It may seem strange, but "help on help" can be quite useful. The PowerPoint Help facility is powerful and includes many features that you can use but which may need a little introduction. In **Chapter 9**, I'll describe the features of PowerPoint Help and show you how to use them.

Finally, there are two appendices and a glossary in this book. Appendix A discusses some of the hardware issues around using PowerPoint, and Appendix B serves as a useful command reference to PowerPoint.

To Sum Up

One way to look at PowerPoint is as a focused word processor. Much, if not most, of the functionality of PowerPoint is already included in many word processors such as Microsoft Word. You can insert text fields, partition screens, include clip art, video, or sound, produce graphs, and more. The difference between PowerPoint and Word, however, is that PowerPoint screens are preformatted, making design a lot easier. In addition, the clip art supplied with PowerPoint offers more variety than is included with the Word package, and the clip art viewer makes it a lot easier to use.

As part of Microsoft's newest Office suite, PowerPoint helps demonstrate the next phase of software that includes common user interfaces, common features, tight integration, and single-vendor packages. You may not find that PowerPoint answers all of your presentation needs, but it will go a long way in helping you produce professional, understandable presentations. I hope the hints and guidance in this book help you get the most out of this package.

—Tom Badgett
Knoxville, TN

CHAPTER 1

Getting Started

Everything has to start somewhere. Your beginning with PowerPoint may have come as you installed the Microsoft Office suite of products or when you decided you needed a presentation product and chose this one, or you may be beginning with PowerPoint with this book.

Whatever your status with PowerPoint, this chapter is a good starting point or a good place to refresh your memory if you already have a little experience with this software.

What is PowerPoint?

PowerPoint is a Microsoft Windows- and Windows 95–based presentation package. It is a standalone product, but most notably is an integral part of the Microsoft Office suite. Prior to Office 95—the Microsoft Office suite designed as a companion to Windows 95—the current version of PowerPoint was 4.0. PowerPoint for Office 95 is version 7, presumably a plan by Microsoft to bring PowerPoint into line with the current Microsoft Word offering, which is version 7.0 in the Office 95 suite.

You will use PowerPoint to design and build slides to support a variety of presentations. It is a good tool for preparing a series of overhead projector foils, producing 35mm slides, printing title or accent pages for a company report, preparing computer-based slide shows, and more.

If you've never used presentation software, you'll be pleased at how easy PowerPoint is to learn. If you have some experience with presentation software, you'll find a lot to like here. PowerPoint's built-in slide designs, interactive Wizards, Auto Clip Art, and formatting tools can make the job go faster, help make sure your designs are complete, and help keep your presentations consistent.

PowerPoint and Windows 95

PowerPoint is designed for the Microsoft Windows 95 environment and carries many features of other Microsoft products, especially Word 7. As a Windows product, PowerPoint is easy to learn and has a user interface that is consistent with other Windows applications. In addition, when you use software that is fully Windows-compliant, you gain the benefit of interoperability through *OLE* (object linking and embedding). PowerPoint, like most of Microsoft's latest Windows applications, supports an advanced object-linking protocol that makes it fairly easy to share data among different applications.

PowerPoint and Other Microsoft Software

OLE is only one of the features of PowerPoint made possible by the Windows environment. Because Microsoft is interested in making the learning curve for PowerPoint as short as possible, the company has designed it to look and act like its other products and to work well with them.

From a screen appearance standpoint, PowerPoint is closer to Microsoft Word 7 (Word for Windows 95) than to anything else. See Figures 1.1 and 1.2 for a comparison of the two opening screens. As you can see, PowerPoint 7 and Word 7 look very similar.

(Your versions of these screens may look a little different from these figures, depending on optional settings and your Windows display configuration.) Obviously this kind of interface consistency makes the transition from one product to another extremely easy. Many of the tool buttons you find in Word are also available in PowerPoint. And, even when the actual menu selections aren't the same, the main menu titles are similar. Both products have File, Edit, View, Insert, Format, and Tools menus, and the Format bars of the two products are very similar, when you look at software screens with documents loaded.

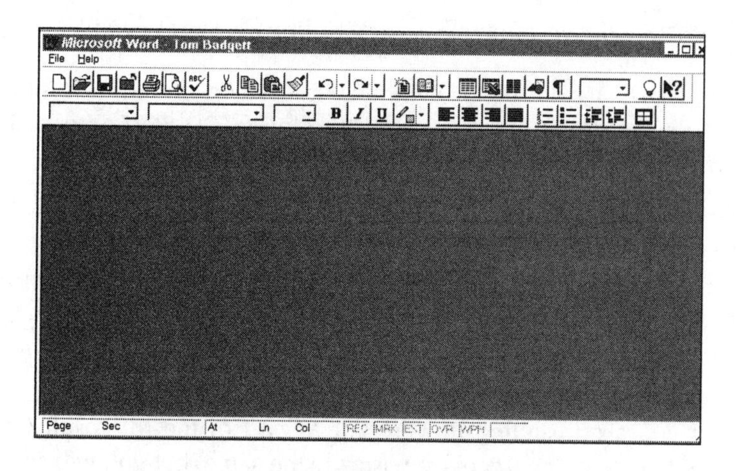

Figure 1.1 *Microsoft Word 7 opening screen.*

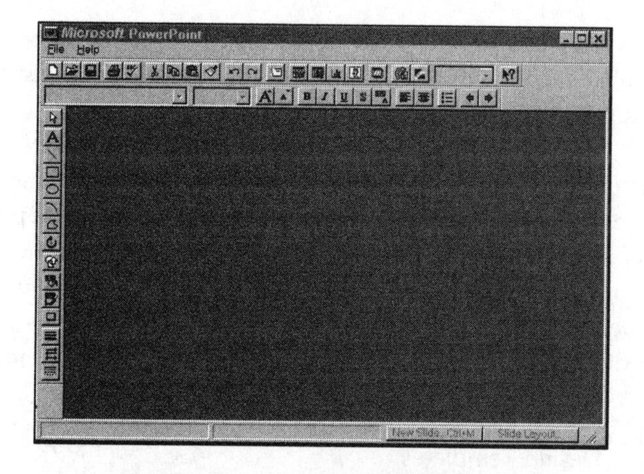

Figure 1.2 *PowerPoint 7 opening screen.*

These two applications are also linked in ways other than through OLE. For example, when you want to edit a PowerPoint presentation outline, you can click on a **Report It** icon on the toolbar to launch Word and load the outline. When you are finished, you can exit Word and return to PowerPoint.

Installing PowerPoint

Installing PowerPoint is a simple process that resembles the installation of any other Windows-compliant program. The basic process is listed below:

1. Insert Disk 1 from the PowerPoint distribution diskette set into one of the floppy drives, or place the distribution CD-ROM into a CD-ROM drive.
2. From the task bar, click on **Start** and choose to pop-up the Run dialog box.
3. In the Command Line: field of this dialog box, type **a:\setup** (or **b:\setup** if you placed the diskette in the b: drive) and press **Enter** or click on **OK**. The initial Setup screen is displayed.

NOTE

If you are installing PowerPoint as part of the Microsoft Office 95 suite, the initial process is basically the same, but you will see screens that deal with all of the Office applications, not just PowerPoint.

4. Accept Setup's defaults of directory and components to be installed, or customize the installation as required. Select the type of installation from the Installation Type dialog box.

PowerPoint Setup is similar to all Windows installation programs, so this part of the setup process should be straightforward. If you choose the **Typical** installation, there isn't much for you to do except insert new diskettes when Setup calls for them. If you select **Complete/Custom** installation, then you can choose which components of the software you want to install. Choose this option if you want to save disk space or make other custom choices in your installation of PowerPoint. Setup gives you the following options:

Design Templates	4577K
Presentation Translators	498K
Genigraphics Wizard & GraphicsLink	450K
PowerPoint Viewer	1633K
Help for Microsoft PowerPoint	1425K
Microsoft PowerPoint Program Files	9024K

For the most complete installation, choose all of these options. That way you won't have to use Setup again to add or remove components, and you won't be surprised or frustrated when you try to do something that PowerPoint supports but you didn't install. Of course if you don't have enough disk space to install everything, specify what you have room for; you can always add and remove components with Setup later if necessary.

PowerPoint Files and File Management

When you install PowerPoint you have the option of accepting Setup's default directory of `C:\Powerpnt`, or you can specify another directory of your choice. Once you have specified the main directory for PowerPoint files, Setup creates additional directories under this main directory for Setup and Template files. You don't make this choice.

Setup also creates additional directories under the MSAPPS directory under your Windows directory. If you are using other Microsoft applications, the MSAPPS directory already exists. If not, PowerPoint Setup will create it for you.

The following section is a brief discussion of the various file groups that you can select as part of the PowerPoint installation.

Design Templates

PowerPoint *templates* are professional presentation designs that you can use as a starting point for your own presentations. If you don't install templates, you can still fully use PowerPoint, but the designs you use will be solely your own.

Presentation Translators

Most programs like PowerPoint include built-in conversion utilities to import data from and export data to other applications. If you don't install these files you may not be able to import data from external applications. If you do install these files, you should be able to share text and graphics files easily with most major applications.

Genigraphics Wizard and GraphicsLink

This set of utilities lets you prepare presentations for transmission to Genigraphics Company to make 35mm slides or color overhead foils. This type of capability is increasingly common with presentation software. Genigraphics is only one of several companies that offer this type of slide preparation service.

PowerPoint Viewer

The PowerPoint *Viewer* is a standalone presentation program that lets you load and display a presentation generated with PowerPoint. Using the Viewer alone, you can display PowerPoint presentations without the full-sized PowerPoint program being installed. You cannot edit or create presentations with the Viewer, but you can load and present them.

Help for Microsoft PowerPoint

Chances are that you'll want the online Help files in addition to the program files. These files give you access to online Help and the electronic manual, the pop-up Cue Cards that offer hints on designing presentations, and a hands-on tutorial. I don't recommend that you try to install PowerPoint without these files.

Microsoft PowerPoint Program Files

You can't run PowerPoint without these files. On the other hand, you *can* make a very basic installation by installing just these program files. There would be a lot you couldn't do if this was all you installed, but you could run the program. You might want to use this choice if you have limited disk space and only need the bare bones.

A Quick Windows and PowerPoint Primer

Before you can use PowerPoint effectively you should be thoroughly familiar with the Microsoft Windows environment. I can't teach you all there is to know about Windows within a short section of a book about PowerPoint, but it might be a good idea for you to scan this section, even if you are an experienced Windows user. That way we can agree on terms and processes. That'll make it easier for you to understand my instructions about using Windows-based PowerPoint features.

The Windows Screen

Microsoft Windows 95 provides a graphical user interface for your computer data and applications. The main Windows 95 interface is the *Desktop screen*, which consists of several application windows (the exact number depends on how many applications you have installed). Inside each application window is a group of icons that represent programs or utilities within that application group.

Figure 1.3 shows a Windows 95 Desktop screen with basic components, including the Microsoft Office Shortcut toolbar. If you are not running Office, your desktop won't look just like this. And, of course, the Windows 95 Desktop is very dynamic. You can insert shortcuts and other objects to customize your operating environment. The sample in Figure 1.3 is just one possibility.

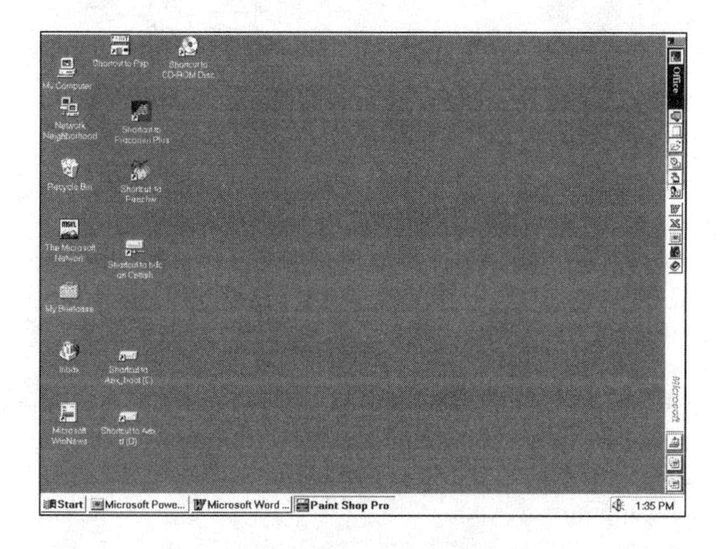

Figure 1.3 *Windows 95 Desktop with Office Shortcut toolbar.*

When you install a new application such as PowerPoint inside Windows 95, the Setup or Install program may create an application window, if it is a standard Windows program, and it will insert an entry onto the Start bar so you can access the program easily.

Once the Windows 95 Desktop is displayed, you can start PowerPoint by clicking on the **Start** button at the bottom of the screen, selecting the **Program** entry to display a list of available programs and program groups, and then choosing **Microsoft Office** or **PowerPoint**, depending on how you installed the PowerPoint application. Windows 95 operates a little differently from earlier versions of Windows. Once you open a menu bar, you can move the cursor bar up and down without holding down the mouse button. Then to launch an application you need only click once; no double-click is required.

When PowerPoint starts, the main PowerPoint screen, complete with the Tip of the Day, is displayed (see Figure 1.4).

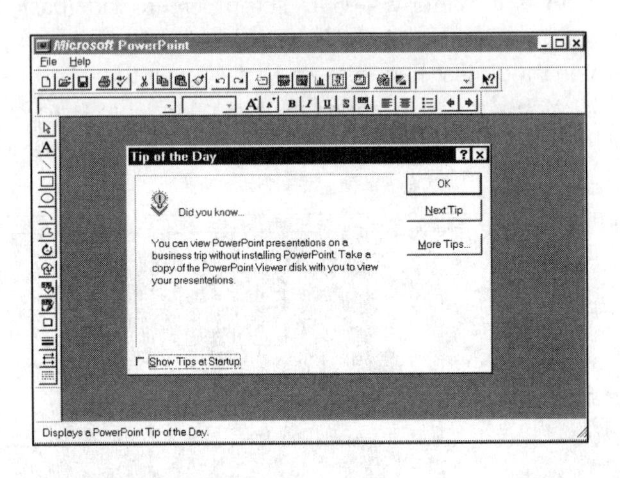

Figure 1.4 *Main PowerPoint screen with Tip of the Day.*

The main PowerPoint screen shows graphically the power of the Windows environment. These screens are full of little pictures (*icons*) that represent programs or program features. You select them with the mouse by clicking or double-clicking on the appropriate icon.

Using the Mouse

The mouse is a great improvement to computer interaction; it seems easy and natural when you watch someone with experience use it. When you first sit down with a mouse, however, it is a pretty awkward experience. I can't teach you to feel comfortable with the mouse; that only comes with experience. I *can* offer a couple of hints that make using the mouse easier, and I can share a couple of terms that you'll see throughout this book.

First of all, as you move the mouse pointer around the screen, notice that the shape of the pointer changes depending on what type of on-screen object is under the pointer. When the pointer is over an object that can be selected, the pointer is an arrow point. When the pointer moves over a part of the screen that can hold text, on the other hand, the pointer changes to an I-beam. This is the *insertion point*; it shows that you are pointing to a text portion of the screen. If you click on the screen with the I-beam showing, a text insertion point is fixed and the next text you type will appear at that location.

NOTE

If you run out of desk before you have moved the mouse pointer where you want it, simply pick up the mouse and move it to give you room to move.

NOTE

You can resize a PowerPoint object by moving the mouse pointer to the edge of the object until the pointer changes to a double-ended arrow. Press and hold the left mouse button and drag the edge of the object to the new position.

NOTE

As you move the mouse, keep your wrist on the desk and move the mouse with your hand. If you try to move the mouse by moving your whole arm, you will have less control and you will get fatigued easily.

Your mouse probably has two buttons, usually termed left and right. The *left* mouse button is the main one. When I instruct you to click or double-click or to hold down the mouse button in this book, I mean the left button. Some applications don't use the *right* button at all, but in PowerPoint you can use the right button to display additional menu choices. For example, if you press the right mouse button when the mouse pointer is inside a slide in the PowerPoint editing window, you will see a pop-up menu with some frequently used selections on it. You can then slide a pointer up and down the list to choose from these selections:

Cut
Copy
Paste
Ruler
Guides

Slide Layout
Slide Color Scheme...
Custom Background...
Apply Design Template
Pick Up Object Style
Apply To Defaults

If you place the pointer within one of the displayed toolbars and press the right mouse button, you'll see another menu for customizing the toolbar displays. The toolbar menu includes these choices:

Standard
Formatting
Drawing
Drawing+
AutoShapes
Animation Effects
Toolbars...
Customize...

You can tell which of these choices is active because a check mark appears in front of the active choices. Some of these are toggles. The first click enables the selection and places a check mark ahead of the name in the pop-up list; a second click disables the choice and removes the check mark.

When I tell you to *click* on a PowerPoint object, I mean to move the mouse pointer over the object and press the left mouse button momentarily. A double-click means to place the mouse pointer over an object and press the left mouse button twice in quick succession. A *double-click* operation can be a little complicated for some users. For one thing, there is sometimes a tendency to move the mouse pointer between clicks. This moves the pointer off the object you are trying to select, so the double-click doesn't take effect. In addition, you need to double-click with a close-spaced rhythm. If you leave too much space between the clicks, you won't make the selection you want. Luckily, in Windows 95 the double-click is not required as often as it was in earlier versions of Windows. A single click, or simply moving a cursor or pointer and releasing the mouse button, sometimes will suffice.

Sometimes you want to select a menu item without actually executing it. When a double-click is required to start a specific menu item, you can use a single click to highlight or select the item. You can also drag a highlight cursor or selector by holding down the left mouse button while you move the cursor. A menu or dialog box selection that requires a single click will be executed when you move the highlight bar over the choice and release the mouse button.

When you are working with text, you can generally *select* a portion of text by placing the mouse pointer at the beginning of the block of text you want to select, holding down the left mouse button, and moving the highlight across as much text as you want to select. Once selected, the text can be manipulated as a unit or block.

You may want to point to an item without selecting it, as when you want to view the ToolTips for a toolbar button. To point to a screen object, simply move the mouse pointer over the object and pause without pressing any mouse button.

Understanding Menus

All Windows 95 programs—or even programs designed for earlier versions of Windows that are running in Windows 95—have similar menu schemes. Figures 1.5 and 1.6 show close-ups of the menu bars for Word 7 and PowerPoint 7.

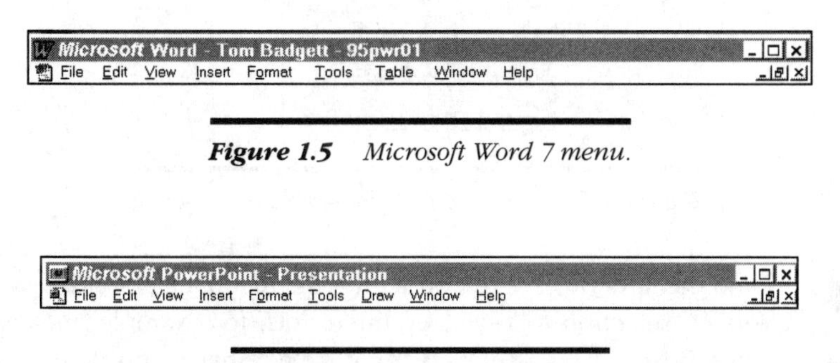

Figure 1.5 *Microsoft Word 7 menu.*

Figure 1.6 *PowerPoint 7 menu.*

Notice the similarity between these menus. They are arranged in a horizontal fashion (similar to the style first used by spreadsheets like Lotus 1-2-3). When an application is active, you are working in the main part of the screen. You may be entering information into a spreadsheet, typing in a word processor, or, in the case of PowerPoint, inserting text or graphics into a presentation slide. When you want to use a menu selection, you can access it in two ways:

- Use the mouse to point to the menu item and pull down the list.
- Press and release the **Alt** key to activate the menu, use the cursor movement keys to highlight the item you want, then press **Enter**. You can also press the underlined character in the menu name to activate the menu. In the PowerPoint menu in Figure 1.6, for example, you can access the View menu by pressing the **V** key after you press the **Alt** key to activate the menu bar.

Figure 1.7 shows a PowerPoint screen with the Format submenu pulled down from the main menu bar.

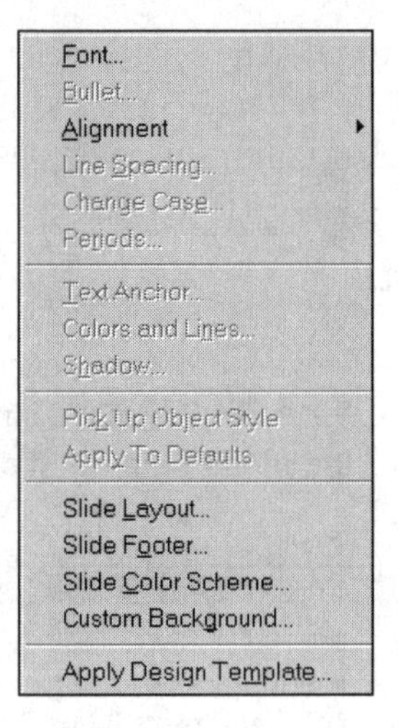

Figure 1.7 *PowerPoint Format pull-down menu.*

NOTE

Some menu choices give you additional feedback about the way they work. A selection followed by three dots, for example, means that a dialog box will be displayed if you select that menu item. Once the dialog box is displayed, you can provide additional information or answer questions to get the desired results. (See the discussion of dialog boxes later in this chapter for more information.)

A menu item followed by a right-facing triangle () means that a submenu will be displayed if you select that item. Figure 1.8 shows one such submenu displayed along with a pull-down menu from the main menu bar.

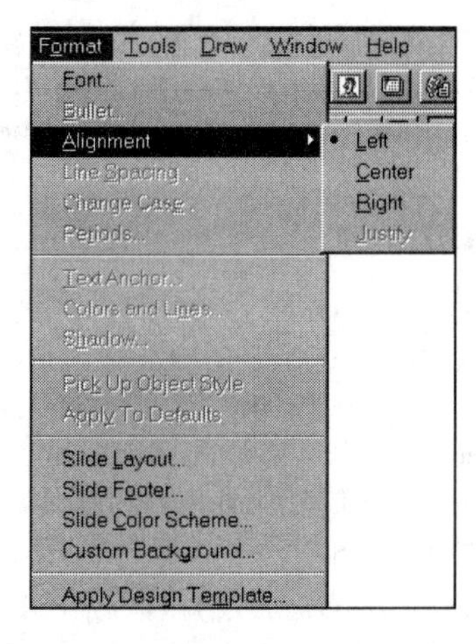

Figure 1.8 *Second menu beside main menu.*

You can start some menu choices with a keyboard *hotkey combination.* These alternatives are shown beside the menu entries. See Figure 1.9 for an example of hotkey prompts on a pull-down menu from PowerPoint.

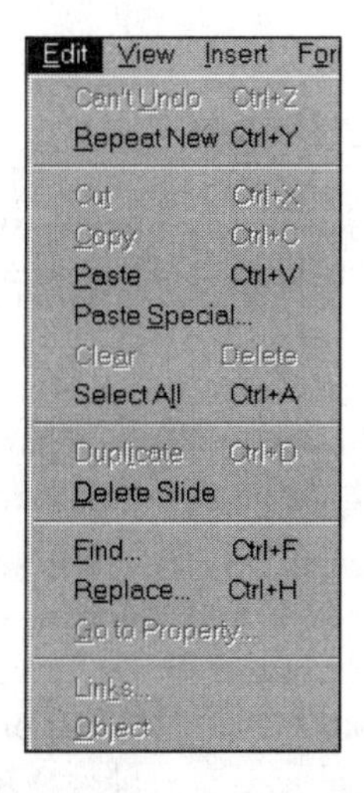

Figure 1.9 *PowerPoint Edit pull-down menu.*

Notice that the choices on a pull-down menu also have one character in each selection underlined. After you pull down the menu, you can either use the mouse to highlight and choose a selection or you can simply press the keyboard character that is underlined in the selection you want. You don't have to press the **Alt** key in combination with the keyboard key in these submenus.

Understanding Toolbars

With a full-featured application such as PowerPoint, the menu structure can become extremely complex. Remembering where each choice is and how to use it can be difficult. That's why PowerPoint uses additional ways to get into its features. One of these is the *toolbar.* The PowerPoint toolbar is located directly under the menu bar. It consists of 20 standard buttons with pictures to help you understand what each button does.

Below the toolbar is the *Format bar.* This object-based feature lets you format text and other PowerPoint objects by accessing pull-down lists and icons.

To access a PowerPoint command or feature from the toolbar, just click on the button (*tool*) that represents the desired feature. The tool is a visual representation of a menu choice, a macro, or an internal command. If you frequently use commands other than the ones supplied on the standard toolbar, you can easily customize the display to include the features you want (I'll show you how to do that in the next chapter).

Understanding Dialog Boxes

A *dialog box* is an interactive pop-up display that asks for more information before conducting the operation selected from a menu. Figure 1.10 shows a typical PowerPoint dialog box.

Notice that there are several features of this dialog box that are common to most dialog boxes. The dialog box is definitely a separate entity from the rest of the display, for one thing. It is well-defined, and it carries a title.

Along the right side of the dialog box are several buttons. Which buttons appear depends on the function of the dialog box, but you are almost certainly sure to find a **Help** button, a **Cancel** button, and an **OK** button. If there isn't an **OK** button, there will be a button that says **Go on** or **Execute**. For example, if you display the Slide Show dialog box (select **View Slide Show...**), the selection to close the dialog box and continue is **Show**. This is obvious, given the title of the dialog box and the menu choice you made to display it.

In addition to these buttons, most dialog boxes include one or more areas for user input. You may be asked to specify a disk drive, a directory, or a file name, or to make selections by clicking on buttons. A *button* is a (usually) round object that is selected or deselected by clicking with the mouse. When a button is *selected* it is colored dark, or, in the case of three-dimensional buttons, it appears to be depressed. These are *toggles*. The first time you click on it, the button is selected. On the second click it is de-selected.

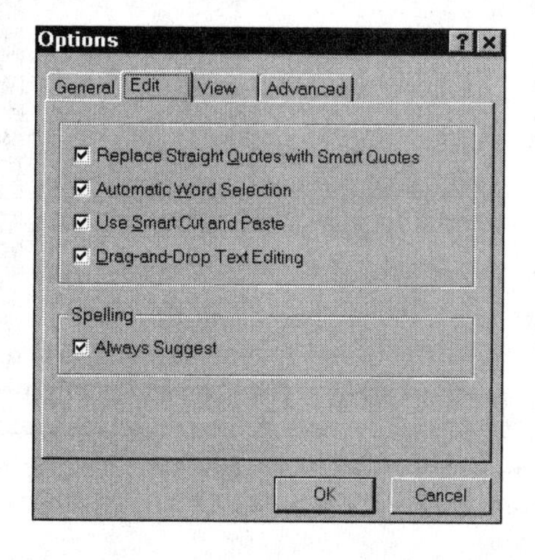

Figure 1.10 *Typical PowerPoint dialog box.*

Understanding Scroll Bars

Most of the time you work with a Windows application, all you are seeing on the screen at any one time is a portion of the total display. In a word processor, for example, you can see only a portion of one page of the document. In PowerPoint you usually are looking at only one slide at a time, even though there may be a dozen or even dozens of slides in the total presentation.

To see other parts of the document or presentation you can use *scroll bars*, the gray horizontal and vertical devices at the bottom and side of the screen. Notice the vertical scroll bar in Figure 1.11. Click on the upward-facing arrow to move one slide up in the presentation; click on the downward-facing arrow to move one slide down in the presentation.

In addition, there is a small box between the arrows on the scroll bar. This shows how far from the top or bottom of the file you are. You can grab this box with the mouse and drag it up or down on the bar to move rapidly across several slides.

Scroll bars frequently appear in dialog boxes as well, to let you select an item in a window that contains too many items to appear in the dialog box at one time.

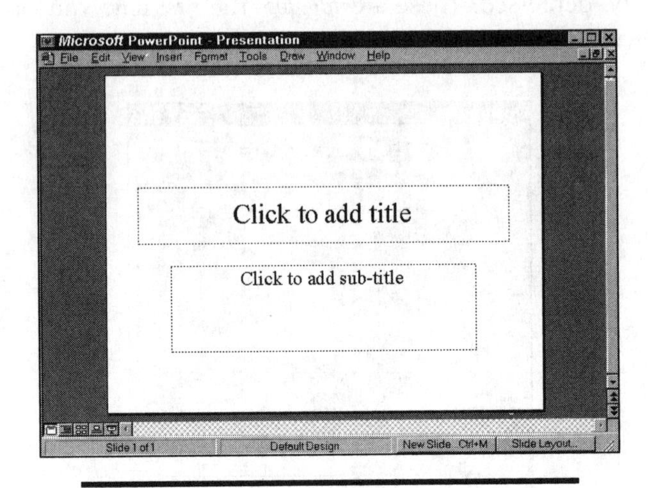

Figure 1.11 *PowerPoint screen with scroll bars.*

Arranging Windows

As a Microsoft Windows product, PowerPoint supports some *multitasking*. That means you can work on more than one presentation at a time, copy or move information from one presentation window to another, and view multiple presentations simultaneously to compare them.

As you work with multiple PowerPoint windows you may nee to rearrange the open windows to make them easier to view, to move one out of the way, or to access a different presentation. There are several ways to display multiple PowerPoint windows. Each time you open a new presentation, PowerPoint overlays the latest presentation window over previous ones. After you have three or four of these open, it will be impossible to see previous displays. Use the **Window Arrange All** menu sequence to have PowerPoint shrink these windows and place them on the screen where you can see them all at once. Figure 1.12 shows a screen with three presentations open.

Even with just three presentation windows open at once, however, it is nearly impossible to see any detail in any of the screens. Another way to display these windows so you can tell what is open is to use the **Window Cascade** command. This stacks up the open windows like a deck of cards fanned out so that you can see the presentation titles, but you can only see the contents of the topmost presentation. Figure 1.13 shows a PowerPoint cascaded display.

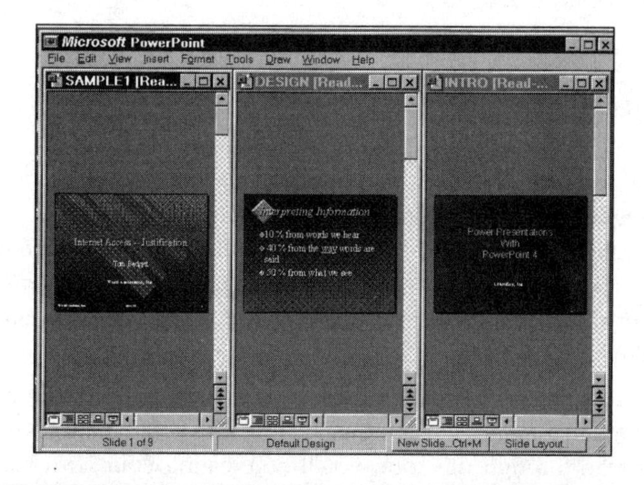

Figure 1.12 *PowerPoint screen with three open presentations.*

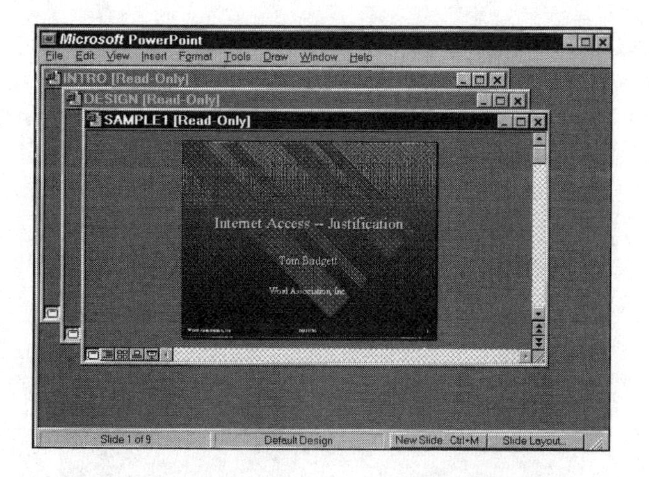

Figure 1.13 *PowerPoint cascaded window display.*

You can activate any of these cascaded windows by simply clicking on the title bar of the one you want. Then you can enlarge the display by clicking on the **Restore** button (the upward-facing arrow) at the far top right of the window. When you want to go back to another of the windows, first shrink the current presentation by clicking on the double-ended arrow on the right of the menu bar. Then you can click on the title of another presentation window and enlarge it as before to work with it.

To Sum Up

Whether you are new to Windows 95 or have a lot of experience with other Windows programs, you shouldn't have much trouble getting up to speed with PowerPoint. After a little practice manipulating the PowerPoint menus, toolbars, and presentation screens, it should feel very natural. Just remember that the Windows user interface provides a standard of data presentation and manipulation that is similar to what you'll find in other major programs.

In the next chapter, you'll walk through a tour of PowerPoint that will show all of this program's major screens and features. If you practice with your software as you read through this tour, you'll be creating your own basic presentations with PowerPoint quickly.

CHAPTER 2

A Weekend Tour of PowerPoint

PowerPoint is a powerful application. You can use it to produce professional presentations, to create complex slides and slide shows, and more. Like most complex applications, there is a lot to learn to become proficient in using it. However, because PowerPoint is a Windows application and because it is part of the larger Microsoft Office suite, there is much you can accomplish with only a cursory introduction to presentation design theory and to PowerPoint itself.

In this chapter, you'll learn the important concepts behind PowerPoint. You'll become familiar with its major screen components, and you'll use it to actually produce a useful presentation. If you step through this chapter and try the examples I show you, you'll end up with a strong working knowledge of PowerPoint.

Starting PowerPoint

First, let's talk about how to start PowerPoint from inside Windows 95. Windows 95 approaches document loading and creation a little differently from previous versions of Windows, but you can still launch applications such as PowerPoint directly.

When you install PowerPoint as part of Office 95, you have the advantage of the Office Shortcut toolbar. Unless you have modified the toolbar, it displays, among other choices, Start a New Document and Open a Document. Notice that there are no icons that represent PowerPoint or the other Office 95 applications. Instead, to open an existing PowerPoint presentation, choose **Open a Document** from the toolbar. Office displays the Open a Document dialog box shown in Figure 2.1.

Figure 2.1 *Office Shortcut toolbar Open a Document dialog box.*

Use the directory and file lists to choose the file you want to open. When you select a PowerPoint presentation file, the PowerPoint application is automatically launched, then the chosen presentation is loaded.

To create a new PowerPoint presentation with the Office Shortcut toolbar, click on **Start a New Document** to display the dialog box shown in Figure 2.2.

From this screen you have three general choices for starting a new PowerPoint document. Click on the **General** tab on the Start a New Document dialog box to display the Blank PowerPoint presentation type. Double-click on this icon to launch PowerPoint with a blank presentation. This lets you start from scratch and design your own presentation from the ground up.

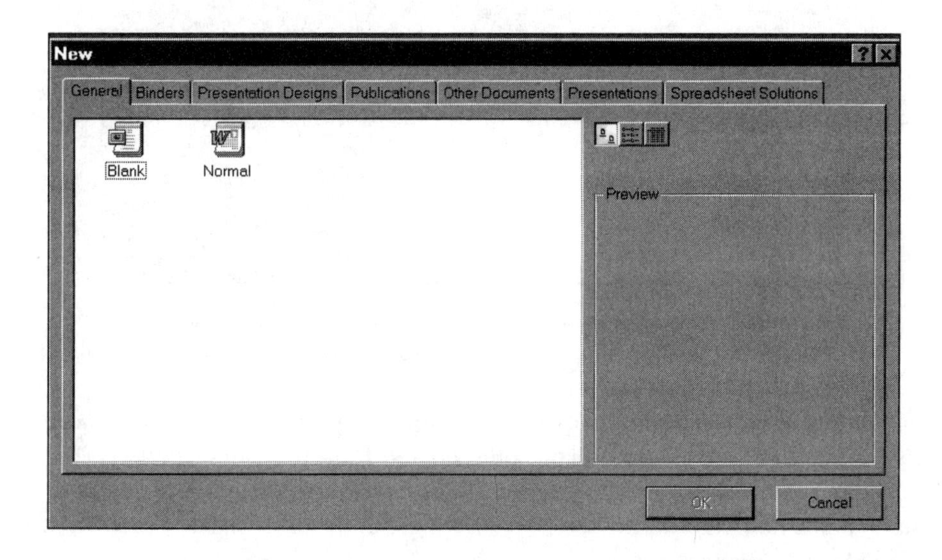

Figure 2.2 *Windows 95 Start a New Document dialog box.*

If you'd like to start a new presentation with one of the many PowerPoint templates loaded, click on the **Presentation Designs** tab to display the available PowerPoint templates. Choose the template you want to use and double-click on it. PowerPoint is loaded with the chosen template as the default. You can single-click on any of the template folders in the Presentation Designs window to see a preview of a template prior to choosing it as the default for PowerPoint.

You can click on the **Presentations** tab to choose one of the PowerPoint presentation designs (see Figure 2.3). These preformatted presentations help you design your own presentation based on the type of story you want to tell. Choose one to communicate bad news, for example, another to report progress, and so on.

If you're not using Office 95 (or you choose not to use the Shortcut toolbar), you can launch PowerPoint from the Start menu. Click on **Start**, slide the cursor up to the **Programs** entry and choose **Microsoft Office** from the pop-up list. From this display you can choose **PowerPoint** to launch the program. Once PowerPoint is loaded, you can choose templates or preformatted presentations, or you can design your own presentation from scratch.

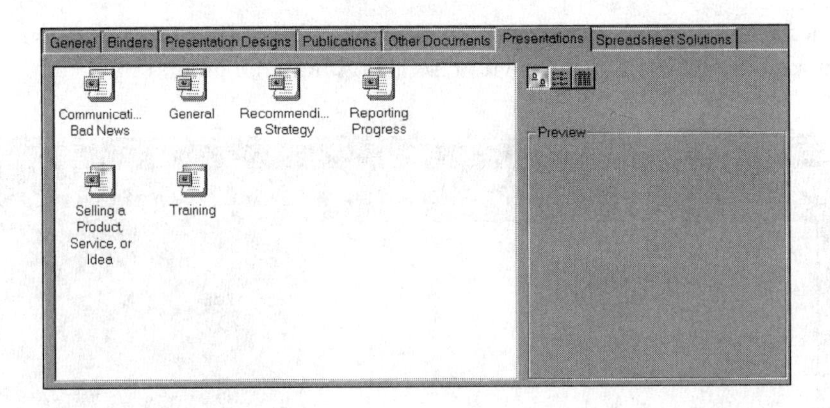

Figure 2.3 *Presentations tab from Start a New Document dialog box.*

However you choose to load PowerPoint, the main program screen is eventually displayed. If you choose the blank presentation from the General tab or if you launch PowerPoint from the Start menu, you should see a blank PowerPoint display similar to Figure 2.4. Refer to this illustration as I discuss each of the labeled components in detail.

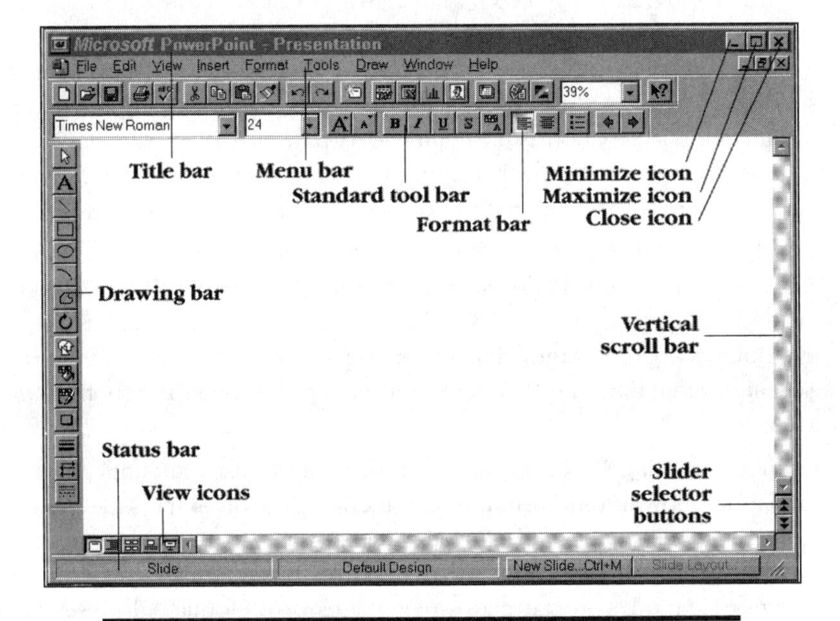

Figure 2.4 *Main PowerPoint screen with components labeled.*

The PowerPoint Screen

Now let's look at the major PowerPoint screen components one by one, so you'll understand how each functions before you start using the program itself.

The Menu Bar

The PowerPoint *menu bar*, like the menu bars of all Windows-compliant programs, is a horizontal strip just below the title bar. (See Figure 2.4 for the location of these screen elements.) I described how to use menus in Chapter 1. In Figure 2.5 you can see a close-up of the PowerPoint menu bar.

Figure 2.5 *PowerPoint menu bar.*

Each of these nine menu choices holds additional selections that you can display by clicking on the menu bar or by using the Alt-Key combination, as discussed in Chapter 1. If you pull down a submenu list and some of its choices are light gray instead of black, that means you can't use them.

Why would a menu item appear that PowerPoint wouldn't let you use? There are a number of reasons, depending on the menu choice. However, the general reason is that PowerPoint (and all Windows-based programs) shows which commands aren't available. This works much better than letting you make the choice and getting an error message such as "Sorry. That command not available."

One example of commands that are on the menu but that can't be accessed are the **Cut** and **Copy** commands on the Edit menu. If there is nothing selected on the active screen, then you can't copy it or cut it. Therefore, these options will be grayed out. Also, if the clipboard is empty there is nothing to paste into the current document or presentation, so the **Paste** choice on the Edit menu will be grayed out.

There are many other situations in which a given menu item may not be available for use until some prerequisite condition is met. If you encounter an inaccessible menu item that you really want to use, find out what the prerequisite is, satisfy it, then try the command again.

In the following pages, you'll find a PowerPoint command and menu reference. Use these figures as a quick reference to the commands available under each main menu choice. You can also see from these screens what the shortcut keys for some commands are. For more detailed information about each PowerPoint command, refer to Appendix B, Menu and Command Reference.

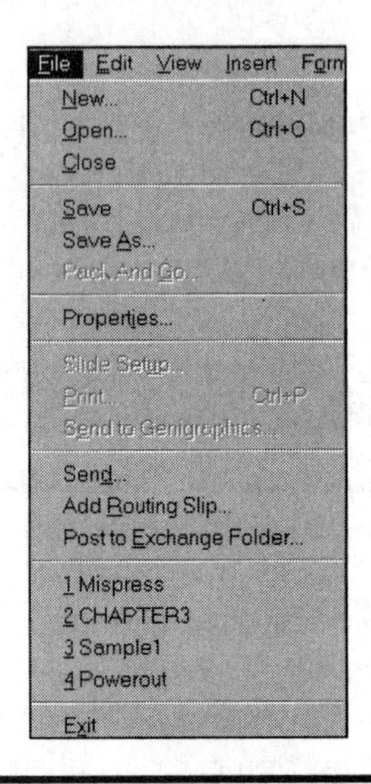

Figure 2.6 *PowerPoint File menu.*

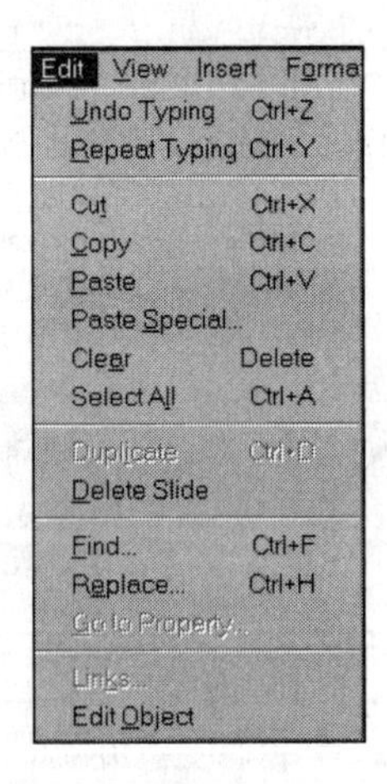

Figure 2.7 *PowerPoint Edit menu.*

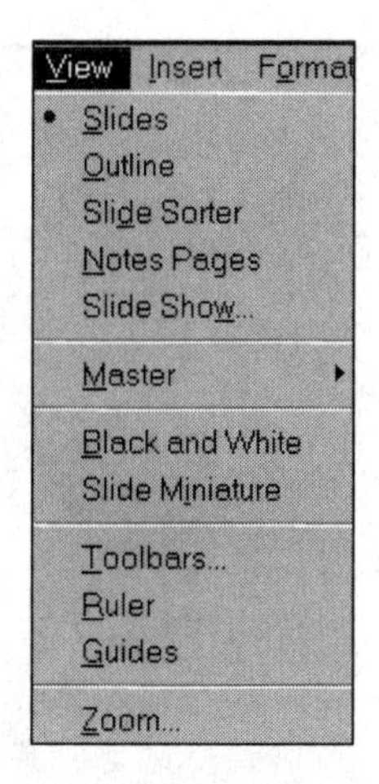

Figure 2.8 *PowerPoint View menu.*

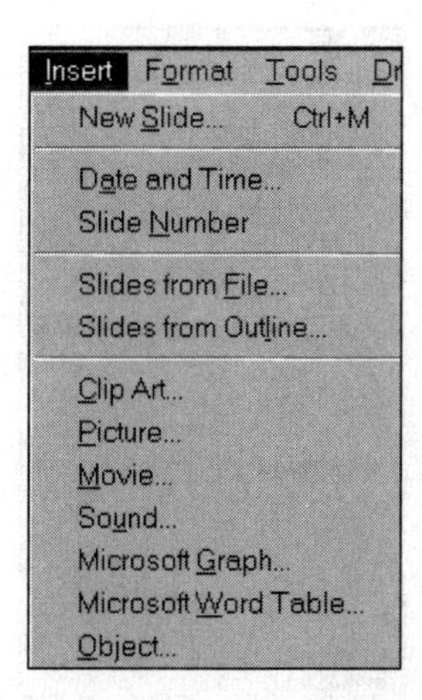

Figure 2.9 *PowerPoint Insert menu.*

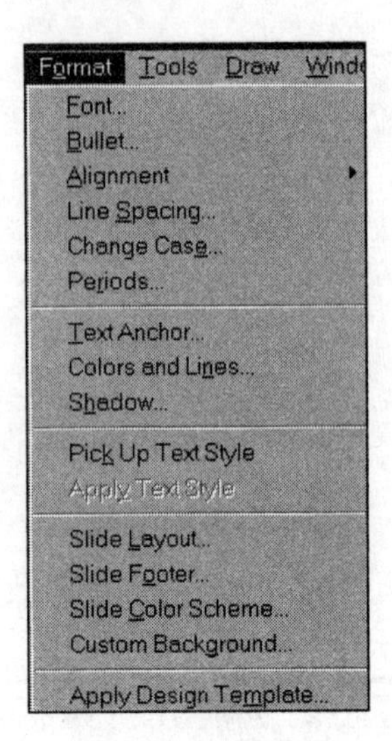

Figure 2.10 *PowerPoint Format menu.*

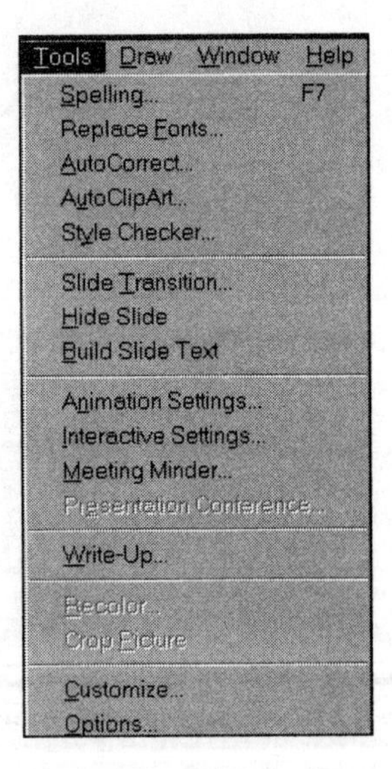

Figure 2.11 *PowerPoint Tools menu.*

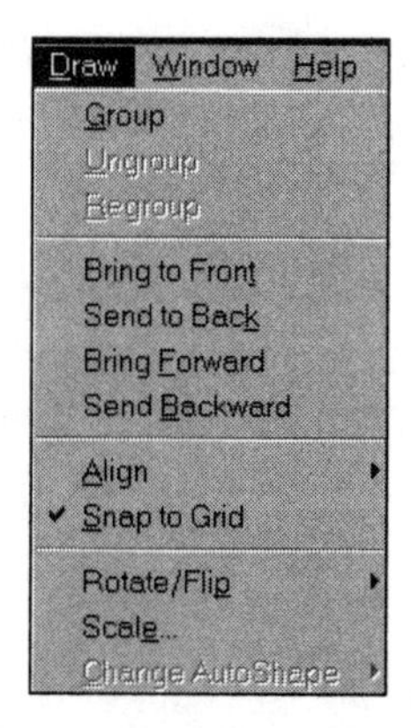

Figure 2.12 *PowerPoint Draw menu.*

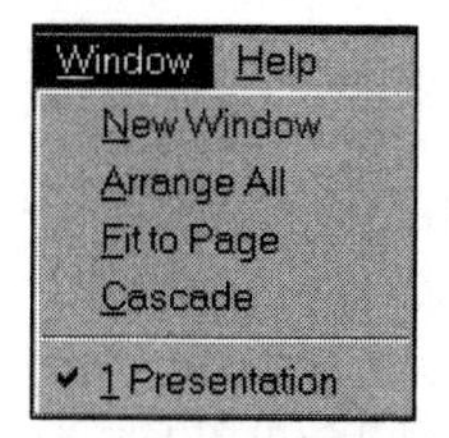

Figure 2.13 *PowerPoint Window menu.*

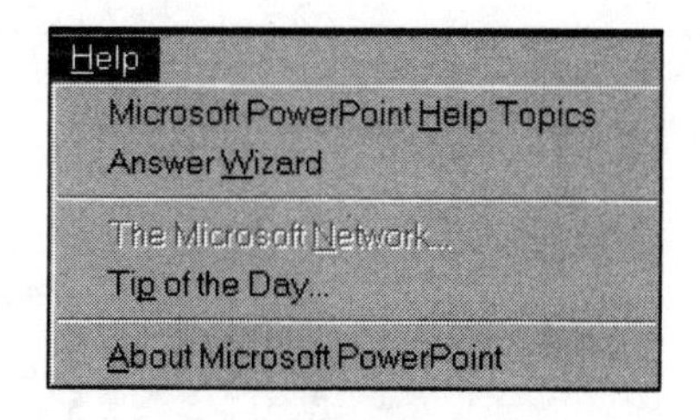

Figure 2.14 *PowerPoint Help menu.*

Remember the conventions of menu displays. A menu item followed by three dots means that a dialog box is displayed as a result of that menu choice. A right-facing triangle means that there's a submenu under that menu item. A control key combination shown after a menu entry means that you can bypass the menu bar and start that command by pressing the control key combination. If there is nothing displayed after a menu entry, you can launch that individual command by highlighting it and pressing **Enter**, or by clicking on the entry.

The Toolbar

The concept of a pictorial toolbar evolved as designers and users realized that certain menu commands are used heavily and are sometimes cumbersome to use or difficult to remember. In general, it is easier to scan a toolbar and pick out a picture to conduct a certain task than it is to remember which menu and which submenu to access to execute a specific command.

PowerPoint installs with three default toolbars but is configured with six toolbars. In addition, you can customize the toolbars by adding or removing commands through the Customize dialog box. (Figure 2.4 shows the standard toolbars and their placement.)

To access a command represented by a toolbar button, simply point to the button and click once. If you can't remember what a particular toolbar button does, point to the button and wait about one second. PowerPoint's automatic ToolTips displays a one- or two-word description of that button's function.

Below is a toolbar reference that shows a close-up of each toolbar with labels that indicate what each button does. The toolbars that appear on the PowerPoint screen by default are shown first, then the ones that you can install through the Toolbars pop-up menu are shown.

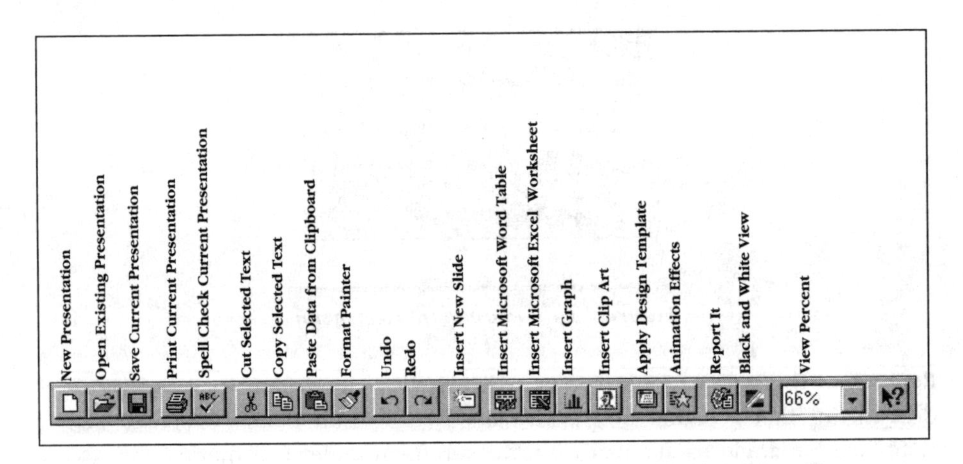

Figure 2.15 *Standard PowerPoint toolbar with labels.*

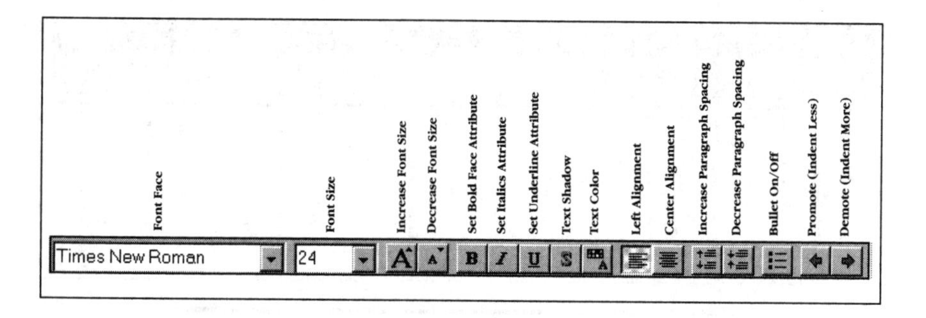

Figure 2.16 *Format PowerPoint toolbar with labels.*

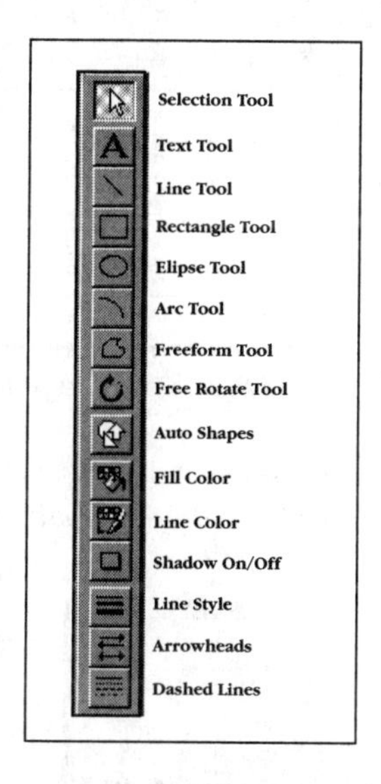

Figure 2.17 *Drawing PowerPoint toolbar with labels.*

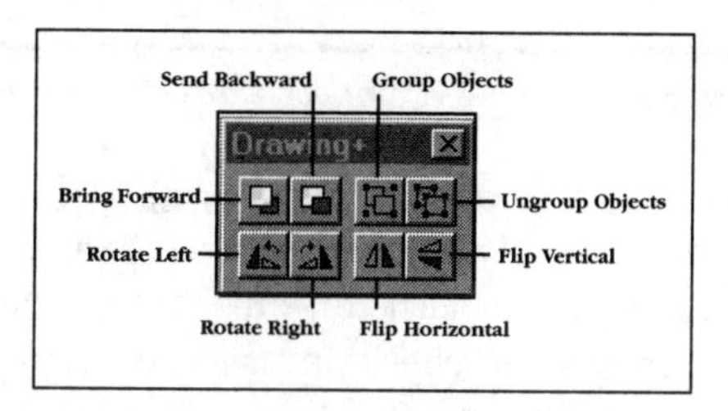

Figure 2.18 *Drawing+ PowerPoint toolbar with labels.*

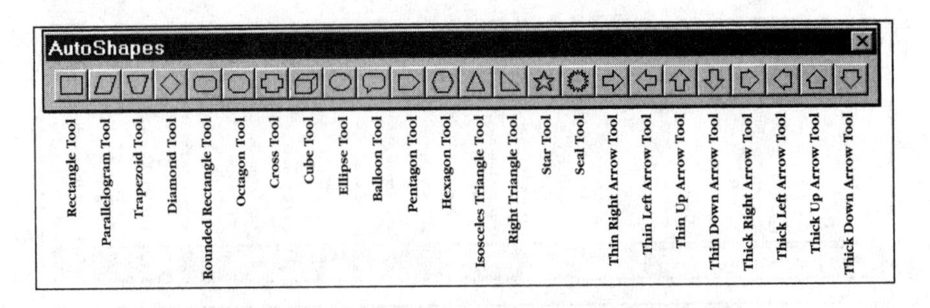

Figure 2.19 *AutoShapes PowerPoint toolbar with labels.*

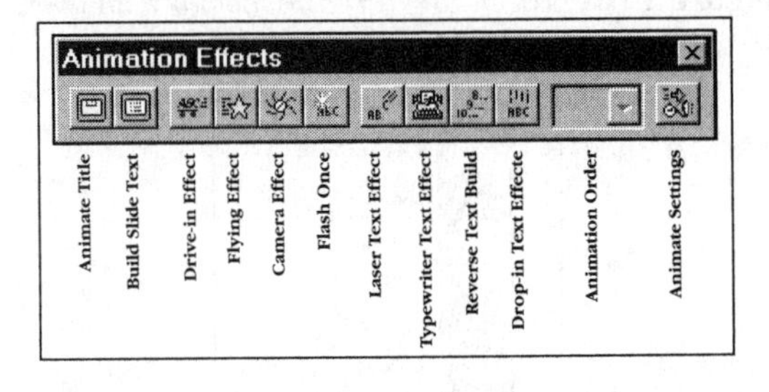

Figure 2.20 *Animation effects PowerPoint toolbar with labels.*

You can add and remove PowerPoint toolbars easily. Point to any toolbar and press the right mouse button to display the Toolbars menu shown in Figure 2.21.

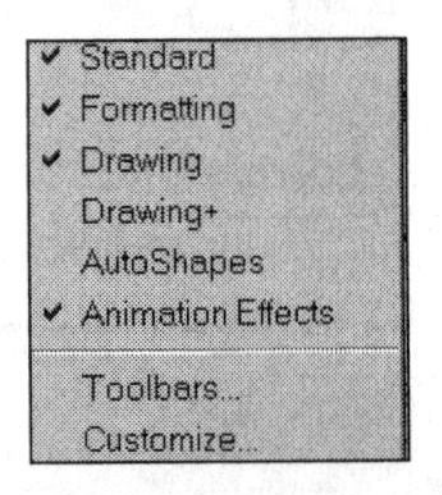

Figure 2.21 *PowerPoint pop-up Toolbars menu.*

Notice that the default toolbars (Standard, Formatting, and Drawing) have a check mark beside them in this menu. That means they are being shown on the screen. These choices are toggles. If you click on any toolbar name that has a check beside it, PowerPoint removes the check and also removes that toolbar from the screen. If you click on a toolbar name that does not have a check beside it, PowerPoint adds a check and also adds that toolbar to the screen display.

To add your own choice of buttons to any toolbar, first display the toolbar you want to change. Then point to it and click the right mouse button to display the Toolbars menu again. Choose **Customize...** from this menu to display the Customize Toolbars dialog box shown in Figure 2.22.

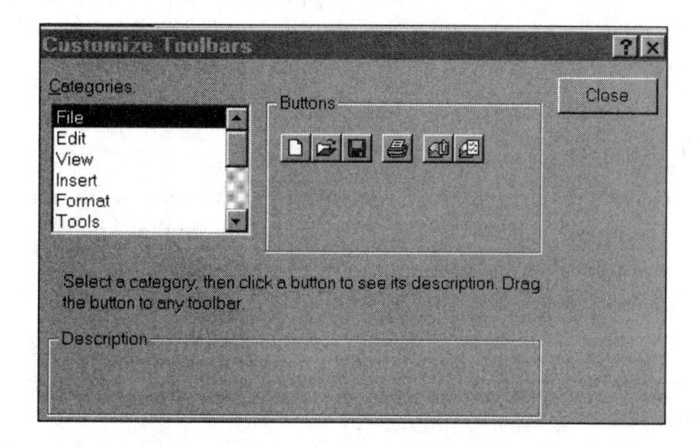

Figure 2.22 *Customize Toolbars dialog box.*

In this dialog box, highlight the name of the menu from which you want to select a command. PowerPoint displays the available toolbar buttons for that menu selection. To install one of these buttons onto a toolbar, grab the one you want, drag it to the toolbar, and drop it. PowerPoint automatically resizes the toolbar to accept the new button. You can repeat this process as often as necessary to install additional buttons on the toolbar. If you change your mind about a tool button you already have placed on a toolbar, just grab it and drag it off of the bar. When you drop it, the button will disappear and will be removed from the toolbar.

In addition, with the Customize Toolbars dialog box displayed, you can even move tool buttons from one toolbar to another. To install the same tool button on more than one toolbar, simply repeat the drag and drop process from the Customize Toolbars dialog box as often as necessary to place the button on as many toolbars as you like.

One more thing. You can change the shape of toolbars by placing the mouse pointer anywhere within a toolbar that is outside the displayed buttons. Hold down the left mouse button and drag the shape of the box to a horizontal, vertical, or square orientation. You can also drag an entire toolbar to any location on the screen you wish. Once you have moved a toolbar from its default position, the familiar Windows 95 "x" for closing a dialog box appears in the upper right corner of the toolbar. You can remove any toolbar by clicking on this **x**, or by deselecting it from the Toolbars menu.

Note that some PowerPoint commands generate their own toolbars. If you insert a graph, for example, a toolbar to support the graphing operation replaces the default toolbars until you close the graphing utility and return to the regular PowerPoint screen.

The Format Bar

As you saw in the previous section, PowerPoint considers the Format bar one of the available toolbars. However, because of the somewhat special nature of its operation, I wanted to give a little attention to this toolbar.

The Format bar is used to format the text on a slide or within other presentation materials such as audience handouts or speaker notes. This is very similar to the Format bar included with Microsoft Word, but it has features specific to presentation applications.

The PowerPoint Format bar includes the usual text formatting features, including boldface, underline, italics, text alignment, and bulleted list. The typeface and font size selections are there too, in the form of pull-down lists like the one in Figure 2.23.

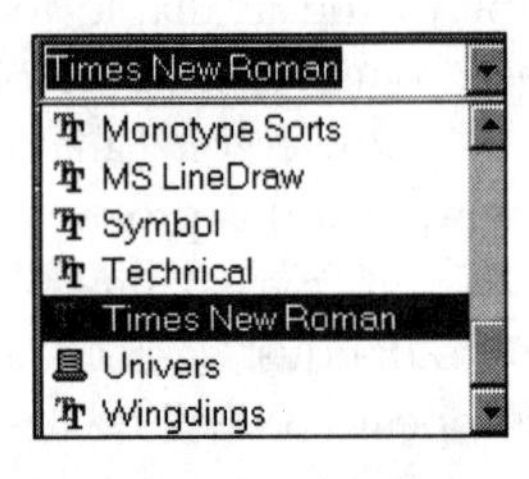

Figure 2.23 *Format bar pull-down typeface list.*

There are additional text formatting tools on this bar as well. For example, you can decrease the size of the current font by clicking on the **Decrease Font Size** button. Increase font size with the **Increase Font Size** button. You can see the results of each click right on the screen.

You can specify text color with the Text Color dialog box and you can create shadowed text easily by selecting text and then clicking on the **Text Shadow** button.

NOTE

PowerPoint is smart enough to know you want to change text formatting for the whole word in which the insertion point rests; you don't have to select a word to format it. To change the format of more text than a single word, select it first.

Finally, left- and right-facing arrows on the Format bar let you promote or demote outline levels on a PowerPoint slide screen.

Creating a Presentation

PowerPoint presentations can be simple or very complex. It depends on the message you're trying to impart with your presentation. A simple message requires a simple presentation design; a more complex message calls for a more complex presentation design.

NOTE

Each PowerPoint presentation is contained in a single file. This one file, which you name when you save the presentation for the first time, stores the slides, speaker's notes, handouts, outline, and the formatting information that gives your presentation its particular appearance.

In the next chapter, you will learn a few tips on planning and designing a presentation. In this section I'll show you how to begin with a basic concept and turn it into a series of slides in PowerPoint. If you step through this exercise, creating the sample presentation discussed here, then it should be fairly easy for you to substitute your own topics and design ideas for what is shown.

Sample Presentation Overview

For this exercise, I'll show you how to construct a simple presentation about a topic you already know. Then you can use this same procedure to build another presentation about a topic of your own.

Let's assume that you want to build a brief presentation to tell someone about this book. You will provide a little background on the publisher (only what you can gather from the book itself), then you will show how the *Teach Yourself...* series fits into the other computer offerings from the publisher (I'll show you that). You will describe the general features of the series, present some specifics about this book in the series, and show the audience where to get more information.

Think for a moment about how to present this information within the framework of what you already know about PowerPoint. Remember that this presentation material is designed to support an oral presentation and not to stand alone, so the slides we create will carry minimal information.

One way to help design a new presentation is to list the general topics you want to cover, as I did above. Next, create a simple storyboard by drawing squares on a piece of paper and labeling them. These squares represent the individual slides in your presentation. For a simple presentation, this may be all the planning you need. PowerPoint includes a number of tools to help you build a presentation, so you can let the individual slides evolve as you work with the software.

The drawing in Figure 2.24 shows my first attempt at a storyboard for this presentation. I didn't try to design each slide fully. I only wanted to get a general idea about the order of the information, to determine how many slides would be needed, and to identify the key slides in the presentation.

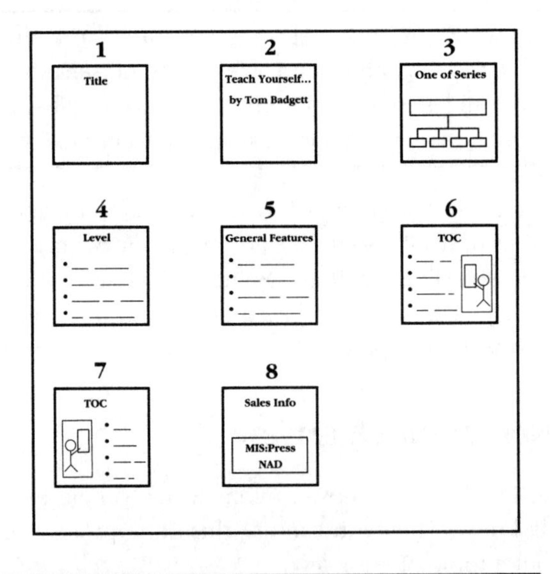

Figure 2.24 *Sample presentation initial storyboard.*

As you can see, this presentation will contain only eight slides. This is not very many, but it is enough for a short presentation and is enough to help the audience retain the information you present. With this much background and planning, let's get on with building this presentation in PowerPoint.

Starting a New Presentation

Starting a new presentation in PowerPoint is similar to creating a new document file in Word or another word processor. Use the **File: New (Ctrl-N)** menu sequence to display the New Presentation dialog box shown in Figure 2.25.

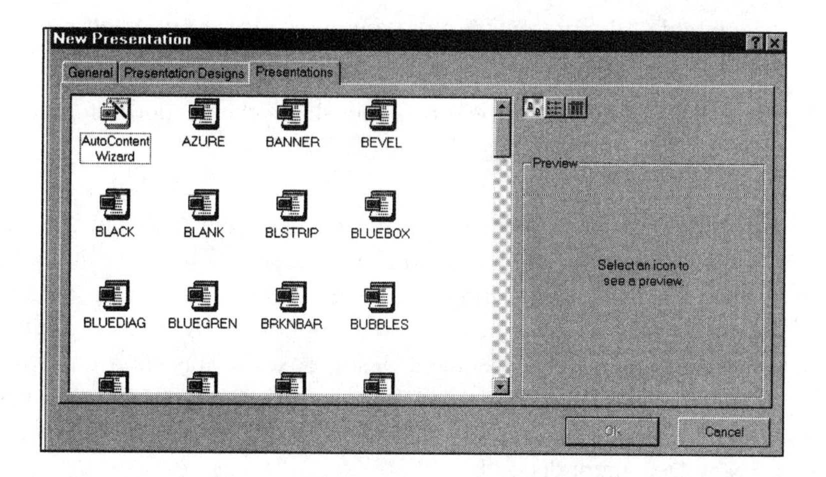

Figure 2.25 *New presentation dialog box.*

NOTE

Remember that you can also start a new presentation by clicking on **Start a New Document** on the Office Shortcut toolbar.

As you can see, there are many choices for starting a new presentation. This is the PowerPoint part of the Start a New Document dialog box discussed earlier in this chapter. There are three tabs on this dialog box: General, Presentation Designs, and Presentations.

If you are familiar with PowerPoint 4.0, you might be used to choosing the **Pick a Look Wizard** to step you through the initial presentation design. With PowerPoint 7, however, you either choose from a Presentation Design, which establishes the template to use, or you select a preformatted presentation, depending on the type of message you want to convey.

Initial Presentation Design

There are several decisions you can make as you create the presentation; these decisions come before you enter any information onto the slides. You need to decide, for example:

- The mood of the presentation or type of data to be presented
- The template design or background color to use
- What information will appear on every slide—the header or footer
- The format of the slides.

Some of this information is specified when you choose a tab from the Start a New Document dialog box or when you make a selection from within a tab. Other choices you will make during the design of the presentation itself. You can experiment with different presentation beginnings by choosing different options from the Start a New Document dialog box. For this short example, I'll show you how to design a presentation from scratch. Once you finish a hands-on design start to finish, try a different presentation with a new beginning from the Start a New Document dialog box.

To start this presentation, click on the **Presentation Designs** tab to display the PowerPoint templates. PowerPoint 7 comes with 60 templates you can use as excellent starting points for your own custom designs. Locate the folder labeled Blue Diagonal in the Presentation Designs tab. You can click once on this folder to get a preview of this template. Double-click on **Blue Diagonal** to select it and display the New Slide dialog box, shown in Figure 2.26.

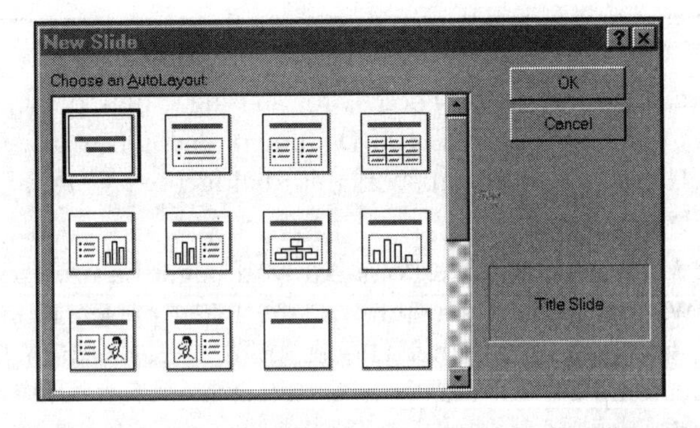

Figure 2.26 *New Slide AutoLayout dialog box in PowerPoint.*

Notice that the default selection is a Title Slide. You may choose one type of slide layout for the title and another for other slides in the presentation. Click on **OK** on this dialog box to accept the default title slide for your new presentation. Your screen should look like Figure 2.27.

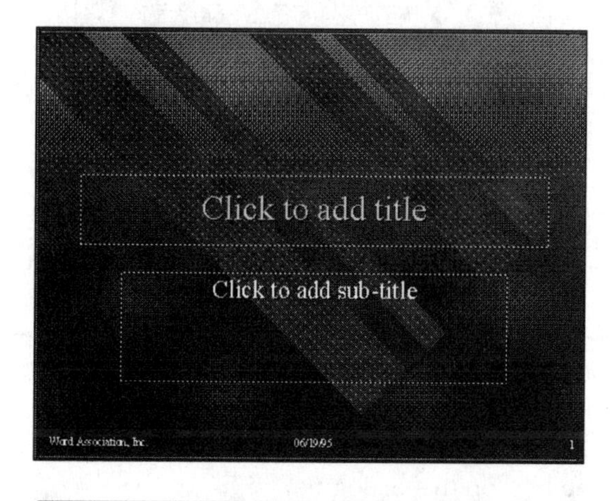

Figure 2.27 *Title slide from a new presentation.*

Next we'll add some formatting that will appear on each slide as the presentation develops. First, add a footer with your company name, personal name, email address, or other information you want to keep in front of the audience throughout the presentation. Do this by selecting the **Format** menu entry from the main PowerPoint menu and choosing **Slide Footer** to display the Slide Header and Footers dialog box shown in Figure 2.28.

Click in the box beside **Slide Number** to enable slide numbering, then click in the **Footer** box. You can now enter the footer text in the footer field. I have entered a company name in this field. Enter whatever data you want to appear on each slide in the presentation. You can also click on the **Don't Show on Title Slide** box to remove the footer information from the title slide, which is usually a good idea.

NOTE

The Preview box on the lower right side of this dialog box shows you how each change you make affects the appearance of your presentation slides. When you choose **Slide Number**, the number box on the Preview slide appears in boldface, for example.

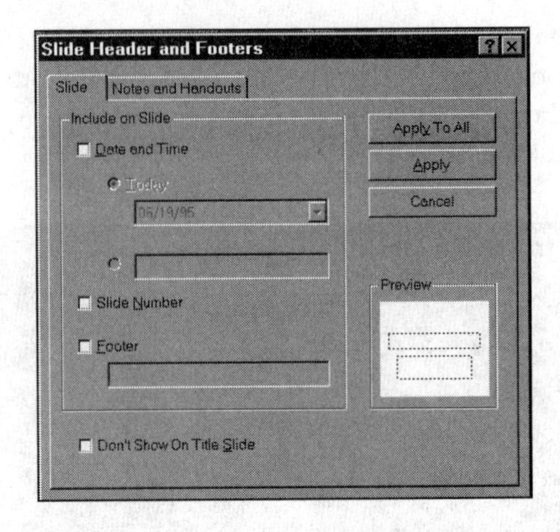

Figure 2.28 *Format Slide Header and Footers Dialog.*

You can also choose to insert the date and time onto each slide by clicking on the **Date and Time** box on this dialog box.

If you click on the **Apply** button, the formatting you specify will appear only on the current slide. Click on **Apply To All** to make the changes appear on all of your slides. However, if you checked the **Don't Show On Title Slide** button, then the title slide will not show the footer information you have specified.

Next you need to format the handout and outline pages so that the footer information appears on these presentation objects as well. Do this by clicking on the **Notes and Handouts** tab of this dialog box. Notice the similarity between this tab and the Slide tab. You can specify the header and footer information for the slide show outline and audience handouts by clicking on the appropriate buttons, just as on the Slide tab.

I prefer to have the footer text at the left side of the slides with the page number on the right. The default is to place the date on the left, the page number on the right, and the footer text in the middle of the slide. To change this default, click on **View**, select **Master** and then choose **Slide Master** from the secondary menu. Now you can click on any of the information in the slide footer to select it; then grab an edge of one of the frames around a single piece of footer information and drag it where you want it to appear.

To make your slides appear like the ones in this example, grab the date and time frame at the bottom left of the master slide and drag it up toward the center of the slide. Next, drag the footer text into the left corner. Slide the date and time frame into the center of the footer area on the master slide. Finally, select **View** and choose **Slides** to return to the slide view of your presentation.

You have one slide—the title slide—on your new presentation and you have specified the footer format for the entire presentation. You are ready to complete the title slide and then to insert additional slides to finish the presentation.

Now save the presentation. Use **File: Save As...** (or use the **Save** button on the toolbar) to display the Save As dialog box. Enter the name **MISPRESS** in the **File Name** field of this dialog box and click on **OK** to save the presentation to the default presentation directory. At this point, the Summary Info dialog box appears. Add any data you wish to the fields in this box and click on **OK**.

Creating the Slides

With the title slide displayed, click where the slide prompts "Click to add title" and type the title of the first slide:

MIS: Press

Click in the field that prompts "Click to add sub-title" and type:

Teach Yourself... Series

Press **Enter** twice to add spacing after this subtitle. Notice that PowerPoint automatically maintains formatting. Now type the last line of the subtitle text:

The Fast and Easy Way

This information comes right out of the book. The finished slide should look like Figure 2.29.

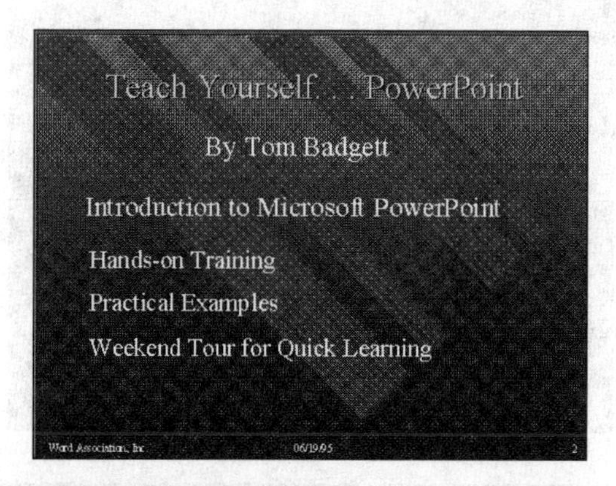

Figure 2.29 *Completed Slide #1 in sample presentation.*

Click on the **New Slide...** button in the status bar at the lower right of the PowerPoint screen to display the New Slide dialog box shown in Figure 2.30.

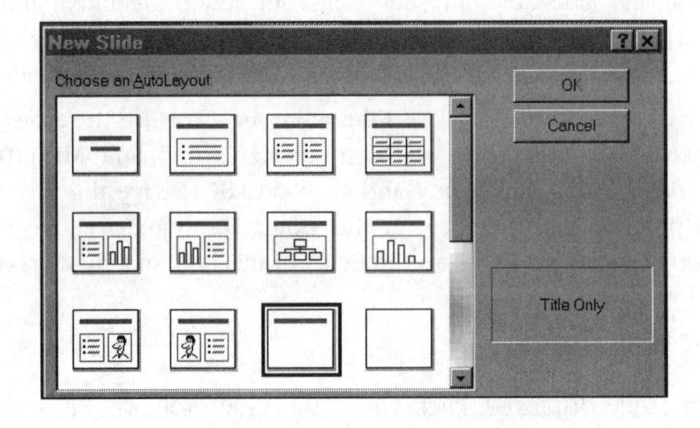

Figure 2.30 *New Slide dialog box.*

Use the scroll bar (at the right of the Choose an AutoLayout window on this dialog box) to move the display down to show more of the available slide types. Choose the next-to-last AutoLayout slide on the third row, which has a single dark line at the top and has the rest of the slide blank (this is one slide to the left of the blank slide). To choose this slide, double-click on it, or select it by clicking once and then clicking on **OK**. The display should look like Figure 2.31.

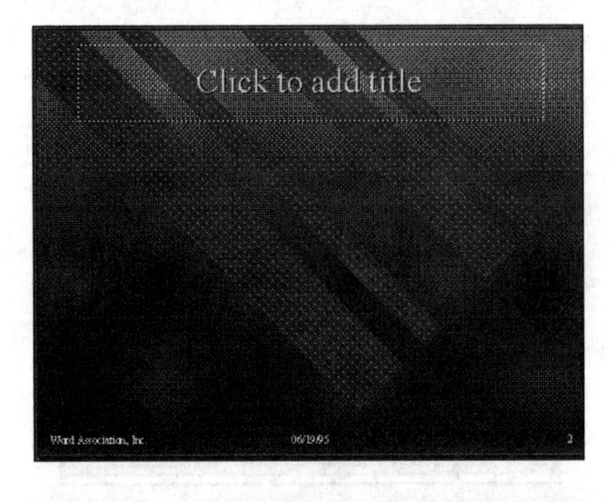

Figure 2.31 *Blank slide (Slide #2 in presentation).*

Notice that the footer information and slide number data you specified earlier appear on this slide. To continue building this new presentation, click where the slide prompts "Click to add title" and type the following title:

Teach Yourself... PowerPoint

Using Text

Select the text tool from the Drawing toolbar at the left of the screen by clicking on it. (The text tool looks like a capital A.) Notice that the mouse pointer changes from the arrow point to a plus sign (sometimes called a *cross hair*). Move the *cross hair* below the slide title under the Y in Yourself. Click the left mouse button to set the text insertion point. Type the second line of the slide:

By Tom Badgett

Now use the text tool four more times to complete the slide. The text tool is canceled and the default pointer is selected when you finish entering information into a text field.

NOTE

You can drag a text box to preset the size before you start typing, or you can simply click once to position the insertion point and let the box grow as you type.

You can enter more than one line of text into a text field by pressing **Enter** at the end of each line, but as soon as you click outside the current text field, the text tool is canceled. When you finish, the slide should look like Figure 2.32.

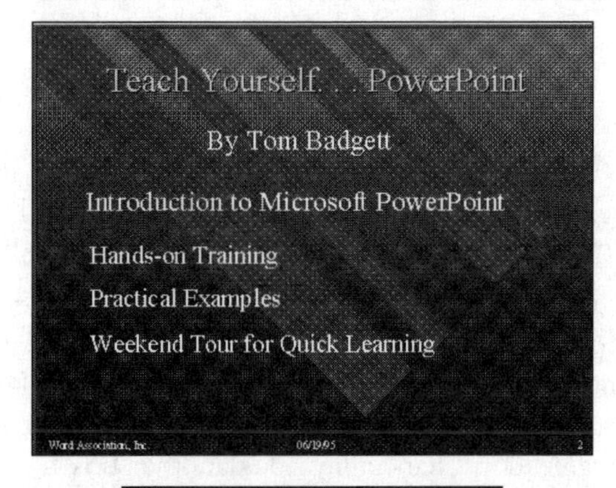

Figure 2.32 *Finished Slide #2.*

NOTE

You could have selected another type of slide that would do more of the text formatting for you, but I wanted to show you how to create your own text fields simply with the text tool from the Drawing toolbar.

Click on the **New Slide...** button at the bottom of the PowerPoint screen and once again choose the AutoLayout slide with the space for a single-line title (the same one you selected for the last slide). Click where the slide prompts "Click to add title" and type the title of this slide:

Teach Yourself: One of a Series

Select **Insert: Object...** to display the Insert Object dialog box shown in Figure 2.33.

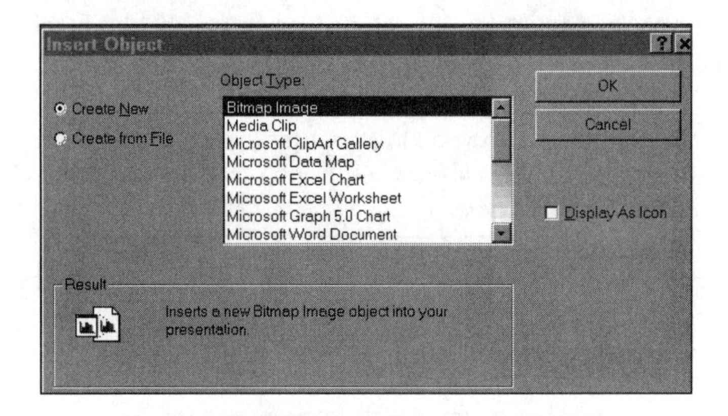

Figure 2.33 *Insert Object dialog box.*

Use the scroll bar at the right of the Object Type window of this dialog box to locate the MS Organization Chart 2.0 entry. Double-click on this line to launch the Organization Chart utility (see Figure 2.34).

Notice that a sample organization chart is already on the screen. You will use this basic chart with one change. Click on the first **Co-worker** button (with the right-facing line). The mouse pointer changes to a Co-worker icon. Move the pointer to the first box on the left of the second line of the organization chart and click. The Organization Chart utility adds another box to the left, creating a display with one box on the first row and four on the second.

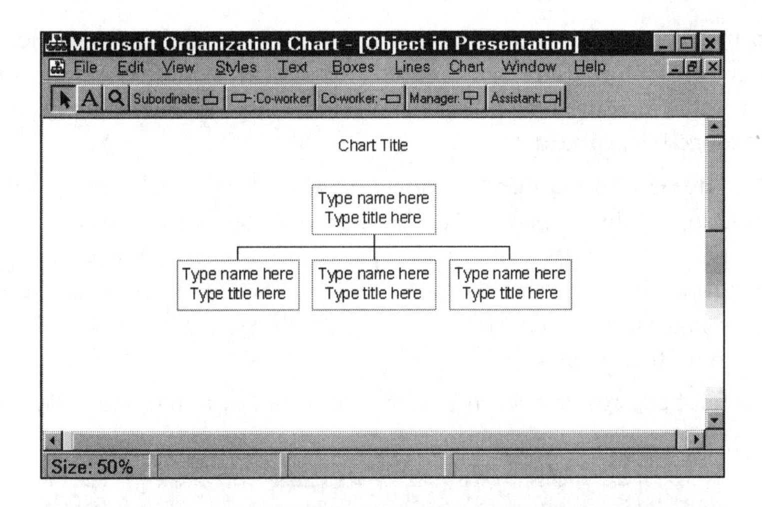

Figure 2.34 *Microsoft Organization Chart application screen.*

Click on the top box in the chart to select it. Now you can enter data for the place holder information. This doesn't work like the "Click here to add title" prompt on the main PowerPoint screen; you'll have to select the entire line with the mouse. Move the pointer to the left of the line, press and hold the left mouse button, and move the mouse to select the line. Now what you type next will replace the prompt line. Type the name:

MIS: Press

NOTE

You can also select the prompt line by pressing **Enter** or **Tab** after double-clicking on the box. This will select the entire title line. Now press backtab (**Shift-Tab**) to select the Name line and start typing. To delete a prompt, press **Enter** or **Tab** to select the line and then press **Del**.

In the same way, enter the title in this first box:

Computer Books

Now start with the left box on the second row of the chart and enter a name into each box. The box names, left to right, should be:

Welcome to...

Teach Yourself...

Power of Power Programming

Power Shortcuts...

Click in the second box on the bottom row (Teach Yourself...) and select **Text: Color** on the Organization Chart menu bar to display the text color bar. Click on a red bar to change the text color to red. This will produce red text against the default orange background.

Select **Boxes: Box Color** to display another color bar. Click on the white box at the top of the color bar. The background color of the Teach Yourself... box changes to white. (Actually, you will see a black box unless you click on the box again or click outside the box to deselect it.) Now you have red text on a white background, which highlights the Teach Yourself... box and makes it stand out from the others.

Your finished organization chart should look similar to the one in Figure 2.35.

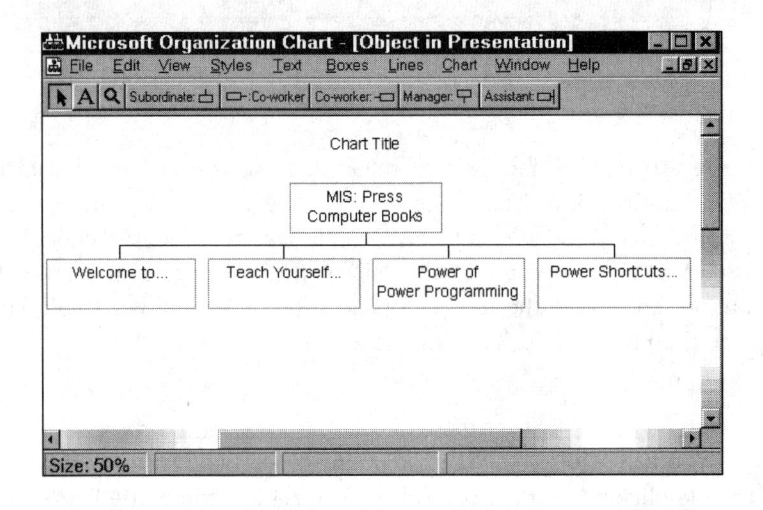

Figure 2.35 *Completed Teach Yourself... organization chart.*

Use **File: Update MISPRESS** from the Organization Chart main menu to place the completed chart onto the presentation slide. Use **Exit** and **Return to MISPRESS** to close the Organization Chart application and return to your slide. The organization chart you just constructed will be overlaid onto slide.

Click anywhere inside the organization chart to select it. Notice the handles that appear on each edge of the chart. Grab a handle on the bottom horizontal edge of the chart and drag the edge until it is nearly at the bottom of the slide. Grab the top horizontal handle and drag the edge until the top of the chart is near the middle of the slide. Now you have an organization chart that is big enough to read, but it is distorted. Drag the left and right edges to change the aspect ratio of the chart so it looks more legible. The resulting slide should look like Figure 2.36.

Figure 2.36 *Completed Teach Yourself... series slide.*

Click on the **New Slide...** button to display the New Slide dialog box. Choose the next-to-last slide from the third row, as before. This is the slide with space for a title and the rest blank. Click on the **Click to add title** line on this slide and type **Levels**. Use the mouse to select the text that you just entered, then click three times on the **Increase Font Size** button on the Format bar. This will enlarge the title.

Click on the text tool icon on the Drawing toolbar and move the mouse downward arrow about halfway between the Levels title and the bottom of the slide. Click once to set the text insertion point. Type the following, pressing **Enter** at the end of each line:

Beginner/Intermediate

IBM/PC

and Compatibles

Now click on the **New Slide...** button to display the New Slide dialog box. Choose the second AutoLayout slide (double-click on it). This slide is the one with a title line at the top and a bulleted list at the bottom of the slide. Click on the **Click to add title** prompt and type the title for this slide:

General Series Features

Click on the "**Click to add text**" prompt to enter the first line in the bulleted list:

Basic and instructional

Press **Enter** to move to the next line in the list. Repeat this process until you have entered all six items in the list, as shown in Figure 2.37.

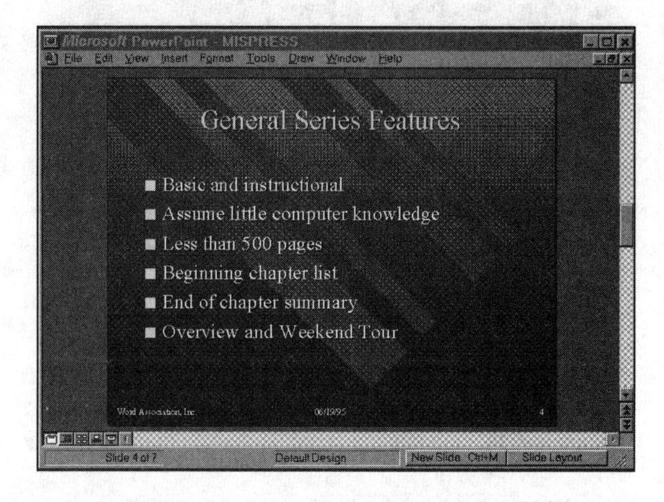

Figure 2.37 *Completed General Series Features slide.*

Click on the **New Slide...** button and choose the third AutoLayout slide down from the top in the left column. This is the slide with a title at the top, a bulleted list on the left, and a clip art image on the right. Add the title shown below at the top of the slide. Press **Enter** after the first line of the title to type the second line:

Teach Yourself...PowerPoint

Table of Contents

Next, click the mouse inside the top of the "Click to add text" box. Enter the five lines of the bulleted list for this slide:

Introduction

Getting Started

Weekend Tour

Designing Presentations

Using Templates, Clip Art and Wizards

Double-click on the clip art image at the right of this slide to display the ClipArt Gallery dialog box. Click on **People** to display only the people clip art. Choose the last clip art image on the fourth row. This is the drawing that shows a presenter standing at a podium ("Man at Podium"). Click **Insert**. The finished slide should look Figure 2.38.

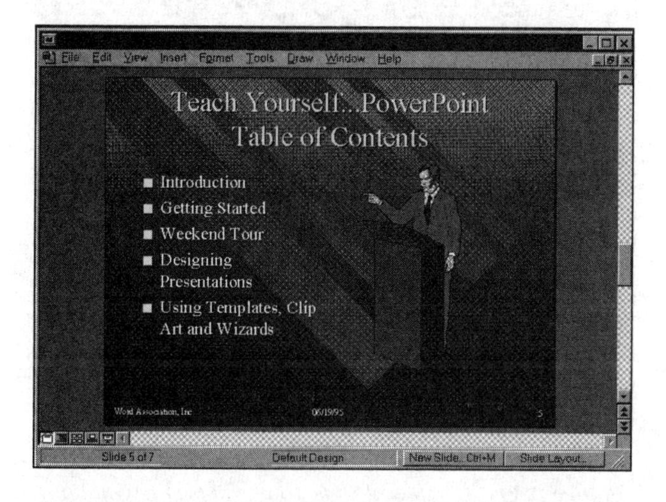

Figure 2.38 *Completed Slide #5 in sample presentation.*

Click on the **New Slide...** button and choose the third slide from the top in the second column from the left. This is the slide with a bulleted list on the right and a clip art image on the left. Enter a title for this slide:

Teach Yourself...PowerPoint

Table of Contents (2)

Enter the rest of this book's table of contents as a bulleted list at the right side of the slide:

Computer Slide Shows

Printing

Presentation Output

With Microsoft Office

Using Help

Hardware & Software

Menu/Command Ref.

Double-click on the clip art icon on the left of this slide to open the ClipArt Gallery. Choose the next-to-last image on the fifth row from the bottom of the People Clip Art list. This is the image that shows a presenter with a black board ("Teacher"). The finished slide should look like Figure 2.39.

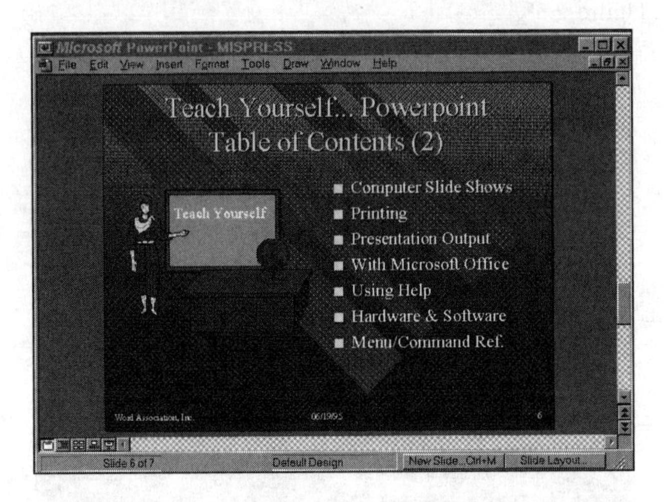

Figure 2.39 *Completed Slide #6 in sample presentation.*

Click on the **New Slide...** button to display the New Slide dialog box one last time. Choose the next-to-last slide in the list on the first screen, which is the one with a title at the top and the rest of the slide blank. Enter a title:

Sales/Purchase Information

Select the text tool from the Drawing toolbar and click near the middle of the slide to open a text box. Type the name and address of MIS: Press as found inside the front of this book. Press **Enter** at the end of each line to start a new line:

Special Sales Director

MIS: Press

a subsidiary of Henry Holt and Company, Inc.

115 West 18th Street

New York, NY 10011

Select the rectangle object tool from the Drawing toolbar and, starting at the upper-left corner above the first line, drag a rectangle around the name and address information on this slide. The default fill color is applied and the box is displayed in the foreground, covering up the text.

Select **Draw: Send Backward** (also on the Drawing+ toolbar, Figure 2.18) to send the new box to the background and make the text visible. The box should still be selected. You can tell this by the presence of handles around the edges of the box. If the box is not selected, click on one edge of the box to reselect it. The handles should appear.

Point to the Drawing toolbar and press the right mouse button. Choose **Drawing+** to add the second drawing toolbar at the left of the PowerPoint screen. Click on the first icon at the top of this toolbar and choose red from the color samples displayed. The background of the selected box around the name and address should change to red.

Finally, format the text. Use the mouse to select the text inside the red box. Click on the **B** button on the Format bar to bold the text. Click on the **Text Color** button on the Format bar to pull down the text color bars, and then choose **White**. The text inside the red box should change to bold white.

Select **File: Save** to store the latest version of your presentation. The final slide should look like Figure 2.40.

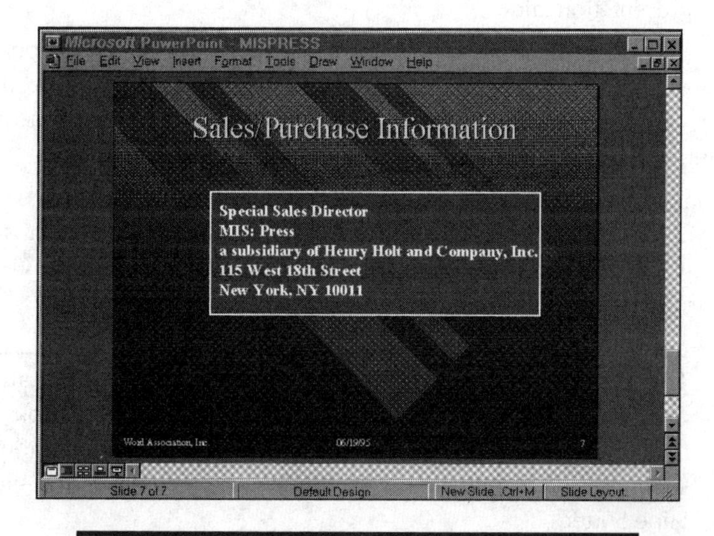

Figure 2.40 *Finished Slide #7 in sample presentation.*

Congratulations! You have taken a basic presentation idea, designed a series of slides around it, and produced these slides in Microsoft PowerPoint. In doing so, you have used many of the features you'll need from now on to make PowerPoint work for you in building successful presentations.

Your next step probably should be to come up with a design of your own. Think about something you already know about—or, like this book, something you can learn about easily—and design a series of slides to support a discussion of that topic. You could use an idea from your job that you already had to present to others or something that you will soon present to someone else. You could choose a topic that you want to discuss at home with your children or spouse, or you could let your children help you select an idea from their current school work. (You'd be surprised at how quickly children take to the presentation idea!) Remember, for additional hints on designing presentations, refer to Chapter 3.

Printing and Presenting the Data

Now that you have a finished presentation, what do you do with it? That depends a little on how you will use the presentation—this one or the ones you create for yourself—but in this section you'll learn about the major options you have with PowerPoint. Later in this book, you'll get additional information on outputting presentation slides.

At the very least you'll probably want to review the presentation you just created to see how things fit together and to decide whether you need to reorganize any of the information. There are a couple of ways to do that quickly in PowerPoint.

Especially for a short presentation like this one, the Slide Sorter view is an excellent way to get an overview of the slides you have and to see how they fit together into an overall presentation. Choose **Slide Sorter** from the View menu to see your presentation all together on one screen, as in Figure 2.41.

NOTE

There is an icon at the bottom of a full-screen slide that lets you choose Slide Sorter view quickly. Click on the icon that looks like four rectangles on a slide (the third icon from the left at the bottom of your slide). Return to full slide view by double-clicking on any slide in the Slide Sorter.

If everything looks all right in the Slide Sorter, click on the first slide in the presentation to select it, and then choose **View: Slide Show...** to display the Slide Show dialog box. Accept the default of showing all slides with Manual Advance by clicking on the **Show** button. PowerPoint will display the first slide in your presentation as a full-screen image and will wait for you to press the left mouse button or any keyboard key to advance to the next slide. Press the right mouse button to bring up a menu, and choose **P** to back up a slide. (You can also use the right and left cursor keys to move forward and backward in the presentation.)

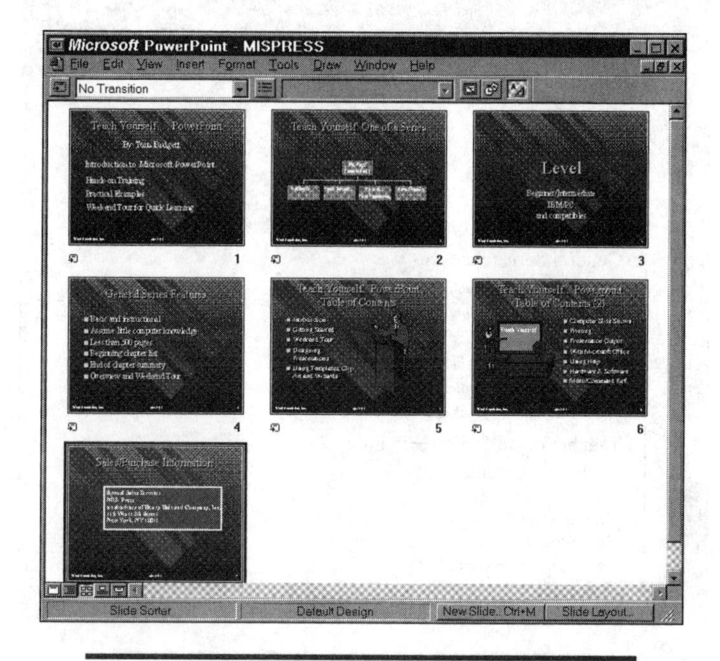

Figure 2.41 *Slide Sorter view of sample presentation.*

Notice that the full information you asked PowerPoint to include is now printed at the bottom of each slide: the company name you specified, the current date, and the slide number. You can return to the Slide Sorter view at any time by pressing **ESC** on the keyboard. When you advance past the last slide in the presentation, PowerPoint automatically returns to the Slide Sorter view (or whatever view was current when you started the slide show).

Remember that as you created the slides, PowerPoint was also creating some additional material for you. This material is described in the following sections.

Outline View

For one thing, there's an outline of the presentation that you haven't seen yet. To get a look at the automatic PowerPoint outline, select **View: Outline**. You should see the slide titles and text in an outline format, as in Figure 2.42. (You can also click on the second icon at the bottom of the slide display—the icon that looks like lines on a page—to display the outline view of your presentation.)

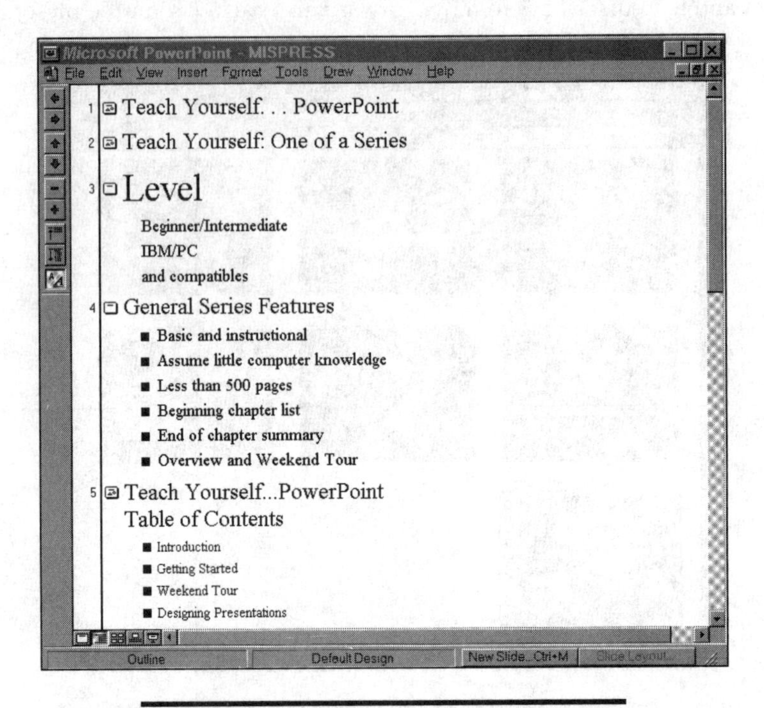

Figure 2.42 *Sample presentation outline view.*

You can easily print the outline with the File Print dialog box by selecting **Outline** in the Print what field. If you'd like to add more to the outline, simply type the additional data where you'd like it to appear. Just keep the notes or outline information within the boundaries of the correct slide. Then, even if you change the position of a slide in the Slide Sorter view, PowerPoint keeps your additional notes with the proper slide on the outline. Remember, however, that the outline is a view of the slide; adding text to an outline means it will show—and print—on the slide itself.

Note, too, that you can change the position of slides from within the outline. Those of us who have years of experience working with text documents and outlines probably find this view very comfortable. For example, to move a slide down in the presentation, simply place the insertion point on the first line of that slide in the outline, and then click on the down arrow on the outline toolbar to the left of the outline display. Notice how the order of slides changes.

Speaker's Notes View

Another view is the Speaker's Notes view. You can display this view with the **View: Notes Pages** command sequence, or by clicking on the **Notes Pages View** icon at the bottom of the screen (fourth icon from the left). Figure 2.43 shows a Notes view for the fourth screen of the sample presentation.

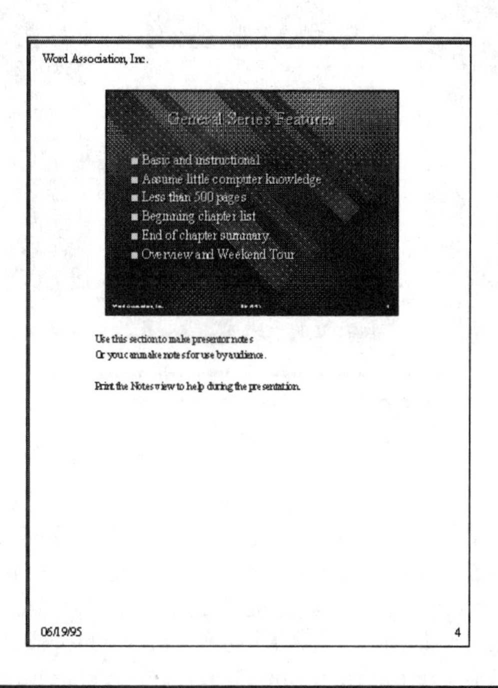

Figure 2.43 *Notes pages view for sample presentation after notes added.*

As you can see, this is a split-page view that places each slide at the top of a page and leaves room at the bottom for information about the slide. This is a convenient tool to use for speaking notes.

Riding along with the notes pages is a Notes Master sheet that helps you do some additional formatting to the notes pages you print. Select **View: Master** to display the Master menu. Then choose **Notes Master** to view the Notes Master page, as shown in Figure 2.44.

By formatting the master page, you establish the format for all notes pages associated with the current presentation. You can grab the slide image and move it around the page, add more graphics elements, and create master text.

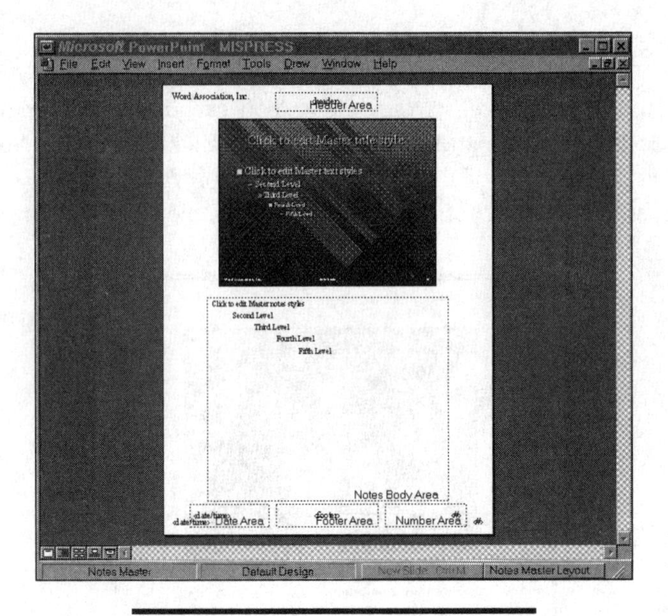

Figure 2.44 *Notes master page screen.*

Handouts

There is another way of looking at your presentation—one that is designed to serve as a handout for the audience. You can create handouts that contain two, three, or six slides per page. To create handouts, first use the **View: Master** command sequence to display the Master menu. Choose **Handouts Master** from this menu to display the Handout Master screen shown in Figure 2.45.

You can use the Handout Master screen to add formatting, text, or graphics to the handout sheet. To generate handouts, use the **File: Print** command to display the Print dialog box. Click on the down arrow at the right of the Print what field to produce a display like the one in Figure 2.46. Select the type of handout you want to create and click on **OK**.

The handout sheets can be helpful in providing an audience follow-along pages or sheets to carry away with them to help improve information retention.

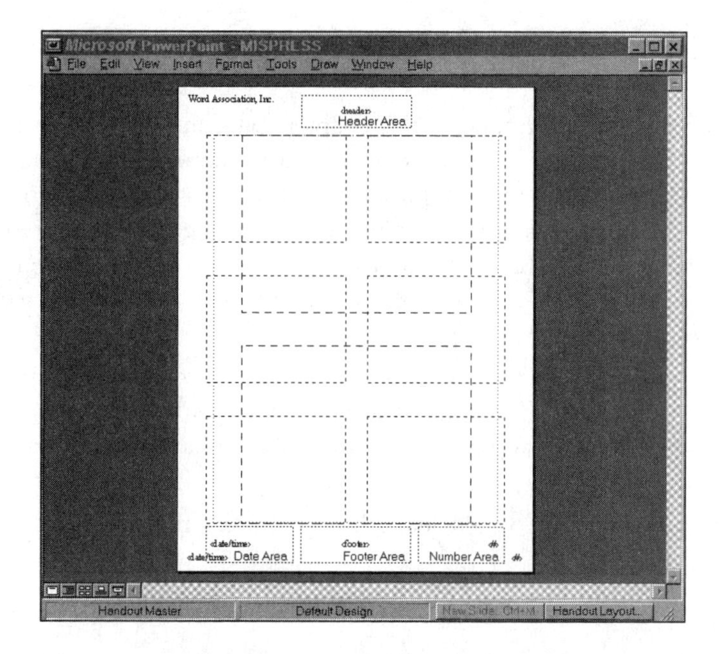

Figure 2.45 *Handout Master screen.*

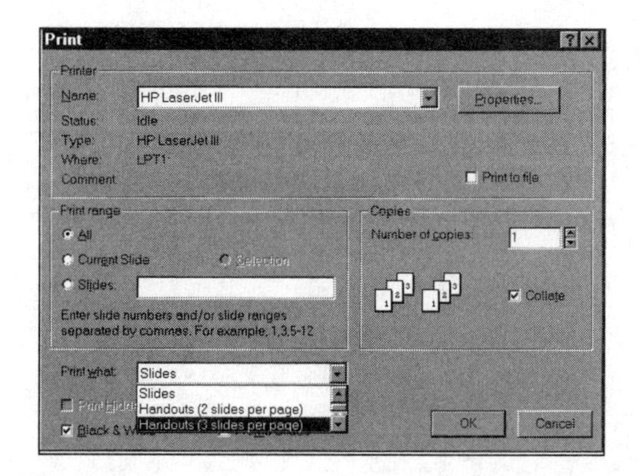

Figure 2.46 *File Print dialog box with Print what list.*

To Sum Up

You've covered a lot of ground in this chapter. Later in this book, we will step together through some of these same areas, but in more detail. In addition, you should try redoing this sample application with content of your own. We covered a lot of information about designing and producing your own presentations with PowerPoint. With the basic information in this chapter—screen components, menus, toolbars, views, clip art, and more—you have all the experience you need to produce your own presentations.

So why wait? Pick a topic from work, home, or school and start working with PowerPoint right now. At the same time, spend some more time with this book refining your skills and going beyond what we have covered in this introduction.

In the next chapter, you'll learn how to make the presentation design process easier.

CHAPTER 3

Designing Presentations for PowerPoint

PowerPoint helps make the job of designing and producing professional and meaningful presentations a lot easier than in the old days of colored pens and flip charts. The computer tools coupled with the drawings, text tools, and forms packaged with the software help just about anybody look like a professional presentation designer.

However, the presentation business has reached the same stage that desktop publishing achieved several years ago. The tools are more powerful, are easy to use, and are widely available, but those of us who have little or no experience in producing presentations can't always use these tools effectively.

A detailed treatise on professional presentation design is beyond the scope of this book—and beyond the expertise of your author. However, there are some design considerations that are easily learned and that, when considered during the design of your presentations as a whole and of the individual slides, can make your work more effective.

That's the topic of this chapter. I'll share some experience that can help you do a better job with the tools PowerPoint offers. As you study these hints, keep in mind that PowerPoint is not designed as a standalone presentation tool. The slides and screens you design with it are intended to be accompanied by a human presenter. Even if you have used music and narration as part of a high-end presentation design with PowerPoint, you may well stand up to control the presentation, to answer questions, or to add personal comments during the show.

With that in mind, part of the planning and design of a PowerPoint presentation should focus on how the human presenter and the material you design can work together to achieve the ultimate goal. I'll discuss general considerations about using PowerPoint presentation material, I'll show you ways to help plan a presentation, and I'll talk about some of the issues involved with designing individual slides.

General Design Considerations

Let's look at some general ideas first. Presentations enhanced with PowerPoint carry a lot more weight than the old-fashioned kind because of the way people gather information. Here's what research shows:

- 10% of what we learn comes from the words we hear.
- 40% of what we learn comes from the way the words are said.
- 50% of what we learn comes from what we see.

So, up to 50% of the information you provide your audience comes from what you present on your PowerPoint slides. That doesn't mean you can back off from preparing for the presentation, or that you should downplay the importance of text and facts. After all, the other 50 percent of what your audience learns comes from what you say and how you say it.

The key to successful presentations is twofold. As you design any presentation, be aware of the power of the visual part of it, but don't forget that the audience also expects to hear something. What the audience sees should be designed to supplement what is being said. The two methods of presenting information work together. You've probably noticed yourself that it can be distracting or even irritating to try to read a lot of material while someone is talking. You tune out the words to concentrate on the visual, or you skim the visual to listen to what is being said.

Therefore, the visual component of a presentation should be brief. You can shorten on-screen presentations by breaking some of the long-standing rules of language you were taught in school. A bulleted list, for example, doesn't always require a subject and verb, and you can use creative symbols in place of standard bullets to enhance the visual. That way the bullets themselves become part of the message. (See Figure 3.1.)

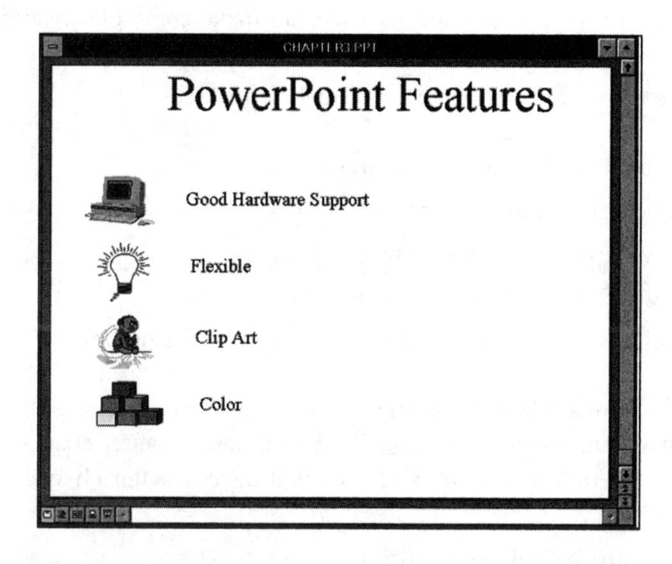

Figure 3.1 *Bulleted list without standard English and with custom bullets.*

The goal is to help the audience grasp the information as quickly as possible and to help them retain it. Whatever you can do to make the experience a visual one will enhance the process.

Some of the same design rules and guidelines you would use for desktop publishing or photographic composition also apply to presentations. After all, the components of a presentation are slides or pages—individual units that are linked together to form the whole. The difference between PowerPoint slides and a printed page or a photograph, of course, is that you can use sound and even motion in addition to layout, color, shape, and shading to get your message across. The key to successful presentations is to use the tools at your disposal in a creative way that is appropriate to the audience you hope to reach and to the message you hope to convey.

In designing a presentation, keep the ultimate goal in mind. Do you want the audience to remember specifics, or is a general idea the more important consideration? In a sales presentation, for example, is it more important for the audience to remember technical specifications and statistics, or do you want to convey a concept or an overview of what the product can do for them or for their business?

There is no set answer. The correct response to that question depends on the type of selling you are doing and what you want the viewer to do, think, or feel at the end of the presentation. But we can make some observations on how to accomplish either of those goals.

To leave the viewer with a concept, feeling, or idea:

- Use motion video and photographs.
- Reduce the amount of text on-screen.
- Show people doing something with the product.
- Show people who appear pleased or satisfied.
- Emphasize *what* is being done over *how* it is being done.

Remember, we retain visual information such as pictures better than text. So whenever you can, impart ideas visually. You'll have a better chance of keeping the audience interested, and the audience will have a better chance of retaining the information.

To emphasize factual details over concept:

- Use text and charts.
- Use no more than six lines per slide.
- State and restate ideas, using different methods and terms.
- Simplify screens.
- Use photographs or art to help the viewer link raw data to the real world.

Whatever the ultimate goal of the presentation is, you can see from the two lists that there are similarities in design concept. The common guideline is to keep things simple yet heavy on the visual to improve information retention.

The sample slide in Figure 3.2 is relatively simple and should be easy for the viewer to understand, interpret, and remember.

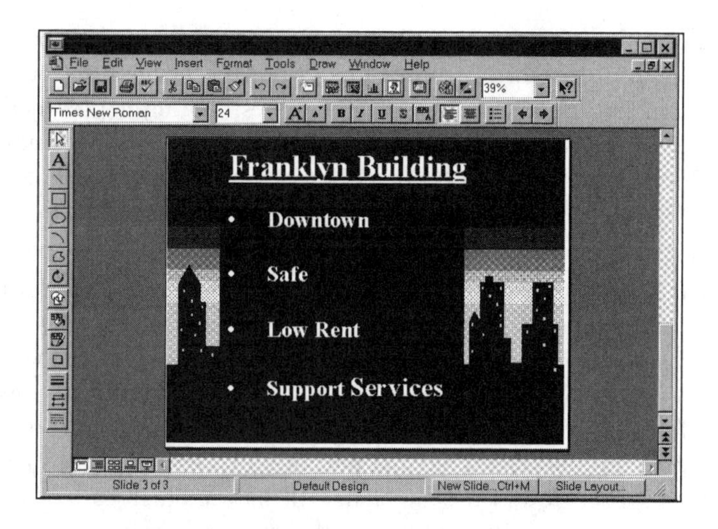

Figure 3.2 *Simple slide easy to interpret.*

The sample slide in Figure 3.3, on the other hand, is too complex. It has too much information on the screen, and would not be easy for most viewers to understand. Remember that presentation slides are designed to augment what a speaker says, not to carry all of the information.

Figure 3.3 *Complex slide difficult to interpret.*

Another important concept is to design presentations for random control whenever possible. In other words, it strengthens your presentation if you can jump over certain slides or backtrack to previous ones. During a presentation, you should be aware of the level of audience understanding. If it becomes obvious that the audience is confused or (worse) bored, you should be able to back the show up or branch to an entirely different segment.

You can do this with interactive buttons on some or all presentation screens, and by having presentation screens that don't appear automatically. A presentation that is under the control of the presenter, who can select slides by clicking on objects that aren't obviously interactive, is much more flexible than one that proceeds automatically. In fact, PowerPoint is set up fairly well for this with its HyperText feature. While you can't make just any object a HyperLink, you can install specific icons that will serve that purpose. By designing icons that appear to be part of a background design or that fit into another part of the overall screen, you can make a link to another slide that is not obvious but that is readily available during the presentation.

Another technique you can use to help you during a presentation is to install an object on every screen—either an obvious or a secret symbol—that jumps to a screen with a complete list of screens and interactive buttons. This display is used as an interim step to any slide in the presentation. That way you need to insert only a single link on each slide. The link is always to the interim slide list. The slide list contains as many links as there are slides in the presentation. Such a screen does a couple of useful things for the presenter. It lets you step back and review any screen as the result of an audience question or if you forget something. It also lets you skip slides if you realize you are running out of time or if you sense that the audience is not following some part of the presentation. The sample screen in Figure 3.4 illustrates this concept.

With a relatively simple presentation, this type of preplanning may not be necessary. But for a lengthy or complex presentation, if you haven't designed a way to back up or to jump to a specific location within the presentation, it may be difficult to respond to forced branching easily.

Another way to use this branching technique is to maintain two presentations, one behind the other. One presentation is a summary and can be used for audiences that need only cursory information. The other offers more detail and can be used for different audiences or to expand on an idea if the audience wants it.

In other words, by including links on the summary slide to another slide with more detail, you have the ability to compress or expand the information you present depending on audience needs. You might create a series of summary screens, and include on each one a button that could branch to a more detailed description of the topic if necessary during the presentation.

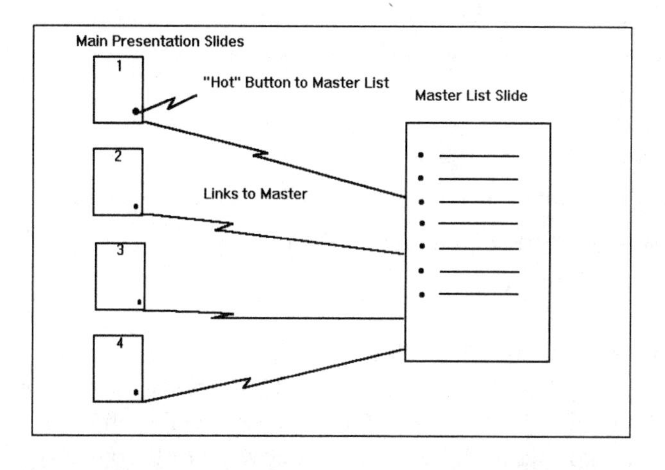

Figure 3.4 *Concept diagram of presentation with master list.*

Another way to break up the information is to have a series of slides that uses common terms for the concepts you are trying to convey. These slides would be enough for nontechnical or inexperienced audiences. When you have to make the presentation to a more savvy audience, on the other hand, you could expand it with more technical information and details.

The basic advice is to be creative. Look at the message you want to get across, consider the audience, and be aware of the broad range of presentation tools available in PowerPoint. Also, while there are some general rules that apply to all types of presentation design, rules are meant to be broken. The dynamic nature of PowerPoint promotes experimentation. If you think of something that might work, try it. Then don't hesitate to listen to feedback from users and viewers of your finished product and to make changes as necessary.

In the next section I'll talk a little about how to start with a basic idea and work toward a presentation design. This is an individual process that you're going to have to develop on your own. However, experience born of practice can help point you in the right direction.

The Design Process

Garrison Keillor, National Public Radio show host, always said he just started talking until he thought of something to say. Unfortunately, too many speeches and presentations are designed just this way. It is better to carefully plan all aspects of the show:

- What to say
- What you want the audience to learn or do as a result of what you say
- What type of room you will do the presentation in
- How you will dress

Making a presentation is a little like flying an airplane: while you are doing it there is so much going on that if any one thing goes wrong it could endanger the whole show. If, as in flying, you have planned well from the beginning, then one or two mishaps along the way won't throw you off course or cause you to crash and burn.

Your approach may be different, or you may use some of these steps in a different order, but the general approach to designing a presentation should include some or all of these elements:

- Brainstorming
- Outlining
- Storyboarding
- Scripting
- Building the presentation
- Testing and debugging

We will discuss each of these processes in the next part of this chapter.

Brainstorming

Brainstorming can be a complex or a fairly simple process, depending on what you are trying to accomplish. We've all used the term at one point or another, but we usually mean something fairly simple. "Let's brainstorm and see if we can come up with a name for the dog," we might say. Then everyone sits around and throws out ideas until somebody hits on one everyone will accept. If you take brainstorming to another, more serious level, however, you can accomplish surprising things with it.

The first step in using brainstorming to help you design a presentation is to ask yourself some basic questions:

- WHO?
- WHAT?
- WHEN?
- WHERE?
- WHY?
- HOW?

These general questions can take more specific forms:

1. Who is the audience?
2. What does the audience know or believe about the subject of the presentation?
3. What does the audience expect to learn or achieve as a result of the presentation?
4. What do I want to accomplish: educating, motivating, informing? What should the audience feel, know, or do differently after the presentation?
5. When and how often will the presentation be delivered?
6. Where will the presentation be delivered, and under what conditions (what kind of room, what atmosphere, what time of day, etc.)?
7. Why am I giving this presentation?
8. How can I most effectively achieve my goals with the resources available?

Some of the answers you need will be immediately obvious. Your supervisor may tell you to prepare a show on a specific topic, perhaps, and will tell you in general what to say and what should be accomplished. Or you may be considering a presentation as the result of a request from a field office or sales force. You may decide to do it yourself as a result of a perceived need to train or inform some of your staff. In these examples, the goals are rather clear and the process fairly obvious.

Other questions may not be so obvious, such as what the audience already thinks or knows about the subject, how you will be most effective in achieving your goals, and what resources you have at your disposal. One tried and true technique for answering these questions, and others you probably haven't thought of, is brainstorming.

Brainstorming is most often associated with a group effort, and it can be effective in that context. But group brainstorming should be preceded by considerable individual effort. The brainstorming process works like this:

1. Use a notepad or word processor and write a topic word or phrase at the top of a page. This should be the general topic if you are designing a presentation.
2. Spend the next 10 to 20 minutes thinking about the topic.
3. Write down every word or phrase that comes to mind during that time. Don't edit, judge, or qualify what you write down. Put on the paper or on the screen everything that comes to mind during the session, even if you can't see how it relates to the topic at hand.
4. When you have to force the ideas or when 20 minutes have passed, stop the session.
5. Don't try to consciously think about the topic for several hours—8 to 24 hours is a good break time.
6. Start another session by reading your previous work quickly.
7. Repeat steps 1 through 6 several times to build a long list of words and phrases. You are through with this first phase of brainstorming when it becomes difficult to come up with new topics.

This part of the brainstorming process can take from a couple of days to a few weeks, depending on the project and how much information you are trying to uncover.

You should be prepared to write down or record new ideas at any time. This is part of the brainstorming process. Relax and be creative. Don't worry about order at this point, but leave room under each item for subtopics. Figure 3.5 shows the result of one brainstorming session about a presentation on the Internet.

When you reach this stage of thinking, you should have a fairly lengthy list of words, phrases, and ideas. They may seem unrelated at this point. You may scan the list and wonder how you came up with such a wildly scattered set of topics. That's okay. You're now ready to try the next part of the process.

Internet
Global Growing at 1 Million/Month Business Difficult to use Need software Access difficult What does it cost? Training? Hardware? Why use it? Who is using it? Cost? Is Sam on it? Who is the bicycle guy?

Figure 3.5 *Internet brainstorming list.*

It is still too early to throw away anything from the list. All you want to do now is group the items, or expand the list for further brainstorming. First, use a separate screen or piece of paper for each of the words or topics you created before. If you ended up with 75 words and phrases, then you should have 75 pieces of paper with one word or phrase at the top of each one. Now go through the previous process (steps 1–7) with each piece of paper. You will end up with 75 sheets (or whatever the original number of topics was), with a collection of words and phrases on each sheet.

At this point you should begin editing the lists, making decisions about which ideas and concepts fit within the general limits of the current project and which ones are obviously beyond the scope of it.

NOTE

Don't throw anything away. A particular page of ideas may help you later or may support a totally different project sometime in the future.

You are ready to begin sorting your topics and ideas. Start by reading the major headings at the top of each brainstorming sheet. If you find entire topics that seem not to fit the current project, lay them aside.

Now arrange the major topics in order of importance. Just stack the individual sheets in descending order. Highlight the important ideas under each major topic (use a highlight pen on paper or boldface type on your word processor). Finally, extract the important subtopics under each main topic into a list organized by order of importance.

The resulting material could take several forms, depending on your personality, the level at which you started, and the type of project you are working on. Whatever the form, you should have a list of topics for the current presentation. Now, consider each of these topics or groups of topics in the light of our WHO WHAT WHEN WHERE WHY HOW guidelines presented earlier in this chapter:

- Which of these is most important?
- How can you present the ideas most effectively?
- In what order should they appear?
- What resources do you have to help you present them?

At this point you may want to bring other people into the process. Make an informal presentation that shows what you have accomplished, including your goals for the presentation, and ask for creative input. Whether you are primarily responsible for the project and are just asking for help, or whether you are part of a team charged with designing the presentation, be sure to give the others involved a definite deadline for their feedback. This should be no more than a few days after you make your initial presentation to them. In addition, make the following clear:

1. The form of feedback you wish: written report, telephone call, another meeting, sample screens.
2. The date, time, and place to submit input.
3. Project goals and the nature of their involvement.
4. Project schedule and whether you will want additional help in the future.

You should now be ready to start an outline. Don't try to outline a presentation until you have finished brainstorming, which is the creative part of the design process. An outline is only an organizational tool. It will help you put in the proper order the creative data you collected during brainstorming.

Creating an Outline

I have worked with a lot of writers and presentation designers, each a creative individual with their own approach to getting the job done. With few exceptions, the general attitude among these people about outlining is fairly negative. Far too many people view an outline as unnecessary baggage in the creative process. That's far from the truth. And the longer or more complex the project, the more important outlining becomes. Whatever preconceived notions about outlining you bring to the presentation table, try to set them aside. Outlining is a useful tool that augments the creative process.

The purposes of an outline are:

- To help organize
- To highlight important areas
- To identify minor ideas or concepts
- To discover irrelevant ideas or concepts

In addition, a well-designed outline can help others see your vision for the presentation. I find that having one or more people review an outline can help you identify weaknesses and omissions in your work before you have progressed too far to make changes easily.

While there are some classic outline forms from which to choose, you can safely design your own. Remember that the outline is an organizational tool, so the more organized the outline is, the better it can do its job. The formality of your outline style should vary directly with the number of people you expect to read it. If your outline is simply for your own reference—a way to guide you toward a storyboard design—then adhering to strict outline format is less important. If, on the other hand, you expect to distribute the outline to several other people, a more formal approach is desirable.

NOTE

PowerPoint has a useful outline view of each presentation. This outline is simply another view of the slide show. You can use the outline view to help you visualize the organization of your presentation. But the outline process I am talking about here is more formal and is designed to help you understand the overall presentation—slides and narration. This outline should be created in Word 7 or another quality word processor.

Here are some outlining guidelines you may find helpful:

1. Use a consistent numbering system that ranges from high to low level. The classic form is Roman numerals at the highest level, followed by capital alphabetic characters, then numbers followed by periods, and so on. Your word processor can provide a workable numbering system.
2. Provide at least two entries at each level (no A. without a corresponding B., no 1. without an accompanying 2.).
3. Use consistent style: single words and phrases (topical outline) or sentences (sentence outline) at each level.
4. Use parallel headings and subheadings so that the same type of material is placed in similar levels.
5. Use consistent wording among entries at the same level.
6. Use main headings that represent slide topics to make storyboard development easier.
7. Use headings that convey sufficient information for other readers to understand.

A fragment of an outline for the sample presentation about this book (described in Chapter 2) is shown in Figure 3.6. Obviously this is not the only format, but it is a basic design that should serve your personal needs and the needs of others in your organization who may have occasion to review it with you.

Teach Yourself...PowerPoint Outline

I. Introduction
   A. Who is MIS: Press?
   B. Teach Yourself... Concept

II. Title and Features
   A. What is PowerPoint?
   B. Author
   C. Features

III. Series Concept
   A. Other MIS: Press Computer Books
   B. Where Teach Yourself... Fits

IV. Target Level
   A. Audience
   B. Coverage

V. General Features
   A. Teach Yourself vs other books
   B. Series Goals

Figure 3.6 *Sample show outline—Teach Yourself....*

If you conduct the brainstorming and outlining steps properly, then when it comes to building the storyboard, the hard work is done. All you will really need to do is use the main outline headings as slide titles and fill in the description from the subheadings on each slide.

If you are designing an *interactive presentation*, or one that includes some direct branching (discussed earlier in this chapter), then you may want to build a flow chart between the outline and the storyboard. A *flow chart* shows graphically any branches or decision points that occur in the show. In an interactive application, the user/viewer can change the direction of the presentation at certain points as the result of prompts or other stimuli. A simple flow chart is shown in Figure 3.7.

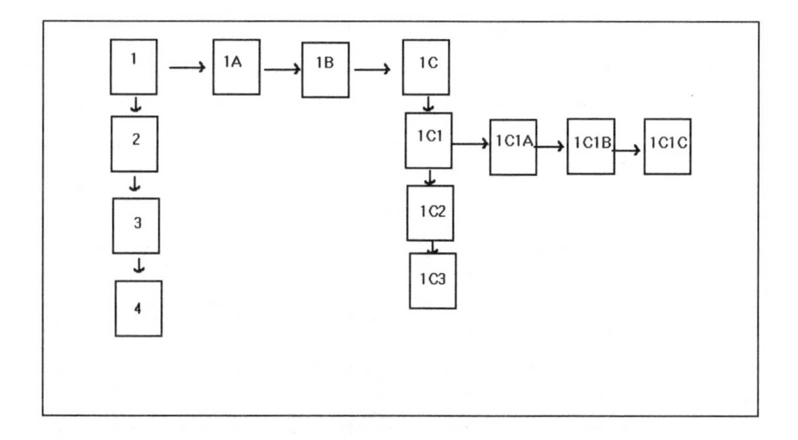

Figure 3.7 *Sample presentation flow chart.*

When the outline is finished you are ready to draw a simple storyboard. We will show you one way to do that in the next section.

Using a Storyboard

Think of a *storyboard* as a graphical representation of the outline. A storyboard can be a simple hand drawing on a yellow pad or a complex, well-drawn creation. Whether you draw a storyboard by hand or use a computer-based drawing tool, the storyboard is an important part of the creative process. Particularly as presentations get more complex, you'll ultimately save time by drawing a storyboard before you start actually constructing the presentation in PowerPoint.

I'll submit to one exception to this storyboard rule. In PowerPoint, the Slide Sorter view can help you visualize your presentation. You can use it to build a storyboard while you construct the presentation. In this case you are using PowerPoint to construct a storyboard that is really part of the presentation itself.

For all but the simplest shows, however, the best approach is to rough out the story line on paper. The idea is to use the outline as a basis for drawing a simple representation of each slide you will have in the program.

Think of a PowerPoint presentation as a series of slides, modules, or events—some of them placed sequentially (end to end), and some of them lying parallel. One of these lines contains the images (slides) you will use during the presentation. Associated with each slide is another unit that represents music, sound, or narration. In addition, you can specify a special effect (fade, wipe, dissolve, etc.) as the transition between slides.

The sample storyboard fragment in Figure 3.8 shows this concept. Any art such as drawings or photographs is shown, plus placement of text, windows, and other special effects. You can note on the drawing what sound, if any, will be associated with each slide.

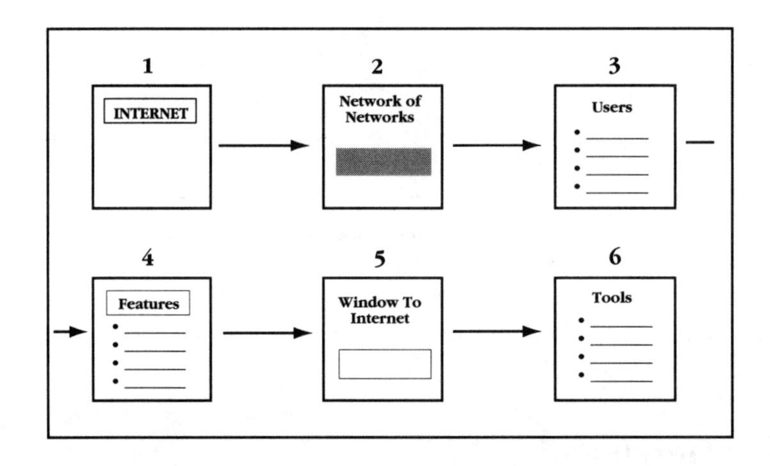

Figure 3.8 *Presentation storyboard fragment.*

The first storyboard after the outline can serve as a doodling session—part of the initial planning. This is a chance for you to put in a primitive visual form the outline you have developed during brainstorming. As with other steps in the design process, you may have to go through this procedure several times to refine the design, locate problems, add new ideas, and get input from other members of the design team or other experts in your organization.

If all of this seems overly complicated, don't let it be. You won't spend very long on any of these steps for a simple presentation, and for a longer presentation, focusing on an organized procedure can make the whole process relatively easy. Besides, storyboarding in particular can be fun. It is not difficult or complicated, and it can make designing the final presentation a lot easier.

Working with a storyboard can accomplish a number of important goals:

- Establish the order of the slides.
- Determine the number of slides.
- Create the general design of each slide.
- Identify special effects (sound, video, wipes, etc.).
- Determine what resources are needed to produce the slides.
- Give other team members a vehicle for reviewing the presentation and making changes.
- Provide an archival copy of the information.

As you work with sound, artwork, and other resources, you may want to brainstorm again. Try writing artwork and sound ideas next to each topic or on the storyboard. Don't worry if your ideas seem strange when you think of them—write them down! Later, what seemed like a bad idea may be the unique angle you were looking for, or it may make you think of an even better way of doing something.

As you refine the storyboard, add additional information. This makes the process of building the actual application in PowerPoint even easier. You may wish to include notes on the file names for any graphics or scanned images, or to jot down a list of resources and their locations beside each slide drawing.

For a relatively simple presentation, your storyboard will likely include every slide. The storyboard for a complicated presentation, however, may show only the first slide or two in a multislide series so that you can track modules of information.

What you learn while working with the storyboard can feed back to the outline, causing you to change the basic design of the presentation. The visual process is a good polishing step that helps you to see how a show shapes up.

Remember that you are trying to tell a story, make a point, sell an idea, or change an opinion. How you do this depends on the audience, the material being presented, and your own personality. There are, however, a few recognized ways of telling a story. For example, you can begin at the beginning with little detail, then build until you have provided the audience with a lot of information:

The computer may seem like a new idea, but the conceptual design for machines we use today is more than 100 years old....

On the other hand, you can start with some piece of important information well into the story, then bring the audience up to date a little at a time:

Today's desktop PC can process information at more than 112 million instructions per second, speed and power that....

Consider these ways of organizing information for a story:

1. **Deductive Organization**: Moves from the general to the specific.
2. **Inductive Organization**: Moves from the specific to the general.
3. **Chronological Organization**: Begins at the beginning and describes a sequence of events in the order in which they occurred.
4. **Process Organization**: Presents the steps involved in a process or procedure where each step must occur in a given order.
5. **Agenda Organization**: Presents information in a random order, frequently without logic. However, a successful agenda organization must tell the audience what the order is.

You can design other ways to organize a presentation that are combinations of these methods. In fact, it is rare to see a clean organization that strictly follows one of these presentation designs. It is more important to know the audience, to understand what end result is desired, and to select a combination of tools and organizational methods to achieve this goal.

You should accept the fact that your carefully planned design will change when you begin production. While the outline and storyboard are excellent organizational tools, they shouldn't become overpowering or cause limitations in your thinking as you work on the script and prepare the slides for the presentation.

Writing the Script

Like a movie script, the presentation script provides a textual representation of all of the elements of the final show. Whereas the storyboard is a visual representation of all or part of the show elements, everything that will be part of the presentation should appear on a script, including:

- Slide descriptions
- Text and how it will be presented
- Slide number
- Duration of each module
- Narration (if any)
- Sound effects
- Music
- Graphics elements
- Video

A portion of a PowerPoint presentation script is shown in Figure 3.9.

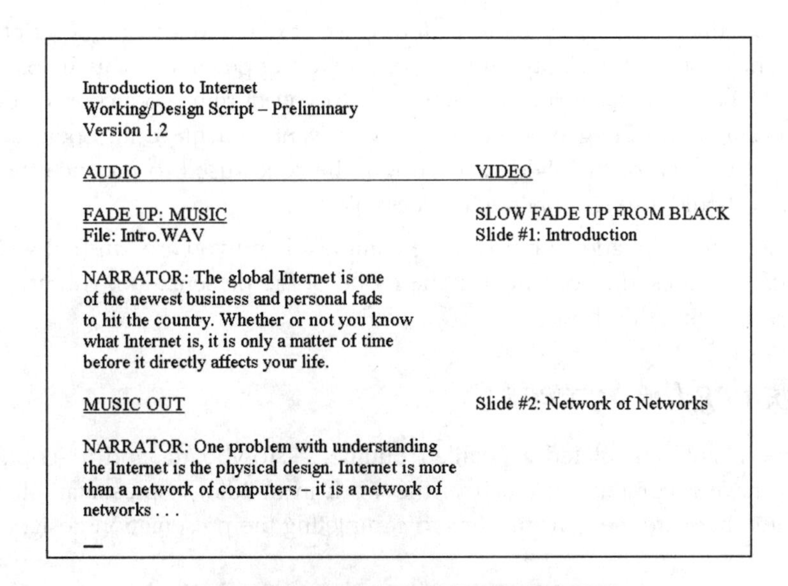

Introduction to Internet
Working/Design Script – Preliminary
Version 1.2

AUDIO	VIDEO
FADE UP: MUSIC File: Intro.WAV	SLOW FADE UP FROM BLACK Slide #1: Introduction
NARRATOR: The global Internet is one of the newest business and personal fads to hit the country. Whether or not you know what Internet is, it is only a matter of time before it directly affects your life.	
MUSIC OUT	Slide #2: Network of Networks
NARRATOR: One problem with understanding the Internet is the physical design. Internet is more than a network of computers – it is a network of networks . . .	

Figure 3.9 *PowerPoint script fragment.*

Like storyboarding, scripting is a personal activity. You can design your own script format and style, but you should keep these ideas in mind:

- Who will use the script?
- Are several people working on the production?
- How complex is the production?
- How will the presentation be produced?

The answers to questions such as these will help you determine how serious you need to be about designing a complete and consistent script style. Here are some guidelines or suggestions to help you develop your own style:

1. Split the page, placing audio information on the left side of the page and visual information on the right.
2. Number the scenes or slides in each module.
3. Include file names or other information where possible.
4. Write instructions in all upper case, and narration in upper and lower case.

Remember that while you want to include a lot of detail in a working script, you also want to strive for clarity and an uncluttered appearance. This helps those who may be unfamiliar with the show to help you during production or during the proofing and testing process. Just as you want to achieve an open, uncluttered feel to each of the slides you design, the script used to produce the presentation should also feel open and accessible.

When the script and storyboard are completed and you are satisfied with the order of the slides, the content, and the mood of the presentation, you are ready to begin building the show.

Designing the Screens

Once you have completed a detailed outline, a storyboard, and a script, you already have accomplished much of the work in building a presentation. From this point, here are the general steps to completing the presentation design:

1. Construct individual slides or screens by creating titles and adding text or graphic elements.

2. Set the duration or control (how the slide will change).
3. Add sound, music, or narration as required.

After the elements of the presentation are in place, test it to make sure that everything functions as you intend and that the program produces the desired effect.

In some ways, a slide or a computer screen is like a printed page. Taken together, all of the elements in either medium create a *layout.* A layout is the arrangement of the elements that make up the page or screen. Some of the possible elements of a PowerPoint screen are:

- Text
- Graphics
- Photographs
- Boxes and other static objects
- Motion video
- Color space

No single element of a layout is intended to stand on its own. Every slide element should relate in some way to every other element and, in some cases, to one or more elements on previous or following slides.

If you change the typeface or typestyle used for a heading, for example, it may change how much information will fit on the page and it may require a change in the type used for the rest of the screen. (See the section on fonts later in this chapter for more information on using typefaces.) If you open up a screen with more colored space, you may not be able to fit all of the elements you had on the screen before. And, if you change the font or background on one slide, you should consider making the same changes to other slides in the presentation for consistency.

Here are general guidelines to remember as you work on slide design:

- Each slide should address a single concept or idea.
- Slides should follow a logical progression, each building on the other.
- In general, a simple design is best.
- The viewer must be able to digest each slide quickly and easily.
- Use no more than six lines of text on any one slide.

- Use upper and lower case text, NOT all caps.
- Choose a color appropriate to the mood you want to convey.
- Avoid using too many colors (five colors per slide maximum).
- Use photographs and video wherever possible.

In addition, be aware of how most of us view a page, a screen, or a photograph. The scanning pattern usually is a reverse "S" that starts at the upper left corner, moves to the middle toward the right side, zooms to the left about three-fourths of the way down, and exits on the lower right. Obviously, items you want to emphasize should be placed at points on the "S" that reinforce the natural scanning pattern.

Consider using motion to focus the viewer's eye on the desired area of the slide. In PowerPoint you can insert short video clips, for example. You could also insert a brief sound element to encourage the audience to focus on a particular slide. I'll show you later in this book how to use such features of PowerPoint to enhance a presentation.

As you design each screen, remember this general rule: Visual material augments a presentation. It adds information to what the speaker is saying or helps the audience to retain or interpret what the speaker is saying. Don't use motion video, animation, or any other technique simply because you can; use it because it is the proper thing to do in a given situation.

One way to think about this is to ask what questions a visual may answer. If it provides information about *where* something is, *how* something works, *how much* is involved (cost, quantity, etc.), *who* is involved or affected, *when* you do something or use something, or *why* this information is important, then that visual is doing its job.

A number of attention-getting concepts can help you enhance a PowerPoint presentation. I've summarized some of them in Table 3.1.

Use the guidelines in Table 3.1 along with the other guidelines you learn in this chapter. For example, the table shows that ALL CAPS get more attention than upper and lower case (initial caps) text. However, you don't want a chart with all text in upper case because it is too difficult to read. We are used to reading text in upper and lower case. Use all caps for headings, titles, and other text you want to emphasize, then revert to normal initial caps for the rest of the text.

In the following sections, I'll give you additional suggestions for using specific slide elements as part of your presentation design.

Table 3.1 elative impact of presentation screen elements.

High Interest	Low Interest
Photos	Words
Color	Black & White
White (Blank) space	Solid copy
Bold type	Italic Type
ALL CAPS	Lower case
Large type	Small type
Wide lines	Thin lines
Large area	Small area
3D	2D

USING TEXT CHARTS

I've spent a fair amount of time in this chapter talking about the many color and graphics tools you can use to enhance PowerPoint presentations. However, you shouldn't ignore the importance of text. At least half of business-oriented presentation material is still text-based. With PowerPoint you can use motion and music to augment what is on the screen, but it is still true that you will likely be using a lot of text charts as part of your PowerPoint shows.

A *text chart* is used for tables of organization, flow charts, timetables, sales presentations, and summaries. The name notwithstanding, text charts may incorporate a variety of graphic elements—scanned images, graphs, and clip art—as well as grids, boxes, lines, and shading, along with basic text.

At its simplest level, a text chart may be nothing more than a bulleted list. After all, one of the reasons for designing a PowerPoint presentation in the first place is to convey some type of information. The advantage of PowerPoint is that you can organize and present this text information in creative ways to catch and keep the viewer's attention and to improve retention of the data. Language, properly applied, is still a good way to present information.

Here are some of the ways a text chart can help you to convey information in a PowerPoint presentation:

- Presents information that includes too many data types or too much information to present logically in a graph.
- Lists exact values instead of graphic approximations.
- Shows information that covers a very broad range between the highest and lowest numbers.
- Shows data when the exact amount is critical.

The guidelines for designing a text chart slide are generally the same as for any other slide:

- Choose typefaces and type sizes carefully.
- Place relatively small amounts of data on each slide.
- Keep information on each slide closely related.
- Highlight the benefits or results of your ideas.
- Be as specific as possible; avoid generalities.
- Keep each sentence or phrase as short as possible.
- Keep slides in a series consistent by using the same combination of fonts and by using similar size and layout ratios from slide to slide.
- Use both upper and lower case characters, not all upper case (except for titles or other emphasis).
- Drop extra or unnecessary words, even if incomplete sentences result.
- Generally, you should avoid the use of hyphens; they can break up the flow of data.

Designing with Text (Fonts)

I've talked about general concepts of using text in your presentations. Now let's look at text elements in more detail. The characters you put on the screen are an important part of your message. Not only does the typeface you select help convey information, it also imparts a mood or style that is an integral part of the message.

What is a *typeface*? It is a distinctive shape and design of type that makes a collection of letters recognizable. Typefaces are generally identified by name, such as Times Roman, Helvetica, Palatino, and Century Schoolbook. In addition to the design of characters, you can also control the size of text in PowerPoint.

The size of the type you use is measured in *points.* One point is equal to 1/72nd of an inch, so 72-point type is about one inch tall. In most typefaces, 12-point type is standard for printed pages and is also a readable on-screen size. A 30- or 50-point size is appropriate for titles and headings or for a bulleted list when the viewer will be a longer-than-normal distance from the screen.

Most typefaces can be presented in different styles and stroke weights. Examples are bold, italic, bold italic, or shadow. A font is a collection of all of the characters available for a particular typeface and style. Times Italic, for example, is a font, as is Palatino Bold or Helvetica Bold Italic.

As you choose type for a presentation slide, also be aware of serif and sans serif designs. Serif type includes finishing strokes at the end of main strokes. Most typefaces use serifs; serif type is usually easier to read than typefaces without serifs (sans serif type).

Times is a serif type: **Times**

Helvetica is a popular sans serif type: **Helvetica**

Notice the difference between a font and a typeface. A typeface is a named shape or design of character, whereas a font is a collection of all of the available characters in a particular typeface in a specific style.

PowerPoint supports a wide range of text styles, sizes, and colors. However, you should work with a limited number of fonts and styles within any given presentation. It is best to stick with the same type style for the same positions across all slides. For example, if you have a series of slides that includes a title or header line on each slide, all of the title text should use the same font and (usually) the same font size. Likewise, captions for the images on these slides should all use the same size and font, running text or bulleted lists should be the same, and so on.

Two or three fonts on the same slide should be the maximum. You might use one basic type style for body copy—the text used in the middle of the screen for description or for lists—and one or two accent faces for captions or emphasis. Accent faces can be an italic, bold, extended, or condensed version of the basic body type, or they can be a related new font. Related type means type of the same general style. You don't want body copy of clean, modern Helvetica, for example, mixed with large titles drawn in florid Old English.

As a general rule, sans serif fonts are a better choice for presentations than serif fonts. Serifs tend to disappear or blur, particularly if you are projecting the image.

Size of type is important in any page, screen, or slide design. Presentation professionals have some guidelines about type size, but the most general rule is, Can the audience read it? You can find this out by testing the presentation with coworkers or friends in an environment similar to where the presentation will be given.

A good rule of thumb is that the maximum viewing distance from a presentation screen is six times the screen diameter. So, if you are projecting images onto a 30- x 40-inch screen, you should plan the presentation so that no one in the audience must sit further than 20 feet away (40 in. x 6 = 240 in./12 = 20 feet). If you are making the presentation on a standard 14-inch PC screen, on the other hand, no one in the audience should sit further than about 7 feet away (14 in. x 6 = 84 in./12 = 7 feet).

Test these guidelines by simply pushing your chair away from your PC. By the time you get six or seven feet away from the screen, reading anything other than fairly large type becomes difficult. In addition to using appropriate size type, you can make the reading process easier through the use of color, accent shapes, and so on.

Designing with Color

Color is an extremely important part of screen design—perhaps even the most important. Compared to a black and white image, such as an overhead projector slide prepared with a standard black type printer, a color image:

- Accelerates learning, retention, and recall by nearly 80%.
- Improves comprehension by more than 70%.
- Increases willingness to read by up to 80% .
- Improves selling efficiency by as much as 85%.

While color is important in your PowerPoint presentations, it is also important not to place too many colors on a single slide or screen. In general, five colors should be the maximum. Most of your screens probably will use even fewer colors than that, unless you are including a full-color photograph or drawn image.

Another way to look at color is to determine what the overall message of the screen or presentation is, then to choose a color appropriate to that message. For example, one study by the Wagner Institute for Color Research in Santa Barbara, California, showed how people react to different colors in interior design. The study showed that blue is a favorite color that elicits positive responses, while red triggers an emotional response. Green is a comfortable color and yellow gets attention more quickly than any other color. Gray says "exclusive" or "quality," while white projects a message of sophistication or refinement. Black, on the other hand, is not appealing to most viewers.

Some of the same general guidelines hold true for presentation material. Studies have shown that different colors cause different responses. Red, for example, is an emotional color that can actually make a person's heart beat faster. Red denotes excitement and may mean stop or danger, depending on the viewer and the context. It also takes longer for the eye to process red than any other color.

Dark blue, on the other hand, projects a stable, trustworthy, and mature message. It can encourage fantasy, but it also has a calming effect, so don't use blue if you want the audience excited or upbeat.

Light blue is considered youthful, masculine, and cool, while the message of green is growth, positive, organic, or go. Green can help people feel comfortable in unfamiliar places. Choose green carefully, however, because many of us carry a prejudice against institutional green—the green of classrooms and chalk boards.

White is a pure color that denotes the sensation of cleanliness, honesty, sophistication, refinement, or delicate things. Used properly with other colors, white can be useful in attracting an upscale audience.

Use black for serious topics or to project the concept of heaviness or death. You should use black carefully, but it can be useful, particularly for some backgrounds.

Gray is a color of integrity. It says exclusive, neutral, cool, mature. Creative people usually feel comfortable being around gray.

Brown is considered a wholesome color that is associated with organic themes and is unpretentious. Yellow, on the other hand, is emotional and positive. It can also denote the concept of caution. Yellow is interpreted by the eye faster than any other color. It can be a good choice for drawing attention to a slide or screen area, but it can also incite anger or irritation.

Another emotional color is orange. It evokes positive or organic feelings. Orange is also considered a neutral color that can help the viewer adapt to other colors. Orange and blue in combination denote strength. Gold is a conservative color and is stable and elegant.

Both purple and pink are youthful colors. Purple is also considered contemporary in mood and pink is often associated with feminine or warm topics. In fact, all pastel colors are youthful and can be feminine. They also denote the concept of swiftness and sensitivity. Finally, any metallic color produces an image of elegance, wealth, and long-lastingness.

Here's a more general way to look at color. Different colors usually are associated with specific feelings or moods. Cyan and blue are cool colors, while yellow and red are warm colors. Magenta and green, on the other hand, are transitional colors that can take on qualities of either warm or cool, though magenta is basically a warm color while green is a cool one.

As you design slides, you should generally use dark colors for backgrounds and lighter colors for text and illustrations, because the eye is naturally drawn to the lighter areas in the foreground. This is the same concept used by photographers and painters to focus attention within a scene. Notice especially people pictures printed by professional photographers. The faces—already lighter than the surrounding features—sometimes are made extra light to force attention on them. The same concept holds true when designing presentation slides. A dark background with light foreground helps keep the viewer focused on what is most important.

The Tektronix company is a leader in color printer technology. It advises that, from a viewer perspective, the most popular colors for backgrounds, in order, are:

1. Dark blue
2. Black
3. Gray
4. Brown
5. Red
6. Green
7. Purple

Also, if you design a chart that arranges items by color, or that uses color to code or flag certain concepts, you should consider arranging the items by color in the order in which the colors appear in the natural spectrum:

1. Red
2. Orange

3. Yellow
4. Green
5. Blue
6. Indigo
7. Violet

Your presentations should consist of logical groupings of color. You should use the same range of colors within a logical section of your presentation, and you should use colors that are close together on the color chart. If you switch color schemes too often or too suddenly it is jarring to the audience.

Using Photographs

I said earlier that you can use photographs to help the viewer relate the information on the slide to the real world. Look at the examples in Figures 3.10 and 3.11. The first illustration shows a bulleted list against a plain background. The second sample shows the same list against a photograph.

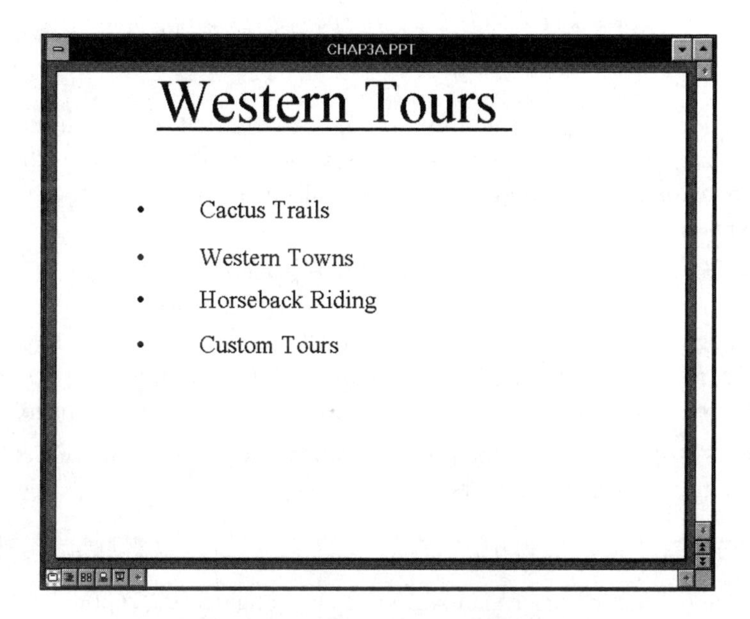

Figure 3.10 *Bulleted list with plain background.*

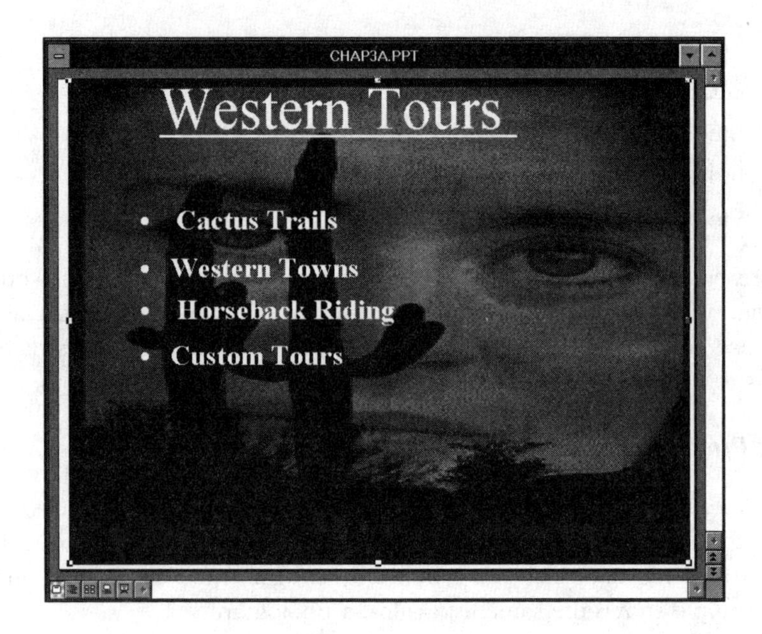

Figure 3.11 *Bulleted list with photograph background*
(photo by Tom DeMoss, Words and Pictures, Tucson, Arizona).

The text information is presented in the same way in both cases, but the photographic background—even if only a hint of an item is shown—helps the viewer relate the textual information to something real. Also, a photograph can improve data retention.

A list that deals with automobiles could be placed over a picture of a car, for example. General sales information could be presented over a picture that suggests selling: a store interior, a shopping mall, or a cash register. If you don't have or can't get a photograph, use a graphic image as the next best choice. You can use something you have drawn from scratch or a clip art image.

Where do you get photographs and other images for your presentations? There are many places to look, including:

- Company brochures, letterheads, business cards, or catalogs
- Annual reports, user manuals, sales aids, engineering reports
- Art used by other members of your organization in previous presentations
- Product samples, intracompany reports, letters

- Clip art, software samples
- Custom-drawn art using a graphics package
- Video tape still frames

You can scan many of these images into the computer in a format that PowerPoint can use directly. Most scanners produce black and white images.

This works for presentations if you can either use colored text, place the photograph inside a color border, or colorize the image with a transparent overlay.

If you want a color image, or if you don't have access to a scanner, check your local telephone book. There are companies that offer scanning services. They will take your image, scan it, and return a computer .TIF, .PCX, or other file format compatible with PowerPoint.

There is a wide variety of sources for images to use with PowerPoint. Just be careful how you use images from outside sources. You can't legally scan an image from a magazine or a book, for example, and then use it for your presentation (without permission from the publisher, that is), though it might be tempting to do so.

One good source of still color images for your presentations is video tape or a video camera fed directly into a video capture board. Most video hardware includes some form of software driver to let you capture a still frame image. All you need to do is set up your camera on a tripod, light it to show what you want, and take a few seconds of tape. Then hook up your VCR player to the video capture board, take a snap shot, and you are ready to go.

This technique lets you capture shots from physical images such as computer keyboards or hardware, parts of your company, equipment used by your company, or scenes of your town or area. Once the image is captured and stored in a graphics file format, you can use it as a background or as a picture inside a window just as you would any other graphics image from your computer.

New technology from Eastman Kodak makes it easy to insert high quality color photographs into your presentations. The Photo CD technology lets you take slides or negatives to your local drug store (or professional photo finisher) and send them away for translation to Photo CD format. Kodak and other companies supply software to convert these digitized photographs to .PCX, .TIF, and other graphics formats that you can use with PowerPoint.

USING GRAPHICS

PowerPoint presentations are built around the concept of using graphics—either colored graphs that represent numerical data or clip art. As I have said, you can use photographs and other elements, but clip art or one of the PowerPoint internal graphs is an easy way to enhance a presentation.

PowerPoint supplies about 1,000 clip art images from a variety of categories. These images are designed to suggest a concept or idea, to add color and shape to your slides, and to provide the audience with images that help with data retention. In addition to the 1,000 or so clip art images, PowerPoint includes preformatted slides that reserve space for clip art. All you have to do is click on the **Clip Art** icon, and PowerPoint opens up the ClipArt Gallery display so you can choose the image you want to use. These are professionally designed slides that help you build quality presentations easily.

Do you want to present complex numerical data in a form the audience can easily interpret? The built-in PowerPoint graphing feature is there to help out. Use a graph any time you want the audience to understand concepts and trends instead of precise numbers. In fact, you might use a text chart of the actual numbers coupled with a graph to provide the full picture.

USING VIDEO

Motion video is still not the most common feature in presentations, mainly because the hardware and software to support it is still relatively expensive and rare. However, PowerPoint supports video and can help you enhance your presentations with interesting video clips.

Motion video is usually displayed in a small window that takes up only a part of your whole screen. One reason for using a small window within a screen display is storage limitations. Standard full-motion video presents information at a rate of 30 frames (screens) per second. Since each of these screens is a graphics image, storage requirements for this amount of information at full speed on a full screen can be staggering.

To get around this limitation, some full-motion video limits the size of the display screen and the resolution of the display. For many types of video, these limitations are not serious. After all, being able to see real-time, full-motion video as part of a presentation is probably worth a slight reduction in image quality.

Keep in mind that we remember things in picture form, not in words (and motion pictures are more lifelike than still pictures, which are more lifelike than drawings). Therefore, anytime you can use video as part of a presentation, you have increased the likelihood that the audience will remember the message you are trying to get across.

Remember, too, that the video component of a given slide doesn't have to carry the majority of the information. Just as you can use a background with a still photograph, you can place motion video so that it enhances other information. This can help the viewer focus on a topic or help the audience relate the data you are presenting to something in the physical world. (Use this technique carefully, however, as we all like movies and you don't want to pull the audience entirely away from what you are saying or what else you may be presenting on the screen.)

On the other hand, you can open a motion video window and let the person or the action in the sequence tell the whole story while the live presenter simply waits until the end. Such sequences should be short for a couple of reasons. Full-motion video requires a lot of storage space, so if you do very much of it during a presentation you may find yourself needing a larger hard disk than most budgets allow. And, any motion video sequence is there to augment or enhance the presentation, not to *be* the presentation. Use it for variety and to enhance interest, not to show a movie.

Testing the Presentation

Presentation testing is a fairly continuous process. As each module is completed, you probably will step through the slides and see how things fit. As you put modules together into a larger unit, you'll test them, and so on. If this is a one-time presentation to a small group, then you can probably view the show yourself and decide whether it achieves its goal. If the presentation will be used several times and you're looking for specific results, then the testing process needs to be somewhat more involved.

You may work alone during the initial design and production stages, but as you start building the final presentation you should get as many people as possible involved. If the show is for internal viewing, as with training or educational material, then you can use coworkers to view the presentation and offer critiques. You should schedule two or more showings to different audiences at different times and evaluate their feedback carefully.

Test audiences should feel free to tell you honestly how they react to your work, and you should be prepared to separate their comments and criticisms from personalities. Try to elicit honest opinions and use them in conjunction with your production expertise and what you know about the goals of the production to draw your own conclusions about the quality and value of the product.

One way to help test viewers open up is to prepare a questionnaire for them to fill out after they have seen the show. However, you have to be careful how you construct the questions in such a survey, and make sure they are not weighted in any direction. Another technique that may help a critical audience relax during a session is to make the presentation during a lunch break or over special refreshments during an afternoon break.

After you have received feedback, make whatever changes in the production you think should be made based on the comments received. Then schedule at least one more showing to see if the problems were corrected. Again, through personal contact, memos, or a pre-show presentation, make it plain that you appreciate everyone's involvement and that you have made changes in the show based on their previous comments. However, you should also make it clear that the previous comments were taken under advisement and the resulting changes were made on the basis of a variety of inputs, including that from other professionals.

Of course the final testing is done in the field, before a live audience. Always be aware of audience reaction during a presentation. If this show or a similar one will be used repeatedly, you may want to devise a questionnaire for each audience. Such regular evaluations, over time, can help you polish and refine a program, removing any unclear or unnecessary components.

To Sum Up

There's a lot of material in this chapter, from brainstorming about the overall design of a presentation to specifics on creating individual slides. You won't use all of these techniques in every presentation, of course, but the concepts in this chapter can help you to create professional and effective shows.

The important thing to remember about your presentation design is that you have a message to impart to an audience, and the whole purpose of your PowerPoint presentation design is to help convey that message. Use the concepts in this chapter to help you do that. Hopefully, some of this information will get you thinking in the right direction as you set out on your own to use the tools provided by PowerPoint to design a presentation.

In the next chapter, I'll give you more detail on using PowerPoint Wizards, clip art, and templates.

CHAPTER 4

Using PowerPoint Templates, Clip Art, and Wizards

Computer software has changed in dramatic ways during the past few years. When I first started working with personal computers there was no software at all; you just used BASIC and Assembler to develop your own applications. Those of us who came out of the minicomputer world longed for a real language—COBOL or FORTRAN—but that was years away.

Eventually, we started getting basic applications such as spreadsheets and databases. Even these were minimal programs that required a lot of configuring and programming by the end user. Some of us made a fair amount of money in those early days by taking what were marketed as finished applications and modifying them so that they did what the customer wanted, or, in some cases, so that they did anything at all. A lot of that early software didn't even work, believe it or not.

Today we get quickly released software with a few bugs or shortcomings, but it works. This software includes useful tools to help beginners get a lot out of the program in a hurry. Microsoft's PowerPoint is one good example of this trend. Embedded within the program are a number of utilities, tools, and templates that make developing presentations easy. Not only that, the built-in features help beginners learn about design so that they can avoid mistakes in the finished presentations. This chapter explains how to use the built-in templates and utilities to produce your own slides and presentations.

Available Templates

A PowerPoint template is a predesigned presentation in which the appearance of the masters (Slide Master, Outline Master, Handout Master, Note Master) and slide colors have been designed to achieve a particular look. You can start a new presentation with a particular template, or you can apply a template to an existing presentation. When you apply a template, the slide backgrounds, the appearance of the master screens, and so on, take on the look of the template.

To use a template with a new presentation, select **File: New** and click on the **Presentation Designs** tab on the New dialog box. By default PowerPoint displays the available templates as folders in a Windows dialog box. You can also display full file names or file names with other data such as file size and creation date. Note that with Windows 95 you are not limited to the previous eight-character file name restriction.

In addition, any existing presentation can be saved as a template that can be used as the basis for the design of future presentations. If you are familiar with Microsoft Word, then you know how Microsoft uses templates to predesign certain aspects of a word processor document. Presentation templates work in a similar way.

If you are familiar with PowerPoint 4, you will see some familiar names in the list of templates in this chapter. However, take a second look. Although many of the names remain, some of the designs have been changed, and there are additional templates you won't find in PowerPoint 4. This version of PowerPoint also includes additional templates in the Presentations Tab of this dialog.

There are 60 templates supplied with PowerPoint 7.0. (This book was based on a very early version of PowerPoint 7. The version you have probably has even more templates.) If you display the New dialog box, you can click on each template name and view a preview of the design in the preview area of the dialog box. You can also get a fair idea about the appearance of each template from the name.

NOTE

I describe these templates from the perspective of a 1024 x 768 display showing 256 colors. If your display adapter is using only 16 colors at 640 x 480, the color schemes will appear different from what I describe. Of course, if your display is using a 24-bit or other high-end color display, you also will see a different template from what I describe.

The first template in the list, for example, is a multishaded blue background with strong blue and black bars stored under the name Azure. All of the templates with PowerPoint 7 are appropriate for 35mm slides, for on-screen shows, and for projection presentations directly from your PC.

PowerPoint lets you adjust the shading and colors of the designs after you select a template. You'll want full, deep colors for 35mm slides and projected computer shows. You'll probably get better results for overhead presentations with templates that use some color but that have white or light backgrounds. You can switch to black-and-white templates with shades of gray and a light background if you're printing your presentations on a black-and-white printer.

To change to an overhead color scheme from the default supplied with PowerPoint, select a template you want to use, then click on **Format** and choose **Slide Color Scheme...** to display the Color Scheme dialog box shown in Figure 4.1.

There are two tabs on the Color Scheme dialog box: Standard and Custom. On the Standard tab there are several color choices. The first is the default. It includes a full range of color appropriate for 35mm slides or high resolution projection. Other color schemes change the color mix, from darker backgrounds to black and white or shades of gray. By choosing a template and then experimenting with the color scheme, you can derive the right combination for your topic and method of presentation. For example, a template with a lighter background is appropriate for use with an overhead projector. The same template in black and white may be a good choice for inclusion in a printed report as a cover or section separator.

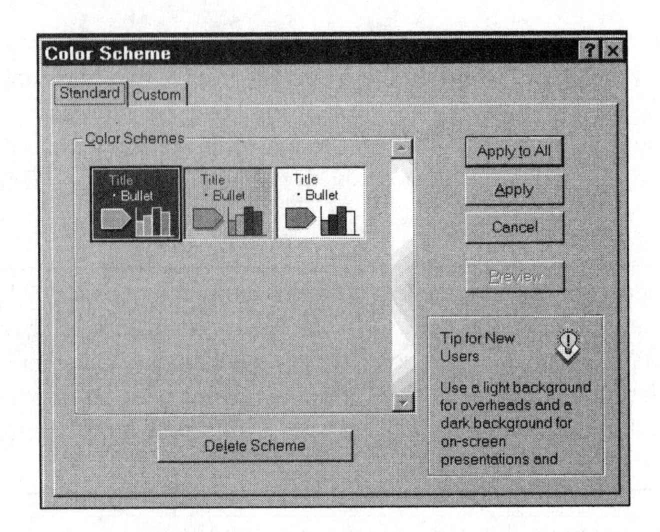

Figure 4.1 *Color Scheme dialog box.*

There are two other ways to change a template's appearance easily. First, you can click on the **Custom** tab of the Color Scheme dialog box. This displays the screen in Figure 4.2.

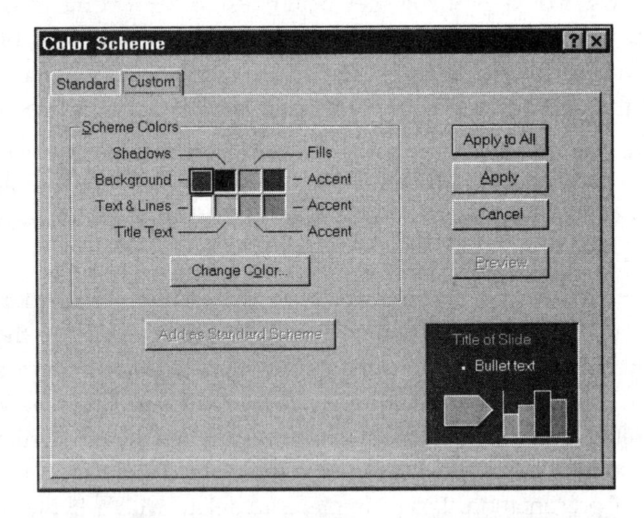

Figure 4.2 *Custom tab from Color Scheme dialog box.*

Adjust individual color components by double-clicking on one or more of the labeled color squares to display the Color dialog box (see Figure 4.3). Choose the color you want from this display, then click on **OK** to close the Color dialog box and insert the selected color onto the Custom tab of the Color Scheme dialog box.

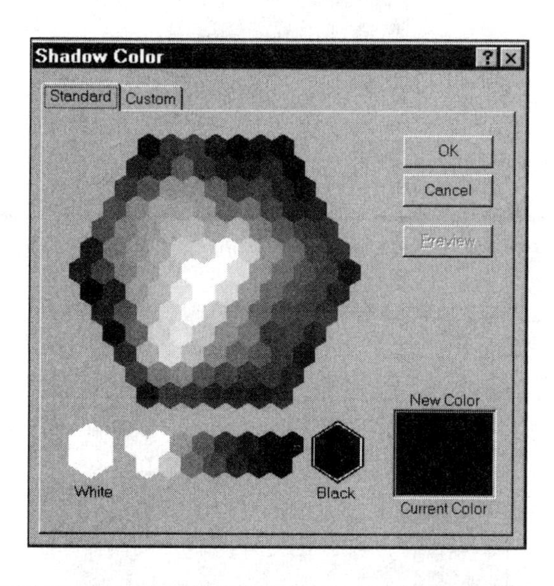

Figure 4.3 *Color dialog box from Custom tab of Color Scheme dialog box.*

In addition, you can click the right mouse button while pointing to a slide you want to change. From the pop-up menu, choose one of the formatting or color choices. Some of these choices display secondary menu choices. For example, if you have set a black-and-white scheme from the Color dialog box, this pop-up menu includes another black-and-white choice. You can specify grayscale from this pop-up menu, for example, or light grayscale, high contrast, or other choices to fit the presentation. Figure 4.4 shows the basic pop-up menu.

The second way to customize the appearance of a template is with the Custom Background dialog box, which you can display by clicking on **Format** and then choosing **Custom Background**. Figure 4.5 shows the Custom Background dialog box with the pattern pop-up list displayed. Choose from this list to change the texture of the template. You'll learn quickly that, in addition to the standard textures, you can choose pictures or other backgrounds stored on disk. Together, these choices let you build a wide range of custom templates.

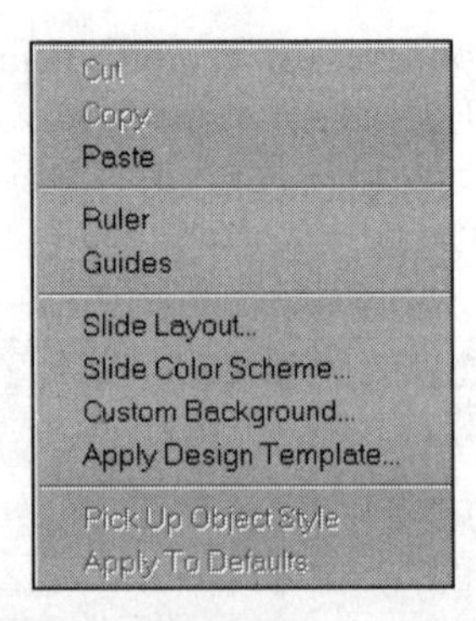

Figure 4.4 *Right-button Template Format pop-up menu.*

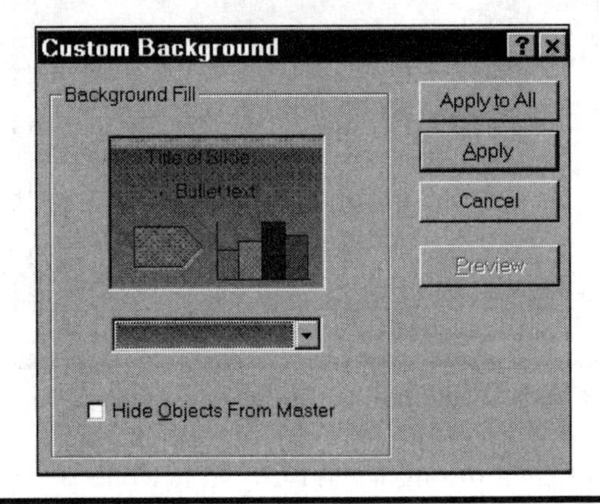

Figure 4.5 *Custom Background dialog box from Format menu.*

In the next section, I'll provide a quick reference to the templates supplied with PowerPoint. Accompanying the template name is a screen shot of the black-and-white overhead template to show you how the template is designed. I've used the black-and-white template because it reproduces better in this book. I've also included templates from the Presentation Designs and Presentation Tabs of this dialog.

Azure

This template may remind you of a printed award or certificate, or it could appear to you as an abstract background in deep blue and black. It has a three-dimensional border with drop shadow. This design evokes a modern mood and would be appropriate for any strong topic.

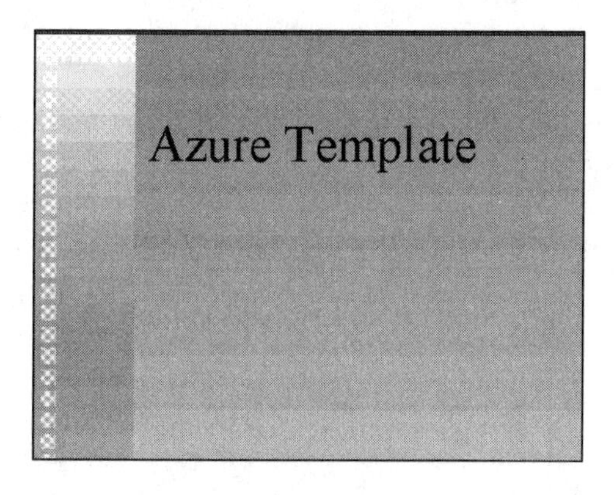

Figure 4.6 *Azure template.*

Banner

The Banner template is similar to the Azure template, but the line is horizontal and wider than with Azure. The top of the slide is separated from the body of the slide by a shadow border. The color versions have a two-tone scheme with buff over dark green or orange over yellow, depending on the type of display adapter you are using.

Figure 4.7 *Banner template.*

Bevel

This template is basically the Azure template with the addition of 3-D graphics on the four sides. Color versions add a light green background with shadows.

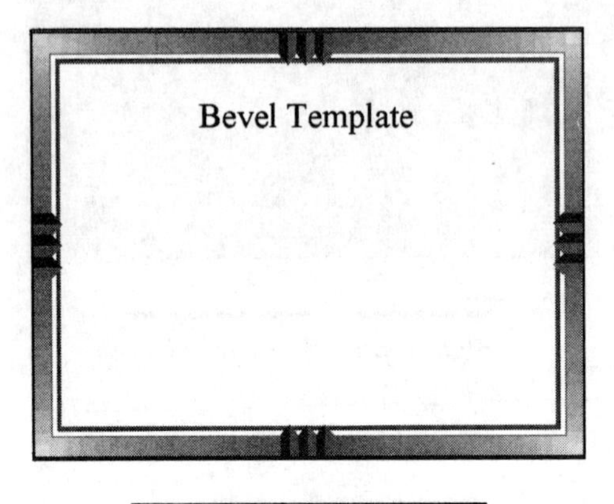

Figure 4.8 *Bevel template.*

Black

This is a simple template with a graduated black strip down the left side of the screen. Use this template when you want to present a modern or clean-cut image. The color overhead slide has a gray vertical strip down the left side. The slide show version is designed in silver and black in graduated shades with yellow letters. All of these templates produce a modern, striking mood.

Figure 4.9 *Black template.*

Blue Boxes

The black-and-white version of this template puts three gray boxes around the slide window. In the color version, you get light and dark blue borders around the slide window and bright yellow lettering. This template offers a crisp, clean design that is particularly good for lists.

Figure 4.10 *Blue Boxes template.*

Blue Diagonal

The Blue Diagonal template isn't blue at all in the black-and-white version, of course, but the color versions do present a pattern of dark blue diagonal lines on a lighter blue background. In black and white, the pattern is a pleasant gray and white.

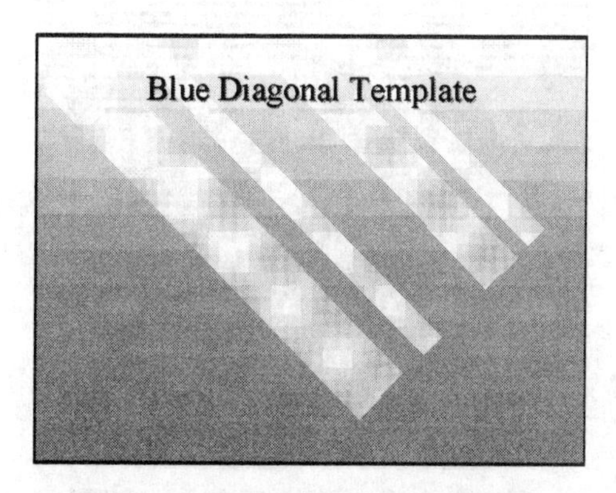

Figure 4.11 *Blue Diagonal template.*

Blue Green

This template places a wide line/thin line pattern behind the main slide window. In color, these lines are light and dark green.

Figure 4.12 *Blue Green template.*

Blue Stripes

The Blue Stripes template has a background of horizontal alternating dark and light stripes. The black-and-white version has gray and white stripes, and the color versions have alternating dark blue and black stripes.

Figure 4.13 *Blue Stripes template.*

Broken Bar

This template uses a wide bar followed by variable-width smaller bars to separate the title area of the slide from the body of the slide. The color versions use dark and light blue bars with a graduated deep red background.

Figure 4.14 *Broken Bar template.*

Bubbles

For a light, party look to your slides, try the Bubbles template. This could be a good choice for posters or announcements or any time you want to evoke a less-than-serious mood. The background color is a graduated deep blue.

Figure 4.15 *Bubbles template.*

Checks

As the name implies, this template places a series of small squares or checks in a vertical bar at the left of the slide. The color overhead version of this template uses a very light, graduated green and white color scheme for a pastel look. The slide show version combines a graduated green with deep black accents and orange lettering for a modern, attractive scheme.

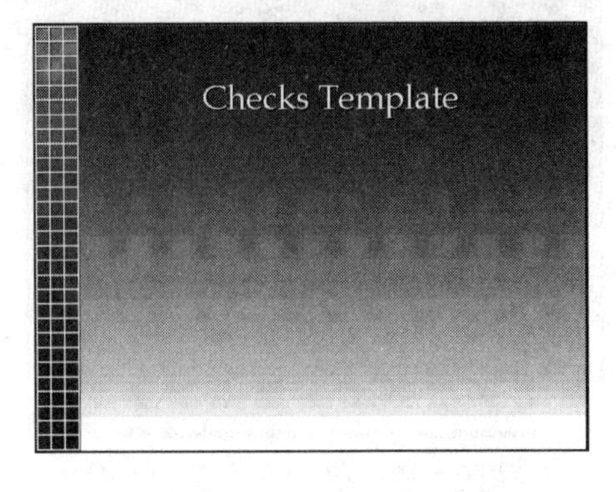

Figure 4.16 *Checks template.*

Cheers

This template uses a party motif with streamers scattered around the border of the slide screen. In color, this slide has a light and dark pink design with bright yellow text.

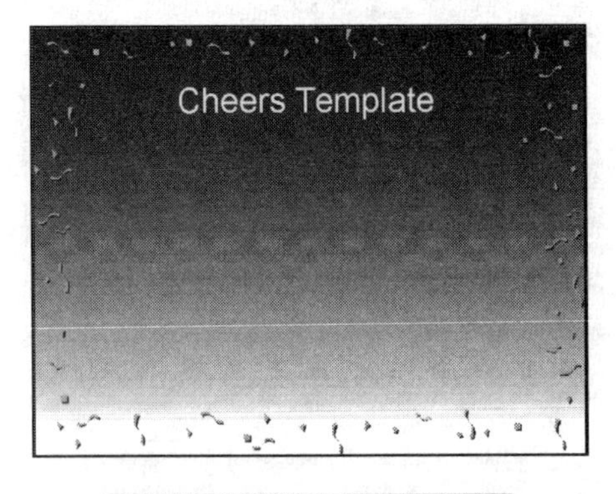

Figure 4.17 *Cheers template.*

Color Boxes

The Color Boxes template is a clean design with a small right angle of shaded boxes in the lower right-hand corner of the slide. In color templates the boxes are various colors, with a white background in the overhead version and a black background in the slide-show version.

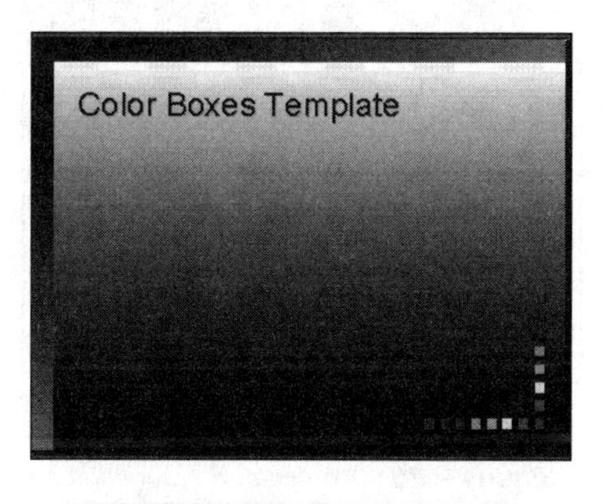

Figure 4.18 *Color Boxes Template.*

Confetti

As the name implies, the Confetti template is based on a scattering of shaded color chips, which are placed around two edges of the slide screen. In color you get multicolored chips on a clean, white background (overhead slide version) or multicolored chips on a crisp, black background (slide show version).

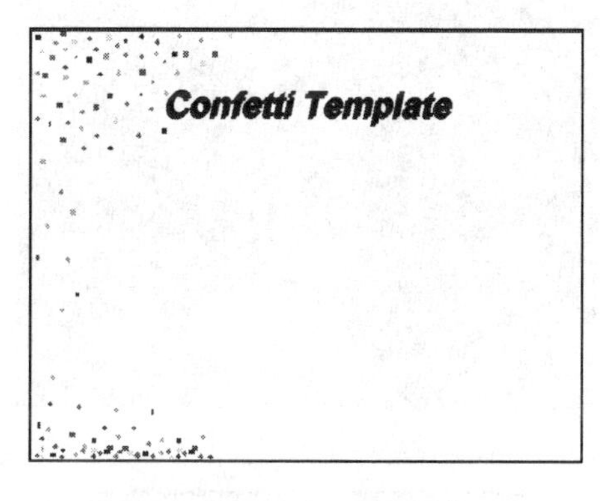

Figure 4.19 *Confetti template.*

Contemporary

This slide presents a bold, strong statement with a bright, white background accentuated by broad, deep red horizontal stripes.

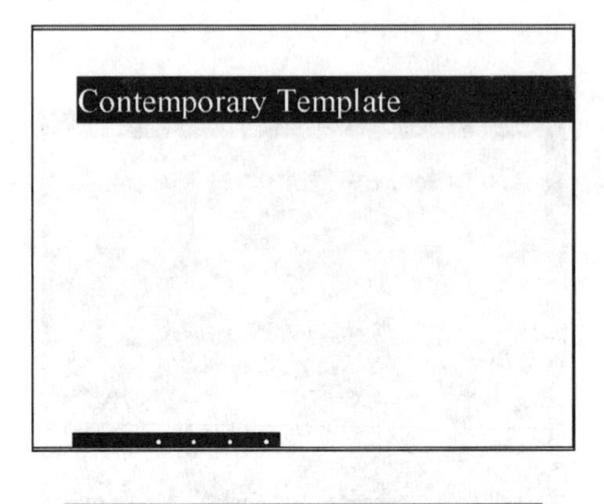

Figure 4.20 *Contemporary template.*

Diamond

The Diamond template is simple and clean. It has a single three-dimensional diamond shape in the upper left corner of the screen. The lettering overlays the diamond. The slide show version of this template is particularly interesting, with a graduated black to pastel green background, a blue green diamond, and yellow text.

Figure 4.21 *Diamond template.*

Double Lines

The Double Lines template is similar to the Banner template (see Figure 4.7), except that the separating line is graduated. In color, this line is purple, green, and black with either a white background (overhead) or a black and violet background (slide show).

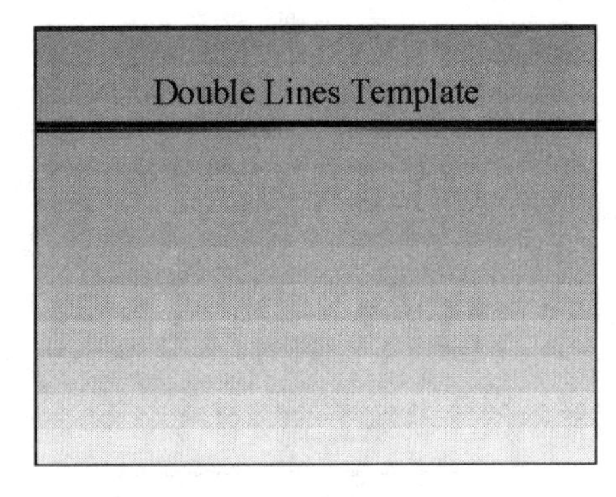

Figure 4.22 *Double Lines template.*

Drop Star

This template evokes a diplomatic mood, with a shaded vertical ribbon terminated in a three-dimensional star. In color, the template uses a multihued green strip, with a white background in the overhead version and a deep black background in the slide show version.

Figure 4.23 *Drop Star template.*

Elegant

The Elegant template uses the same background pattern as the Blue Diagonal template (see Figure 4.11). The color of this template is, indeed, elegant, in shades of purple and black.

Figure 4.24 *Elegant template.*

Embossed

The Embossed template has a modern design composed of straight lines accented by an integral square in one of the horizontal lines. The color versions are based on a light and dark green color scheme, which is pastel in the overhead slide version and has a metallic look in the slide show version.

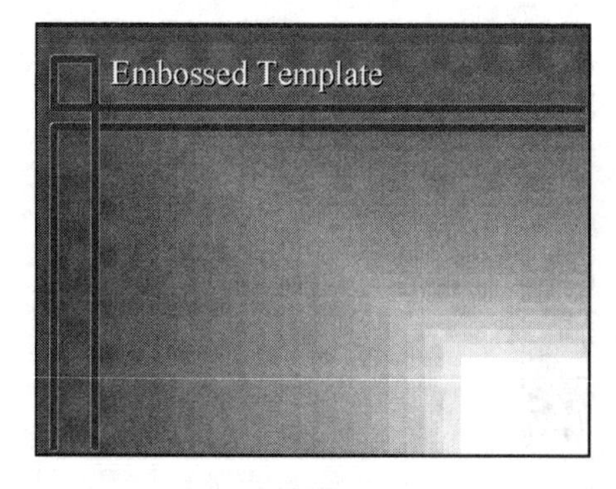

Figure 4.25 *Embossed template.*

Fiesta

As you might expect, the Fiesta template has a party feel similar to the Cheers template (see Figure 4.17). The black-and-white version is, in fact, very similar to the Cheers template. The color versions use a blue, purple, and yellow color scheme instead of the pink tints of Cheers.

Figure 4.26 *Fiesta template.*

Flag

The Flag template is based on a flowing, flag-like pattern behind the upper area of the slide. In black and white, the mood is muted with shades of light gray and a white background for the body of the slide. The overhead slide maintains the light gray flag and white background, but adds blue text. The slide show template uses a gray background instead of the white of the overhead template.

Figure 4.27 *Flag template.*

Forest

This is not exactly a primitive forest design, but the little trees in the border do hint at a forest theme. The Forest template is probably not for serious environmental topics, but it is useful when you want to suggest a forest theme.

Figure 4.28 *Forest template.*

Granite

This template provides a multishaded, rough background that does, indeed, look like granite. Use it for strong topics, lists, or motion-oriented topics.

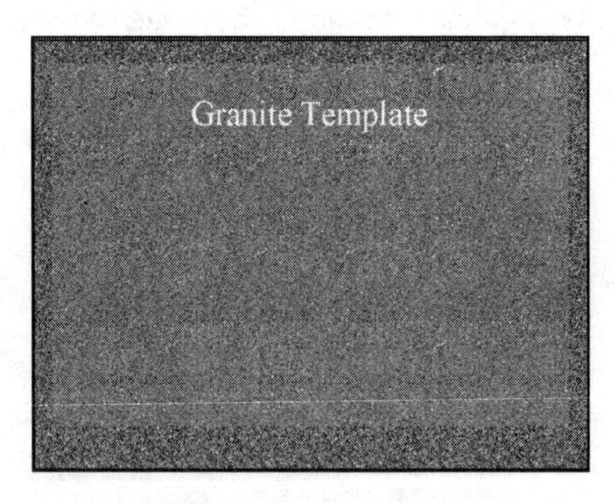

Figure 4.29 *Granite template.*

Grid Work

The Grid Work template uses a three-dimensional series of linked squares around the top and left side of the slide window. In color, this pattern is in deep blue.

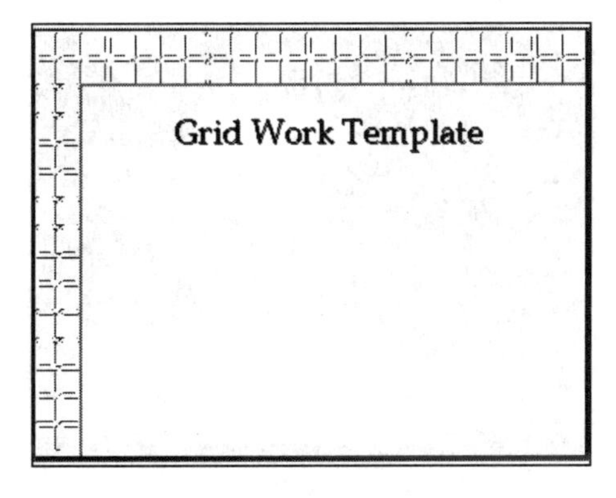

Figure 4.30 *Grid Work template.*

International

This is a simple template that uses a world globe in the lower right-hand corner of the slide window. The black-and-white slide is in shades of gray, while the color versions use dark blue and white.

Figure 4.31 *International template.*

Island

A northern coast mood seems to be the intent of this template. In black and white the slide is a little flat, but in color versions shades of dark green add some interest.

Figure 4.32 *Island template*

Lines on Blue

This is a relatively simple template, but it can serve you well as a background for lists or simple graphics. The graduated grays or blues (on the color versions) present a clean image that should be particularly useful for high tech topics.

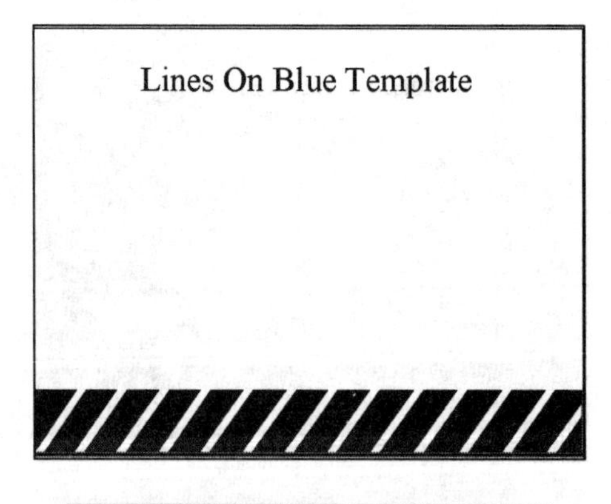

Figure 4.33 *Lines On Blue template.*

Marble

This template uses shadow effects heavily, with a large shaded block in the upper left-hand corner of the slide screen and a shadow effect around the bottom and right edges. In color, these effects are presented in red and pink.

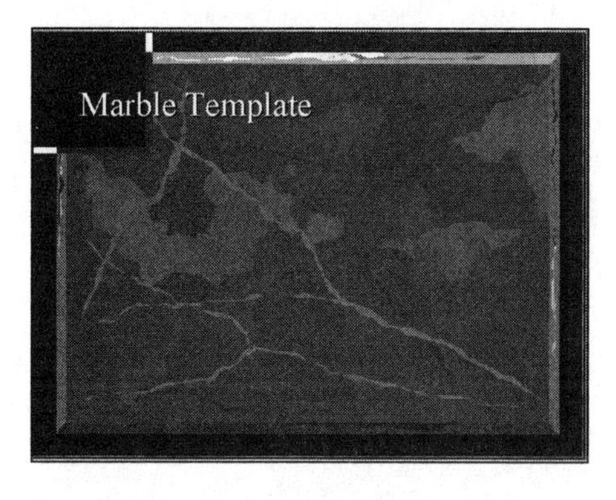

Figure 4.34 *Marble template.*

Medical

This design uses a caduceus as a shaded background. It is in gray in the black-and-white design and in pastel purple and blue in the color versions.

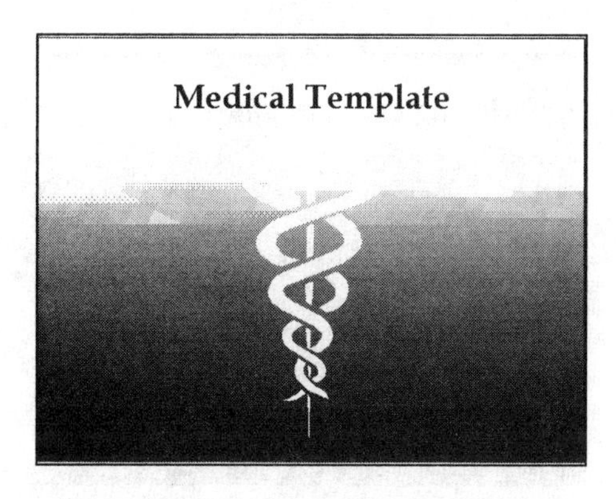

Figure 4.35 *Medical template.*

Metal Bar

This is a modern industrial design that can be used to good advantage for high tech or manufacturing topics. The black and white version is a metallic gray design, whereas the color templates use shades of blue and silver.

Figure 4.36 *Metal Bar template.*

Moving Line

This is another modern template based on crisp horizontal lines. The black-and-white version uses heavy black lines against a white background, while the color versions use red lines and blue text.

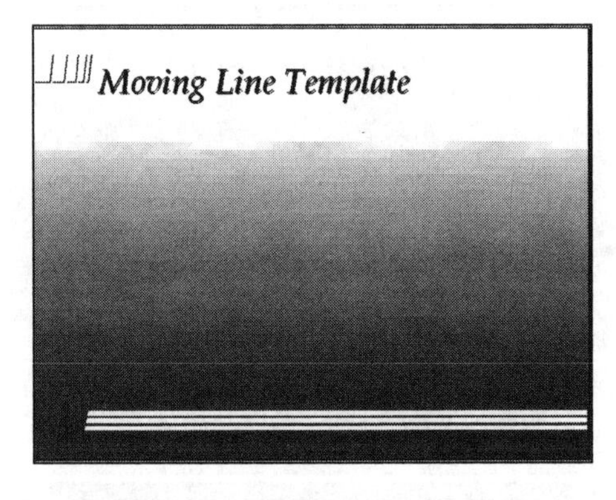

Figure 4.37 *Moving Line template.*

Multiple Bars

This template uses a series of shaded metallic-type bars to frame the left and top section of the slide screen. In color, these bars add a deep blue and red accent to the metallic gray, and the background is green.

Figure 4.38 *Multiple Bars template.*

Multiple Boxes

This template is based on a series of shaded boxes in the upper left and lower right corners of the slide window, accented by a shadowed box in the center of the display. In color, the slide uses shades of lavender, green, and blue for a pastel fifties mood.

Figure 4.39 *Multiple Boxes template.*

Music

This template has a musical theme. It places the text on top of a music staff accented by musical notes. In color, this template uses orange notes and red staff with a blue background.

Figure 4.40 *Music template.*

Neon Lights

The Neon Lights template is another design that evokes memories of the fifties. In black and white the mood is good for manufacturing themes. The grid background accented by graduated shaded boxes on the right of the slide presents a clean design. In color, this templates uses purple, green, and blue shades.

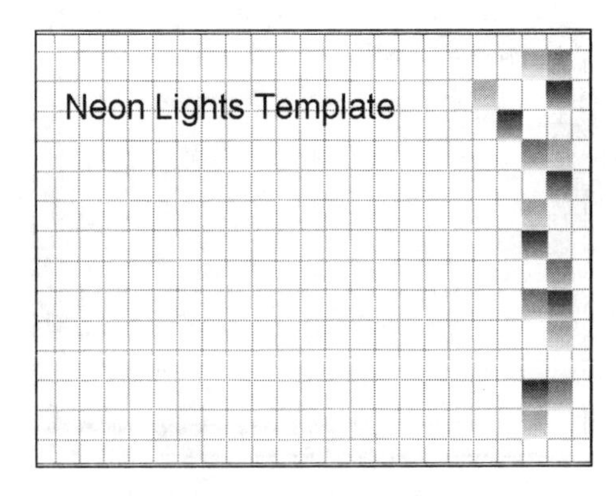

Figure 4.41 *Neon Lights template.*

Pastel

A basic design, the Pastel template should serve well for educational topics or any time you want the slide itself to jump out from the template. The color versions use graduated violet-to-gray shades with either a very light violet or a light green background.

Figure 4.42 *Pastel template.*

Patchwork

Patchwork is a busy design that plays better in color than in black and white. The sharp triangular border can be distracting, so use this design only for strong slides that stand well on their own merits. The color slides use strong shades of black, red, yellow, and blue, but are still potentially distracting.

Figure 4.43 *Patchwork template.*

Professional

This is one of the simpler designs among the available PowerPoint templates. A deep blue background is accentuated by a moderately broad, horizontal red stripe.

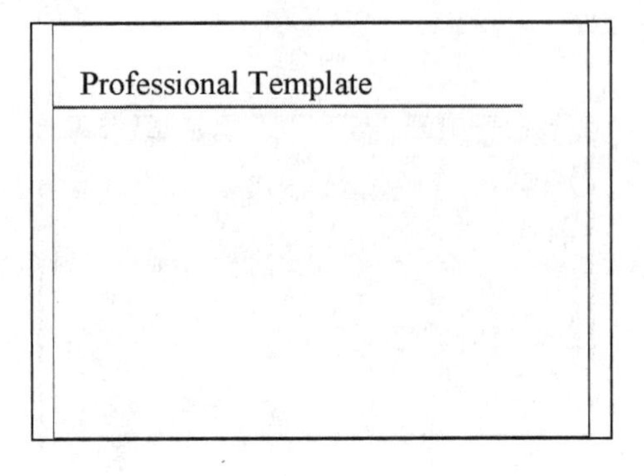

Figure 4.44 *Professional template.*

Red Lines

The Red Lines template is a design based on horizontal lines. In black and white, the template uses graduated gray lines separated by white space. In the overhead color version, the lines are red and the separating space is black. In the slide show version, the overall mood is more muted with dark red lines and lighter accents.

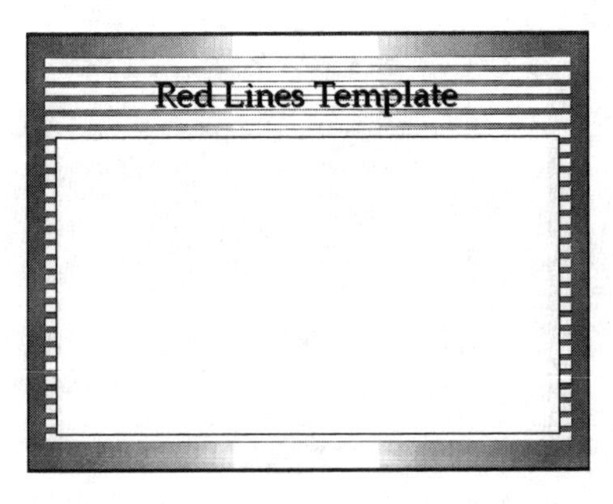

Figure 4.45 *Red Lines template.*

Seashore

The Seashore template offers a seashore theme with a hint of sand dunes and sea grass. The color versions replace the light gray images with dark blue.

Figure 4.46 *Seashore template.*

Shaded Bars

The slides using this template have graduated, shaded bars at the top and bottom, with clean left and right margins. The black-and-white version uses graduated gray and black, while the color versions use purple and sand (slide show) or blue and red (overhead).

Figure 4.47 *Shaded Bars template.*

Side Bar

One of the simplest templates, Side Bar uses a single thin horizontal line under the title, with the remainder of the slide plain. The color versions remain clean and simple. The overhead slide version colors the horizontal line blue; one slide show version uses yellow text, a pink bar, and a blue background.

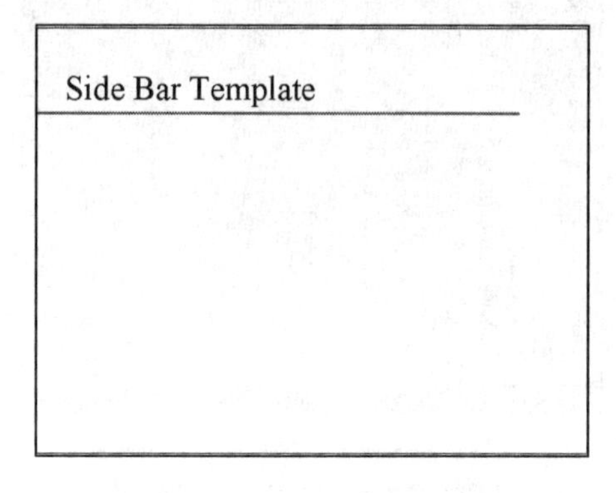

Figure 4.48 *Side Bar template.*

Side Fade

This template uses a wide graduated vertical bar at the left of the slide window and a horizontal double line at the top. The effect is crisp and clean, offering a good accent for presentation material. The color overhead template is presented in shades of green for a cool, pastel effect. The slide show template uses darker tones of sand and black for a metallic look.

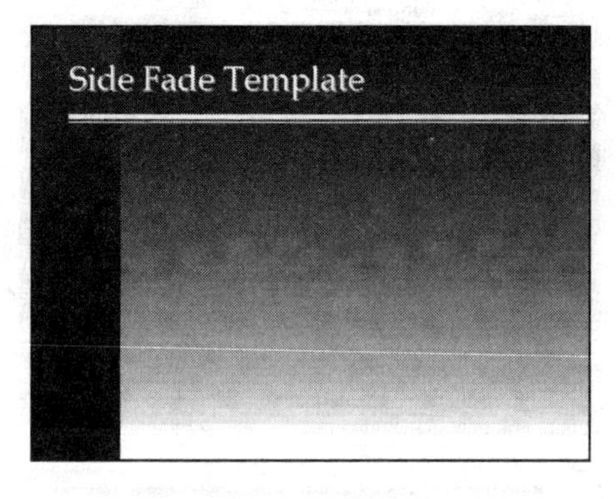

Figure 4.49 *Side Fade template.*

Soaring

This template uses a unique graphic shape as a background for your slides. A sweeping, wing-like shape moves from the lower-right corner to the upper-left corner of the slide window. In black and white, the shape is a light gray. In color, the shape is in shades of light and dark blue. The slide show template adds a dark blue background with graduations to black, offering a futuristic background for your information.

Figure 4.50 *Soaring template.*

Southwest

The Southwest template uses a Western U.S. Indian design on the left border and as a background. The black-and-white template uses a black vertical bar with white accents on the left of the slide with shades of gray as the background. The overhead color template uses fluorescent green and orange as accent colors against a light gray background. The slide show version, on the other hand, changes the vertical bar to pastel earth colors with a black background.

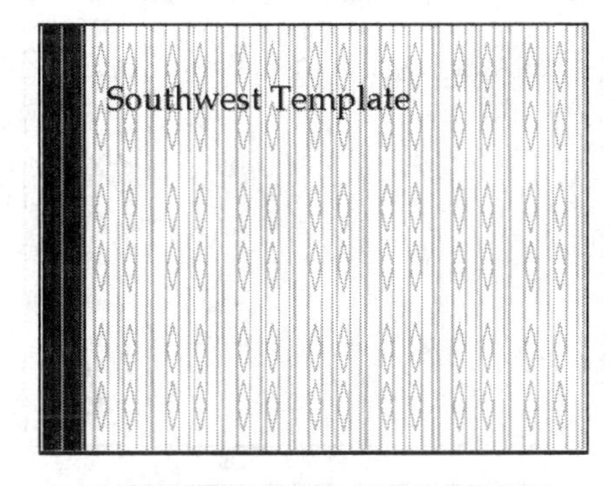

Figure 4.51 *Southwest template.*

Sparkle

A bright star in the upper left-hand corner of this template is accented by double horizontal bars under the title. Use this slide effectively for accenting information, especially with short lists and uncomplicated slides. The color versions use metallic blue shades for emphasis.

Figure 4.52 *Sparkle template.*

Splatter

Like splotches of paint splashed randomly across the slide, the Splatter template adds interesting shape and color to your slides. This is particularly suited for color applications. The color overhead template uses magenta and green against a white background. The slide show template splashes magenta and green against a dark, cobalt blue background.

Figure 4.53 *Splatter template.*

Sunset

Like a greeting card without text, the Sunset template offers an interesting pattern that ranges from black at the top to a yellow-toned sunset shade at the bottom. If you choose light colors for foreground text and graphics, this template can be an effective addition to your presentation.

Figure 4.54 *Sunset template.*

Tablet

Clean, simple lines can help you enhance your slide displays without distracting shapes or colors. The three-dimensional shadow border of the Tablet template helps your slides jump out of the screen. The color versions add a light green shade for accent.

Figure 4.55 *Tablet template.*

Theatre

Add ancient Egyptian symbols to a movie-screen-like box for your slides, and you have an accent that can help promote your information. This design is best used in color. The overhead version adds a green border to the white background, while the slide show template adds a graduated green-to-black background and a gold border.

Figure 4.56 *Theatre template.*

Topline

One of the simpler templates, this one places a wide black line across the top of the slide. You get a graduated blue background with a magenta line in the overhead version. The slide show template has a bright and catchy black and blue background.

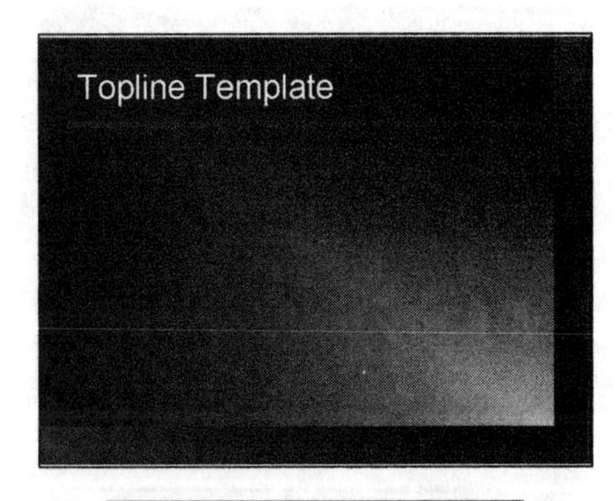

Figure 4.57 *Topline template.*

Travel

A boat and a plane accent this template, which is effective in black and white as well as in color. The color overhead version has shades of blue against a white background, while the slide show puts black images against a cobalt blue background.

Figure 4.58 *Travel template.*

Tridots

This combination of triangles and tiny dots gives a modern, even futuristic feel. This could be a useful template for side-by-side lists and sequential display lines.

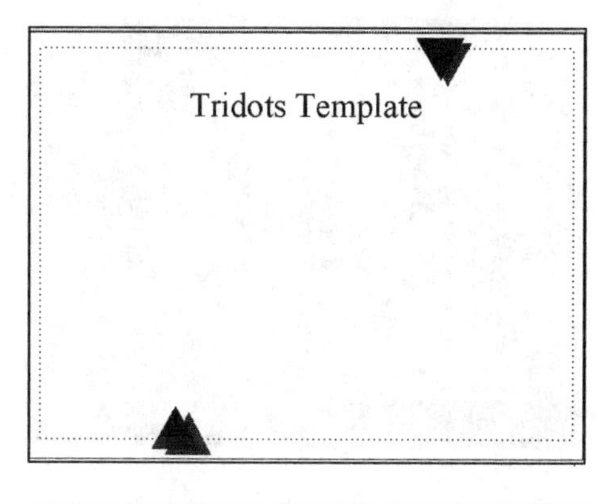

Figure 4.59 *Triangles and Dots template.*

Triumph

This template places an Olympic torch along the left margin of the slide against a gray or red background.

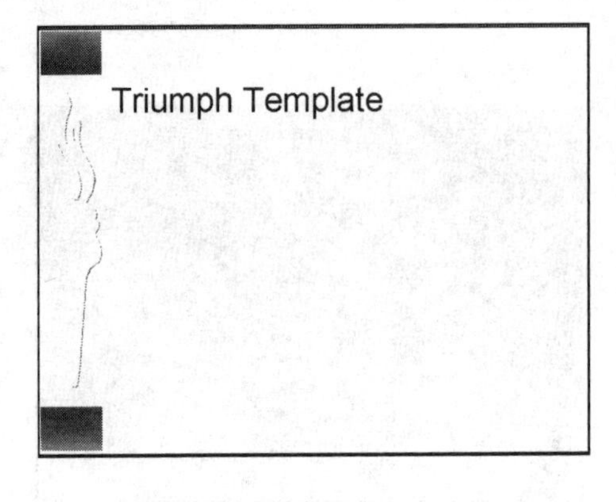

Figure 4.60 *Triumph template.*

Tropical

This template offers a tropical theme with palm tree silhouettes and a setting sun. Use this one in color for best impact.

Figure 4.61 *Tropical template.*

Twinkle

This template is similar to the Diamond template (see Figure 4.21), except that it uses a twinkling star or sparkle symbol on top of the diamond. The color versions add shades of violet and blue or green and black.

Figure 4.62 *Twinkle template.*

Vivid Lines

A clean center area is accented by a group of horizontal lines about three-fourths of the way from the top of this slide format. The title is in a shadow box. The color versions use red and yellow lines.

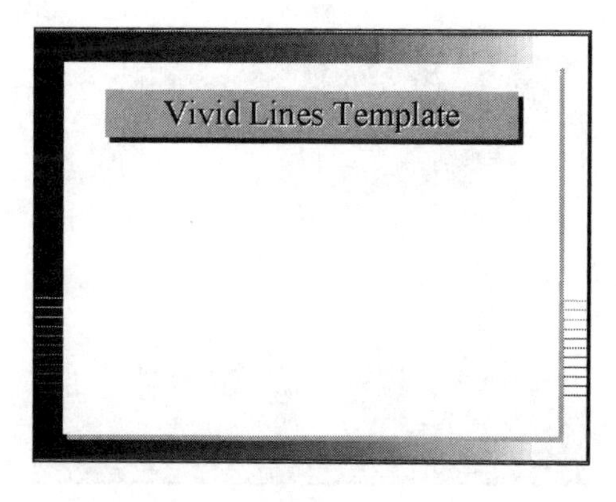

Figure 4.63 *Vivid Lines template.*

Watercolor

This is a fun template, especially in the slide show version. It consists of a light background flanked by multicolored flecks along the right and left borders. Use it anytime you need a light-hearted mood for your presentations. The black and white version is rather flat.

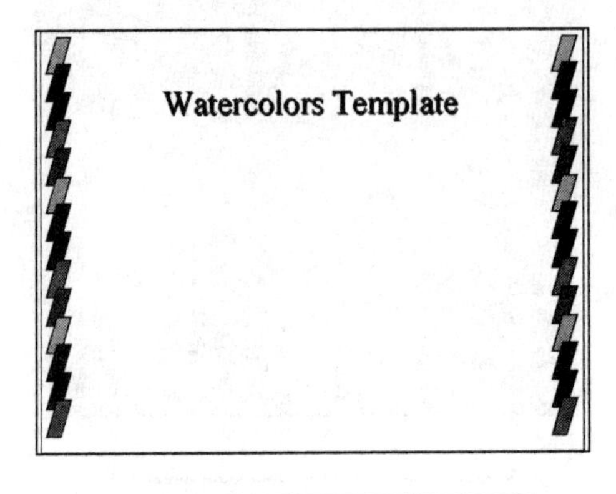

Figure 4.64 *Watercolor template.*

World

The World template places a watermark of a flat global map as the background in the center of the slide. This can be quite effective in black and white or in color.

Figure 4.65 *World template.*

Presentation Design Tab Templates

Additional templates have been added as Microsoft continues to update PowerPoint 7. These templates can be found under the Presentation Design Tab. Your disk may contain additional templates.

Bed Rock

Depending on the text or other art that accompanies your presentation, this template could effect a frivolous or serious mood. The image on the side looks like a piece of heavy rock that has been chipped off and leaned against the side of the slide. The lighting gives it a three-dimensional appearance.

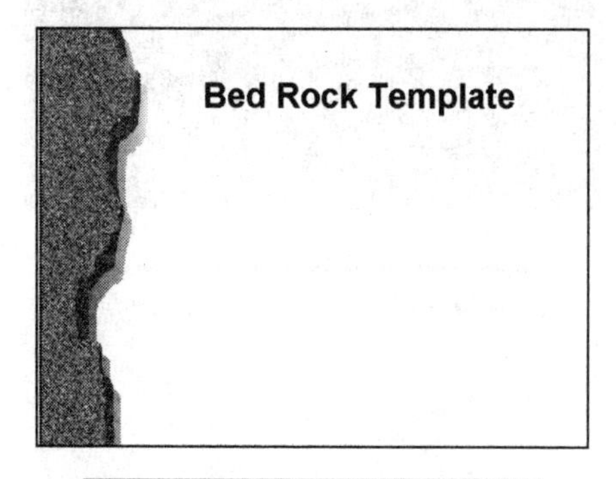

Figure 4.66 *Bed Rock template.*

Blue Weave

This template includes a soft, multi-colored pattern that reminds me of flannel. It could be used for family, home, or craft topics. It looks a lot better in color.

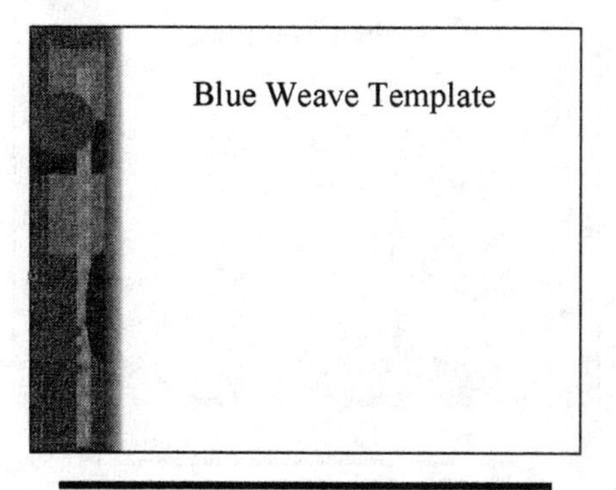

Figure 4.67 *Blue Weave template.*

Brown Marble

This template consists of a brown-colored marble pattern inside a frame. Use this template carefully. Objects you place on this template should be bright and relatively simple.

Figure 4.68 *Brown Marble template.*

Comet

This template looks a little like the Sparkle template. The shaded background with the streaking pattern at the top evokes a clean design with a hint of motion.

Figure 4.69 *Comet template.*

Tatami

This is an interesting pattern in shades of brown and orange. Keep objects on top of it relatively simple and this could be an effective template, especially for times when you want to suggest a warm topic.

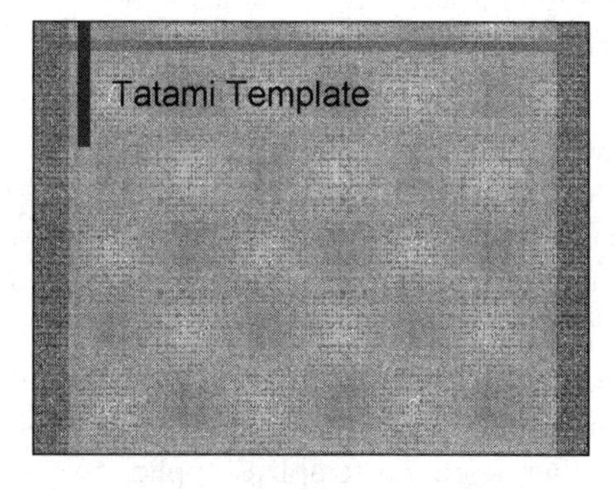

Figure 4.70 *Tatami template.*

Wet Sand

This template suggests vacation or perhaps children. The sand pattern is accentuated by the orange text and small footprint in the lower right corner of the slide.

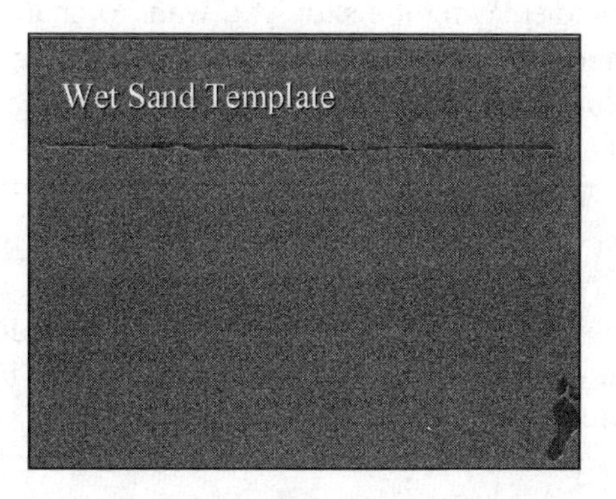

Figure 4.71 *Wet Sand template.*

Using Templates

Now you know which templates are available. In this section, I'll show you how to use them. Try to match the template you use to the topic or mood of your presentation. As you can see from the reference section earlier in this chapter, some of the templates tend toward the frivolous, while others are more serious. Some are colorful and bright, and others are muted and plain. So it is with the topics you'll cover.

You might choose a bright template to liven up a dull subject—sometimes that helps. But use this technique carefully or you will trivialize the subject. Although there are no hard and fast rules, try to consider the relationship between the topic you are covering in your presentation and the mood the template presents.

When you apply a template, any slide design you choose from the New Slide dialog box contains the color scheme and the images that are part of the template design. In other words, a template applies to an entire presentation, giving it an overall mood or look. You can't apply templates to individual slides. You probably wouldn't want to do this because part of creating a successful presentation is developing a look that carries throughout the presentation.

NOTE

You can modify individual slides within a template design, if you wish. You could select a different background for specific slides, for example, or change the color scheme for part or all of specific slides without changing the template design for the rest of the presentation. Do this by displaying the slide you want to change, then by selecting the **Format: Slide Layout...**, **Format: Slide Background...**, or **Format: Slide Color Scheme...** commands to reformat the slide. This is useful for emphasis or to introduce a new section of the presentation.

Remember, however, that you don't have to use a preformatted template for your presentations. You can start with a blank presentation and design the slide color and pattern on your own. In addition, once you have a presentation design you like, you can use the presentation as a custom template. Notice that templates are saved as **.PPT** files. These are Presentation files that are saved without text or clip art.

You can use an existing file as a template simply by specifying the file name from inside the Format Apply Design Template dialog box. Notice that PowerPoint shows you a full directory and path display within this dialog box.

To use another file as a template, simply step up the directory structure to where the file you want to use is stored. When you load a file as a template, the data that goes with the presentation is stripped away and only the background and other formatting are used with the new presentation.

Available Clip Art

Text, backgrounds, and designs aren't the only things that make up a presentation. PowerPoint comes with a full selection of clip art images that can be used to enhance individual slides in your presentation. Some slide layouts include areas for clip art, making it easy to drop in one of these images as part of your slide design. A clip art image is a simple drawing that can be used to suggest a topic or to enhance a list or other text display. You can use photographs or other images with your presentations, of course, but the simplicity of clip art sometimes has an advantage.

The clip art supplied with PowerPoint is grouped into several categories to make it easier to select an image for a particular application. There are far too many clip art images to show them all in this book. To see these images on the screen for yourself, simply open the ClipArt Gallery (select **Insert: ClipArt...**) and choose the category you want to view from the Category window at the top of the dialog box (see Figure 4.72).

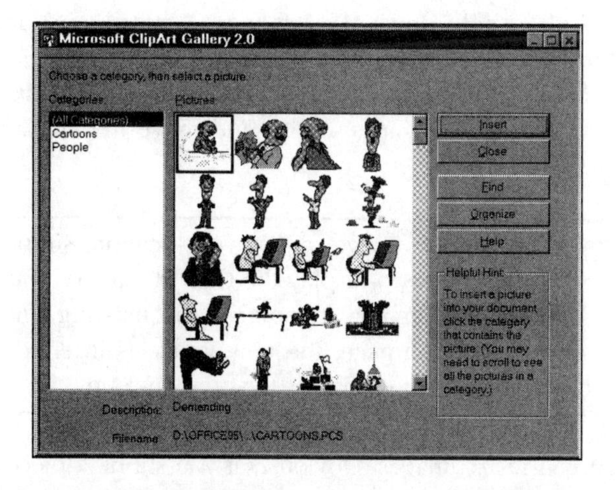

Figure 4.72 *Opening Clip Art Gallery screen with Category display.*

NOTE

If you have installed new software since you installed PowerPoint, then you will be given the opportunity to add new images to the gallery.

Using Clip Art

To use clip art with a layout that includes space for it, simply double-click inside the clip art area to display the ClipArt Gallery dialog box, shown in Figure 4.66. Select the category of clip art you want to use and step through the displayed images inside that category until you find what you're looking for. You can either double-click on the image you want, or select it by clicking on it once and then clicking on **Insert**.

You can add clip art to any slide, whether or not it contains a preformatted area for art or objects. Simply make the slide to which you want to add clip art current, then use the **Insert Clip Art...** command to display the ClipArt Gallery. PowerPoint will reserve a place on the slide for the clip art. When you choose the image you want to use, it will be inserted into this location. The size and position may not be what you want, but you can adjust it after you exit the Gallery display.

When you return to your slide, the clip art image you just inserted is selected. You can tell this by the presence of handles around its parameter. You can grab any one of these handles and drag that side of the image to change the size. Also, with the image selected you can place the mouse pointer anywhere inside the image, then hold down the left mouse button and drag the picture anywhere on the slide screen. This combination of sizing handles and the ability to drag the entire image anywhere you want it on the slide gives you a lot of flexibility in slide design. You can also size and move the clip art you inserted on a preformatted slide.

NOTE

To select a different image for a given location, simply double-click on an existing image to display the ClipArt Gallery dialog box. When you select a new image, it replaces the existing one. If you have resized the existing image, the new image is inserted into the same location and at the same size as the previous one.

Be careful when you resize images. Obviously if you shrink a piece of clip art top to bottom, then everything in it shrinks. You can get some strange looking people, places, and things this way. Try to shrink left-to-right at about the same ratio as you shrink top-to-bottom to keep the aspect ratio of your image the same as the original. Be aware of how the pictures inside an image border change when you start resizing it, and use good judgment in adjusting the borders.

Available Wizards

You could think of a Wizard as a smart template. In reality it is an interactive macro (small program) that steps you through some of the tasks associated with creating presentations in PowerPoint. Two Wizards are supplied with PowerPoint: The Pack and Go Wizard and the Auto Clip Art Wizard. I'll describe each of these Wizards in this section.

Pack and Go Wizard

This is a really simple program that can help you get ready for a road show quickly. Included with PowerPoint is a runtime version of the program, called the *PowerPoint Viewer.* You can use this relatively small program to run a PowerPoint slide show on a laptop or other PC without having access to the full PowerPoint application or Microsoft Office.

The Pack and Go Wizard helps you prepare a floppy disk with your presentation and the Viewer program. When you get to your destination, simply insert the floppy disk into a drive, copy everything on the disk to a hard drive, and run the program **pngsetup** that is part of the Pack and Go set. Then your presentation is ready to go.

To use this Wizard, click on **File** and choose **Pack and Go** to display the Pack and Go Wizard dialog box shown in Figure 4.73.

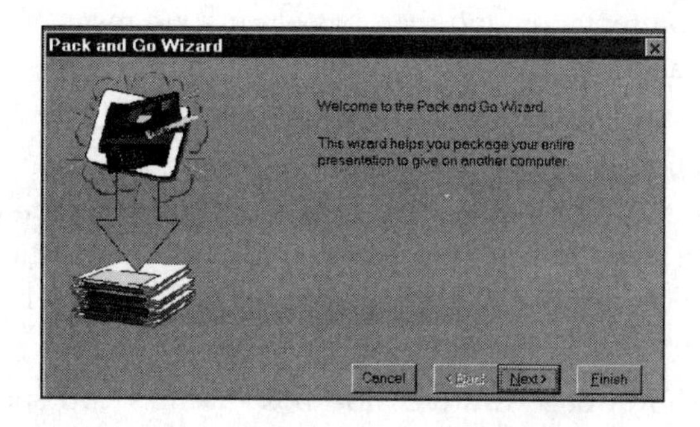

Figure 4.73 *Pack and Go Wizard opening screen.*

If you want to pack the current presentation—the one on the screen when you launched Pack and Go—click on **Next** on the first screen, then click on **Next** again on the next screen. This accepts the default of the current presentation. If you want to pack another presentation, click on the button next to the **Other Presentations** title, then choose **Browse** to display a file manager dialog box. Choose the presentation you want to package from the file manager display. Pack and Go returns to the file selection screen with the chosen file name displayed. Click on **Next** to go on to the next screen.

Specify the disk drive where you want Pack and Go to copy the Viewer and the presentation file you just selected. Click on **Next** to display a dialog box that asks whether you want to include linked files with the presentation. Another click on **Next** and you will see the final screen. You can click on **Finish** to start the copy process and build the Pack and Go floppy.

Auto Clip Art Wizard

After you have created a basic presentation, you can ask the Auto Clip Art Wizard to suggest some clip art to enhance it. With the presentation you want to enhance current, click on **Tools** and choose **AutoClipArt...** to launch the Wizard. As with other Microsoft Wizards, you can answer a few simple questions from the Wizard dialog box, clicking on **Next** each time you're ready to move to the next dialog box.

AutoContent Wizard

If you choose the Presentations tab on the New Presentations dialog box, one of your choices is an AutoContent Wizard. This interactive wizards asks you questions about your presentation and then based on your answers picks a presentation template. In addition, the wizard places text on the slides and use prompts that help you organize information for your presentation.

The wizard chooses templates and pre-formatted presentations from among those available in the Presentations tab of the New Presentation dialog box. This wizard works like other PowerPoint wizards. Read the instructions on each wizard dialog box, click any choice buttons, and click on **Next** when you are ready to go on to the next dialog box.

Figure 4.74 shows one wizard dialog box that lets you specify the type of presentation you want to create.

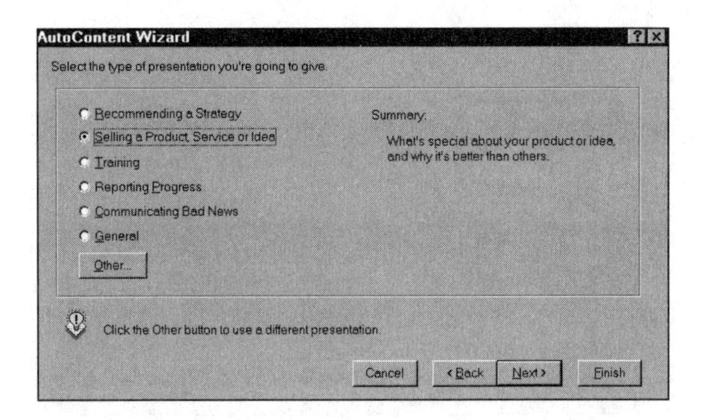

Figure 4.74 *AutoContent Wizard dialog box for choosing a topic.*

If you click on the **Other** button in this dialog box, PowerPoint presents the full list of objects available in the Presentations tab of the New Presentations dialog box. Click on **Next** after you have chosen the type of presentation you want to design.

The wizard designs a title slide for you and inserts a number of slides with text on them. You can use this basic design as a starting point toward your finished presentation.

The precise order of wizard dialog boxes and the dialogs presented depend on the type of presentation you choose from the dialog box in Figure 4.74.

With some presentation choices, you will be given the selection dialog box shown in Figure 4.75.

After the final dialog box in the wizard is finished, a new presentation will be opened in the slide view in PowerPoint. Step through the slides, replacing the "dummy" text with information that fits your own presentation.

Study the list of presentations in the Presentations tab of the New Presentations dialog box. You can bypass the AutoContent wizard, if you wish, and load one of these pre-formatted presentations and add your own material and formatting.

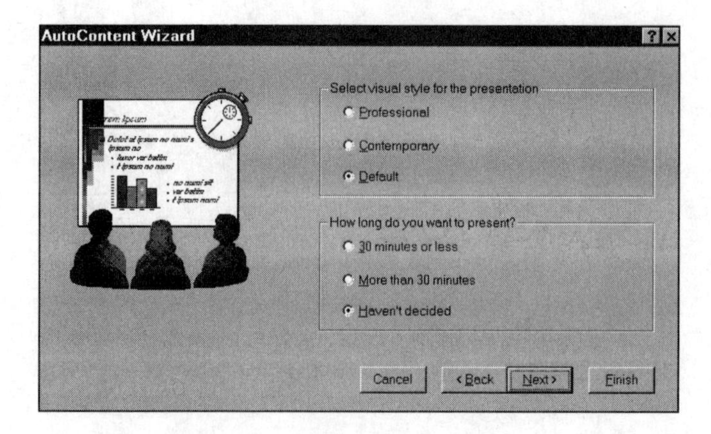

Figure 4.75 *AutoContent Wizard dialog box for choosing length and template.*

To Sum Up

You can use this chapter as a reference during presentation or slide design. The images of individual templates will help you plan your presentations even when you don't have access to your computer and PowerPoint (as when you are at home and your computer is at the office). In fact, as you can see from the material in this chapter, PowerPoint is so rich in material that it may take you a while to become familiar with all of its features. I urge you to use the information in this chapter as a jumping-off place for further study. Use the computer and PowerPoint's screens to teach yourself even more about this useful program.

In the next chapter, I'll give you additional information about designing individual slides in PowerPoint, and I'll offer some suggestions on using PowerPoint for on-screen and projected slide shows.

CHAPTER 5

Computer Slide Shows with PowerPoint

If you have read the previous chapters of this book and have tried at least some of the things I have suggested, you have a firm foundation in PowerPoint. You know how to use the preformatted templates and interactive Wizards to produce a slide show or presentation.

In this chapter I will show you in more detail how to design individual slides—apart from the templates and Wizards—and how to use the screens to actually produce a computer-based slide show. In later chapters I'll show you how to take the basic on-screen material and turn it into overhead projection foils, printed pages, graphics files, or 35mm slides.

Designing Slides

I talked about slide design considerations in Chapter 3. Those general guidelines will help you choose the proper typeface, type size, and colors for a particular application. In this section I'll show you how to use PowerPoint tools to create your own slide designs, either from scratch or by starting with a template and editing it for your own needs.

Review the information on templates in Chapter 4. Also, remember that you can use any presentation you design as a template for future presentations.

Let's start with a blank slide, no template, no design. Do this by selecting the **File: New** command from the main PowerPoint menu. In the New Presentation dialog box, choose the **General** tab and then choose **Blank Presentation**. The New Slide dialog box is displayed. Choose the blank slide from this dialog box. This will open a blank PowerPoint presentation with a vacant title slide displayed. Your screen should look like Figure 5.1.

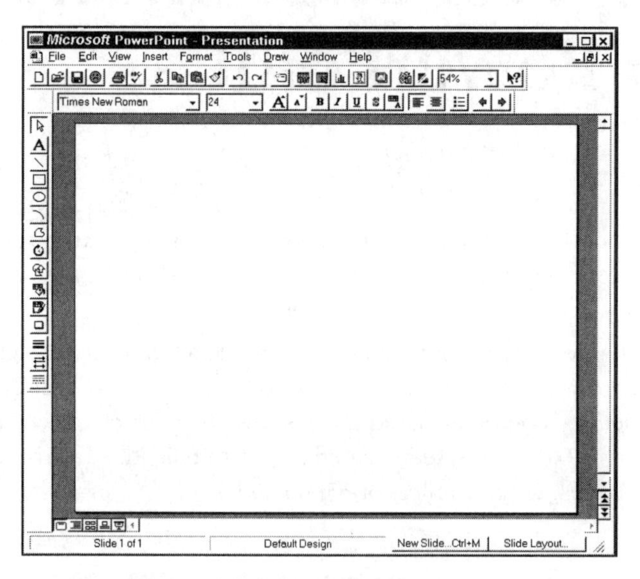

Figure 5.1 *New Presentation with vacant title slide.*

Now let's put some text and graphics on that blank slide. This time we'll use the manual features of PowerPoint instead of the automatic and preprogrammed features.

Adding Text

First we'll add a title to the blank slide. The blank presentation routine automatically inserts a title slide in the front of the otherwise blank presentation. You need only click in the two title areas to add information. However, I want you to understand how these slides are formatted. That way you'll be able to start with a completely blank slide or an AutoLayout slide and edit it to achieve the look you want.

For the purpose of this exercise, let's remove the preformatted title areas from this slide:

1. Click inside the area that says "Click to Add Title." The prompt disappears and a frame appears around the section.
2. Click anywhere on the frame (the wide, dark line that replaced the dotted outline that was there before you clicked inside the area to select it). Black handles appear around the frame.
3. Press **delete** on your keyboard to remove the frame.
4. Repeat the previous three steps to remove the frame that holds the Subtitle prompt.

Now you should have a blank slide with no objects on it.

NOTE

If you click on the **New Slide** button on the Standard toolbar or use **Ctrl+N**, PowerPoint displays the Autoformat dialog box. Choose the blank slide from the lower right-hand corner of the display to get a blank presentation without having to delete the default title slide.

To add text, simply click on the text tool in the Drawing toolbar at the left of the PowerPoint slide window. (The Drawing toolbar could be positioned elsewhere. It can be moved anywhere on the screen.) The mouse cursor should change to a downward-pointing arrow. Move this cursor to the location on the slide where you want the text to begin, then click the left mouse button. That fixes the beginning of the text cell so you can simply type the text you want to insert onto the slide. PowerPoint places a small shaded box around the cursor, indicating that a text window has been opened and is ready for input.

Type one line of text. I've used **This is a Title** for the example and I've placed it at the top of the slide in a title position (see Figure 5.2).

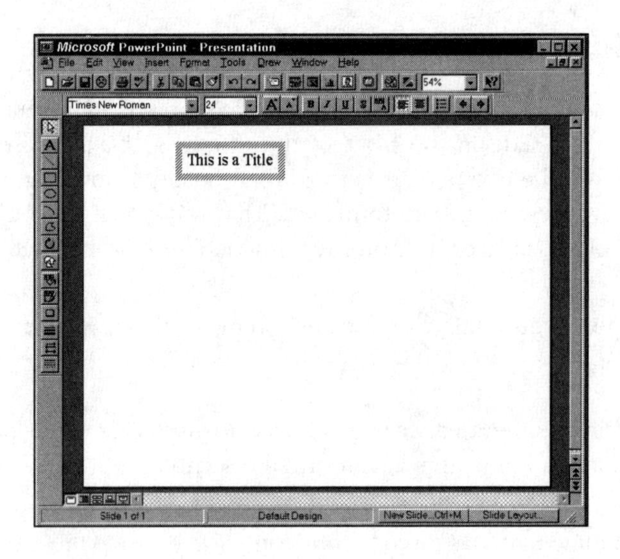

Figure 5.2 *Sample slide with This is a Title inserted.*

As you can see from Figure 5.2 and your own typing, PowerPoint selected a font for these letters for you. Like a word processor, PowerPoint has preset defaults that apply unless you change them.

SPECIFYING FONT AND SIZE

For text, the default font is Times New Roman 24 point. Times New Roman specifies the typeface—the particular design of the characters—while 24 point specifies how big the characters are. A 24-point letter is about one-third of an inch tall, because it takes 72 points to make a character one inch high.

When you type a business letter or a report on a word processor, you will likely use 10- or 12-point type. That's about the right size for most standard text. When you are using text in a presentation, however, the letters generally need to be much larger than those on a normal printed page. In fact, the 24-point default in PowerPoint is much too small for a main slide title. If you use one of PowerPoint's AutoLayout slides or one of the preformatted presentations from the New Slide dialog box, the text in the title portion of the slide is preformatted at 44 points (0.61 inches). That is large enough for projected slides, but may be too small if you are using the computer screen itself.

Here's how to enlarge text. We'll leave the Times New Roman typeface because it produces good general purpose text that is easily read. Use the mouse to select the text you just entered. Do this by placing the cursor to the right or left of the text, holding down the left mouse button, and highlighting all of the text. You could also place the insertion point at the beginning or end of the text, hold down the **Shift** key, and then use the cursor movement keys on the keyboard to select the block.

Click on the **Increase Font Size** button on the Format bar. Notice that the font size increases from 24 points to 28 points. Each click on this button increases the size of the selected text by 4 points.

If you are using very large fonts, the Increase or Decrease Font Size button will change the font size by much more than 4 points. If you start with a 4000 point font, for example, the change is 364 points with each click.

Click four more times on the **Increase Font Size** button to raise the size of the title text to 44 points, PowerPoint's default for preformatted slides.

You can see that this is the new point size by looking at the Font Size window beside the Font name on the Format bar. Each time you click on the Increase Font Size button the number in this window increases by four points. You can see the size of any text on the screen by placing the insertion point within any word and then looking at the number in the Font Size window.

Is a 44-point title big enough for your application? That depends on how you will use the slide or presentation you are creating. You can try a larger font size by simply clicking more times on the **Increase Font Size** button. You can also pull down a list of standard font sizes by clicking on the down-pointing arrow beside the Font Size window, as shown in Figure 5.3.

Try a 72-point (one inch) font for this title by using the scroll bar to the right of the pull-down font size list. This produces a large font that can be seen easily, even on a computer screen presentation. For a larger font, select 96 points (1.3 inches), which is the last standard font on the list.

Want a REALLY big font for a short title? Select the font size displayed in the Font Size window of the Format bar, type in the font size you want to use, then press **Enter**. The standard pull-down list contains fonts that range from a very small nine points to a relatively large 96 points. However, you can type in font sizes from 1 point (too small to see) to 4,000 points (about 55 inches). Obviously you have to adjust the size of the text you're using to fit the application. You can't see a 55-inch character on a 14-inch computer screen, but you might be able to print it if you have a large plotter that can handle images that large. Use **Slide Setup (File: Slide Setup...)** to set the paper size if necessary and use **Printer Setup (File: Print Printer...)** to select the plotter to which you want to print.

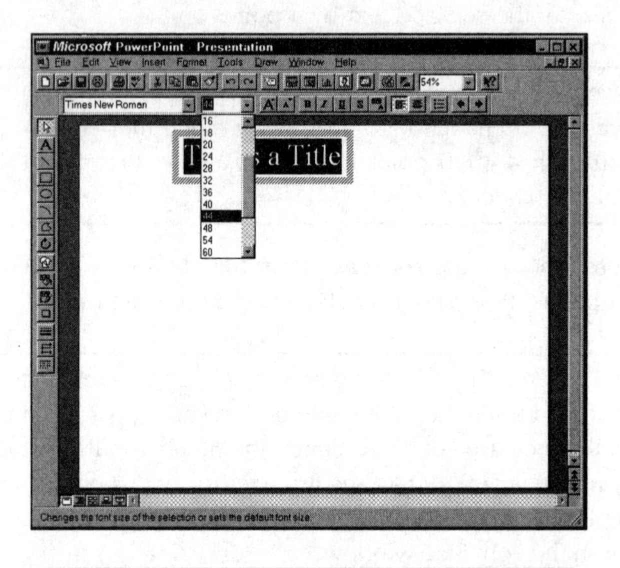

Figure 5.3 *Font Size pull-down list on Format bar.*

SETTING TEXT POSITION

I've shown the text on this slide as a top-of-slide title. However, you can place text anywhere on the slide. Simply select the text tool (as described above) and click on the slide where you want to start entering text.

Suppose you want to position the text in an orientation other than horizontal, left to right. Let's say you want to position the previously-entered title as a corner banner at the upper right-hand area of the slide (see Figure 5.4).

PowerPoint's built-in utilities make this an easy process. Here are the steps:

Select the text by clicking anywhere within the title. PowerPoint places a box around all of the text. Click on the box to place handles around the title (see Figure 5.5).

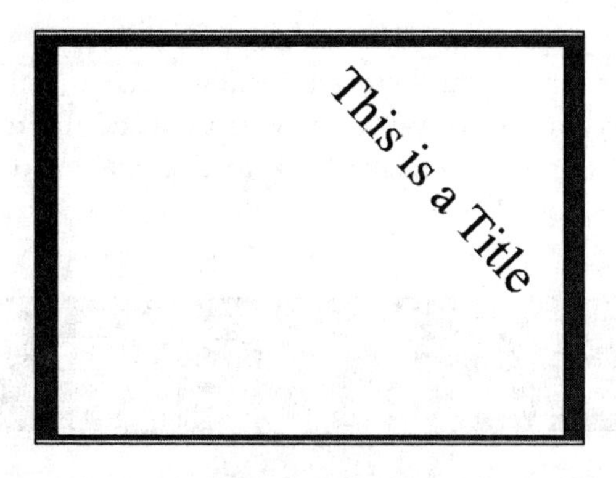

Figure 5.4 *Slide title positioned at upper right corner.*

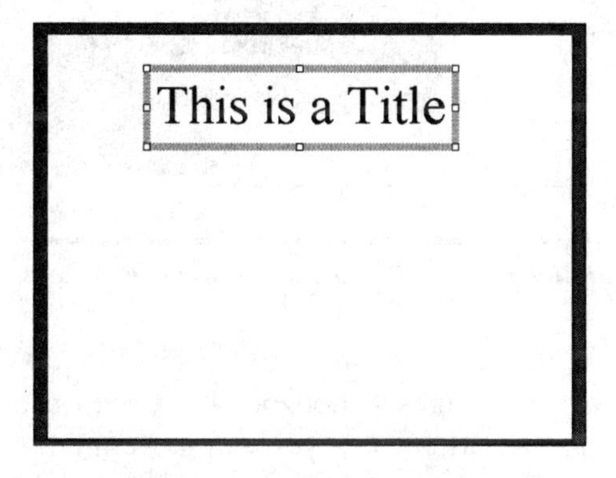

Figure 5.5 *Title text selected.*

Grab the title box and drag it toward the middle of the slide. This is to give you room for the rotation of the text. Use **Draw: Rotate/Flip** to display the Rotate/Flip menu shown in Figure 5.6. You can also choose the rotate tool from the Drawing toolbar.

Choose **Free Rotate** from this menu. The mouse cursor now shows a double circular arrow as well as the standard pointer, indicating that you can rotate the selected text freely in any direction. Move the cursor to one of the handles on the selection box around the title text. The cursor changes again to just the double circular arrows.

Grab the handle by pressing and holding the left mouse button. Now you can rotate the text box around a center point by moving the mouse. Turn the box until it is approximately 45 degrees relative to the upper right-hand corner of the slide. Don't worry if you don't get the angle exactly right. You can change the angle later if you need to. Click anywhere outside the text box to turn off rotation. The mouse cursor changes back to a pointer and the selection box around the text is removed.

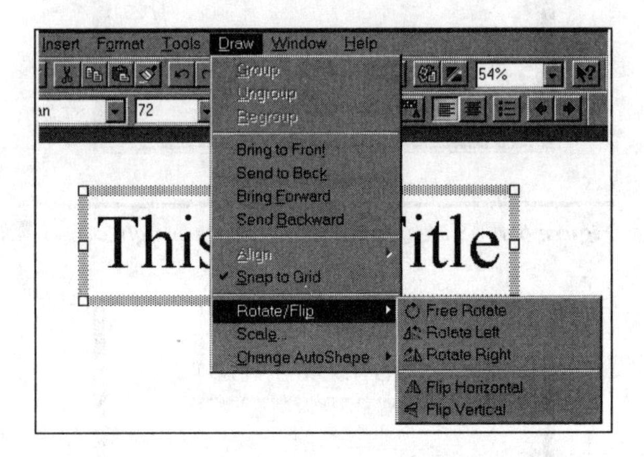

Figure 5.6 *Pull-down Draw Rotate/Flip menu.*

Click anywhere inside the text once more to reselect the text. PowerPoint puts a frame around the text and aligns it horizontally. Click on the frame itself and hold down the left mouse button. Now you can move the box to the upper right corner of the slide. If the rotation isn't exactly right, use **Draw: Rotate/Flip** again to adjust the angle so the text will fit into the corner of the slide. The finished result should look like Figure 5.4.

Another way to change the orientation of text is to enter it in a vertical line instead of horizontally. You could use a short line of vertical text to call attention to a graphic or to help the viewer focus on a different area of the slide. You can enter a vertical line of text easily. Simply select the text tool and position the cursor where you want the first letter in the line of text to appear. Type the first letter, then press **Enter**. Now enter the second letter and press **Enter**, and so on. Press **Enter** twice between words to separate them.

You can select this vertical line of text by clicking anywhere inside the line and then dragging the entire box where you want it on the screen. You could rotate this line of text as well, but it can be difficult to read rotated vertical text. I'm not saying you shouldn't rotate a vertical line, but that you should use good judgment in how much you rotate it and you should keep the amount of text to a minimum.

You should choose the typeface for vertical text carefully. A large bold font is a good choice, perhaps a sans serif font (one without serifs) such as Impact or Helvetica. Also, it is a good idea to keep the number of words in a vertical line small. It is relatively difficult to read text with one character on top of another. In fact, a single word for emphasis is the best choice, but you can use several words. Just be aware that it may take slightly longer for the audience to assimilate multiple words in a vertical format than it would take if the text were conventionally placed. Figure 5.7 shows how you might use a single vertical word to emphasize an idea also presented by clip art. Figure 5.8 shows rotated vertical text.

Figure 5.7 *Vertical text with clip art.*

Figure 5.8 *Vertical text rotated for emphasis.*

Changing Text Color

You can do other things with text besides changing its size and moving it around the slide. For one thing, you might want to change the color of text if you are designing a presentation for projection, for conversion to 35mm slides, or for color printing on overhead foils.

To select a different text color, first select the text either by holding down the left mouse button and highlighting the text you want to change, or by clicking anywhere inside a line of text to select it all. If you select a single word or a single character by highlighting, you can change colors on a character-by-character or a word-by-word basis. If you place a text selection box around a block of text by clicking anywhere inside the line, you'll change the color of everything inside the box at once. Either way, change text color by popping up the **Text Color** selector from the Format bar. Click once on the **Text Color** symbol to display the selector shown in Figure 5.9.

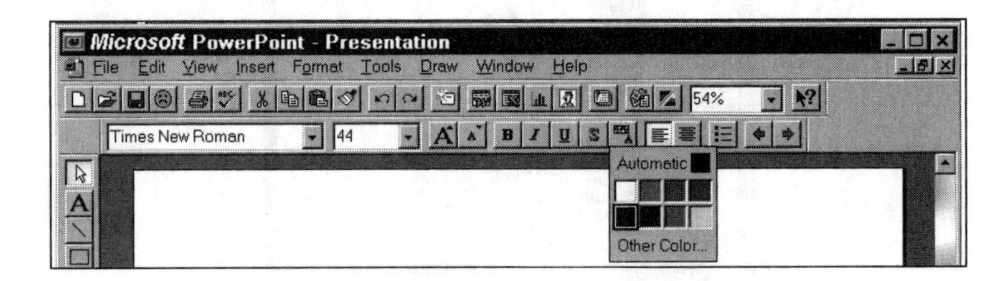

Figure 5.9 *Text Color selector from Format bar.*

NOTE

You can also change text color with the **Format: Font Color** command sequence. This procedure displays the Font dialog box and then pops up the Text Color selector inside this dialog box.

To change the color of any selected text, simply click once inside the square of the color you want to choose from the Text Color selector.

Placing Text Inside Objects

What else can you do to format text? You could place text inside a colored object, for example, or you could enter text and then place an object over or behind it. Suppose you want a colored rectangle with text inside it. In fact, you could use multiple rectangles on a slide to hold different text components. Consider the slide in Figure 5.10.

Figure 5.10 *Slide with multiple text boxes.*

This slide incorporates several text formatting features of PowerPoint: underlining, text color, text over an object, and parallel positioning. Here's how to recreate the slide in Figure 5.10.

Start with the clip art. I've used a cartoon clip art image that shows a woman beside a blackboard in front of an audience. You can find this slide in the People group in the ClipArt Gallery. You can select something else for this exercise if you'd like. Use **Insert: Clip Art** to place an image within the slide. PowerPoint places the selected image at about the middle of the slide at a preformatted size. For this example, we'll move the image from its default position and resize it slightly to make it large enough to hold the text.

First, we'll move the image from the center of the screen to the right edge; not all the way to the edge—but close to the right edge of the new slide. When you insert the slide, PowerPoint automatically selects it. You can tell that it is selected by the presence of handles around the parameter of the image. If the clip art is not selected, simply click anywhere inside the clip art image to select it. Once the image is selected, you can move the mouse pointer inside the image, hold down the left mouse button, and drag the image to the right of the slide. Release the mouse button when the image is positioned where you want it.

Move the pointer over the handle in the lower left corner of the clip art and hold down the left mouse button. Now you can drag the edges of the clip art to make it a little larger. Just pull the lower left corner down and to the left an inch or so.

NOTE

Use care in resizing clip art, photographs, or other images. If you shrink the image horizontally (narrowing the width) without also changing the height, you change the *aspect ratio* of the image. You can determine the proper aspect ratio by looking carefully at the image as you resize it.

Now insert the text. Select the text tool and click inside the blue presentation board to the left of the woman. Type the first block of text. If you are re-creating the sample slide, type **Sales Opportunity!** Click on the box that surrounds the text to select it as a block. PowerPoint places selection handles at each corner and in the middle of each side of the text box. Now you can move the text, size it, and change its attributes.

Click on the **Increase Font Size** button on the Format bar until the size of the text increases to 40 points, as shown in the Font Size window of the Format bar. Drag the text box so that it is centered in the top portion of the blank area of the board.

Next, create the WELCOME banner at the top of the screen. Select the text tool from the Drawing toolbar. Click anywhere near the top of the screen to establish a text entry box. Type **W E L C O M E** in all capital letters with a space after each letter.

Select the rectangle tool from the Drawing toolbar and use this tool to draw a rectangle around the block of text. Do this by placing the pointer to the left and above the text box. Hold down the left mouse button to nail down the upper left corner of the rectangle, then drag the box to the lower right edge of the text box. Make the box considerably larger than the text—it should be a pleasing size around the text. When you release the mouse button, PowerPoint creates a colored box on top of the text. Unless you have changed PowerPoint's defaults, the box is blue and covers up the text. The blue box is selected (you can tell this because there is a line around the box and selection handles on it).

Use **Draw: Send Backward** to move the colored rectangle behind the text. This makes the text visible. Now you should see black text inside a dark blue rectangle. Click on the text inside the colored box. PowerPoint places a white box around the text and opens the block of text for editing. You could type additional text or delete text inside the box at this point, but we don't want to edit the text. We want to change the text's color and its attributes. Click on the box that PowerPoint has drawn around the block of text. You can tell the whole block is selected because PowerPoint places handles on it. Now you can manipulate all of the text as a block without having to select it in the conventional way.

Click on the **Bold** button on the Format bar to change the text to boldface. (You can also use the **Format: Font** command to display the Font dialog box. You can select the bold attribute from this dialog box.) Also select the underline attribute, either by clicking on the **Underline** button or by using the Font dialog box.

Open the Text Color selector either from inside the Font dialog box or by clicking on the **Text Color** button on the Format bar. Choose the white color box from inside this display to change the text color to white. This produces a blue box with bold underlined white text inside it.

NOTE

Although the colored boxes and text seem to be single objects, they remain separate. You can reposition them by moving the text and then dragging the box over it. Or you can group the text and box, making it easy to move them together. Click on a colored box to select it, then hold down the **Shift** key and click on the text. Now additional "star" handles show that both text and box objects are selected. Use **Draw: Group** to join the two. Now you can move them as a single object.

The slide is beginning to shape up, but it has one basic problem, so far. Notice that the color of the board beside the woman presenter is a different shade of blue from the box behind the WELCOME banner. It would probably look better if the two were the same color. I personally like the deeper blue of the box behind the WELCOME text, so here's how to change the color of the presentation board to match.

1. Move the mouse pointer anywhere inside the clip art image and press the right mouse button. PowerPoint selects the image, placing handles around the parameter, and pops up the menu shown in Figure 5.11.

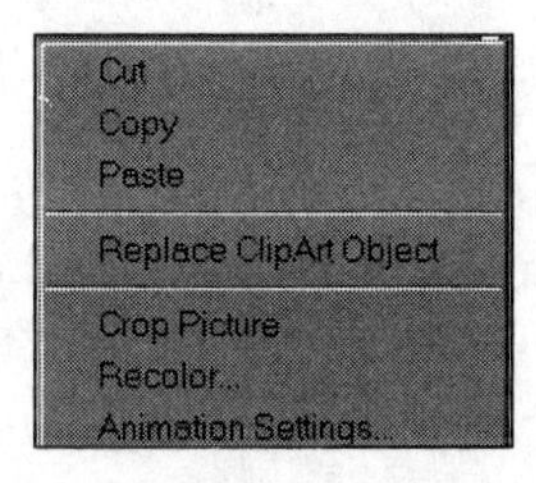

Figure 5.11 *Clip Art Edit pop-up menu.*

2. Click on the **Recolor** menu option to display the dialog box shown in Figure 5.12. This shows all of the available colors in the clip art and lets you change them individually. You can't tell from the black and white image in this book, but the Original and New colors are the same.

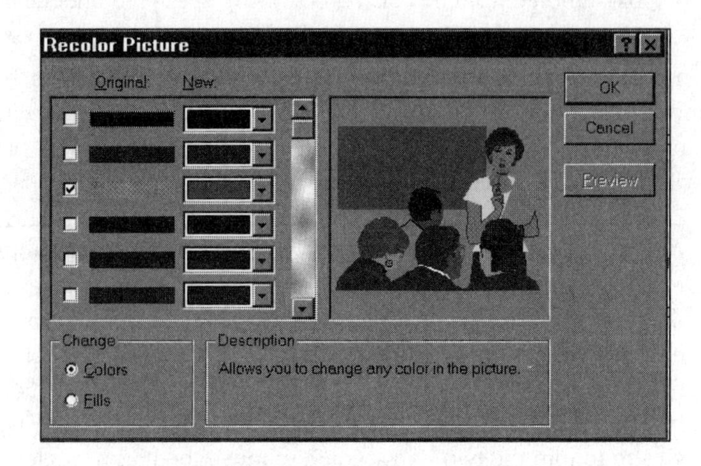

Figure 5.12 *Recolor dialog box.*

3. Click on the blue bar—third from the top—to select it.
4. Click on the down arrow beside the blue box in the New column to display a color selection dialog box.
5. Click on **Other Color...** to display the Colors dialog box.
6. Choose a blue color to match the box behind the WELCOME banner and click on **OK**.

Next, create the bullet list to the left of the clip art image.

Creating Bullet Lists

In this section I'll show you how to quickly create the bullet list in this slide. Then we'll work together on a new slide with a bullet list so you can experiment with additional text formatting.

To create the bullet list to the left of the presenter clip art:

1. Choose the text tool from the Drawing toolbar.

2. Click in the space to the left of the clip art image, near the left margin of the slide.
3. Type the first line of text in the list and press **Enter**.
4. Type the remaining four lines of text, pressing **Enter** after each line (except the last).
5. Click on the frame around the block of text to select all of the text. Handles appear around the frame.
6. Click on the **Bullet List** icon on the Format bar. PowerPoint adds bullets in front of each line, but they are too close to the text.
7. Click after the bullet on the first line to position the insertion point.
8. Press the **Tab** key to move the text to the right. If this moves the text too far, click on the **Undo** icon on the Standard toolbar and type three spaces after the bullet instead.
9. Add a tab (or spaces) after each of the remaining bullets.

Now let's experiment with additional bullet list formatting. Try building your own list by first inserting a new slide. (Click on the **New Slide...** button at the bottom of the screen or use **Insert: New Slide...**.) Again, choose the blank slide in the AutoLayout list—the one with no preformatted sections for title, lists, or clip art.

Select the text tool and click on the slide where you want to start the bullet list. Type the first line of the list. Now you can either press **Enter** to create a list as a single object, or you can click outside the text block to close the box. If you do the latter, then you must select the text tool again, reposition the insertion point, and type the next line of text. If you want more flexibility in positioning items in the list, make each line a separate object. If you are satisfied with the order and don't plan to move individual items to different areas of the screen, then enter the bullet text as a single list.

A basic list of single-line text items is shown in Figure 5.13. I've added a title to this slide as well, and I've enlarged the type from the PowerPoint defaults.

Now you can add standard PowerPoint bullets to the list. Select the first text block (or the only block, if you've entered the list as a single object). Click on the **Bullet List** button on the Format bar. PowerPoint adds a standard bullet to the beginning of each text line within the selected block. If you have more than one block, repeat the process until you have each line bulleted, as shown in Figure 5.14.

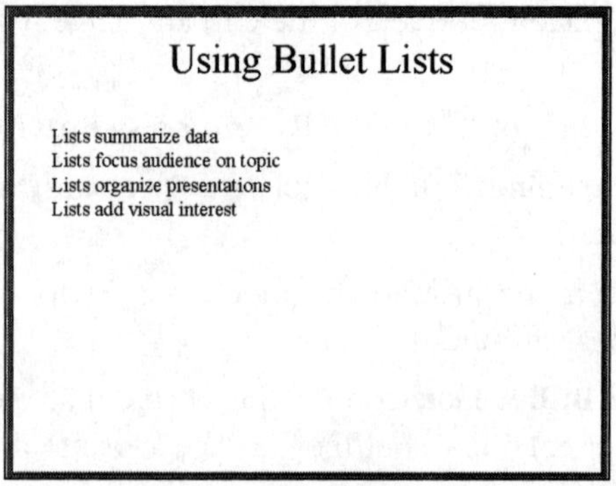

Using Bullet Lists

Lists summarize data
Lists focus audience on topic
Lists organize presentations
Lists add visual interest

Figure 5.13 *Basic text list without bullets.*

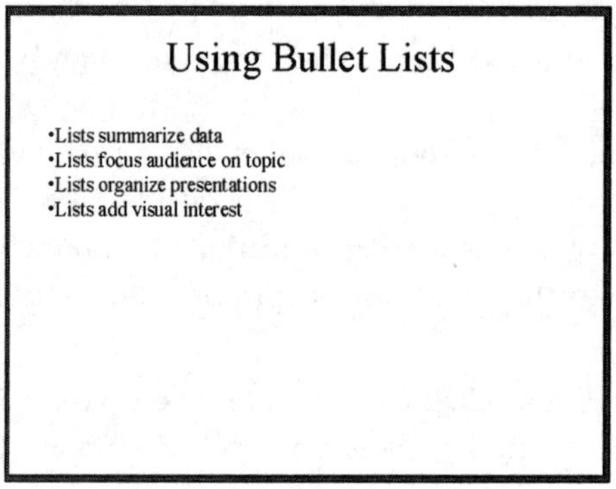

Using Bullet Lists

•Lists summarize data
•Lists focus audience on topic
•Lists organize presentations
•Lists add visual interest

Figure 5.14 *Beginning bullet list.*

Notice that PowerPoint doesn't place any additional space between the bullet and the text. Normally you want to format a bulleted list as a hanging indent paragraph. In PowerPoint, however, you so rarely have a multiline bullet that a simple tab between the bullet and the first character in the text line is sufficient.

To insert a tab after the bullet, click to the left of the first character in each line to place the insertion point between the first character and the bullet. Click on the **Bullet List** button to remove the bullet temporarily and then press **Tab**. Now place the insertion point at the beginning of the line and click on the **Bullet List** button to reinsert the bullet. As you can see from Figure 5.15, the list is more pleasing and easier to read with spaces after the bullets.

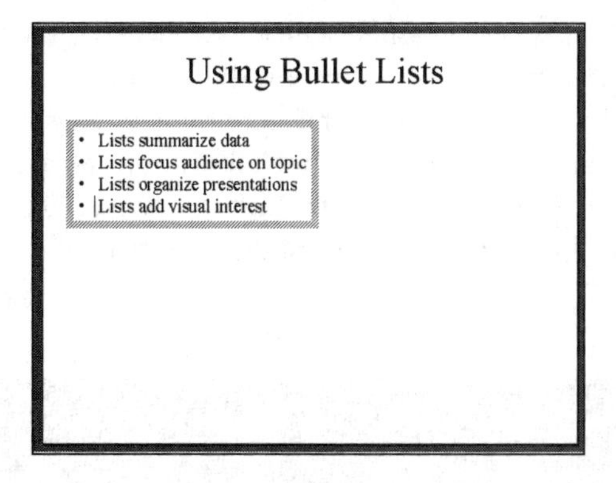

Figure 5.15 *Bullet list with spaces.*

You have used the PowerPoint default bullet settings to create a bullet list. What if you want to use another character for the bullets? This is easily done. Select a block of text by clicking anywhere in the line. This is like selecting a paragraph in Microsoft Word or other word processors. Now use the **Format: Bullet** command to display the Bullet dialog box shown in Figure 5.16.

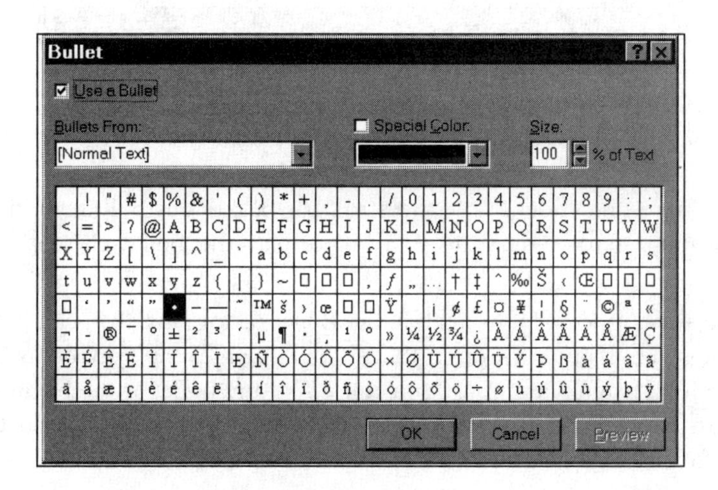

Figure 5.16 *Bullet dialog box.*

Notice that the default bullet is highlighted, and the Use a Bullet button is selected. (This is because you previously inserted a bullet into this line of text. If the selected text did not have a bullet already, then this button would be blank.)

The Normal Text font is in the Bullets From window of the dialog box. There are several interesting choices for bullets on this screen, including boxes of various shapes, special symbols such as the copyright (©) or registered trademark (®), and foreign characters. But that's not all. There are a number of typeface groups from which to choose bullets. To find out what's out there, click on the down arrow beside the **Bullets From** window to display a list of typefaces, as shown in Figure 5.17.

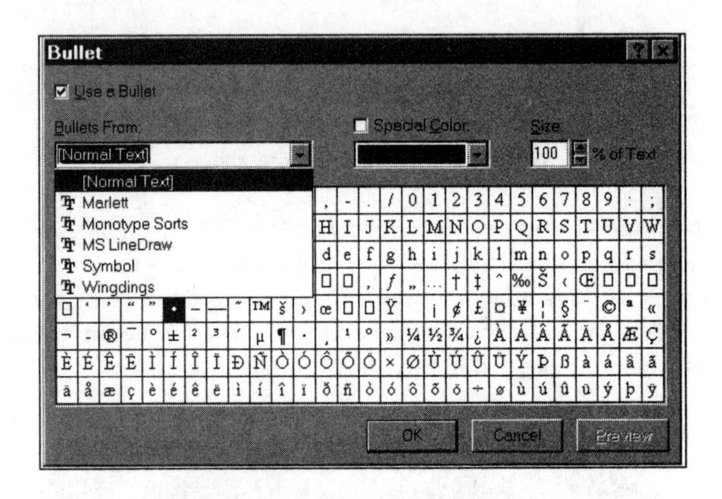

Figure 5.17 *Bullets From typeface list.*

For some interesting choices, use the scroll bar beside this pull-down list to find the **Wingdings** entry. Select this entry to display the bullet choices shown in Figure 5.18.

These symbols look fairly small in the Bullet dialog box. To get a better look at any one symbol, just click on it. PowerPoint enlarges the symbol, as if it were placed under a magnifying glass. You can insert any bullet at the beginning of a line of text either by double-clicking on the bullet or by clicking on **OK** after selecting the bullet you want to use.

Figure 5.19 shows the bullet list with smiley faces as bullets instead of plain black dots. Obviously this is just one of many choices for unconventional bullets for your lists. If you want card suit symbols (diamonds, spades, etc.), for example, select the **Symbol** typeface from the pull-down list instead of Wingdings.

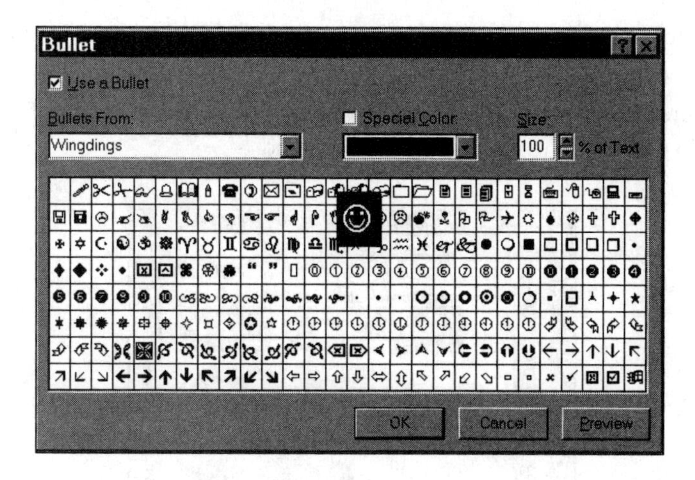

Figure 5.18 *Wingdings bullets.*

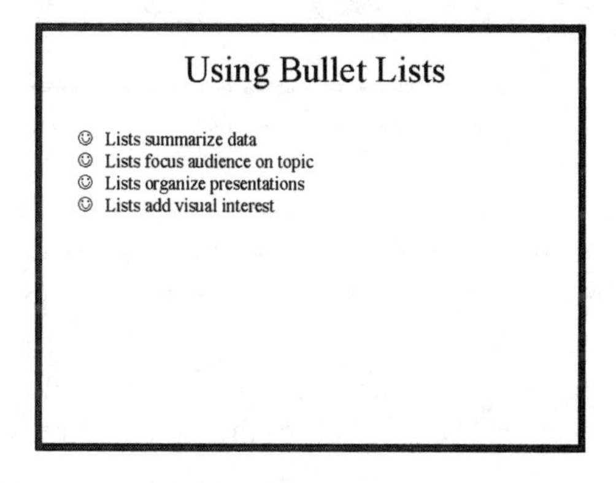

Figure 5.19 *Bullet list with smiley faces as bullets.*

Don't forget that you can change the color of the text lists, including the bullets. I showed you how to do that earlier in this chapter.

ALIGNING TEXT

One more text feature needs to be discussed. When you place two or more objects on a single slide, it may be important to ensure that they are aligned in a particular way. You may want two text boxes to be placed one directly above the other, for example. This can be difficult to achieve when you have different blocks of text that you are trying to keep aligned. Fortunately, PowerPoint includes a tool to make this job easier.

In Figure 5.20 I have added a ruler display to the left and top of the screen. You can do this with the **View: Ruler** command.

Figure 5.20 *Text box slide with ruler display.*

As you move the mouse, you can track the vertical and horizontal position by noting the position of the pointers on the two rulers. Notice that the center of the slide is at 0,0. In conventional screen addressing, the upper left-hand corner is usually 0,0.

To make sure that two text boxes are lined up on the same vertical line (they are the same distance from the left of the slide), place one box where you want it.

NOTE

A text box can be a true box, like the one we placed in the WELCOME banner at the top of the slide, or it can be straight text, such as the bullet list to the left of the clip art. When you select either kind of text box, you can move it as a unit, using the ruler to help you position it.

Next move the mouse pointer onto the left edge of the box and note the horizontal position on the top ruler. Now you know where to position the next box. Grab the next box and drag it to a position where the left edge is on the same vertical line as the first one.

Obviously you can use the same technique to position a series of objects along a horizontal line by using the vertical ruler at the left of the PowerPoint screen.

In addition, you can use these rulers to help you align text or other objects in a block. When you activate a block of text by clicking inside the text, the ruler changes to show the area of the slide occupied by that block. Notice how the rulers have changed in Figure 5.21. Duplicate this display by clicking on the text in the bullet list at the left of the screen. You can see the width and height of the block by referring to the space defined on the rulers.

Figure 5.21 *Rulers showing height and width of text block.*

Remove the rulers with the **View: Ruler** command sequence. This is a toggle command, so the first time you use it a check mark is placed beside the Ruler menu item and the rulers are displayed. The second time you use the command the check mark is removed and the rulers disappear.

Adding Clip Art, Pictures, and Graphs

As you've already seen, effective slides aren't built from text alone. Although text blocks may carry the majority of the information in a slide, other objects can help to emphasize the message of the text or to augment it in different ways.

Using Clip Art

In the previous chapter you learned how to insert a clip art image from the ClipArt Gallery, and also how to move and resize the image. Clip art won't solve all of your graphics needs in PowerPoint, but it can go a long way toward helping you design and create powerful, effective presentations. PowerPoint comes with enough clip art images to help enhance almost any type of presentation. You can also find clip art within other applications such as Microsoft Word, WordPerfect, Parsons Technology Announcement, various calendar, card, and banner programs, as well as drawing programs.

USING PICTURES

You don't have to limit yourself to PowerPoint clip art. As I have mentioned, clip art images are frequently supplied with other applications. These are standard format graphics files that may end in **.PCX**, **.TIF**, or another file format extension. You can insert these images into a PowerPoint presentation with the **Insert: Picture...** command sequence from the main menu. This command displays the Insert Picture dialog box shown in Figure 5.22.

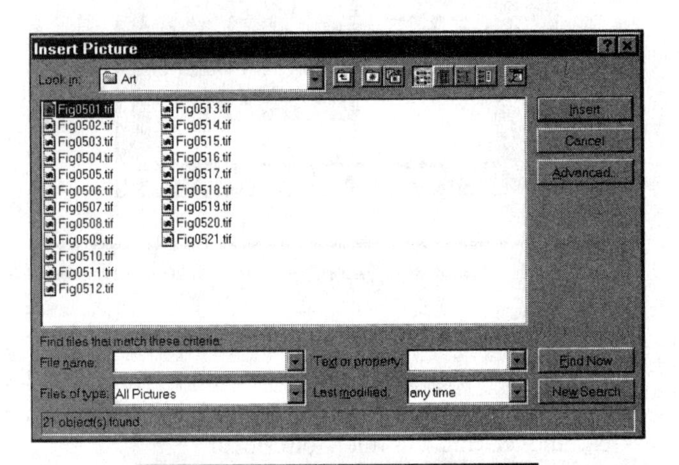

Figure 5.22 *Insert Picture dialog box.*

The default directory will be the current directory or the last directory you used to insert a picture. PowerPoint automatically lists files of known graphics types (All Pictures in the File of type field) that it can convert and import. Among the file types PowerPoint will look for are files with these extensions:

```
*.wmf, *.wpg, *.drw, *.dxf, *.hgl, *.cgm, *.eps,
*.tif, *.pcx, *.gif, *.pct, *.adi, *.cdr, *.plt,
*.pcd, *.tga, *.bmp, *.dib
```

That's a comprehensive list of graphics files. If you want to narrow the list to a specific type of file—such as ***.pcx** or ***.tif**, common formats with scanners and many graphics programs—then simply type ***.pcx** or ***.tif** in the File name window. The description in the Files of type field changes to Tagged Image Format, and the list of files changes to reflect the new file name specification.

Use the scroll bar, if necessary, to step through the list of files, and double-click on the one you want to import into the current slide inside your presentation. You can change directories by clicking on one of the parent directories listed in the Directories window of this dialog box, then stepping down through the list to the directory you want.

Double-click on the file name you want to import, or select the name and click on **OK** to import it into PowerPoint. Once the image is imported into your current slide, you can move it or size it just like the clip art you experimented with earlier in this chapter.

The ability of PowerPoint to import graphics images from a variety of drawing and graphics programs lets you use images created by almost any popular application inside your PowerPoint presentation. If you're using a drawing program to prepare graphics elsewhere in your company, or your business involves CAD design, it is probable that you can use native images from these applications directly inside PowerPoint presentations. Many applications can export files in other than native format, so if a particular program doesn't use a file format that is compatible with PowerPoint import filters, chances are that you can export files into a format that PowerPoint will support.

Using Graphs

As I mentioned in the previous section, you can import images and files from a wide variety of programs. This lets you use powerful graphics, drawing, and image programs to help you support presentation design in PowerPoint. However, PowerPoint itself contains features that can handle many, if not most, of your image needs.

You can import a spreadsheet graph from Excel or 1-2-3, for example; this is what you may want to do if the data on which the graph is based is complex or if you merely want to avoid entering the data a second time. However, if you are dealing with raw data that you want to represent as a graph, you can use PowerPoint's built-in graphing facility.

Click on the **New Slide...** button at the bottom of the PowerPoint display. Select the third slide (the first in the third column at the right) in the AutoLayout display. This slide is preformatted with a title and space for a graph. Your screen should look like Figure 5.23.

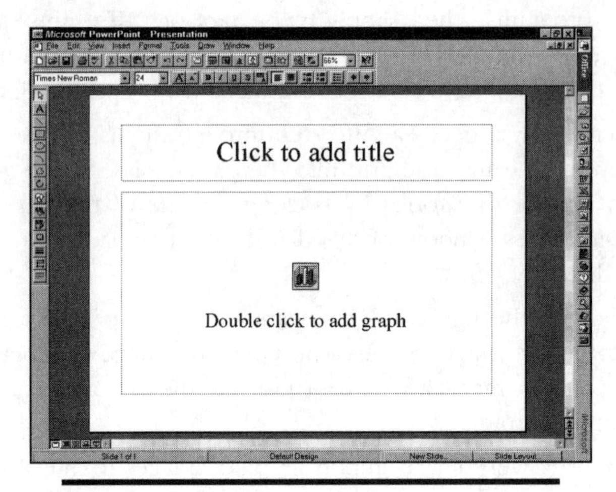

Figure 5.23 *New Slide with Graph AutoLayout.*

Although we are using a preformatted AutoLayout slide in this example, you can add a graph to any slide, whether or not it has a section set aside for one. The graph image works like any other object such as clip art or pictures. Once on your slide, you can move or size a graph image just as you can clip art.

Add a title to the sample slide, if you wish, by clicking in the indicated area and typing the text for a title. I've used the title Sample Graph Slide for this example. Double-click on the graph symbol to open the PowerPoint graphing utility (Microsoft Graph) shown in Figure 5.24.

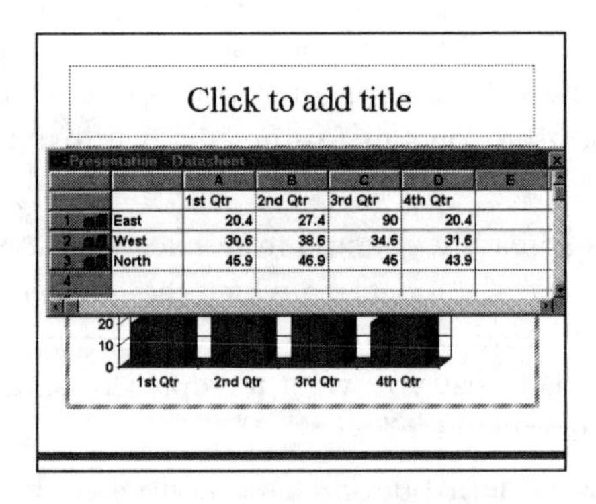

Figure 5.24 *PowerPoint graphing utility.*

Notice that PowerPoint inserts the graphing utility inside the current slide, and that it includes sample data that is used to present a sample graph. The graphing utility window looks like a portion of a spreadsheet window. You can enter new labels and data to replace the existing information and create your own graphic display of raw data.

Suppose you want to compare the number of endangered species in the U.S. with those in foreign countries in graphical form. (This is data right out of the *1994 World Almanac*. Your information might be different, but you can see from this example how to present numerical data as a graph.) Here is the raw information to be graphed:

Table 5.1

Group	U.S. Only	U.S. and Foreign	Foreign Only
Mammals	37	19	249
Birds	57	16	153
Reptiles	8	8	64
Amphibians	6	0	8
Fishes	55	3	11

To use PowerPoint's graphing utility, simply re-create the list inside the graphing utility. Replace the East, West, North titles with Mammals, Birds, Reptiles, Amphibians, and Fishes, and enter the numbers in the appropriate columns. Replace existing data by selecting it with the cross cursor or arrow keys and typing in the new information. PowerPoint automatically updates the graphs in the window based on the new data you enter. Figure 5.25 shows how the screen looks after the raw information has been entered into the graphing utility.

Notice that there are some problems with the display in Figure 5.25. You are probably having the same problems with your graph display, unless you are familiar with Microsoft Excel and have corrected the problems as you entered the data. (Microsoft Graph behaves in many ways like Excel, although it lacks many of its features.)

First, we have entered three columns of data, but the sample graph includes four columns. You can remove this last column by moving the cross cursor onto the **D** at the top of the fourth column, then clicking once to select the whole column. PowerPoint will set the column in reverse video to indicate it has been selected. Press **Del** once to remove the data in that column.

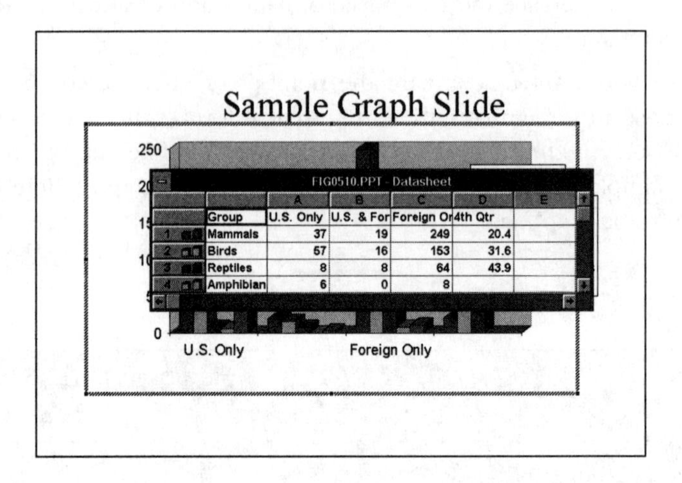

Figure 5.25 *Raw endangered animal data in graph.*

Now only data you want to display is in the spreadsheet, but some of the cells are too narrow to hold the information. You can widen the cells easily by moving the cross cursor into the top of the columns. As you move the cursor over the vertical lines that divide the columns, the shape of the cursor changes from a cross to a double-ended arrow. Try this with column **B**. When the shape of the cursor changes to the double-ended arrow, press and hold the left mouse button and drag the dividing line between columns **B** and **C** to the right, widening the entire **B** column. Drag the line far enough to make room for the whole title, **U.S. & Foreign**.

Repeat this process for the **C** column, making room for the **Foreign Only** title. Notice how the data window and the graph window have changed. PowerPoint redrew the graph as you entered new information into the data window. You can get a look at the graph without closing the data entry window by clicking its title bar and dragging it off the top of the graph. This gives you a picture like the one in Figure 5.26.

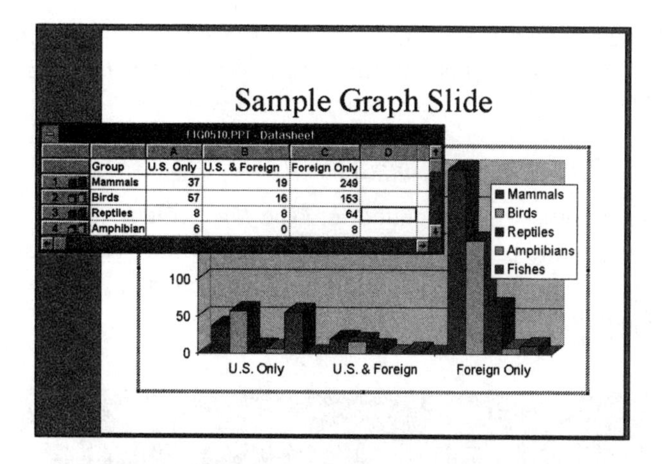

Group	U.S. Only	U.S. & Foreign	Foreign Only
Mammals	37	19	249
Birds	57	16	153
Reptiles	8	8	64
Amphibian	6	0	8

Figure 5.26 *Graph with data entry window to side.*

If you need to edit data you've entered, simply click inside the cell you want to change and type the new data. When all the titles and numbers are correct you can close the data entry window, leaving the newly created graph inserted onto the current slide. To close the data entry window, click on the control panel button (now represented by a color Windows icon) at the upper left corner of the data entry window and choose **Close** (you can also just press **Ctrl-F4**). The result is the slide shown in Figure 5.27.

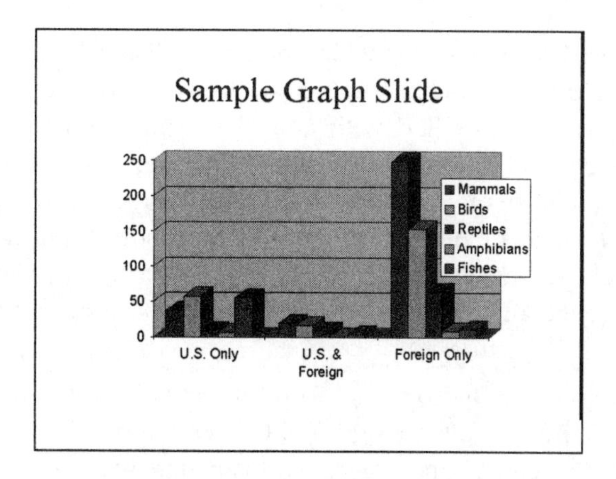

Figure 5.27 *Finished graph slide.*

Notice that the graphic representation of the data can be much easier and quicker to interpret than numbers. Creating a graph with PowerPoint's built-in graphing utility makes the process automatic and easy.

Using Other PowerPoint Objects

Because PowerPoint is well-integrated into the Microsoft Windows environment, you can insert a number of other types of objects into your slides. To insert something into the current slide, use the **Insert: Object...** command to display the Insert Object dialog box shown in Figure 5.28.

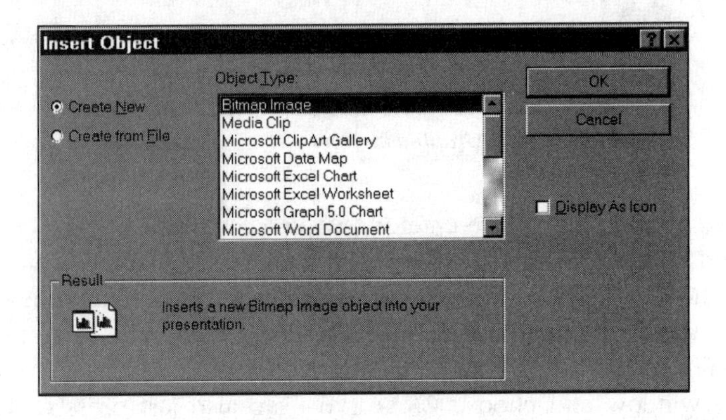

Figure 5.28 *Insert Object dialog box.*

The object types that appear in the Insert Object dialog box depend to some extent on what other resources you have installed on your system. Many Microsoft products are installed with common components in subdirectories within the Windows subdirectory. In general, however, you should find choices for Media Clip, Microsoft Drawing, equations, graphs, Word documents, WordArt, and a range of other objects from Microsoft applications. Just how these objects behave on a PowerPoint slide depends slightly on what the object is, but you can generally expect to insert an object, size it, and move it just as you would clip art or pictures.

I've shown you already how to use AutoLayout slides to create a particular style of slide. The AutoLayout dialog box includes sample slides with placeholders for text, clip art, charts, and so on. You can start with one of these designs and change the placeholder type if you want to build a show of slide types before you insert the actual images. Do this by selecting the placeholder and then clicking on the type of image on the Standard toolbar that you want to use. You can also use the **Insert: Object...** command to display the Insert Object dialog box. When you choose an object type, PowerPoint inserts a placeholder for that object in place of the previous one.

If you are starting with a slide that does not have a placeholder, use **Insert: Object...** and click on the **Display As Icon** button on the Insert Object dialog box. Then when you select an object type, it will be inserted onto your slide as an icon. You can double-click on this icon to launch the utility that lets you insert an object of this type.

Adding Organization Charts

I showed you in Chapter 2 how to use the Organization Chart utility in PowerPoint. I'll just review the process here and add more information to the basics already provided. Click on the **New Slide...** button at the bottom of the PowerPoint screen. Notice that the second slide down in the third column of the AutoLayout window has a section set aside for an organization chart. If you choose that slide, you can add an organization chart by simply double-clicking on the slide's organization chart symbol. For this example, however, select the last slide in the third row—the blank slide. I will show you how to format your own slide and how to find the Organization Chart utility without the AutoLayout prompt.

With a blank slide on the screen, choose the text tool from the Drawing toolbar and create a title for this slide. I used the title OrgChart Sample Slide. Increase the size of the title font to 54 points and underline it. (See the text section earlier in this chapter if you need help remembering how to do this.) Your slide should look like Figure 5.29.

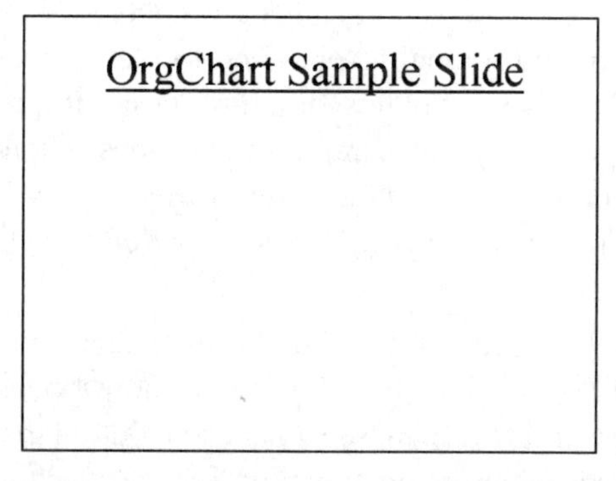

Figure 5.29 *Organization chart sample slide with title only.*

You can insert an organization chart by clicking on the **Insert Organization Chart** symbol on the Standard toolbar or by using the **Insert: Object...** command and choosing **MS Organization Chart** from the Insert Object dialog box. Either way, the Organization Chart utility screen, shown in Figure 5.30, is displayed.

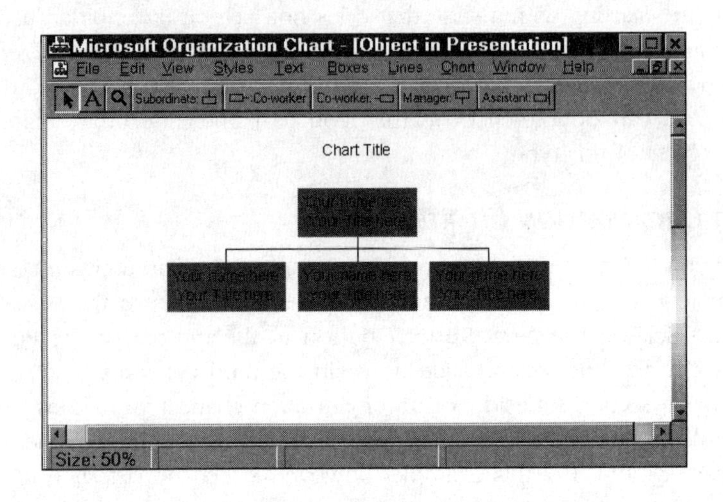

Figure 5.30 *Organization Chart utility main screen.*

This utility is similar to the graphing utility. You use a separate application closely tied to PowerPoint to create the organization chart, then you insert the final image into your slide at a predetermined location at the center of the screen. After the image is inserted, you can size it or move it as with clip art and other objects.

The Organization Chart screen contains a predefined organization chart with a title line and two organizational levels—one top-level box and three boxes at the second level. Each box contains dummy entries for name, title, and two comments. You can see only the name and title lines when Organization Chart opens. To open an entire box, click on one of the dummy lines of text inside a box. Organization Chart expands the box to show all four lines of dummy text, as you can see in Figure 5.31.

Notice that a toolbar beneath the Organization Chart menu bar lets you add text to the area around the chart boxes and add more boxes to the chart. Study the toolbar carefully and you can see that each button has a connective line attached at a different location on the box icon. You choose the appropriate icon to add a box at a specific location on the chart.

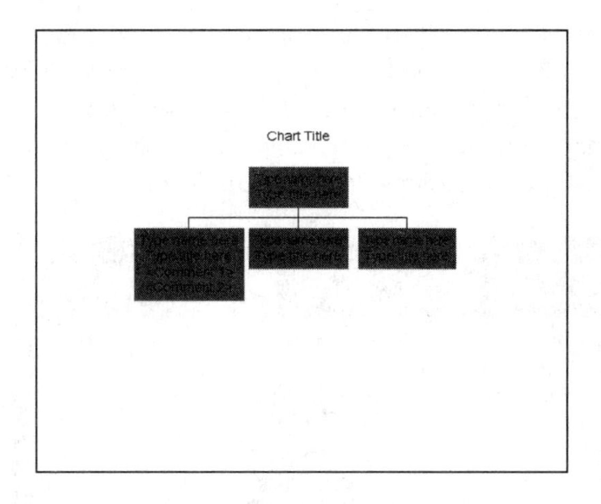

Figure 5.31 *Organization chart with left box opened.*

To change the dummy text on any Organization Chart box, click on the box to activate it and use the mouse to select the text you want to replace. When you start typing, Organization Chart replaces the selected text with what you type.

Organization Chart includes several formatting features to help you design the precise type of organization chart you want. These features are accessed from the Organization Chart menu bar. For example, when you click on the **Styles** menu, Organization Chart displays the organization chart formats shown in Figure 5.32. If you had first selected an entire existing chart—such as the default sample chart—you could change the style of this chart by clicking on one of the designs in the Style dialog box.

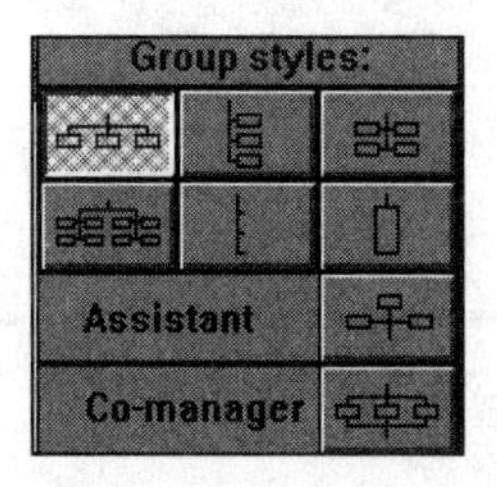

Figure 5.32 *Style dialog box from main Organization Chart menu.*

Select an organization chart by holding down the left mouse button and drawing a box around the chart or chart portion you want to modify. Organization Chart changes the color of the selected chart or chart portion. Now you can use the Styles menu to rearrange the existing boxes. For example, if you click on the second style in the Style dialog box, a top-down subordinate design, the Organization Chart default chart looks like the one in Figure 5.33. Use this design to create deeper subgroups under a main level.

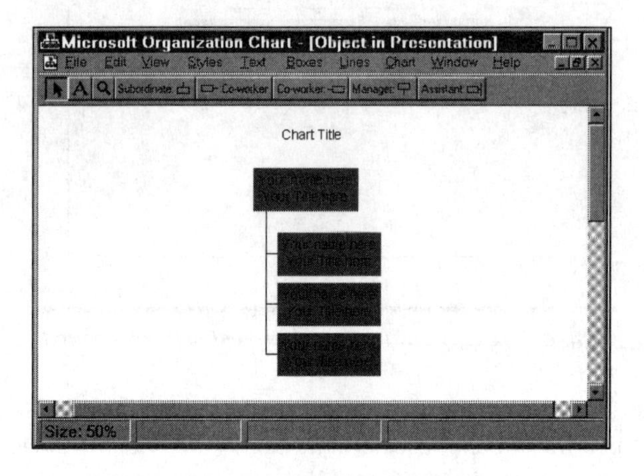

Figure 5.33 *Top-down organization chart.*

Another way to change the appearance of an organizational chart is to change the borders around the boxes or the color or style of the lines between boxes. Make these changes, and others, with the Boxes menu, shown in Figure 5.34.

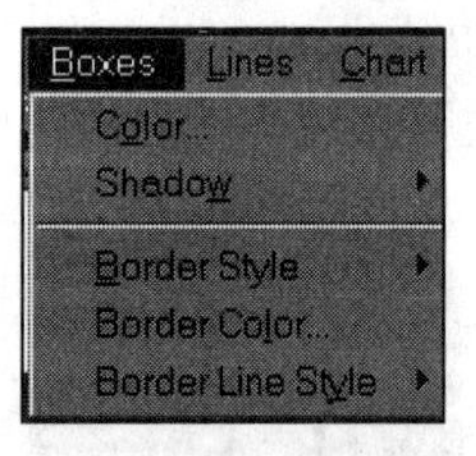

Figure 5.34 *Boxes menu from Organization Chart main menu.*

With these menu selections you can add or remove borders, change the thickness of the lines, change line style and color, or add shadows around the boxes. Use these formatting features to add emphasis to part or all of your organization charts. You can tell by the right arrows beside the Boxes menu entries that additional menu choices are behind each of these selections.

After you have added the text and formatting you want to an organization chart in the Organization Chart utility, use **File: Update** to place the image into the current slide. Then use **File: Exit** to return to PowerPoint. The completed sample slide is shown in Figure 5.35.

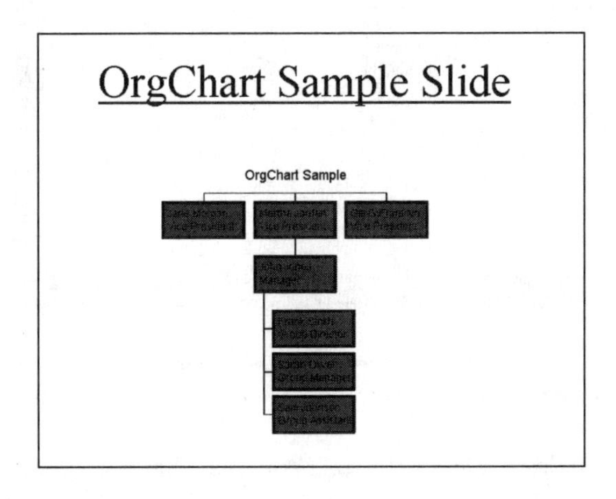

Figure 5.35 *Completed Organization Chart sample slide.*

You can return to the Organization Chart utility at any time by double-clicking on a chart inserted into a PowerPoint slide.

Editing and Building the Presentation

In the previous sections of this chapter you have built a small presentation or slide show. Now it is time to learn how to manipulate these images into a final presentation.

Using the Slide Sorter

The best way to get an overview of a presentation is to turn on the Slide Sorter view. Do this by clicking on the **Slide Sorter** icon at the bottom of the slide display, or by using the **View: Slide Sorter** command sequence from the main PowerPoint menu. Figure 5.36 shows the sample presentation we built in this chapter in Slide Sorter view.

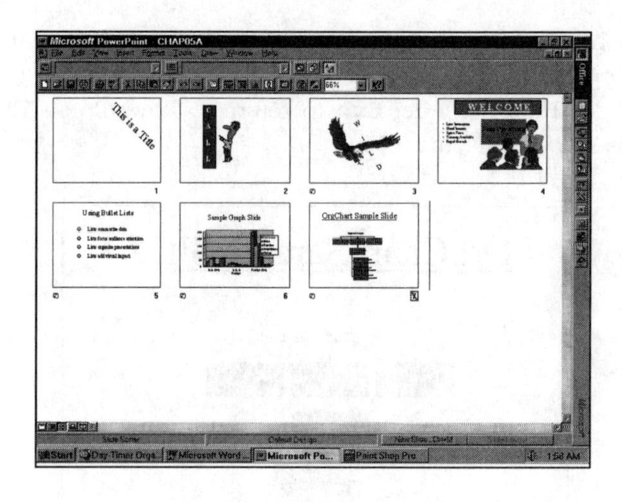

Figure 5.36 *Sample presentation in Slide Sorter view.*

There are seven slides in Figure 5.36. (You may have a couple more or less, depending on how you followed the samples earlier in this chapter.) This view of your presentation shows how the various slides are positioned, and it gives you the opportunity to move them around if you wish. This is also a good place to start when you want to add new slides to a presentation.

Notice that PowerPoint places a large insertion point or cursor within the Slide Sorter view. This shows the current location of the slide pointer. You can use the mouse to place this pointer anywhere in the presentation. You can click on an existing slide to select it and make it the current slide, or you can click in the space between slides to insert a new slide into that location. Once a slide has been selected, you can use the mouse to drag it to any position within the Slide Sorter. Try that now. Move slide number 7, the organization chart, to position 2, right after the **This is a Title** slide. Your Slide Sorter screen should look like Figure 5.37.

Notice that as you drag a slide the pointer changes to a packet or envelope to indicate that you are carrying an object. The entire slide won't move until you place the insertion point in the new location and release the mouse button.

Adding Transitions

After you have the slides in the order you want and you have inserted any new slides, you are ready to work on *transitions.*

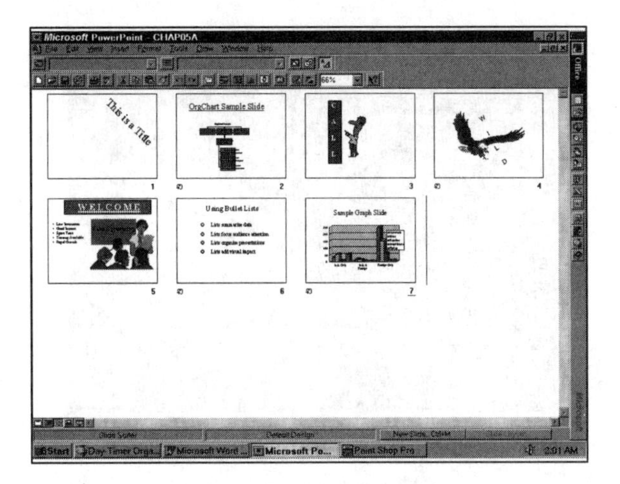

Figure 5.37 *Slide Sorter with #7 in #2 position.*

NOTE

If you are designing a presentation for overhead projections or for conversion to 35mm slides, you don't need to worry about transitions. If you will use the presentation as an on-screen slide show or will project the computer images to a large group, then transitions can enhance the presentation.

A transition setting specifies how PowerPoint will make the change from one slide to the next. You might specify a *fade*, for example, or a pattern that *dissolves* across slides. Such effects smooth the transition between slides. You should either choose an effect and stick with it through most of the presentation, or use *straight cuts* except when you want to emphasize a slide or idea. Too many different types of transitions can be distracting, especially when the slides are changed frequently. Properly used, however, transitions can give you some time between slides for narration and can help guide the viewer and indicate that a slide change is taking place.

To specify a transition, select a slide and then use the **Tools: Slide Transition...** command sequence from the main PowerPoint menu. This displays the Transition dialog box, shown in Figure 5.38.

You can see from this figure that No Transition is the PowerPoint default. That means that when you enter Slide Show mode and press a key or click the left mouse button, the current slide is removed and the next slide is presented without any transition effect between them.

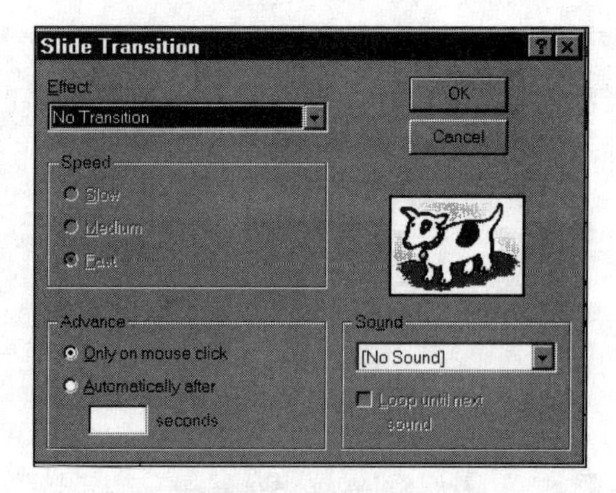

Figure 5.38 *Transition dialog box.*

To view a list of possible transitions, click on the downward-facing arrow to the right of the **Effect** window. Your display should look like Figure 5.39. Use the scroll bar to display the rest of the list, which contains at least 45 transition types.

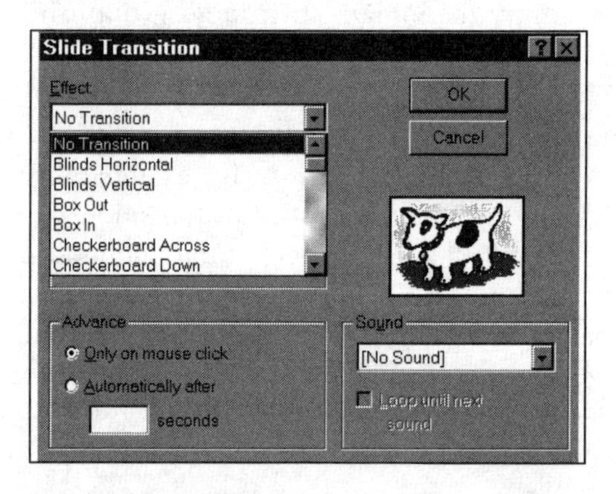

Figure 5.39 *Pull-down Effect list in Transition dialog box.*

To specify a transition, first select a slide, then choose a transition type from this pull-down list. You can also specify whether the transition is to occur at a fast, medium, or slow rate. When you make these specifications, PowerPoint demonstrates the transition on the small slide at the lower right-hand corner of this dialog box. To see the example again, just click on the **Speed** button that you want to review. Even if the button is already selected, you can click on it and get a preview of how the transition will take place.

NOTE

When you choose a transition you are specifying how the current (selected) slide will be presented, not the next slide. If slide #2 is the current slide and you choose a slow dissolve, for example, then slide #2 will appear after slide #1 (or slide #3 if you are backing up through the show) is displayed with a slow dissolve.

Try specifying a transition for slide #2. Pull down the Effect list and use the scroll bar to locate the **Random Bars Vertical** transition. Click on **Slow** in the Speed section of the dialog box and observe the sample transition. Some of these transitions are reminiscent of techniques used in videos or movies, including dissolves, wipes, pattern dissolves, and so on. Experiment with various transition effects to find one (or several) that seem to fit the mood of your presentation.

One possible choice—especially while you are designing a presentation—is Random Transition, which is the first transition choice in the Effect list. If you specify Random Transition for every slide, then as you work with the slides you can view several different types of transitions. This may help you locate one that works best. You could leave Random Transition specified for your actual presentation and it might work fine. However, as I mentioned earlier, too many different effects can become distracting. As with any special effect or formatting, try it out, be aware of your subject and your audience, and use what works for you.

You may want to specify slow transitions for all slides until you have decided what the final effects will be; then you may want to switch to medium or fast. In general, you want the effects to simply take you from one slide to the next, not get in the way of the show.

Presenting the Show

Now you're ready to present the show, or at least to step through it and practice your narration, evaluate transitions, study slide design, and so on. The more complex your presentation design, the more time this stage of design and building will take. It won't take long to step through our simple show, but the same techniques I'll show you here will work for any presentation you design.

To view the presentation as a slide show, simply click on the **Slide Show** icon at the bottom of the screen or use **View: Slide Show...** to present the images in full-screen mode. PowerPoint will display the current slide and then wait for you to press a key or click the left mouse button before going on to the next slide. By starting in the Slide Sorter view and then launching the Slide Show view, you can begin the presentation anywhere you wish by selecting the starting slide from the Slide Sorter.

To advance to the next slide in the presentation, press one of the following keys: the **Spacebar**, **Enter**, the **N** key, down arrow, page down, or right arrow, or you can click the left mouse button. To back up one slide, either click the right mouse button, hold the **Ctrl** key and press the left mouse button, or press one of the following keys: left arrow, the **P** key, up arrow, page up, or **Backspace**.

NOTE

If you need a reminder of what keys do what during a presentation, press **F1** to display a Help dialog box that shows major keyboard and mouse functions (see Figure 5.40).

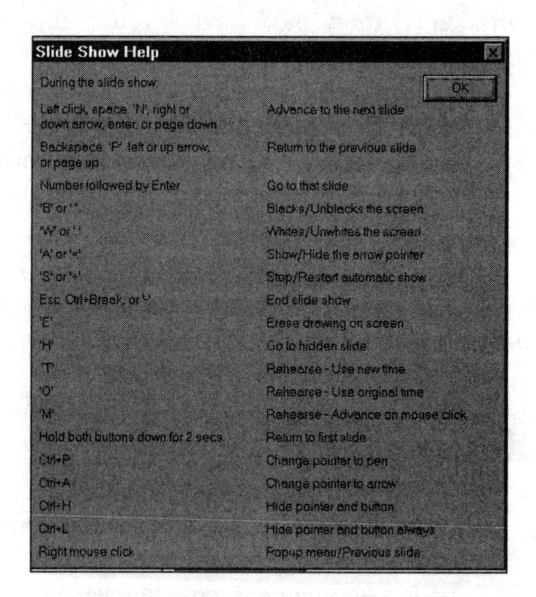

Figure 5.40 *Slide Show Help screen.*

Notice that you can jump directly to any slide within the show by entering the slide number and then pressing **Enter**. To jump directly from slide 3 to slide 7, for example, simply press **7** on the numeric keypad or at the top of the keyboard and then press **Enter**. The slide in the number 7 position will appear, using whatever transition you have specified for that slide.

NOTE

You can also use the Outline view or the Slide Sorter to jump to a specific slide. Click on **Outline View** or **Slide Sorter**, select the slide you want to view in the Slide Show view, then click on the **Slide Show** icon to restart the slide show.

Other Slide Show Utilities

There are other PowerPoint features that can be extremely useful during a live presentation. When you are in Slide Show view, PowerPoint places a small triangle icon at the lower left corner of the screen, but not until you move the mouse pointer after the slide is displayed. You won't see this icon if you use the keyboard or if you just click a mouse button to change slides. After a slide is displayed, however, you can move the mouse pointer to make this icon appear.

Click once on this icon and you will see the pop-up menu shown in Figure 5.41.

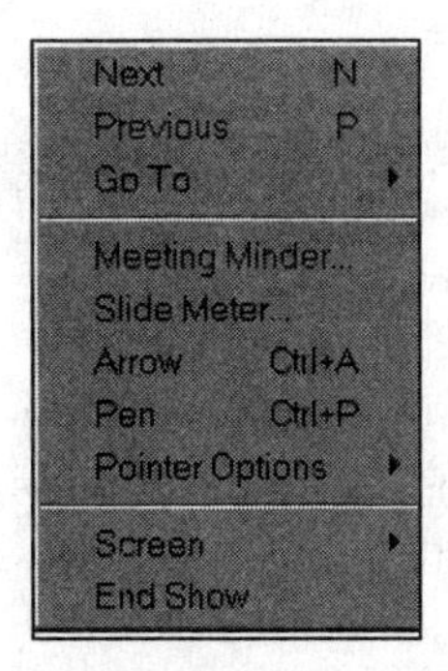

Figure 5.41 *Slide Show pop-up menu.*

You can choose any of these menu items during a slide show presentation. The first three menu items are obvious. Click on **Next** to advance one slide, **Previous** to back up one slide, and **Go to** to jump directly to any slide in the current show.

NOTE

You can display this menu at any time during a slide show by pressing the right mouse button.

The fourth menu choice is the Meeting Minder, a pop-up dialog box that lets you keep track of the progress of the current presentation (see Figure 5.42).

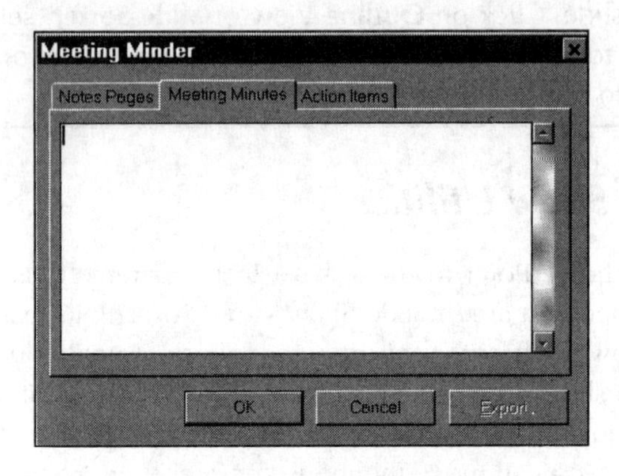

Figure 5.42 *Meeting Minder dialog box.*

Type notes about the meeting (or a complete set of minutes, if you wish), create a list of Action Items for follow-up later, or type new or edited information onto the Notes Pages from this dialog box. Pop this dialog up when you need it and remove it to continue the show.

The fifth choice on the Slide Show pop-up menu, Slide Meter, displays a meter that helps you judge the progress of the presentation. You can see a countdown timer that shows how long the current slide has been displayed, as well as a color-coded display that tells you when a slide has been displayed too long or when your transitions are too quick.

The next three options control the on-screen pointer. Choose **Arrow (Ctrl-A)** to display the default arrow pointer or select **Pen (Ctrl-P)** to bring up the pen. In addition, you can choose **Pointer Options** to control these objects. Choose **Hide Now** to remove the pointer from the screen, or **Hide Always** so that the pointer never appears. And, when you choose **Pen Color**, another pop-up menu displays a number of color options. Choose a color that is easy to see on the slide background you are using.

When you choose the Pen (it looks more like a pencil to me) you can move it anywhere on the slide and then hold down the left mouse button to draw on the slide. What you draw lasts only until you change slides, and it doesn't affect the slides stored on disk. This tool can help you emphasize data or a feature displayed on the screen. Figure 5.43 shows one of the sample slides with drawings on it that were created during a presentation.

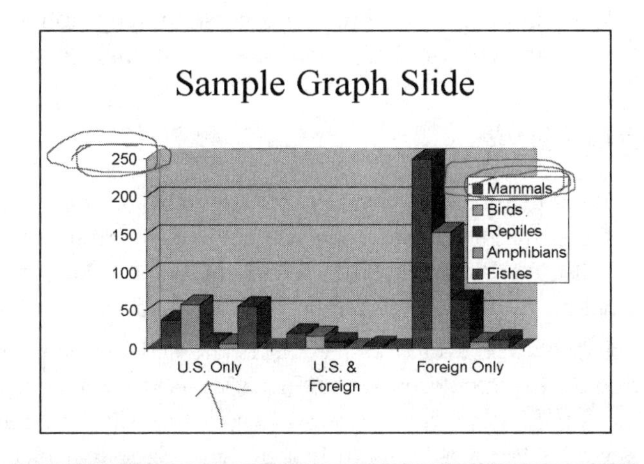

Figure 5.43 *Sample slide with hand drawings for emphasis.*

The Screen option on this Slide Show pop-up menu lets you set the screen color to black (or remove the black), pause a running show, and erase the pen. You might use the black screen option to temporarily remove some slides from a show or to help in transitions.

Finally, use the **End Show** menu item to stop a running slide show and return to the PowerPoint screen that was displayed when you started the slide show.

Exiting a Slide Show Presentation

Press **Esc** at any time during a presentation to return to the screen that you were viewing prior to starting the slide show. If you were viewing the slides in Slide Sorter view before starting the slide show, you will be returned to the Slide Sorter if you press **Esc** during a show.

If you decide one or more slides should not be used for a given presentation, don't delete the slide(s). Instead, select the slide you don't want to use, then use **Tools: Hide Slide** to avoid displaying this slide in Slide Show view. It will still appear in the Slide view, the Slide Sorter, and the Outline.

And, as I mentioned in the last section, you can use the pop-up menu (press the right mouse button) and choose **End Show** to stop a running show.

Using a Build Slide

Another PowerPoint feature you may want to use with presentations is the Build or Progressive Disclosure slide. Although you can use successive slides to reveal information in a list, there may be times when you want to keep the same slide on the screen but have each item in the list appear when you need it.

You will probably use a Progressive Disclosure slide as part of a bullet list. Let's add a slide to the sample presentation we've used in this chapter and create a bullet list as the basis for a Progressive Disclosure slide. In general, to create a Progressive Disclosure slide, you first design a slide that includes a list of information, such as a bullet list. Then you convert the slide to display each item in the list sequentially. I'll show you the steps for completing a Build slide in this section.

To create a Progressive Disclosure slide, your list must be constructed with one of the bullet list AutoLayout forms provided with PowerPoint.

First open the presentation to where a bullet list slide exists, or create a new bullet list slide. Let's add a bullet list slide to the existing presentation as the last slide. Click on the **Slide Sorter** icon at the bottom of the presentation screen to enable Slide Sorter view. Click in the space after the graph (slide #7 in our sample presentation).

Click on the **New Slide** button at the bottom of the screen. PowerPoint displays the New Slide dialog box. Choose the second AutoLayout slide (the first slide in the second column), which has a title and bullet list layout. A blank slide is inserted. Double-click on the blank slide to open it for editing in Slide view. Your screen should look like Figure 5.44.

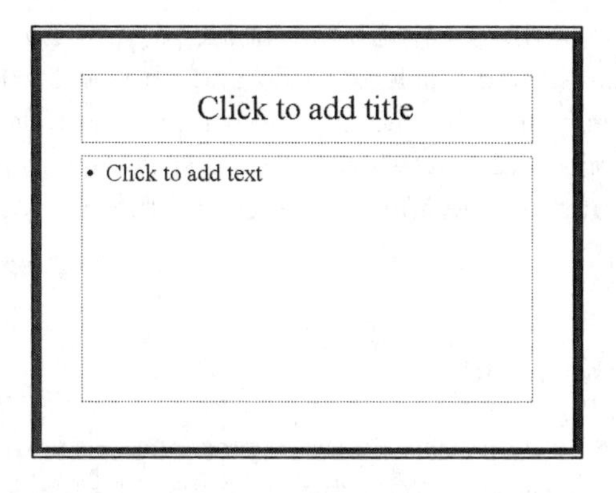

Figure 5.44 *New bullet list slide in Slide view.*

Add a title by clicking in the title area of the slide. I used Progressive Disclosure as the title. Add several lines of bullet text by clicking on the **Click to add** text prompt. Press **Enter** between lines. My finished slide looks like Figure 5.45. This slide gives you a summary of the process for creating a Build or Progressive Disclosure slide.

NOTE

Although you can create bullet lists inside a standard text box, unless you use a pre-formatted bullet list, the build feature will not work properly.

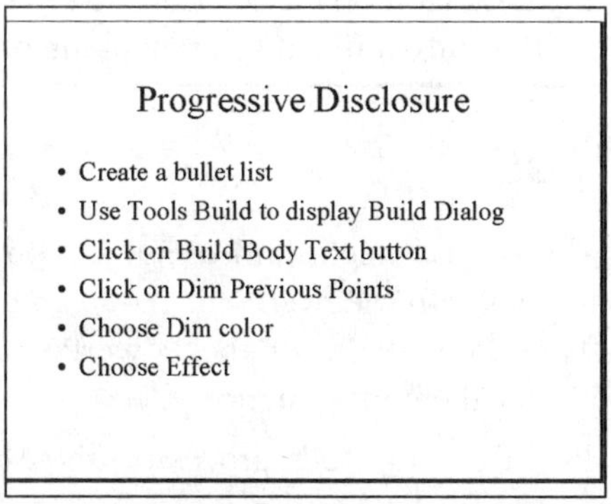

Progressive Disclosure

- Create a bullet list
- Use Tools Build to display Build Dialog
- Click on Build Body Text button
- Click on Dim Previous Points
- Choose Dim color
- Choose Effect

Figure 5.45 *Finished bullet list Build slide.*

Next, select the text in the slide with the mouse or your cursor movement keys. With all of the text selected, select **Tools** and choose **Build Slide Text...**. A check mark appears beside this menu option, indicating that an automatic Build slide has been constructed. Now, during a slide show when this slide is selected, the bulleted items appear one after the other and the previous items are grayed out as new ones appear.

Adding a Blank Slide

When you advance past the last slide in a presentation, you will be returned to the previous presentation view. You may wish to add a blank slide to the end of the presentation so that when you step past the last slide in your show, a blank screen is displayed instead of the Slide or Slide Sorter view of the presentation.

Here's how to create a blank slide to go at the end of your show. Make the last slide in your presentation the current slide. Click on the **New Slide...** button at the bottom of the screen and choose the blank slide from the AutoLayout list (this is the last slide in the list).

Use **Format: Slide Color Scheme...** to display the Slide Color Scheme dialog box. Double-click on the **Background Color** button to display the Background Color dialog box. Choose **Black** and click on **OK**. Click on **Apply** to close the dialog box and return to Slide view with the black slide displayed.

NOTE

Be sure to save your work often as you build presentations in PowerPoint. After you have saved a file for the first time, you can use **File: Save**, the **Disk** icon on the Standard toolbar, or **Ctrl-S** on the keyboard to save the current file to its original file name.

Creating a Play List

A play list is another feature you might find useful as you present on-screen or projected presentations from within PowerPoint. You can create a text file called a play list, and then have PowerPoint or the PowerPoint Viewer load one or more presentations and play them in sequence.

To create a play list, use your word processor, the MS-DOS Editor, or any text editor that can save text files. Place the name of each presentation you want to display on a line by itself, including the **.PPT** extension. To play three presentations, one after the other, your text file would look something like this:

```
PRES01.PPT
PRES02.PPT
PRES03.PPT
```

However, instead of **PRES01.PPT**, you would enter the name of the first presentation you want to run. In place of **PRES02.PPT** you would enter the second file name, and so on. If you have files named **MISPRESS.PPT**, **JOBS.PPT**, and **SALES.PPT**, for example, you could run these presentations in sequence with the following play list:

```
MISPRESS.PPT
JOBS.PPT
SALES.PPT
```

After you have entered all of the names of the presentations you want to include in the play list, save the file in text (ASCII or DOS) format with a file extension of **.LST**. You could save a file as **SHOW.LST**, for example. You can put the file anywhere, but it probably is best to place it inside your PowerPoint subdirectory.

Now you can play the file by opening it from within PowerPoint as you would a presentation. Use **File: Open** from the main PowerPoint menu. When PowerPoint displays the file list, you can select the file you are using for the play file, or you can select another directory to locate the proper file.

When you double-click on the file name or select the file and click on **OK**, PowerPoint scans the file for the presentation names you have entered, loads them into PowerPoint in the order you specified, and begins playing the first slide. Each presentation is presented in the way that it normally would be. If you have set up a presentation for automatic slide advance, that's the way the program plays. On the other hand, if you have established manual slide advance, you must use the mouse or the keyboard to move to each successive slide.

To Sum Up

I can't possibly tell you everything there is to know about formatting slides or presenting slide shows in PowerPoint. There simply isn't enough room in this book. However, we have looked at PowerPoint's major features and I've shown you how to access all of its menus. You can go beyond what I've shown you in this chapter by exploring the menu and toolbars in PowerPoint on your own. A good technique for learning is to set up a simple presentation like the one I used in this chapter. It shouldn't be one you really hope to use so that you don't feel hesitant about experimenting with it. Then you can add slides, edit slides, move slides around, and play with PowerPoint features until you feel comfortable using them. Don't forget the Help feature, which is a strong asset of this product. (I'll show you more about using PowerPoint Help in Chapter 9.)

In the next chapter you'll learn how to set up a printer and how to print presentation data from PowerPoint. Then in Chapter 7 we'll look at ways to create presentation quality output such as overhead projection foils, video tape, and color slides.

CHAPTER 6

Printing from PowerPoint

You may never print a presentation from PowerPoint. After all, the object of this program is to help you prepare slides for display on the computer screen, for projection directly from the computer, for the creation of 35mm slides, or for use with overhead projectors. If your presentations are relatively simple and informal, you may not need to print any of the presentation components.

However, PowerPoint supports more than just presentations. It also supports outlines, speaker notes, audience handouts, and more. Even if you don't print the presentation itself, you may want to print some of the support material that PowerPoint produces along with it.

As I have suggested before, you may want to use PowerPoint to design report covers, section dividers, charts, and other visual material to use in a printed report. Although PowerPoint is primarily designed as a live presentation tool, printed material is a presentation too. And PowerPoint can support these efforts very well. Whatever the reason, if you want to print from PowerPoint, this chapter will show you how to approach it.

Configuring the Printer

When you install PowerPoint, it becomes part of the Microsoft Windows environment. That means that it can use common features of Windows that are available to all Windows applications. This includes the installed printers and other output drivers. In addition, PowerPoint installs a driver to facilitate the production of 35mm slides from your presentation art. This is the Genigraphics Driver, which you will see in your Windows Printer Setup or your PowerPoint Printer Setup dialog box. I'll talk more about how to use this driver—and others—in Chapter 7.

For conventional printer output you will use whatever standard printer you normally use. The majority of business computer installations today have some type of laser printer available, and perhaps an inkjet or a dot matrix impact printer as well. If you are using PowerPoint on a network, you may have several printers at your disposal.

To find out what printers you can use to print PowerPoint information, use **File: Print** to display the Print dialog box shown in Figure 6.1.

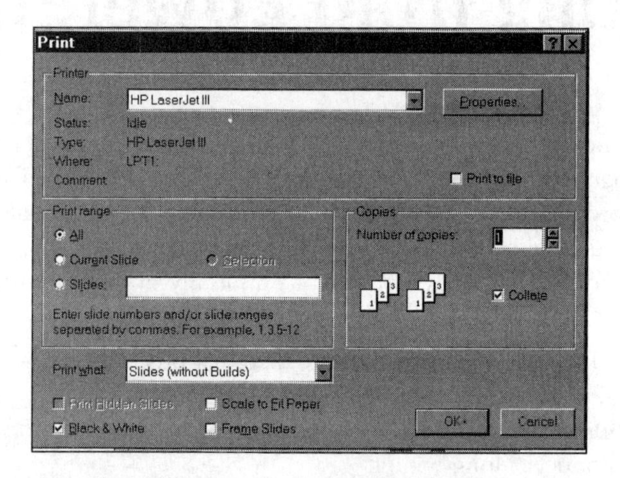

Figure 6.1 *PowerPoint Print dialog box.*

This is the dialog box you'll use to actually print from inside PowerPoint. I'll tell you more about that later. To configure a printer or to choose a printer to use, click on the down arrow at the right of the **Printer** field to pull down a list of available printers, shown in Figure 6.2.

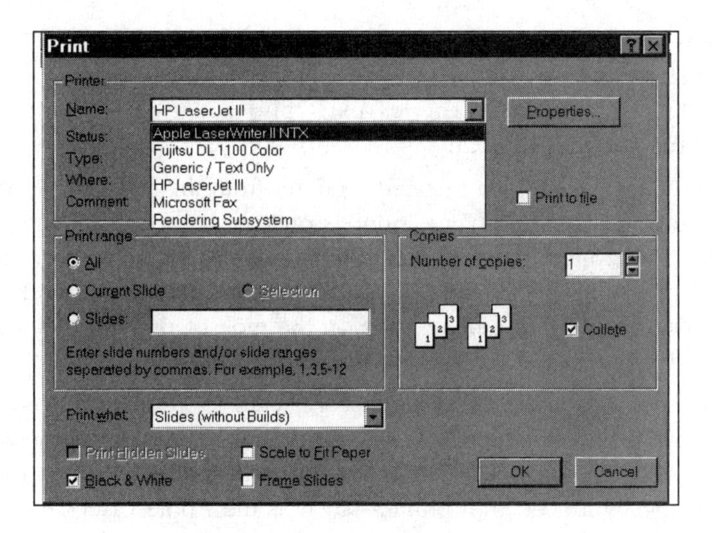

Figure 6.2 *Printer List dialog box.*

Because PowerPoint is a Windows product and is well-integrated into that environment, the printers installed for use by Windows are the same printers you will access from inside PowerPoint. The Windows 95 environment causes the dialog boxes for devices such as printers to vary somewhat from application to application, but if you open the Printers folder inside the Control Panel (chosen from the Settings menu), for example, you will see this same list of printers. It'll just be in the form of separate folders for each printer, like the dialog box in Figure 6.3.

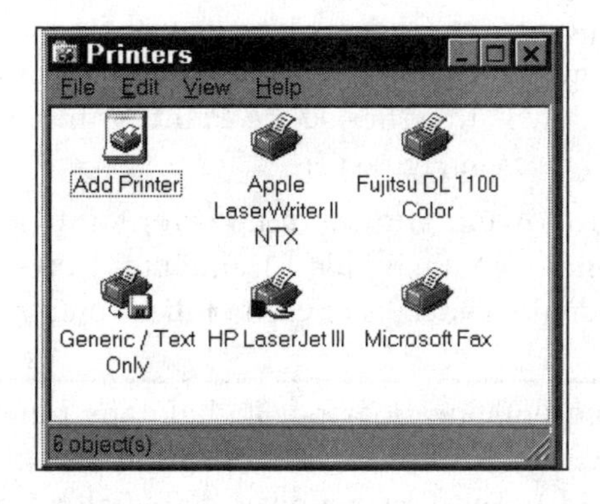

Figure 6.3 *Control Panel Printers folder.*

The system from which this screen shot and the one in Figure 6.2 were taken has six printers available. Actually, there are three printers (Apple LaserWriter II NTX, HP LaserJet III, and Generic/Text Only) and two non-printer drivers (Microsoft Fax and the Rendering Subsystem).

Normally, once you have selected a printer from this list, you won't use this dialog box again until you change printers on your computer or until you want to create a printer file on disk to send to another site for printing or for conversion to 35mm slides. Of course if you are working on a network you may change printers fairly often, depending on the type of printing you want to do or which printer is busy.

Suppose you have an HP LaserJet connected to your local computer, but you want to use the features of a PostScript printer located on the network. You have previously selected the HP LaserJet and perhaps have used it for printing before. To specify a PostScript printer—such as the Apple LaserWriter II NTX—use **File: Print...** to display the Print dialog box. Then pull down the list of printers by clicking on the down arrow beside the default printer name at the top of the dialog. From there you can click on the **Apple LaserWriter II NTX** printer name to select it. With the new printer selected, PowerPoint returns you to the Print dialog box. From this dialog box you can specify how much of the presentation to print and how to print it.

Specifying What to Print

The default output is slides. When you print slides, PowerPoint configures the output in a landscape format (slides wider than they are tall), one image per page. Slides are printed in a 10- x 7.5-inch frame. To specify another type of output, click on the down arrow beside the **Print What** field of the Print dialog box. You'll see the choices in Figure 6.4.

You have the following choices for PowerPoint printer output: Slides (Without Builds), Slides (With Builds), Handouts, Notes Pages, and Outline View. Let's look at additional details of each of these output choices.

If your presentation does not include any build slides (slides with Progressive Disclosure), you are not given the option of printing Slides (with Builds). The first option in this dialog box would be simply Slides.

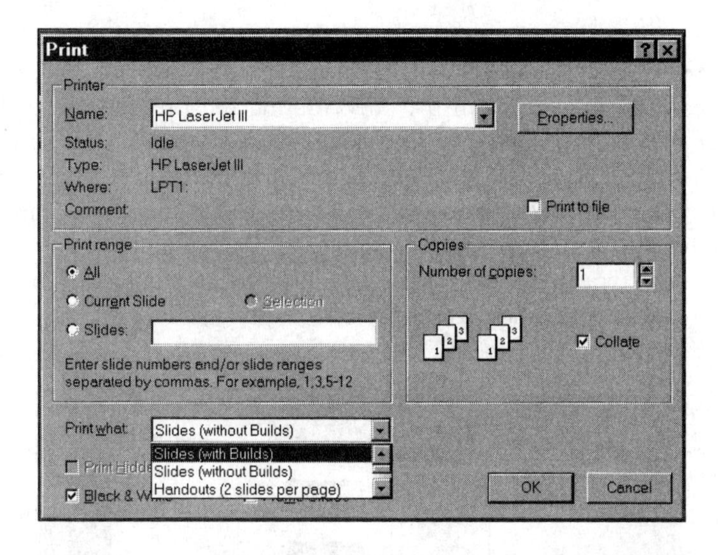

Figure 6.4 *Print What pull-down menu on Print dialog box.*

Slides (with Builds)

This option prints each phase of the build slide as an individual page. If you have six bullet items in a build list, for example, PowerPoint prints six slides—each one showing an additional item in the list. If you have only one build slide in the presentation, then only one slide is expanded in this way; the remainder of the slides are printed with all of the information for each slide on a single page. Slides are printed in a 10- x 7.5-inch landscape format.

Slides (without Builds)

This option prints all slides in the presentation without builds. If you have a slide with six items in a bullet list in build format, this option prints the slide once, showing all of the entries on the bullet list. Slides are printed in a 10- x 7.5-inch landscape format.

Notes Pages

This option prints the speaker's notes pages for the slides specified in the print range. Notes Pages show one slide at a time in a reduced size at the top of a portrait-format page. Each page has room at the bottom or along the sides for notes to accompany the slide. You can use the Notes Pages to help you organize a presentation or you can use them during the presentation to help you remember the main points you want to cover while each slide is displayed. Figure 6.5 shows how a Notes Page prints and is displayed on the screen. PowerPoint defaults to 21 point text on this screen. If this is too small to read comfortably, select the text after it is entered, or position the insertion point when you will type new text, and then click on the font size arrow on the Format bar and choose a larger font.

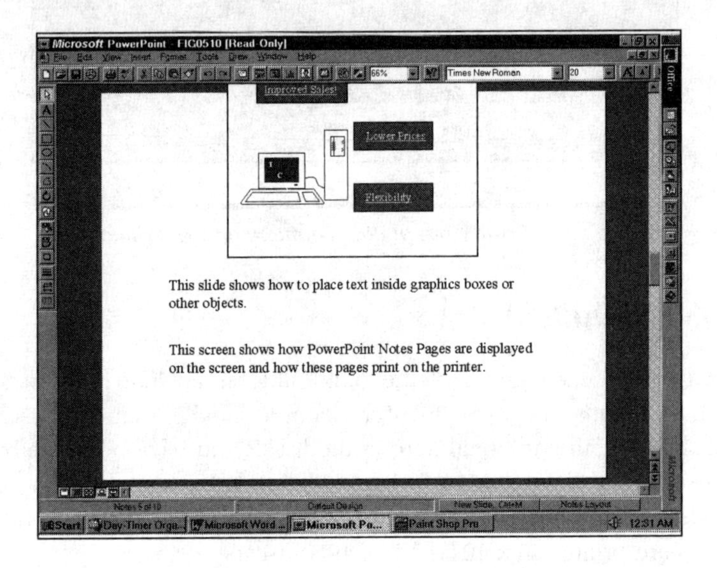

Figure 6.5 *Sample Notes Pages screen.*

Handouts

Handout pages are designed to provide the audience with material about the presentation. You can print handouts with two, three, or six slides per page. When you specify two slides per page, PowerPoint prints two slides, one above the other in portrait format. When you specify a three-slide handout format, PowerPoint places three slides on a portrait page, one above the other. A six-slide format produces a printout with two columns of three slides each on a portrait page.

If your presentation includes more slides than will fit on a couple of handout sheets, you should include slide numbers with the slides. Use **View: Master Slide Master** to display the Slide Master screen. Then click on the **Master Layout** button at the bottom of the screen to pop up a Master Layout dialog box. From there you can choose slide numbers. Grab the number box and place it on the slide where you want it to appear in the show and on the handout sheets. You can also use **Format: Slide Footer** to specify numbers on each slide.

Outline View

When you specify Outline View on the Print dialog box, PowerPoint prints the outline for the current slide show instead of the slide images themselves. The Outline View includes the slide title and any bullet list text that was inserted from an AutoLayout slide.

Special Printing Considerations

There's more to printing a PowerPoint presentation than specifying whether to print slides, presentations, handouts, or outlines.

Specifying Number of Copies

You can specify more than one copy of the items you are printing. Obviously, if you are preparing audience handouts, you may want to print more than one copy. Select the **Copies** field and type the number of copies you want to print, or use the up and down arrows beside the **Copies** field to select the number of copies to print.

Specifying Slide Range

The default slide range to print is All, which prints all of the slides in the current presentation. You can print a single slide by clicking on the **Current Slide** button. This will print the slide that is selected or is being displayed when you start the print routine.

To print a range of slides—from one slide to all of the slides in the presentation—click on the **Slides** button and enter a range of slides in the field beside this prompt. You can enter slide ranges in a number of ways:

X–Y	Print slides X through Y inclusive.
X–	Print slide X and all of the slides that follow it.
A–B, X–Y	Print slides A through B inclusive and X through Y inclusive, but omit the slides between B and X.
X–X	Print only slide X.

Selecting Slides to Print

You can print a selection of slides by choosing the slides to print before launching the Print routine. The easiest way to select a range of slides is to display the presentation in Slide Sorter format. Then hold down the left mouse button and drag a box around the slides you want to print. When the Print dialog box is displayed, specify that you want to print only the selected slides by clicking on the **Selection** button.

This won't work if the slides are not located together in the sorter display, of course. If you need to print a series of random slides, you can hold down the **Shift** key while you click on the slides you want to print. Specify **Selection** in the Print dialog box and the slides will print in the order they appear in the show.

Specifying Print Options

There are six print options that you can select on the Print dialog box. Two of these—Print Hidden Slides and Collate Copies—are selected by default. You can also specify Print to File, print in Black & White, Scale to Fit Paper, and Frame slides. These print options are chosen in addition to the Print Range, Copies, and Print What selections.

PRINT TO FILE

Use this option to create a file of printer commands that can be used to print the specified selection to any printer of the same type specified in the File Print Printer dialog box. If you are using an HP LaserJet Printer, for example, then the print file that results from choosing the Print to File option will contain Hewlett-Packard printer commands to print the specified part of the current presentation. If the selected printer is a PostScript printer, then the file created by PowerPoint will be PostScript commands.

After you click on **OK** on the Print dialog box, PowerPoint asks for the name of the file you want to use to store printer commands. Creating a print file in this way lets you print a PowerPoint slide or presentation on a printer not attached to your computer or on a computer that does not have PowerPoint installed. To use a print file, enter **Copy file name PRN**, where file name is the name of the print file.

NOTE

If you have problems printing a file in this way, add the **/B** (for binary) switch after the copy command. This tells DOS to pass the characters through to the printer exactly as they appear in the file.

Print Hidden Slides

PowerPoint prints hidden slides by default, but you can turn off this default by clicking on the **Print Hidden Slides** button. You may want to hide one or more slides in a presentation that are not appropriate for a given audience, without removing the slides from the presentation. However, if you want to print all of the slides in a presentation—even those marked hidden—you can do this by accepting PowerPoint's default. To avoid printing the hidden slides, click once on this button and none of the slides marked hidden will print.

Black & White

This option prints all slides in black and white, turning all fills on objects to white, or to black and white if the fill uses a pattern. Unbordered objects that don't include text appear with a thin black frame.

Collate Copies

This option—a PowerPoint default—keeps the pages of a presentation together when you print multiple copies. If you print three copies of a ten-page presentation, PowerPoint prints all ten pages of the presentation, in order, three times. Without Collate Copies selected, PowerPoint prints three copies of page one, three copies of page two, three copies of page three, and so on until the print job is completed.

Scale to Fit Paper

The Scale to Fit Paper option causes PowerPoint to print all slides so that they fit the paper selected with your printer.

Frame Slides

If you want PowerPoint to draw a frame around each slide as it prints, click on this button. You may want frames around printed slides for emphasis or to help offset one slide from the other if you choose to print multiple slides to a page (see the next section).

Configuring the Presentation

In addition to specifying what parts of a presentation to print, you can make changes to the format of the presentation that affect the way your slides print. By default, PowerPoint prints slides in landscape format in a 10- x 7.5-inch frame. You can use the Slide Setup dialog box to make additional specifications about the way PowerPoint slides print. Use **File: Slide Setup...** to display the Slide Setup dialog box shown in Figure 6.6.

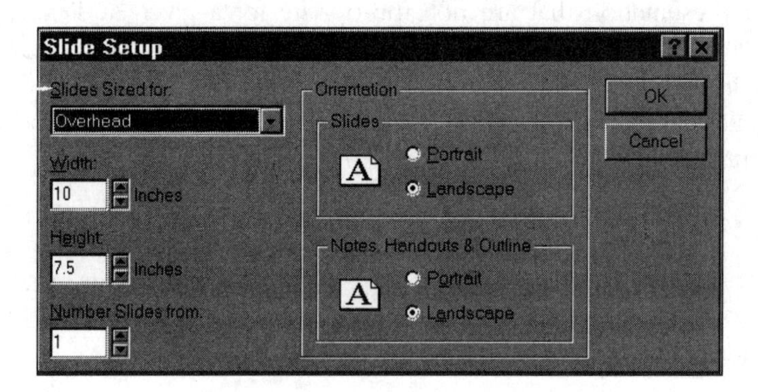

Figure 6.6 *Slide Setup dialog box.*

Setting Slide Size

The PowerPoint size default is for on-screen presentation. You have other choices for slide size, including standard letter paper, A4 paper, 35mm slides, and custom sizes. You can see these choices by pulling down the list in the **Slides Sized for** field of the Slide Setup dialog box. Click on the arrow beside this field to see the list in Figure 6.7.

In the following sections I'll give you more information about each of these choices.

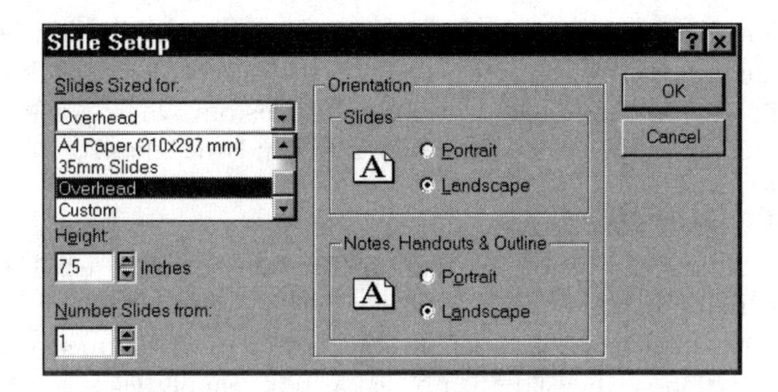

Figure 6.7 *Slides Sized for list on Slide Setup dialog box.*

ON-SCREEN SHOW

This choice sets the size of presentation slides to a width of 10 inches and a height of 7.5 inches. This is an aspect ratio of 3:4.

LETTER PAPER (8.5 X 11 IN)

The Letter Paper choice is basically the same as On-screen Show. This setting assumes a landscape orientation specification. When you print a slide on paper, the slide prints sideways so that you look at the slide with the long portion of the paper oriented horizontally. (You can change the orientation on the Slide Setup dialog box.) This is also an aspect ratio of 3:4. It is the most common selection for printing overhead transparencies.

A4 PAPER (210 X 297 MM)

This choice is for European-sized paper. It sets the slide image size to 26 cm wide (10.83 inches) and 18 cm high (7.5 inches). The aspect ratio is between that for On-screen Show and 35mm Slides.

35MM SLIDES

For 35mm slides, PowerPoint sets the width to 11.25 inches and the height to 7.5 inches, for an aspect ratio of 2:3.

OVERHEAD

The Overhead format is for an 8.5 x 11 in. page with the slide area formatted at 10 x 7.5 inches. By default, overhead slides print in landscape format.

CUSTOM

The Custom setting is what the name implies. When you choose this setting, you can click on the up and down arrows beside the Width and Height boxes on the

Slide Setup dialog box. In fact, you can force the Custom selection by clicking on one of the up or down arrows with any setting visible in the Slides Sized for window. PowerPoint automatically jumps to Custom when you change the height or width from the pre-set values for any standard slide size.

CHANGING ORIENTATION

PowerPoint selects landscape orientation for slides of all sizes. The support material—outlines, handouts, and speaker's notes—prints in portrait orientation. However, you can change these defaults by clicking on the proper button in the Orientation section of the Slide Setup dialog box. Simply click on **Portrait** to change the slide default from Landscape.

Figure 6.8 shows the standard landscape orientation for an on-screen display, while Figure 6.9 shows how the display changes when you switch to portrait orientation.

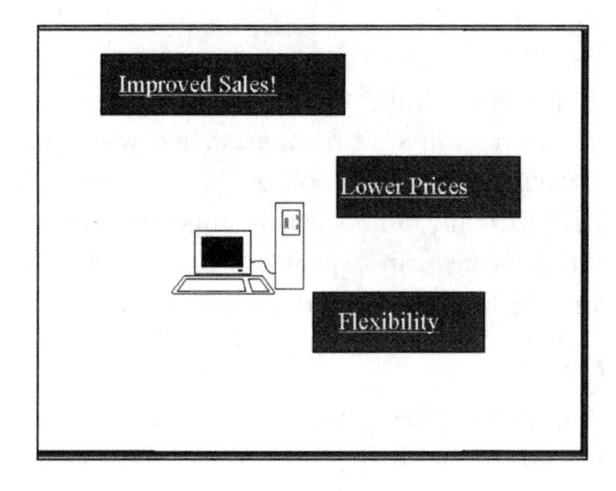

Figure 6.8 *On-screen show in landscape orientation.*

Notice that many parts of a slide can change when you change orientation. In our sample, part of the text is obscured when the width of the display area is reduced by the portrait orientation setting. With other slides you may not see such a dramatic change. You may only notice a narrowing of some of the objects. If your application requires portrait orientation, you should specify that setting before you design the slides.

One application where you may want to change the orientation default is when you are printing overhead projection foils. Although many projectors can handle landscape or portrait orientation, some do a better job in portrait orientation.

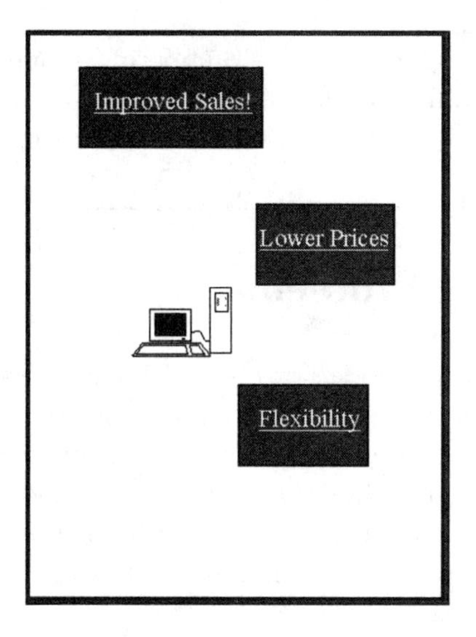

Figure 6.9 *On-screen show in portrait orientation.*

In addition, you may want to use landscape orientation to print handouts, especially if you are putting six slides on a page. A landscape orientation for a page this full may make it easier for the audience to use, depending on the type of slides your presentation includes. You can test the orientation for handouts by choosing **Landscape**. Then, from the Print dialog box, specify only the **Current Slide**. PowerPoint uses the current slide as a starting point and prints the number of slides you specify in the Print what field of the Print dialog box.

Setting Slide Numbering

PowerPoint automatically numbers the slides in your presentation beginning at one with the first slide. You can change the default numbering scheme by clicking on the up arrow beside the **Number Slides from** field on the Slide Setup dialog box. Or, you can select the default number in this field and type a new number on the keyboard.

Normally, when your presentation stands alone as a separate presentation, you will leave this default setting alone. However, there may be times when you want to put two or more presentations together as a single show. In this case you might start numbering the second set of slides after the last slide in the first show; the third show would start numbering after the last slide in the second show, and so on.

NOTE

Even if you specify a slide numbering scheme, PowerPoint won't include a number on the slides unless you have specified slide numbers on the Slide Master. See the discussion on how to do this earlier in this chapter.

Solving Printing Problems

Printing presentations from inside PowerPoint should be straightforward and you should encounter no problems. There are a few situations that may cause some head scratching, however. The best general advice for solving printing problems is to check all of the settings in the Print dialog box and in the Slide Setup dialog box. If these are correct, then your presentation should print as you expect. If you encounter any of the situations described in the following sections, perhaps the suggestions included will help.

Nothing Prints

Suppose you seem to be doing everything right and you get no error messages, yet nothing comes out on the printer. There are some very common causes of this problem.

WRONG PRINTER

Probably the most common cause of nothing printing, if you are connected to a network, is that you have specified the wrong printer. The slides you're printing are coming out, but not on the printer you're watching. In this case, check the printer selected on the Print dialog box (select **File: Print** and pull down the list of printers from the **Name** field).

The same thing can happen if you have specified the wrong printer driver even if you're not on a network. If you are using a PostScript printer, for example, and you send it non-PostScript commands, the printer may print nothing. If you've sent the wrong commands to a printer one or two times, you may have to turn the printer off and then back on again to get it to print correctly, even after you change the printer definition inside PowerPoint.

PREVIOUS PRINTER PROBLEM

In the Windows environment you don't actually print directly to a printer. Instead, Windows sends data destined for a printer to a special area of memory called a print queue, which usually includes spooling some data to disk. That clears the print operation quickly and lets Windows manage printing in the background. Also, you can send printer output from multiple applications without waiting for the previous print job to finish. Multiple print jobs—whether from a single application or from several applications—stack up in one or more print queues and are sent to the printer in turn.

However, suppose one of these print jobs encounters a printer error. Perhaps the printer ran out of paper, or you sent work to the printer and forgot to turn on the printer. Whatever the cause, the print job that encountered the error is stalled, waiting for the printer problem to be corrected.

Luckily, Windows 95 does a much better job of notifying you when a printer problem occurs. You'll probably see an error message on your screen indicating that a problem exists. However, if you're on a network and are sharing a printer with other users, another user may have caused a printer problem and you may or may not hear about it.

You can find out if your print job is stalled and waiting for problem resolution by following these steps. Click on **Start**, choose **Settings** from the pop-up menu, and specify **Printers**. The Printers folder is opened. Double-click on the folder that represents the printer you are using. Windows opens a dialog box for that printer, showing any pending jobs (see Figure 6.10).

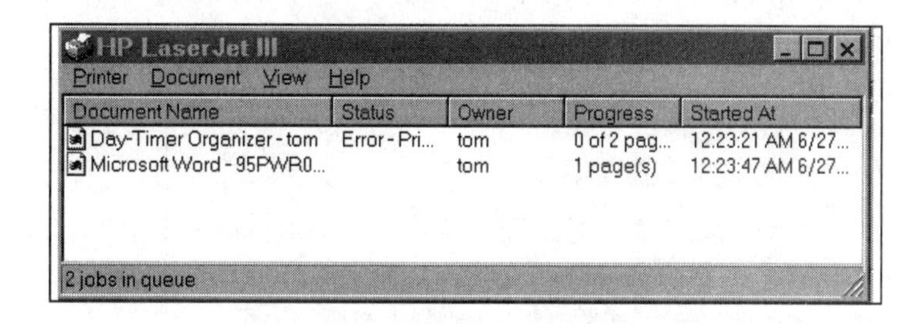

Figure 6.10 *Printer dialog box.*

Select the document that appears to be stalled and click on **Document** on the Printer dialog box's main menu. Choose **Cancel Printing** to remove the selected job from the queue. Correct any printer problems (add paper, push online button, correct paper jam, etc.), then resend the stalled job.

NOTE

You may have a Print Manager error even if you think you have corrected a printer problem. When the printer runs out of paper, for example, the printer stops printing until you add paper. As soon as the printer senses that it has paper, printing resumes as the printer continues to dump the contents of its internal print buffer. It looks as if everything is okay. However, only the information that remains in the print buffer is printed. The data that remains in the print spooler won't resume printing until you start it again or, in the case of a canceled job, until the job is restarted.

Garbled Output

Suppose you print a slide or a presentation and the printer seems to work, but you get only a partial printout or garbled data on the page. This probably means you have selected the wrong printer driver. Depending on the particular printer you are using and the driver you have specified, an incorrect driver may cause no output at all, or it may cause the printout to be unreadable.

One common problem is getting a series of text lines on the page instead of the picture you expected (see Figure 6.11). This probably means you have chosen a PostScript printer driver in PowerPoint, but your printer is a LaserJet or other non-PostScript device.

```
□%!PS-Adobe-3.0
%%Creator: Windows PSCRIPT
%%Title: PowerPoint - FIG0510.PPT
%%BoundingBox: 14 9 597 784
%%DocumentNeededResources: (atend)
%%DocumentSuppliedResources: (atend)
%%Pages: (atend)
%%BeginResource: procset Win35Dict 3 1
/Win35Dict 290 dict def Win35Dict begin/bd{bind def}bind def/in{72
mul}bd/ed{exch def}bd/ld{load def}bd/tr/translate ld/gs/gsave ld/gr
/grestore ld/M/moveto ld/L/lineto ld/rmt/rmoveto ld/rlt/rlineto ld
/rct/rcurveto ld/st/stroke ld/n/newpath ld/sm/setmatrix ld/cm/currentmatrix
ld/cp/closepath ld/ARC/arcn ld/TR{65536 div}bd/lj/setlinejoin ld/lc
/setlinecap ld/ml/setmiterlimit ld/sl/setlinewidth ld/scignore false
def/sc{scignore{pop pop pop}{0 index 2 index eq 2 index 4 index eq
and{pop pop 255 div setgray}{3{255 div 3 1 roll}repeat setrgbcolor}ifelse}ifelse}bd
/FC{bR bG bB sc}bd/fC{/bB ed/bG ed/bR ed}bd/HC{hR hG hB sc}bd/hC{
/hB ed/hG ed/hR ed}bd/PC{pR pG pB sc}bd/pC{/pB ed/pG ed/pR ed}bd/sM
matrix def/PenW 1 def/iPen 5 def/mxF matrix def/mxE matrix def/mxUE
matrix def/mxUF matrix def/fBE false def/iDevRes 72 0 matrix defaultmatrix
dtransform dup mul exch dup mul add sqrt def/fPP false def/SS{fPP{
/SV save def}{gs}ifelse}bd/RS{fPP{SV restore}{gr}ifelse}bd/EJ{gsave
showpage grestore}bd/#C{userdict begin/#copies ed end}bd/FEbuf 2 string
def/FEglyph(G  )def/FE{1 exch{dup 16 FEbuf cvrs FEglyph exch 1 exch
putinterval 1 index exch FEglyph cvn put}for}bd/SM{/iRes ed/cyP ed
```

Figure 6.11 *PostScript commands on printer output.*

Great Presentation Ideas

Courtesy of Projections

This slide effectively incorporates a scanned photograph. Note that the topic, fall registration, is suggested by the leaves in the corner of the slide.

The light, gradient background and simple design for this slide reflects regular feedback that JP Hogan receives from its clients. Companies often want the simplest slides possible because colorful, complex designs distract an audience during a presentation. This Kodak Photo CD image shows principals, offers color, highlights the basic product (foam) and provides a background for the title message.

Courtesy of JP Hogan and Company

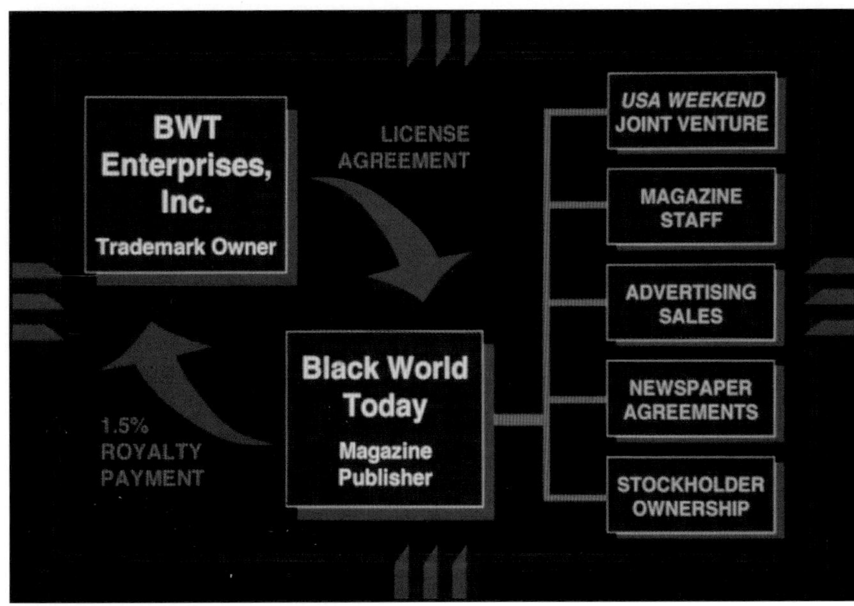

Courtesy of Economic Development Group

This slide, based on a standard PowerPoint template, couples motion, provided by the arrows, with bright colors. You can create this slide with standard PowerPoint tools and a little personal creativity.

This slide, which also uses a standard PowerPoint template, demonstrates how you can scan images and position them creatively on a PowerPoint slide. Notice how the placement of the magazine cover on the far right adds a level of interest.

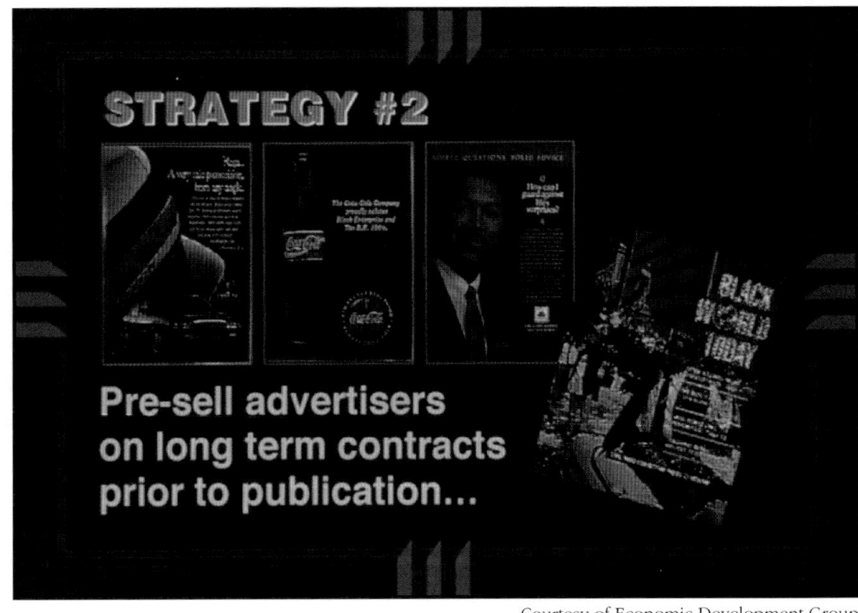

Courtesy of Economic Development Group

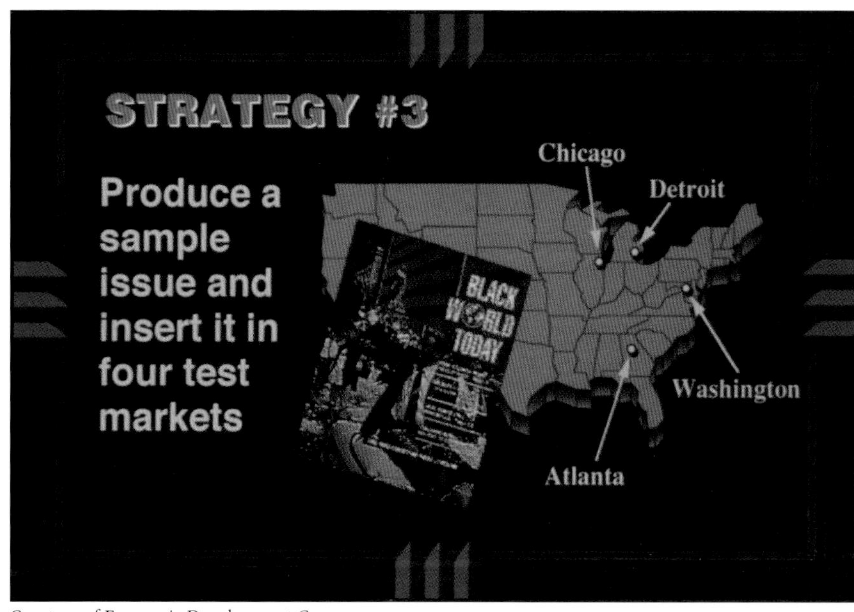

Courtesy of Economic Development Group

The map, coupled with text and a scanned magazine cover, creates a dynamic presentation. The audience will be able to focus on the main concept while viewing the actual magazine cover.

This slide effectively uses color, text, and graphics to tell a complete story. The three-dimensional U.S. map offers quick audience recognition, and the simple gradient background helps the colors in the foreground stand out. The text at the top and the list at the left provide detail, while the spoke-like destination points give the audience perspective. Notice that a simple company logo is displayed in the lower right hand corner.

Courtesy of Projections

Great Presentation Ideas

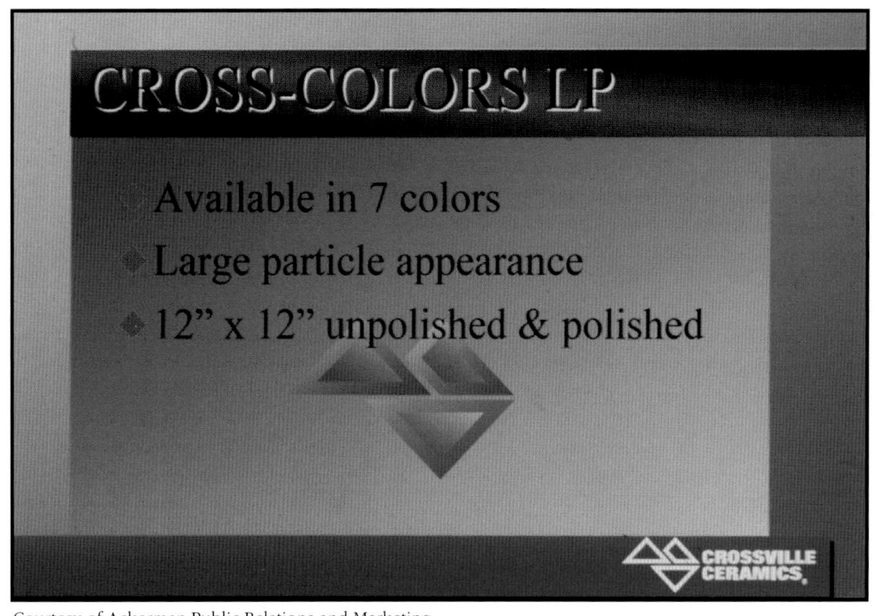

Courtesy of Ackerman Public Relations and Marketing

This slide illustrates an attractive title style on top of a clean design. The short list with colored bullets makes it easy for an audience to interpret the data.

The strength of this slide resides in its simplicity, creative layout and use of color. The shuttle clip art was enhanced with clouds and exhaust that were created with drawing tools. The dark background and sharp contrast enhance this slide's impact.

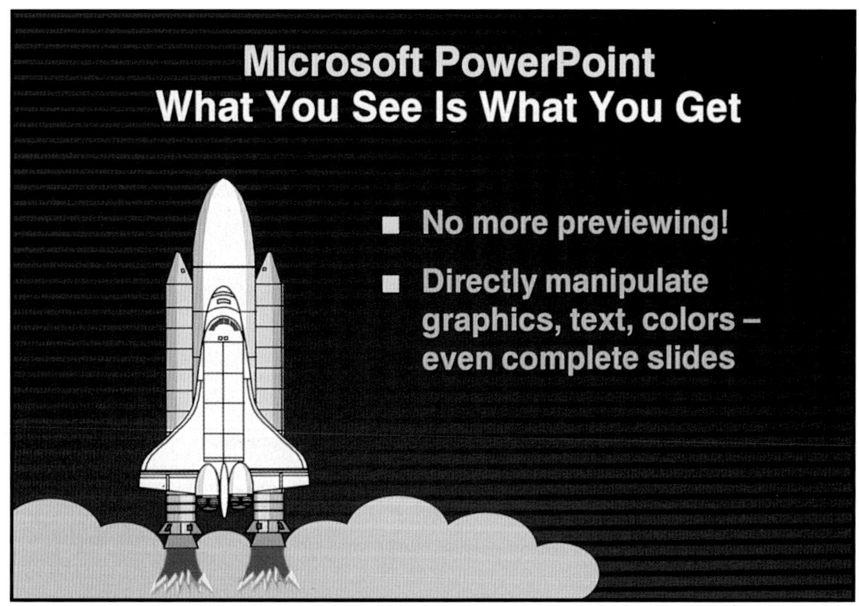

Courtesy of Genigraphics

GREAT PRESENTATION IDEAS

Africa:
Total Annual Precipitation and Average Annual Temperature

Station	Precipitation in	Precipitation mm	Temperature °F	Temperature °C
Agadir	9	229	66	19
Cairo	1	25	72	22
Cape Town	26	660	63	17
Harare	30	760	64	18
Kinshasa	60	1,524	77	25
Nairobi	36	914	64	18
Yaundé	60	1,524	75	24

Courtesy of Genigraphics

Even with its many numbers, this slide works because of a pleasing color scheme and the distinctive background. The clip art map and subtle color reinforce the African theme. The subdued tone could let the slide stay on the screen relatively long to give the audience time to study the numbers.

The standard PowerPoint template forms the basis of this slide design. The projector and the Projections title show an interesting play on the company's name while providing a graphical reference to the numbers being shown. There are several ways to interpret the numbers on this slide: the relative positions on the graphical grid, the length of lines and colors, and the numbers themselves.

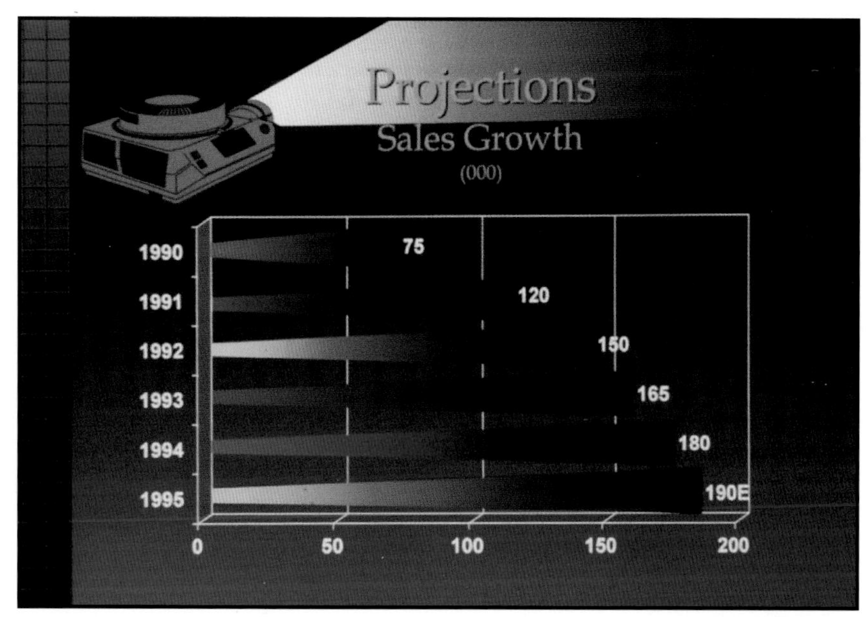

Courtesy of Projections

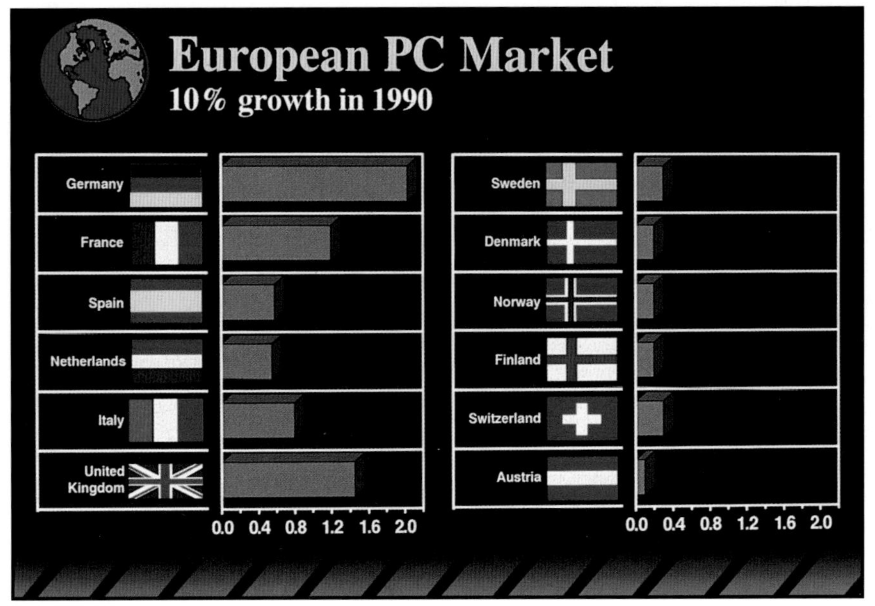

Courtesy of Genigraphics

Even with its high concentration of data, this design presents information clearly. Clip art flags enhance the association of data. The PowerPoint template offers a dark background, brightening and enhancing the color in the clip art.

PowerPoint helps you communicate data relationships clearly with a flow chart. This template enhances the crisp, graphic nature of the design. Extra space around boxes lends clarity while the bold attribute helps emphasize small text.

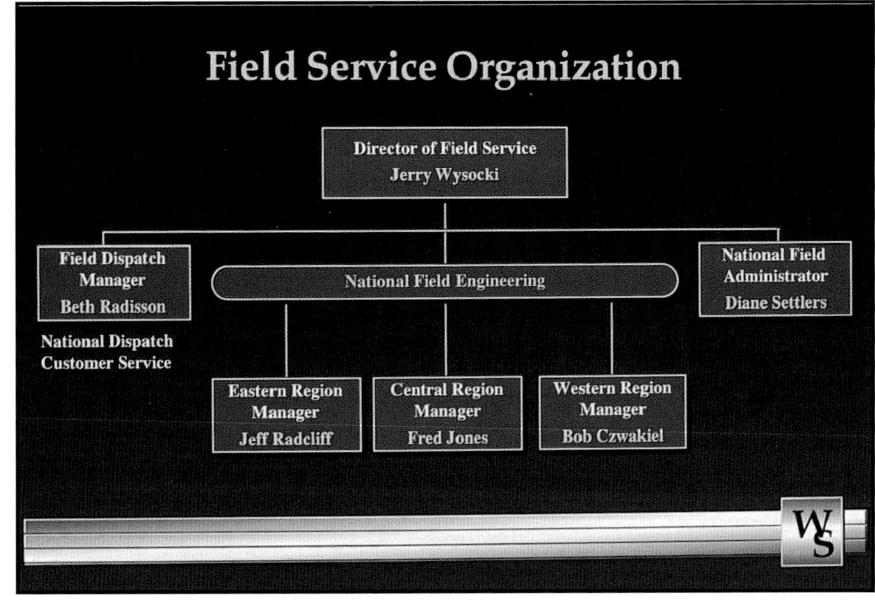

Courtesy of Genigraphics

TITLE IMAGE EVOLUTION

Genigraphics Corporation
Products and Services
1994

The title slide sets the mood for the show, giving the audience a first impression of your company or topic. This slide shows poor formatting: too-large text, too much white space at the bottom, and no color.

Reduce white space, and make the text smaller, and less overwhelming. This slide uses layout space more efficiently.

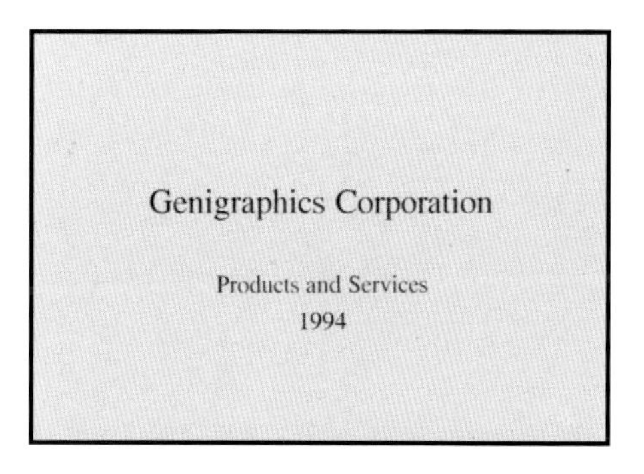

Use a standard company font for titles to promote consistency. This slide also adds a background treatment for atmosphere and depth.

Genigraphic's Joey Schroth used the drawing tools to produce a company logo, and created the sweeping arcs with the arc tool. Other strong points of this slide include: simple and succinct copy, a limited number of typefaces, a dark background with a light foreground, and three simple colors that don't distract from the message.

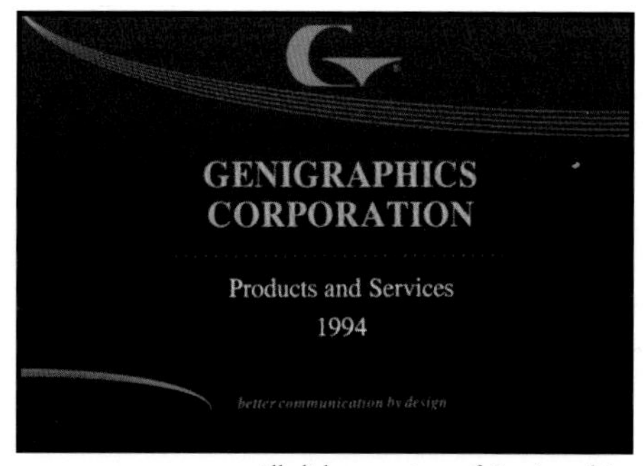

All slides courtesy of Genigraphics

DATA CHART EVOLUTION

Current Presentation Market - Material Overview

Two-thirds of all presentations are given inside the firm. These presentations are almost by definition, informal meetings where people are presenting in a conference room. Twenty-two percent of presentations are delivered in someone's office. This means that presentation graphics programs are being used for one-on-one and one-on-two discussions, not just for podium presentations to large audiences.

Most presentations are in the conventional media: overhead, and paper. Seventy-three percent of all presentations were made on black and white paper and overheads, with twelve percent being color. Once again, evidence that most presentations are informal. Seven percent of media usage consists of 35 mm slides. This number is expected to stay about the same over the next few years. Electronic presentations are growing -- even though they represent only eight percent of all presentations made, some twenty plus percent of all users now give electronic presentations.

This slide is too dense and communicates the specifics of data values poorly. Everything in this copy is important, but it is difficult to interpret.

Use lists whenever possible. Lists reduce text and enhance retention. This data type is a Column Chart. The template adds color and helps the audience focus on the main points.

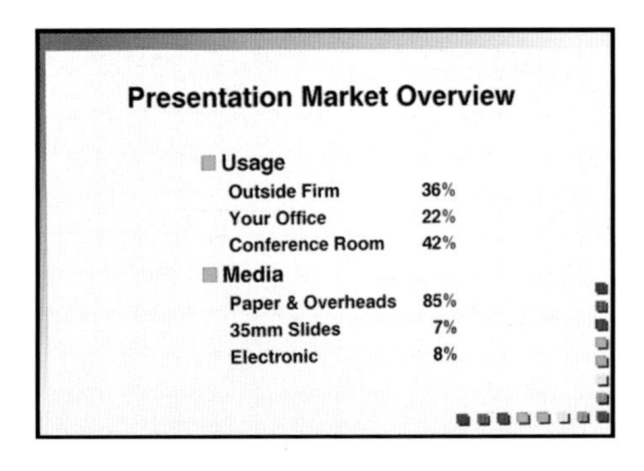

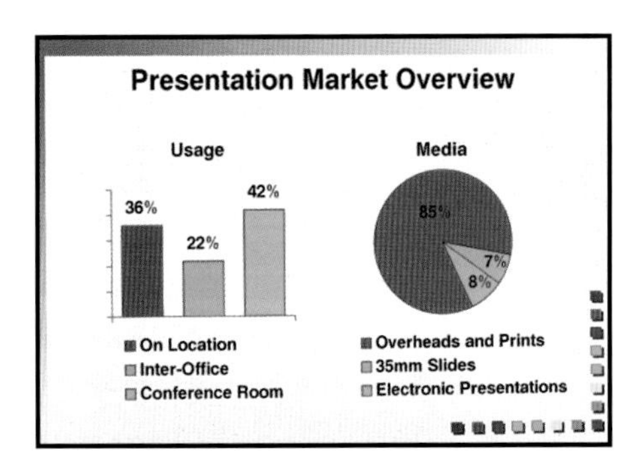

Use charts and graphs to aid data interpretation. Bar charts give side-by-side comparisons of the whole. In general, graphs are visually appealing and communicate data more effectively.

Three dimensional charts have more impact. Limit the number of color to under ten. If too much information is still included in a slide, then separate the information into two slides. This image is well suited for either a color overhead or 35mm slide presentation.

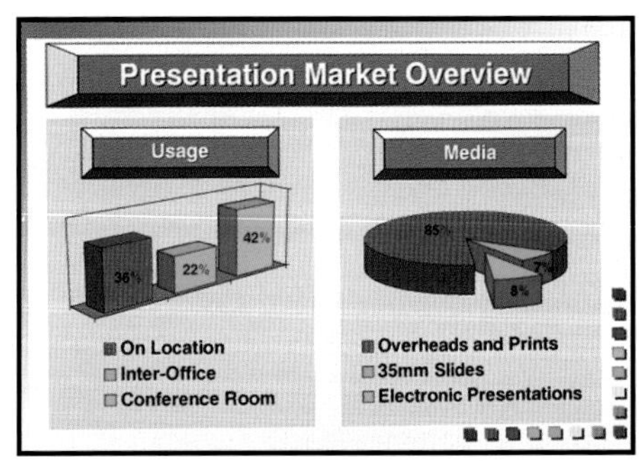

All slides courtesy of Genigraphics

The solution to the problem is to check the settings in the Print dialog box to make sure you have selected the proper printer driver for your printer.

To Sum Up

Printing from inside PowerPoint is a relatively simple process. For the most part you will accept the program's default settings for page size, orientation, and printer. If you want to adjust the settings for a particular output need, or if you have problems with your printer, then the suggestions in this chapter should help you get on the right track.

In the next chapter we will look at additional presentation output considerations, including producing 35mm slides and videos.

CHAPTER 7

Creating Presentation Output with PowerPoint

In the last chapter I showed you how to print the various components of a PowerPoint presentation. But there is more to using PowerPoint than just printing the output as slides, outlines, notes, or handouts on a standard printer. You can also use PowerPoint to create slides that you can use for live presentations or to create 35mm slides or videos.

In some ways you can improve your PowerPoint results by considering the output first. Will you be printing PowerPoint images in color? Is the final output for projection—either 35mm slides or overhead transparencies? Who is the audience? What type of images will you produce?

Before creating any graphic images with PowerPoint, decide what form of media will be used to present the images. Based on the type of media, different rules should be followed. For example, if the final images will be printed on a laser printer and included as black and white images within a business report, there is no need to take advantage of PowerPoint's colors when creating the image. On the other hand, if the images will be converted into some form of color media, such as 35mm slides or overhead transparencies, then color is a vital component of the finished image.

You should consider these questions for each series of drawings you produce in PowerPoint. This will help you visualize the output before you start image design and production. In this chapter, I'll give you some insight into using PowerPoint for these applications.

35mm Slides

Once you have created a presentation that you can show on your computer screen, you can also create 35mm slides as another way of presenting your show.

NOTE

You can create 35mm slides from any PowerPoint presentation, but the results will be better if you establish 35mm format for your slides before they are designed (use **File: Slide Setup**...). This ensures better sizing and formatting.

A slide version of your presentation offers several advantages over computer projection or overhead transparencies. For one thing, you don't have to carry a computer with you when you make the presentation. Almost any hotel, convention center, or company conference room is equipped with a slide projector. However, you may have trouble finding a computer of the type you need, especially with projection equipment.

Slides offer much higher resolution than the computer monitor. If you have a slide reproduced by a slide service, you can get 3500–4000 lines of resolution. Some of these services will enhance the basic computer display to take advantage of this resolution. You'll also find it easy to rearrange a slide show once the slides are produced. You can use a simple hand-held viewer or light table and sort slides at home, at your hotel, or even on an airplane.

Many professional presenters also find that 35mm slides help the speaker make a good impression on the audience. When a speaker arrives for a presentation with a set of slides, it is obvious that considerable time has been spent preparing for the show.

Even if you design a slide show for multiple presentations, a good technique is to prepare a custom title slide for each presentation. That way, when your standard show opens, the audience sees the name of their company or conference, the date, and the topic right at the start. This enhances your image as one who prepares carefully, and it improves audience acceptance of your material.

Besides designing the images for the slide format, there are additional guidelines that can help you prepare a successful presentation.

- Prepare at least two copies of the slides for each presentation. This lets you use some slides more than once, either for emphasis or to fill in weak spots that you discover later. It also gives you a backup set of slides in the event that you lose the primary one.
- Plan on enough slides to carry the show. A good rule of thumb is two to three slides per minute of presentation. If you leave one slide on the screen too long, the audience loses interest and your show loses momentum.
- Learn as much as you can about the room where your presentation will be made. If it can be made totally dark, you can be more creative in slide design. For general designs or when you aren't sure about the location, use dark backgrounds and light letters on your slides. That way, if you have to present in a relatively light room, the material will still be visible.
- Have someone else proofread your slides on the computer or from a printout before you have them converted to film. Don't proof your own slides; it is too easy to miss spelling and other errors. Reenie Feingold, who is the owner of Visual Horizons in New York and is a professional presenter, recommends three steps to slide proofing:
    1. Read first for content.
    2. Read the second time word-by-word looking for spelling errors.
    3. Read the third time from the rear to the front and from the bottom to the top. That way you will evaluate each word as it stands alone without the influence of context. Also check numbers in reverse order.
- Get professional help in slide design. PowerPoint helps you overcome the mechanical problems of creating presentations, but we all can use

some professional design help in telling specific stories. The more complex or the more important your presentation, the more valuable professional advice will be. Remember, you may need only one person in your audience to change their mind, to modify their buying habits, or to say yes to your proposal to make the expense of preparing your professional presentation cost-effective.

- Rehearse your presentation alone and in front of a group. You can learn your presentation in the same way you learn to type or to play the piano. Your mouth seems to remember the right words if you have enough preparation time.

Obviously, if you are designing a presentation for 35mm slide display, you'll need some way to convert the slide images from the computer display to slides. There are two basic ways to create 35mm slides from a computer display. You can either take a picture of the screen or you can save the slides to a file for conversion by a slide service.

Using a Screen Camera

You can hire a slide service to produce film slides from your computer images (see the following section for more information). However, if most of the work you do with PowerPoint involves producing slides, then it may be more cost-effective to produce the slides yourself with a screen capture camera. These cameras consist of a high-resolution black and white or color television monitor, a light mask, a camera mount, and an electronic interface to your computer. Depending on the device design, you may plug in a circuit board to serve as a custom interface between your computer and the camera display, or you may attach the camera directly to your computer's video display adapter or cable. When you display an image on the computer screen, the connection to the screen capture camera displays the same image on the camera display.

You then take a picture of the screen with a quality 35mm camera. The camera may be part of the system, or you may purchase the camera separately or use a camera you already have. Usually these devices include electronic control of the camera. The camera—although it looks in many respects like a standard 35mm camera—may not include a standard viewfinder and other features you usually associate with modern cameras.

The LFR film recorder from Lasergraphics is one example of this type of device. It is capable of 4,000 line resolution. You can use it with either standard

35mm or Polaroid film packs. The LFR attaches to your PC through a custom bus-level interface that includes a graphics co-processor to speed up operation. For more information, contact Lasergraphics, Inc., 17671 Cowan Ave., Irvine, CA 92714, 714-727-2651.

Similar devices include the offerings of Polaroid Corporation and Agfa. In fact, Polaroid offers a number of output options for computer presentation, including multiple film recorders and projection devices. The Polaroid devices use a special interface to attach to your computer. Then you can use Polaroid or conventional cameras to capture screen images to film (see Figure 7.1). For more information, contact Polaroid at 565 Technology Square, Cambridge, MA 02139, 617-386-2000.

Figure 7.1 *Polaroid film recorders.*

Agfa also offers a range of products to support desktop publishing and computer-based presentation. You can get more information from Agfa at 200 Ballardvale Street, Wilmington, MA 01887, 508-658-5600.

Using a Slide Service

A number of companies will produce these slides for you. This is the way to go if you only need an occasional slide or slide show. Generally, the procedure is to create the images you need in PowerPoint. Then you either mail a diskette to the company, or you send the image files over a modem directly to a computer or through an electronic mail store and forward service such as CompuServe.

Most slide production companies can load up the graphics image, edit it, add backgrounds, change the color, and make other minor changes before producing a high-resolution 35mm color slide for you.

For a text slide, never fill up more than 75 percent of the slide with text. Many slide services recommend that no more than twenty words be used in a title or text slide. When creating images with PowerPoint, be sure that the information being depicted in the slides will not be misunderstood by the audience. Misunderstandings can easily occur if too much information is included within the image, or if part of the graphic image does not pertain to the point being conveyed.

Color has a major impact on the visual appeal of graphic images that are created with PowerPoint and converted into slides or overheads. Lines, text, and all graphics should contrast with the background color being used. In most cases, dark backgrounds with light-colored text and graphics work best for slides. The opposite is true for overhead transparencies. Many of the borders and color clip art images available for use with PowerPoint can be edited. This means that the colors of the border or clip art images can be changed to maintain color continuity throughout the presentation.

For more detailed information about putting together a 35mm slide presentation, consider an Eastman Kodak book titled *Slides: Planning and Producing Slide Programs,* which covers the basic rules for developing slide shows. This book does not specifically cover the use of computer-generated images. However, much of the information in this book is applicable.

Many of the service companies will go beyond simply producing slides from your computer images. They can consult on slide design, write scripts, produce custom backgrounds, do color correction, and more. You can also find companies that will produce your initial slides for free so that you can learn about their services and receive suggestions about your presentation. Visual Horizons, for example, offers three free slides from your software. The images will be finished in about three days and returned via first class mail.

When it is time to produce your entire show, you can choose from a variety of slide services and service times. In fact, Visual Horizons, like many other slide service providers, offers 24-hour service for a premium price. This company, and others, can also produce overhead projection slides from your computer files.

In general, when you use a slide service, the company can either use native files from PowerPoint or they may send you additional software that converts PowerPoint data to a format compatible with their equipment. This software may operate as a standalone application, or it may simply install as a printer driver in the Windows Control Panel. Then, when you want to prepare material for conversion by the service, use **File: Print Printer...** to choose the proper driver and send the information to a disk file.

In fact, one such driver is shipped with PowerPoint. You can access it by selecting **Send to Genigraphics** from the File menu. The following sections provide a brief summary of the services available from a few selected service providers.

GENIGRAPHICS

Genigraphics is one of the multi-function service providers that is specifically targeted at PowerPoint. They designed the original templates for version 4.0 of PowerPoint. The Genigraphics Driver supplied with PowerPoint lets you print a presentation to a disk file—complete with job instructions, billing information, delivery requirements, and other data—then send it to Genigraphics electronically. It will be processed at one of Genigraphics' locations and most likely transmitted to Memphis, Tennessee for final production. The Genigraphics office in Memphis is across the street from the Federal Express distribution center, which means that if you submit a job to Genigraphics today you can get finished slides on your desk via Federal Express tomorrow.

To submit a PowerPoint presentation to Genigraphics, load and update the presentation, then use **File Send to Genigraphics...** to display the opening dialog box of the Genigraphics Wizard, shown in Figure 7.2. (If you are specifying 35mm slides, review the information on formatting presentations for 35mm slides in the previous section of this chapter).

This opening dialog box shows you what steps to take to complete the shipment to Genigraphics and provides a phone number to use for help directly from the company. If you click **Next** in this dialog box, you'll see the second screen in this Wizard, shown in Figure 7.3.

The second box is the first screen of a series that lets you specify details of this order. Notice that the left side of this dialog box offers some hints on what to order based on what you plan to do with the current presentation.

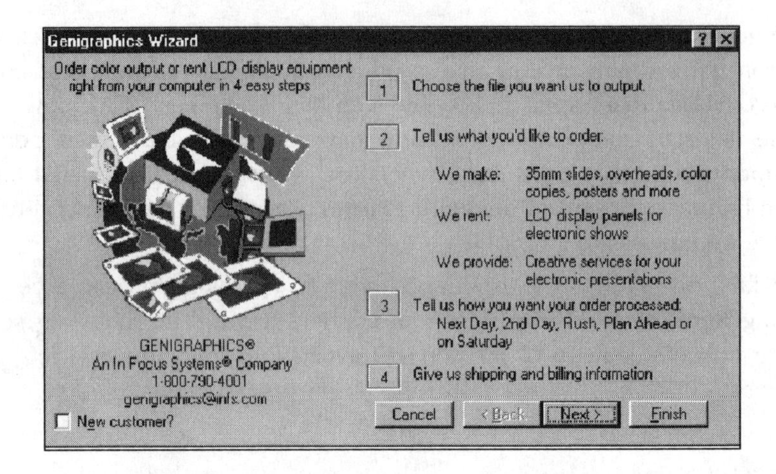

Figure 7.2 *Genigraphics Wizard dialog box.*

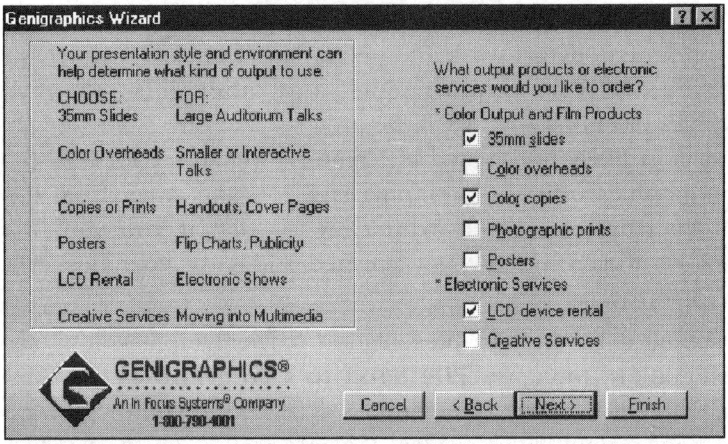

Genigraphics Wizard

Your presentation style and environment can help determine what kind of output to use.

CHOOSE:	FOR:
35mm Slides	Large Auditorium Talks
Color Overheads	Smaller or Interactive Talks
Copies or Prints	Handouts, Cover Pages
Posters	Flip Charts, Publicity
LCD Rental	Electronic Shows
Creative Services	Moving into Multimedia

What output products or electronic services would you like to order?

* Color Output and Film Products
  - [x] 35mm slides
  - [ ] Color overheads
  - [x] Color copies
  - [ ] Photographic prints
  - [ ] Posters
* Electronic Services
  - [x] LCD device rental
  - [ ] Creative Services

GENIGRAPHICS®
An In Focus Systems® Company
1-800-790-4001

Cancel | < Back | Next > | Finish

Figure 7.3 *Genigraphics Wizard second dialog box.*

The right side of this dialog box offers check boxes for ordering Genigraphics services. You can specify one or multiple services. In addition to slides, overhead foils and other products, Genigraphics offers extended services such as rental of LCD projection panels and Creative Services such as slide design, presentation enhancement, presentation consulting, and so on.

Click **Next** to present the next dialog box (See Figure 7.4).

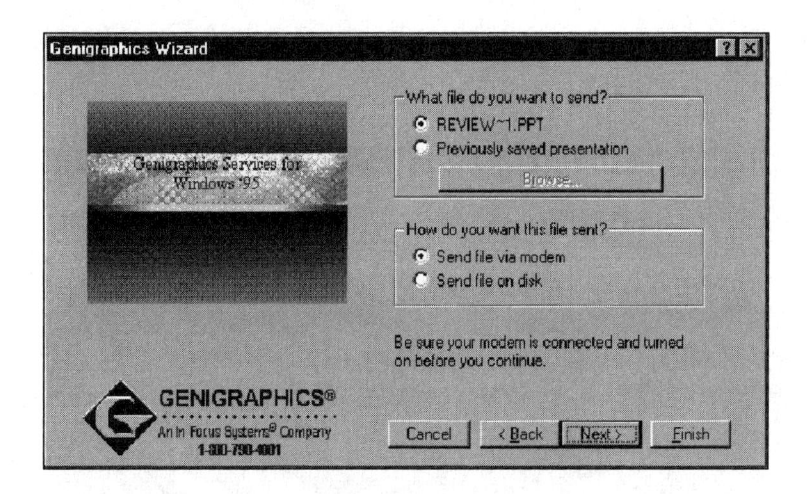

Figure 7.4 *Genigraphics Wizard File Selection dialog box.*

In this screen you can either specify which of the open presentations to send, or you can specify a previously-saved presentation. You can click on **Browse** to display a file manager screen to help you locate a specific file. The preview window at the left of the dialog box shows you the initial slide in the specified presentation file.

You can also choose how to send the file from this dialog box. You can either click on **Send file via modem** to have the Wizard automatically dial up a Genigraphics site and upload your file, or click **Send file on disk** if you prefer to mail or Federal Express the file.

Click **Next** to display the Mount Selection screen shown in Figure 7.5.

The box at the left of the mount selection dialog box gives you tips for when to use different types of slide mounts. You'll probably use plastic mounts for most of your presentations but, if you have a presentation that is heavily used, used in a hostile environment, or is shipped a lot, consider glass mounts.

You can also specify the number of slide sets you want Genigraphics to prepare from your presentation. Depending on your budget, at least two sets is a good idea. This lets you replace slides that become damaged, permits you to have two presentations on the same subject going on at the same time, and lets you easily use the same slide more than once within your presentation.

Click **Next** to go on to the next dialog box.

If you specified color copies in the products and services dialog box, you will see the color copies specifications shown in Figure 7.6.

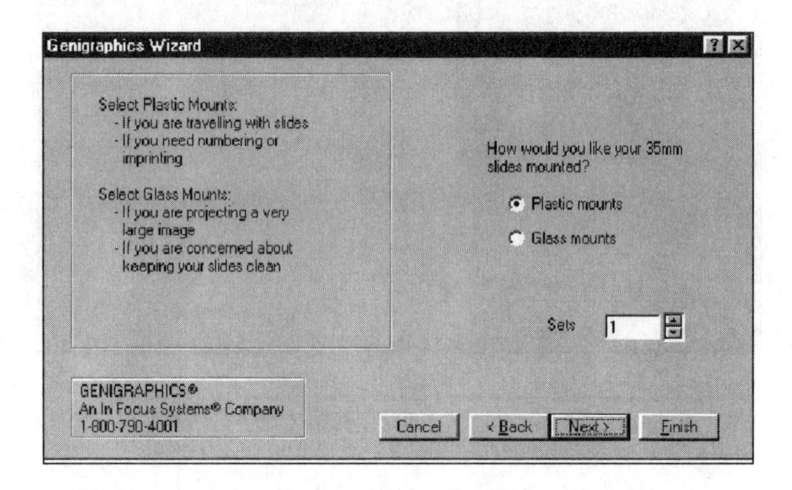

Figure 7.5 *Genigraphics Wizard Slide Mount Selection dialog box.*

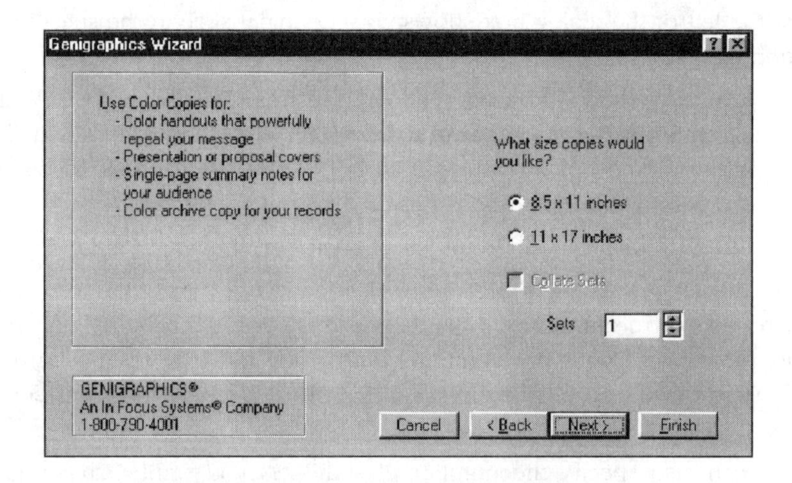

Figure 7.6 *Genigraphics Wizard Color Copies dialog box.*

The dialog box shown in Figure 7.7 may also be displayed during this sequence to let you specify the extended Genigraphics services you want to order.

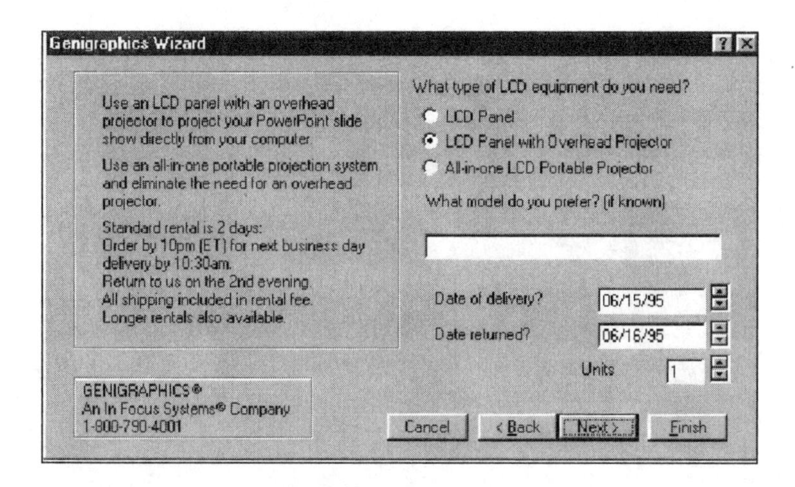

Figure 7.7 *Genigraphics Wizard Extended Services dialog box.*

This interactive Wizard also can help you fine tune your presentation for the type of output you have specified. The dialog box in Figure 7.8 will help you.

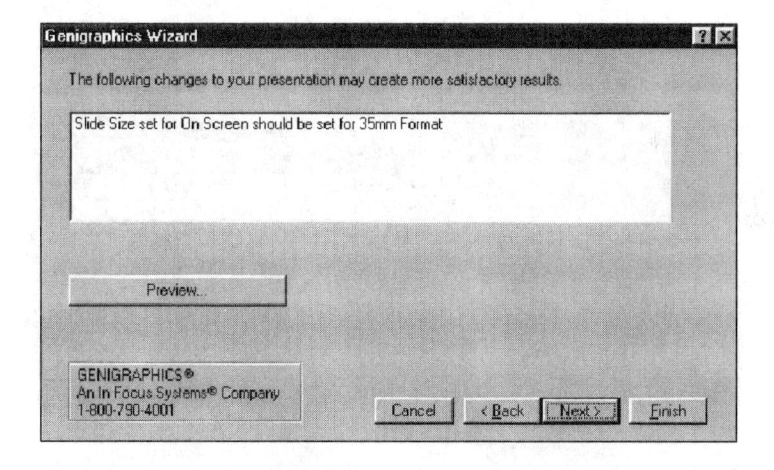

Figure 7.8 *Genigraphics Wizard Help dialog box.*

Once you have specified all of the products and services you want to order, the order processing dialog box shown in Figure 7.9 will appear.

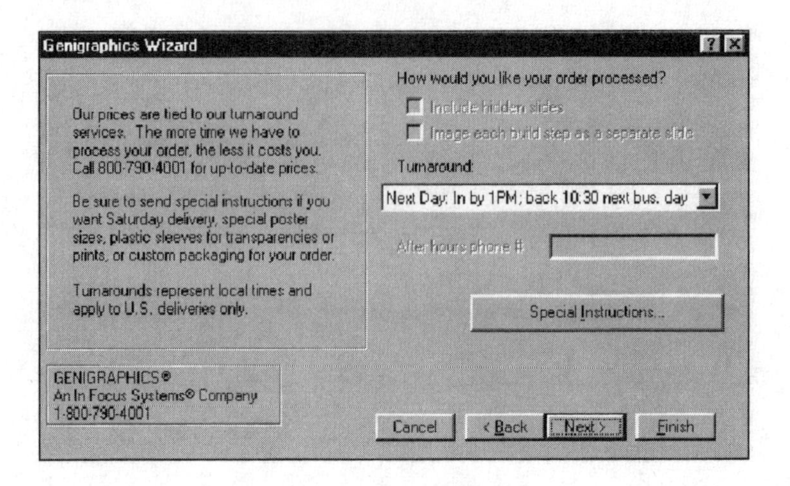

Figure 7.9 *Genigraphics Wizard Order Processing dialog box.*

Use the pull-down list in the middle of this dialog box to choose shipment method and time (See Figure 7.10).

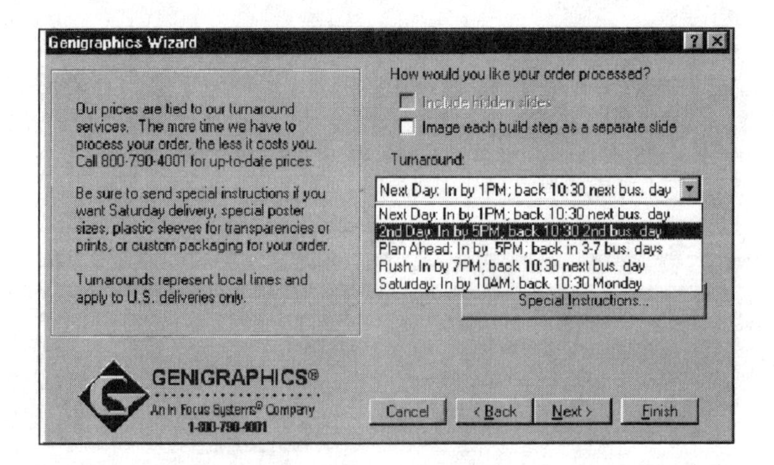

Figure 7.10 *Genigraphics Wizard pull-down turnaround list.*

The Special Instructions button lets you add instructions of your own. Click **Next** to bring up the shipping instructions dialog box shown in Figure 7.11.

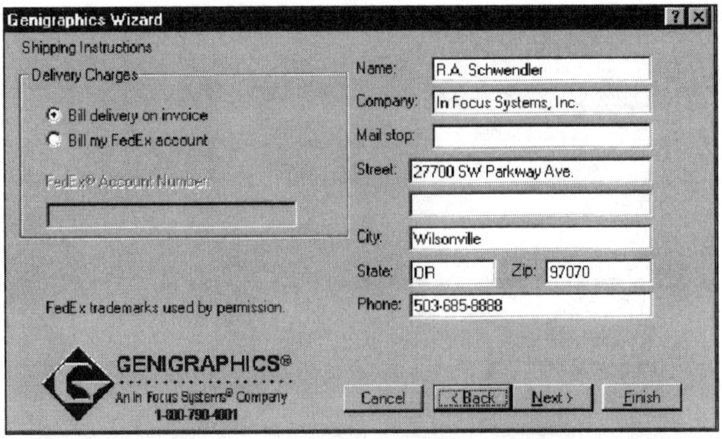

Figure 7.11 Genigraphics Wizard Shipping Instructions dialog box.

Click in the button next to the listed method for paying for the shipping charges. If you tell Genigraphics to bill your Federal Express account, then you can enter your account number in the box under these buttons.

The next dialog box asks for the method of payment for the Genigraphics services (See Figure 7.12).

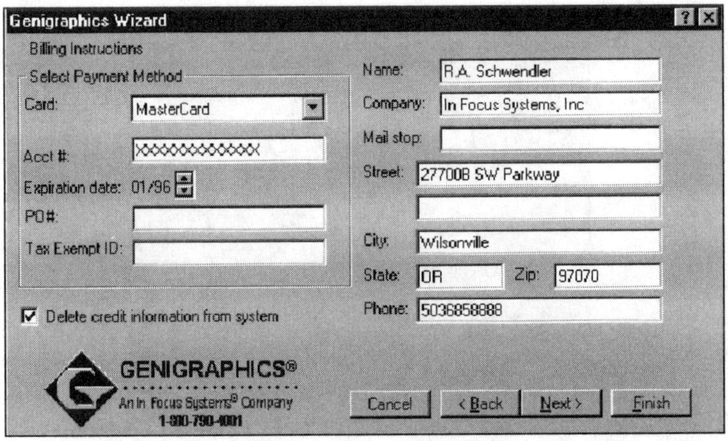

Figure 7.12 Genigraphics Wizard Billing Instructions dialog box.

Click **Next** to display the order summary dialog box shown in Figure 7.13.

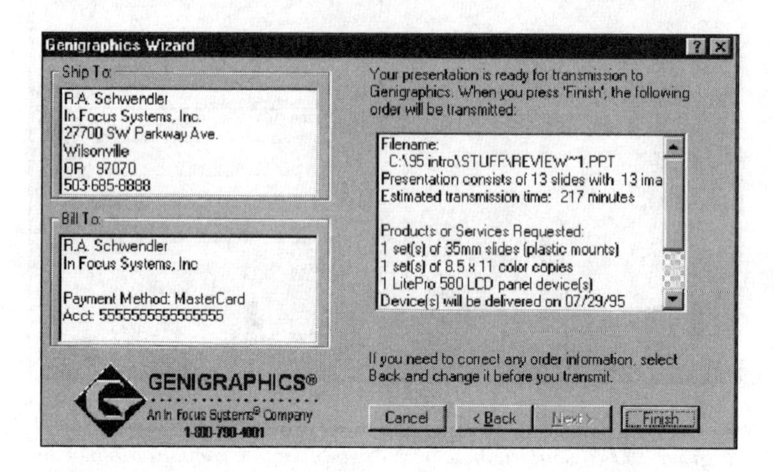

Figure 7.13 *Genigraphics Wizard Order Summary dialog box.*

When you click **Finish** on this dialog box, the Wizard automatically loads the utility that transmits the file to Genigraphics. The first time through this routine you will be asked for information about your modem, serial port, baud rate and the like. The Link program then dials the number and starts the transfer. You will see a progress report dialog box like the one shown in Figure 7.14.

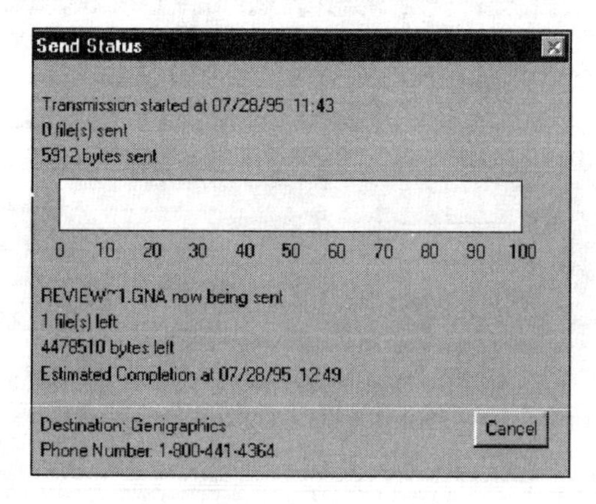

Figure 7.14 *Genigraphics Link Transmission Progress dialog box.*

GRAPHEXEC VISUALS

Graphexec Visuals offers custom presentations or straight slide conversions from PowerPoint as well as a variety of other packages. You can supply the company with a rough idea of your presentation and let their professionals design slides for you. A proof will be sent for your approval if time permits.

You can either mail diskettes with PowerPoint slides for conversion to film, or you can use the Graphexec bulletin board to upload the files. If you have access to a modem, this is the best choice. You save shipping charges, the images arrive at the Graphexec offices immediately, and there is less chance of losing your files.

In addition to preparing 35mm slides and overhead foils, Graphexec can supply full color prints from your PowerPoint disk. You can use these prints for inclusion in printed reports, as section dividers, or for report covers.

As with many presentation services, Graphexec can also scan your color or black and white prints so you can insert them into a PowerPoint presentation. Services such as these let you access the images you need without the expense of purchasing a high-end scanner.

Graphexec Visuals, 1991 Highway 54 West, Fayetteville, GA 30214, 404-487-2165.

VISUAL HORIZONS

Visual Horizons offers one of the most complete ranges of services in the industry. You can send completed PowerPoint presentations and have Visual Horizons convert them to 35mm slides or overhead foils. If you'd like to try this company's services, send three images to get three free slides as a sample. The company's Transgraphic software helps you set up images for conversion, asks about deadlines and special requirements, then calls up Visual Horizons and uploads the images. Then you can choose from a variety of services and deadlines.

In addition, you can send Visual Horizons an outline or ideas about your presentation and have their professionals help you design the slides and offer suggestions on presentation design. In fact, this company will pick up your presentation at just about any point in the process and step you through the rest of the procedure to complete the package. You can let them add colors or backgrounds, insert graphics, and more. Visual Horizons also supplies helpful booklets that show you how to design and proof your presentation for a professional result.

Visual Horizons, 180 Metro Park, Rochester, NY 14623, 716-424-5300.

Overhead Projection

In addition to 35mm slides, PowerPoint is excellent for creating either black and white or color overhead transparencies. Since an overhead transparency is similar to a typical 8.5 x 11 inch piece of paper, but will be projected onto a wall or screen to be seen by many people, the rules for creating transparencies are a cross between printing a hard copy of the final PowerPoint image and developing a slide image. As with slides, the key to creating an effective overhead is to keep the message simple.

To create a black and white overhead, the printed PowerPoint image can be copied onto overhead transparency stock using almost any copy machine. Many office supply stores and computer stores sell overhead transparencies that may be used with a copy machine or with a laser or dot-matrix printer. Before you put the transparency material directly in to your laser printer, make sure your printer can use it without damage.

Although you should be able to use copy machine transparencies in your laser printer, your particular machine may have problems with it. Some office supply stores and discount houses offer laser machine transparency material that is known to work with most printers; your best bet is to use this stock instead of the standard copy machine variety.

The NEC LC-890 technical manual, for example, cautions that transparencies for use with this LED printer must be able to withstand the high fusion temperatures of up to 170 degrees C (338 degrees F). In addition, only transparencies that are 0.10 mm or thinner and have been treated to prevent static buildup should be used.

The user manual for the Hewlett Packard LaserJet III includes the caution, "Use only overhead transparencies recommended for use in laser printers." In addition, HP recommends that you use a straight exit path for the transparency sheets. HP LaserJet printers turn the printed page once at the end of the print cycle so that it exits the printer face down, collating the sheets. You can bypass this step by opening a rear exit door on the printer. This reduces the possibility of curling, which can be caused by that final sharp turn while the transparency material is hot from the printer.

You should also watch your printer carefully as the transparency sheets exit. Remember, they are extremely hot and may tend to stick together when they stack up. To avoid this possibility, print one page at a time. Or, you can simply take care to remove each page as it is printed so the pages don't stack up in the printer output tray.

These guidelines are probably good ones for most modern page printers. Check your printer manual and your printer supplier. Many printer manufacturers will sell you transparency material as well as other specialty output material, either through approved distributors or through a division of their own company.

Creating color overhead transparencies is slightly more complicated. Unless a color laser printer (or other color output device) is used, the PowerPoint image must be sent to a company such as Visual Horizons for conversion to color transparency. There is a growing number of color printers available to handle your color output. Whereas a full color printer used to cost anywhere from $5,000 to $20,000, you can get acceptable color output today for under $3,000. In fact, there are a few color printer models available at slightly less than $500 that might do all the color output you need for your presentations.

Hewlett-Packard offers at least two relatively low-priced color printers. In addition, the Fargo Electronics Primera Color Printer, a dye-sublimation device, is priced under $1,000. You can use wax-based inks for medium quality draft and proof output, then change to dye-sublimation when you want photo quality output. All you need to do is change paper and ribbon. You could take color prints from printers of this type and create overhead transparencies by simply running them through a color copier at your local copy center. Compared to the $5 to $10 the service bureaus charge for overhead foils, the $1 to $2 for an overhead slide done this way is a real bargain. Besides, you can use these color pages directly in annual reports and other printed documents.

Computer Projection

Many of the presentations you make with PowerPoint will be displayed right on the computer screen. If you have a small group that can sit around a table or a desk, all you need is a standard computer screen for everyone to see the material.

When you want to use the computer as a presentation platform for larger groups, however, you need a way to enlarge the image so everyone can see it. One way to do this is to convert your computer's signal to a television signal. Once that is done, you can attach your computer to projection TV devices or large screen monitors, or you can dub to video tape. See the discussion on using video tape later in this chapter for details on how to do this.

Another way to project your computer image is to connect the computer display to a projector that enlarges the image and projects it onto a wall or a screen. There are a number of devices that can do this, but they all work in generally the same way. Figure 7.15 shows a conceptual diagram of a computer projection device.

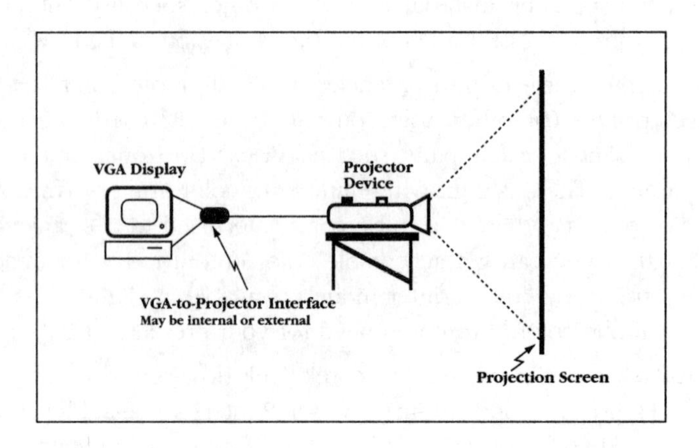

Figure 7.15 *Typical computer projection diagram.*

In general, a projector connects to your computer's video adapter and then projects the information onto the wall or screen. These devices may include their own projection hardware, or they may make use of projectors integral to other equipment. For example, a projector adapter may display the computer's image on a small flat screen, which can be positioned on top of an overhead projector. The overhead projector then projects the screen image onto the wall.

The quality of a projected image may not be as good as an on-screen image, but today's projectors can produce very high-quality images. The main consideration in selecting one of these devices is the environment in which you will be making presentations. It takes a lot of light to make a projected image sharp, readable, and exciting in a room that is lit like a standard office. The 3M company, for example, recommends an overhead projector with at least a 7,500 lumen output for computer projection in conjunction with an LCP display panel. You may get by with less, but your images will appear washed out. If you can darken the room, the image improves, but the best projected images still come from high-output units. Figure 7.16 shows a typical computer projector that can help you enhance your computer-based presentations.

Figure 7.16 *Typical projector*

The following list includes sources for computer projection hardware:

Boxlight Corporation

17771 Fjord Drive, NE
Poulsbo, WA 98370
206-779-7901

Eiki International, Inc.

26794 Vista Terrace Drive
Lake Forrest, CA 92630
714-457-0200

Proxima Corporation

9440 Carroll Park Drive
San Diego, CA 92121
619-457-5500

Sharp Electronics Corporation

Sharp Plaza
Mahwah, NJ 07430-2135
201-529-8731

Spectrel International

1308 Bayshore Highway 100
Burlingame, CA 94010
415-343-5987

In addition to straight projection, some companies—such as Proxima Corporation—offer control devices that help you concentrate on the audience and the topic instead of the mechanics of manipulating the computer and the presentation. The Proxima Cyclops interactive pointer system, for example, lets you stand in front of an audience and control your PC-based presentation with an infrared pointer (see Figure 7.17).

Figure 7.17 *Proxima Cyclops interactive Pointer System.*

Whatever projection and control system you choose, make sure that it functions properly with your computer and that it provides the quality and control features you need. Without a doubt, this kind of hardware gives you more freedom in designing PowerPoint presentations. You can take advantage of the sound, video, and other computer-based features of PowerPoint, which you can't do if you elect for overhead or 35mm slide projection.

PowerPoint and Multimedia

It is getting more and more difficult to separate multimedia from conventional computing. The majority of new computer packages today include at least a CD-ROM drive and interface, and an increasing number of off-the-shelf machines include audio boards and speakers. These two components—CD-ROM and audio—offer a level of capability those of us with several years of computer experience couldn't even imagine just a short while ago.

CD-ROM Drive

With a CD-ROM drive, you have access to over 600 megabytes of read-only storage that can include high-resolution pictures or drawings, motion video, clip art, utility programs, and sound. Figure 7.18 shows a typical external CD-ROM drive with the caddy that holds the CD platter itself. Other designs fit inside your computer in place of a 5.25-inch floppy drive. In addition to storing images and digitized sound, many of these CD-ROM players will play back standard audio CDs with the addition of a software control package.

Figure 7.18 *Typical CD-ROM drive and carrier.*

These features are important to PowerPoint users because they open up a variety of image types and a wider variety of images that can be made a part of your PowerPoint presentation. You can purchase photographs, clip art, music, sound effects, drawings, movie clips, and more on CD-ROM at reasonable prices for inclusion in your PowerPoint productions. (I've listed a few suppliers of these and other support products at the end of this section).

Sound Card

A sound card offers the same kind of enhancement for your PowerPoint presentations. You can attach a microphone, CD player, or other audio source to record digitized sound into disk files. These files can then be attached to individual PowerPoint slides to be used as background sound, music, or narration. Combined with video tape output (see the discussion on using video tape later in this chapter), PowerPoint slides with sound narration can produce a self-running instructional presentation.

Refer to the information with your sound card for details on recording and playing sound. Once you have a **.WAV** or a **.MID** file recorded to disk, you can insert the file into your PowerPoint presentation fairly easily. First, load an existing presentation or start a new one. Make the slide to which you want to add audio the current slide. Use **Insert: Object...** to display the Insert Object dialog box shown in Figure 7.19.

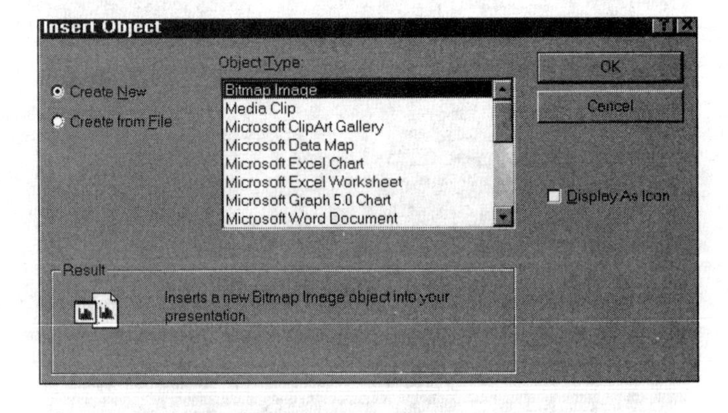

Figure 7.19 *Insert Object dialog box.*

Click on the **Create from File** button at the left of this dialog box. This tells PowerPoint that you want to use an existing sound file, and it opens the File Selection window shown in Figure 7.20.

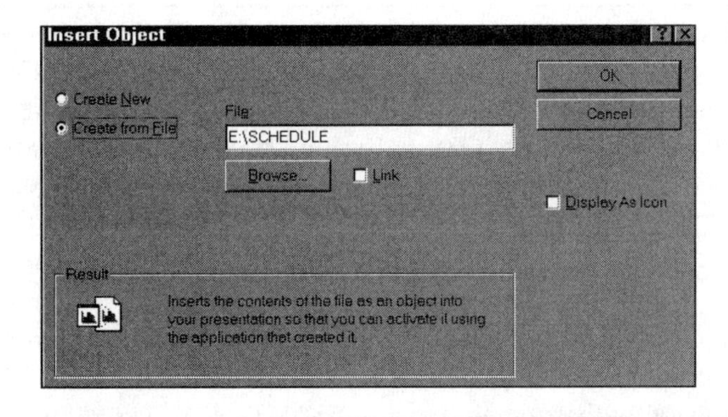

Figure 7.20 *File Selection window on Insert Object dialog box.*

NOTE

You can create new sounds on the fly by accepting the Create New default in PowerPoint. If you accept this default, PowerPoint loads the Media Player utility to let you record a new sound for use on the current slide. I prefer to create the sound files first.

Either enter the path and file name of the sound file you want to use, or click on **Browse...** to open the Browse dialog box shown in Figure 7.21.

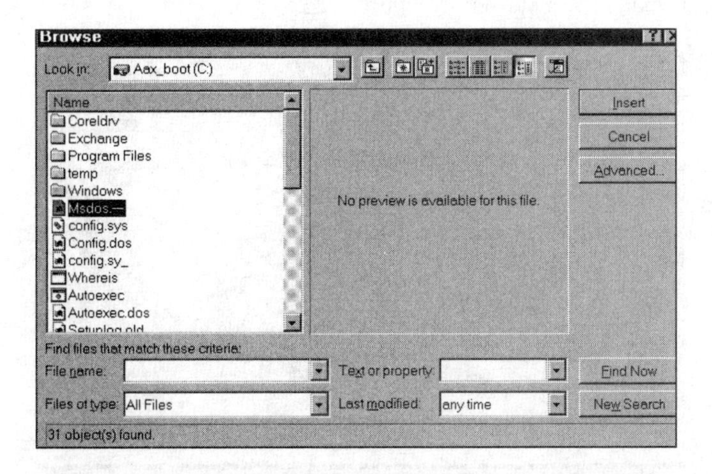

Figure 7.21 *Browse dialog box from Insert Object dialog box.*

Choose a directory and a sound file from the Browse dialog box. Double-click on the file name or select it and click on **OK**. PowerPoint inserts the path and file name into the Insert Object dialog box.

NOTE

If you want to experiment with sound and you haven't recorded your own, use one of the **.WAV** or **.MID** files from the Windows subdirectory. There are several files there that you can use as trials. On the Windows 95 distribution CD-ROM, for example, look in the `\cdexpo` directory for a list of interesting sound files you can use for experimentation.

NOTE

If you are using short sound effects or music bridges, you will probably use **.WAV** files. These are digitized recordings directly from a microphone or other sound device. For longer background music, consider **.MID** (MIDI) files. These are programmed files that require a fraction of the storage space of **.WAV** files. You could use a relatively small **.MID** file to provide background music throughout an entire presentation, for example. A **.WAV** file of that duration would require more disk space than you're likely to have.

By default, PowerPoint displays **.WAV** files as a microphone icon and **.MID** files as the Media Player icon. If you'd like to specify your own icon to represent sound files on your slides, click on **Display As Icon** on the Insert Object dialog box. This displays the default icon for the selected file type and adds a Change Icon button (see Figure 7.22). Click on the **Change Icon** button to display the Change Icon dialog box shown in Figure 7.23.

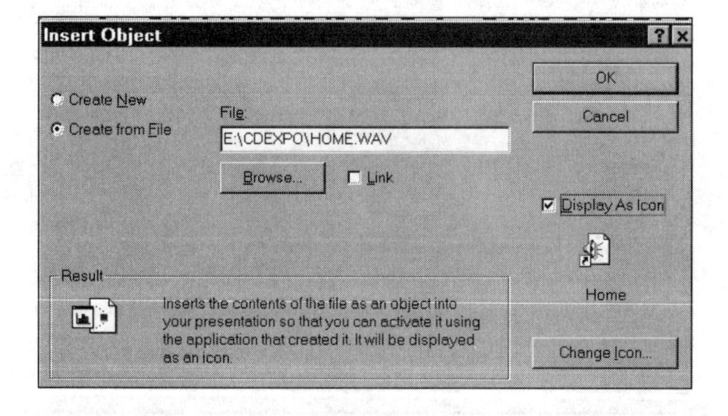

Figure 7.22 *Insert Object dialog box with Change Icon button.*

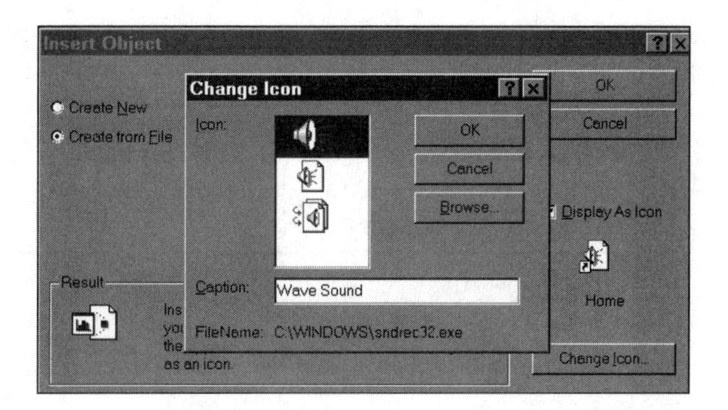

Figure 7.23 *Change Icon dialog box.*

Notice that the current and default icons are shown. You also have the option of selecting another icon from a file on disk. If you click on the **Browse...** button on the Change Icon dialog box, PowerPoint again opens a file selection dialog box so you can specify a directory and file from which to select the icon.

NOTE

Many executable (program) files include icons. You can use their icons by specifying the particular file name. You can also use any file with the extension **.ICO** as an icon. The distribution CD-ROM with Windows 95 includes several icon files in the `\products\demos\scenes` directory and in the `\cdexpo\bitmaps` directory. On your Office 95 CD-ROM you'll find icon files in the `\winword\wordmail` and the `\schedule` directories.

When you have selected the icon you want to use, click on **OK** to return to the Insert Object dialog box. The new icon appears on the dialog box under the Display As Icon prompt. Click on **OK** once more to close the Insert Object dialog box and return to your document. PowerPoint inserts the icon you have specified at the center of the current slide. You can leave it there or grab it and drag it to another position. To play the sound, double-click on the icon.

If you insert a **.MID** file with a long playing time, you can play another sound file—such as a sound effect—on top of it. For example, you could insert a **.MID** file on one of the first slides and start it playing to provide background music. Then, on that and subsequent slides, use additional sound inserts for sound effects or narration.

You may have your own sound and music to include with PowerPoint presentations. If you need help with sound effects or music, contact one of the vendors in the list below. This is by no means an exhaustive list, but it will get you started.

Creative Support Services

1950 Riverside Drive
Los Angeles, CA 90039
213-666-7968
800-468-6874

Killer Tracks

6534 Sunset Boulevard
Hollywood, CA 90028
213-957-4455
800-877-0078

Multimedia Arts, Inc.

3900 West Alameda Avenue
Suite 1700
Burbank, CA 90068
818-972-2625
800-468-9008

The Music Bakery

660 Preston Forest Center
Suite 300
Dallas, TX 75230
800-229-0313

The Music Library

80 South Main Street
Hanover, NH 03755
603-643-1388
800-545-0688

Valentino, Inc.

500 Executive Boulevard
PO Box 534
Elmsford, NY 10523-0534
914-347-7878
800-223-6278

Motion Video

In addition to inserting music and sound into your PowerPoint presentation, you can make use of full motion video in a PowerPoint slide window. This is another impressive benefit of PC-based multimedia. Use the same technique as with sound to insert a motion video clip into a PowerPoint slide. Access the Insert Object dialog box (select **Insert: Object...**) and click on **Create from File** to open the File Selection window. Either enter the name of the motion video file or use the **Browse...** button to locate the file you want from the directory and file name display.

The video and sound component of PowerPoint uses the Windows Media Player utility, so it is capable of accessing any files the Media Player can play. Which files are supported depends on what hardware and software drivers you have installed. You can learn something about what to expect by opening the Control Panel, then choosing the Multimedia icon. Figure 7.24 shows the Multimedia icon visible in the Control Panel. Figure 7.25 shows the Multimedia Properties dialog box that is displayed when you double-click on the Multimedia icon in the Control Panel.

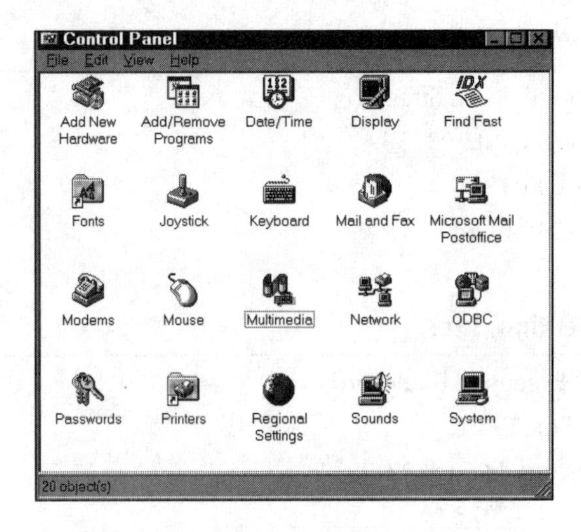

Figure 7.24 *Windows Control Panel display.*

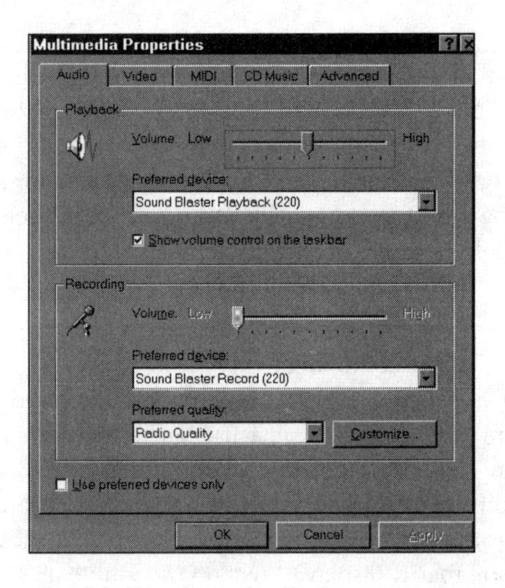

Figure 7.25 *Control Panel Multimedia Properties dialog box.*

For motion video, you may find files with various extensions. One common extension is **.AVI**. Locate a file with an **.AVI** extension from inside the

PowerPoint Insert Object dialog box. When you double-click on the file, PowerPoint inserts an icon containing the file's first video frame onto the current slide. The dialog box in the middle of Figure 7.26 comes from a sample video file that ships with Windows 95 (`\funstuff\videos\highperf\goodtime`).

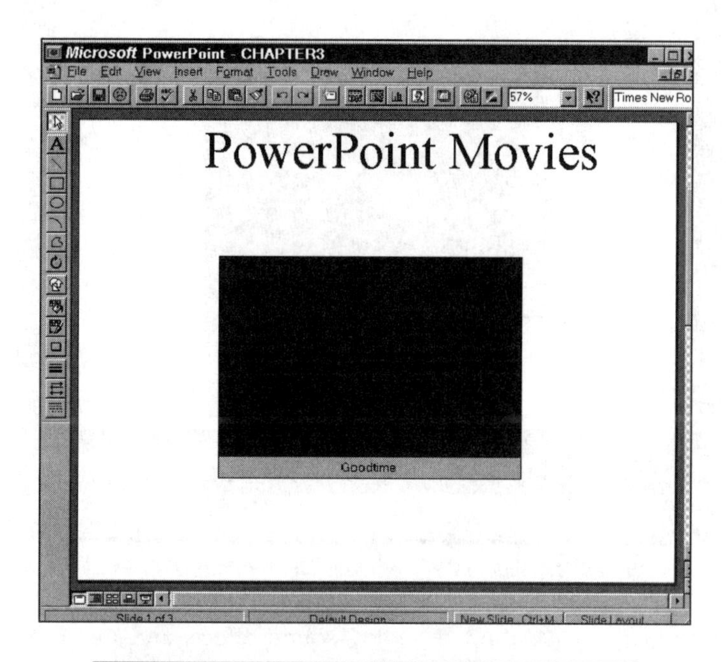

Figure 7.26 *Sample video icon on PowerPoint slide.*

As with sound files, you can play a video clip inserted onto a PowerPoint slide by double-clicking on the icon. PowerPoint launches the Media Player in the background, and opens another window on top of your slide. (Notice that this second window opens. The icon that represents the video clip does not play.) Figure 7.27 shows how the Media Player launches and plays the video represented by the icon on the slide.

The video clip window is opened as a very small square. When the video dialog box is inserted into a slide, you can grab any of the window borders and drag them to enlarge the box. The larger the box, the lower the quality of the video display. Because of the video technology used with the standard player, you won't get a full-screen display even when you click on the Maximize button. You can make this motion video segment a part of a video tape presentation of slides as well. See the Video Tape section later in this chapter for information on how to do this.

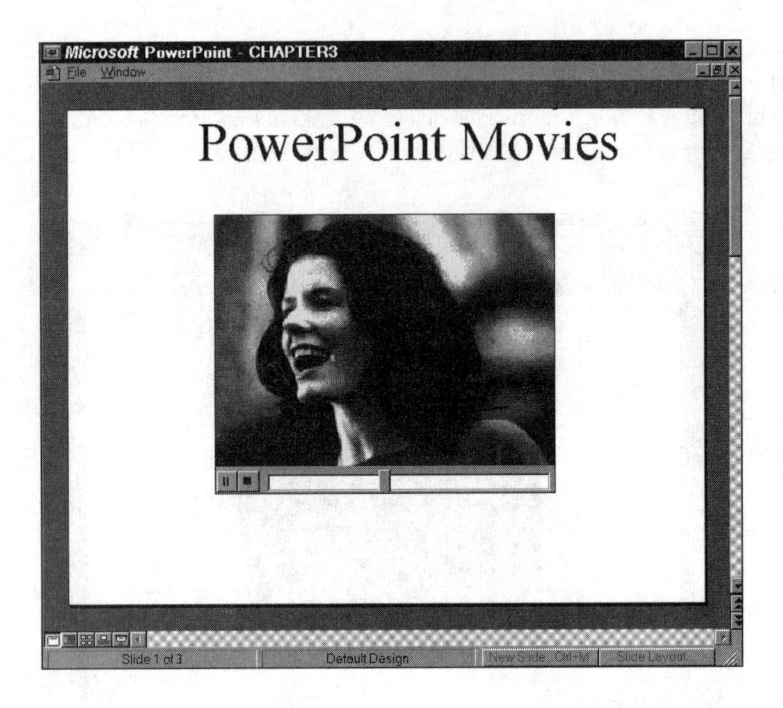

Figure 7.27 *Media Player video clip on PowerPoint slide.*

Just as you can purchase canned audio—sound effects and music—for use in your presentations, you can also purchase film clips on CD or video. These range from stock footage designed for presentation applications to historical film fragments. I've listed a few suppliers of stock footage below. Contact one or more of these companies to get help in enhancing your PowerPoint and other computer-based presentations.

Alpha Technologies Group, Inc.

6921 Cable Drive
Marriottsville, MD 21104
410-781-4200

Archive Films

530 West 25th Street
New York, NY 10001
212-620-3955

Bliss Interactive Technologies

6034 West Courtyard Drive
Austin, TX 78730
512-338-2458

BMUG, Inc.

1442a Walnut Street, Box #62
Berkeley, CA 94709
510-549-2684

Jasmine Multimedia Publishing, Inc.

1888 Century Park East
Suite 300
Los Angeles, CA 90067
310-277-7523
800-798-7535

Mediacom

PO Box 36173
Richmond, VA 23235
804-794-0700

Video Tape Library, Ltd.

1509 North Crescent Heights Boulevard
Suite 2
Los Angeles, CA 90046
213-656-4330

Video Clips, Inc.

22 Fisher Avenue
Wellesley, MA 02181
617-235-5617

WPA Film Library

5525 West 159th Street
Oak Forest, IL 60452
708-535-1540
800-777-2223

Other Presentation Types

The variety of methods available to you for presenting information created with PowerPoint is almost unlimited. In addition to conventional PC-based presentations, projecting your PC images, and using 35mm slides, you can use custom presentation hardware, convert your show to video, and more. I'll discuss a few of these options in this section. However, as you work with PowerPoint and become more comfortable with designing and giving presentations, keep your ears, eyes, and mind open to other options that can enhance your message and keep your audience interested.

VideoShow

One of the many ways to present PowerPoint images is with General Parametrics Corporation's VideoShow. This is a standalone presentation system that uses PC-compatible disk files to produce an electronic slide show similar to projecting a presentation from the PC (see Figure 7.28). VideoShow is essentially a video projector, except that you don't use your computer. It is a standalone device that uses disk files created by your computer to present video slides.

Figure 7.28 *VideoShow.*

PowerPoint files can easily be transferred into VideoShow format by installing a Windows driver and printing the show or individual slides to a disk file after selecting the VideoShow driver. Press **Enter** with the Print dialog box displayed; the file name will be translated into VideoShow format and placed in whatever subdirectory PowerPoint image files are saved in. VideoShow files can be placed in any subdirectory by entering the appropriate path when the file name is entered.

Using VideoShow, PowerPoint files can be displayed on any RGB video monitor or video projector. Files can be linked together using special effects, and exciting presentations can easily be developed. VideoShow uses PowerPoint files that are saved on floppy disk. To use the product, a computer is not required (after the images are created). VideoShow is similar to a VCR (both in size and in function) for displaying computer images. After you insert a floppy disk containing graphic files, VideoShow will display the files in any order and will let you add different types of effects for enhancing the presentation. VideoShow can be programmed to provide a self-running presentation, or, with the use of a remote control unit, VideoShow can be used as a visual aid during a speech.

General Parametrics offers another interesting product to support presentations—the VideoShow Presenter. This is a handheld computer-compatible video screen with a control pad. A cable connects the Presenter to your PC, and the 4-inch color display in your hand helps you manage the show. From the control pad you can access any image in the show instantly, privately preview any image without showing it on the screen or projector, or review speaker's notes on the screen.

For more information about VideoShow or VideoShow Presenter, contact: General Parametrics Corporation, 1250 Ninth Street, Berkeley, CA 94710, 800-223-0999 or 510-524-9954.

Video Tape

Once you have your PowerPoint presentation planned and produced, you can show it to your audience in a variety of ways. With today's computer technology, the option of converting your show to video tape is relatively easy and inexpensive. All you need is a plug-in board or external interface to convert your computer's display to video format. Then you can attach a standard video recorder to the output of this converter and step through your presentation, recording it to tape. Figure 7.29 shows a typical connection diagram for attaching your computer to a VCR.

If you are using a sound card with your computer and have attached sound or narration to your PowerPoint presentation, you can also output the audio portion of your show to the VCR to create a standalone, self-running presentation that anyone can view. Of course you can also record audio information on video tape after you convert the PowerPoint images to video. There are numerous video service companies (one is probably located in or near your town) that will add music and narration to your basic slide show for a reasonable price. If you are working for a relatively large company, there are probably video production facilities available to you to help you enhance your PowerPoint/video production.

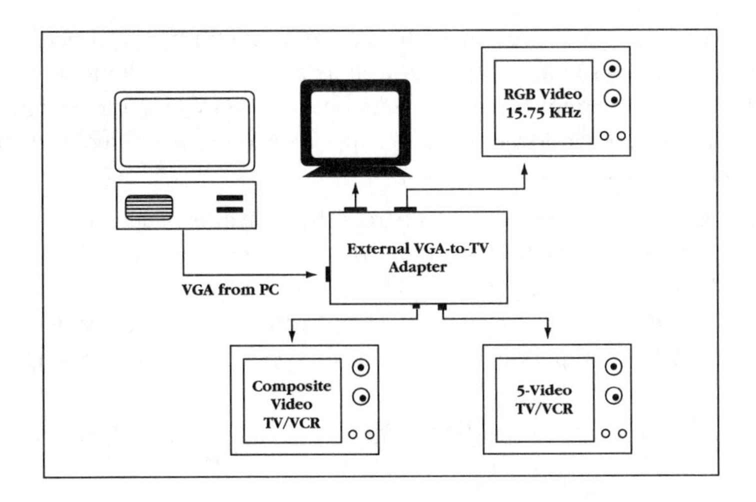

Figure 7.29 *Typical Computer-to-VCR connection diagram.*

The hardware available for PowerPoint to video conversion is varied in function and in price. Many products available to do the job are part of a more comprehensive package designed to support full desktop video editing. If you intend to expand to more advanced video work, this kind of product is a good investment. On the other hand, if all you really want to do is convert your PowerPoint shows to video, then you can use a simpler (and lower-priced) unit. In the following sections I'll give you a summary of a few of the available products to help you use video with PowerPoint. Obviously there are other products available. Ask your local computer dealer and check the mail order advertisements and magazines for more choices.

Notice that you can use these devices not only to produce video tape, but also to enable you to show your computer shows on a standard television monitor. This is a good choice when you are presenting PowerPoint shows in a location that is wired for television instead of computer video projection. Many conference rooms have a number of large screen television monitors around the room or are equipped with a large screen projection TV. Using a VGA-to-video interface lets you plug directly into these display devices to present your PowerPoint show to a large audience directly from your computer.

BRAVADO

The Truevision Bravado encoder is more of a multimedia device than a presentation device, but the two applications are beginning to merge in today's high-end software such as PowerPoint. Bravado is a multi-function board that supports composite or S-Video output as well as audio. This multimedia board also lets you display a variety of components on your VGA monitor, including text, graphics, and video windows. Bravado supports live motion video as well as static computer displays.

Like many other video output boards, the Bravado includes standard VGA circuitry, so you don't need a separate VGA adapter. The Bravado accepts two stereo or four monaural inputs. Amplified audio output lets you use the audio portion of the board with standard speakers without the requirement of a separate amplifier. Line outputs to carry audio to a video recorder or amplifier system are also available.

Truevision, Inc., 7340 Shadeland Station, Indianapolis, IN 46256, 317-841-0332.

Genie and VINplus

Jovian's VINplus is a low-cost hardware/software combination that handles the VGA-to-TV conversion for your PC. You connect the external box to the VGA port and install the required software to output composite or S-Video signals for video recording or television monitor display.

For about three times the cost of VINplus you can purchase the Jovian Genie, a hardware-only device compatible with PC or Apple computers. In fact, you can connect PC and Apple computers to the Genie input simultaneously and convert their outputs to TV signals one at a time. Separate NTSC and PAL models are available for Genie and VINplus.

Jovian Logic Corporation, 47929 Fremont Boulevard, Fremont, CA 94538, 510-651-4823

PC-TV Encoder Box

The PC-TV Encoder is a small, flat box that sits outside your PC and converts standard VGA signals into television signals. It supports displays up to 640 x 480 resolution in full color, and it can display on a television monitor and VGA display simultaneously. Television outputs include S-Video and composite signals. PAL and NTSC models are available. No separate software driver is required. You simply connect your VGA signal to the input, and a television monitor, recorder, or other television device to the output. A separate encoder card that plugs inside your PC also is available if you prefer to have the converter inside the computer instead of outside.

Yuan Technology, USA, 1223 S. Dorsey Lane, Suite 203, Tempe, AZ 85281, 602-966-1557.

PORTASHOW AND VIGA VGA+

PortaShow is an external box that converts your computer's VGA display signal to video. You plug the output of your VGA display card into the PortaShow, then connect your VGA computer monitor to the VGA output of the PortaShow.

At the same time you can connect a composite or S-Video device to another PortaShow port. Notice that the PortaShow uses your computer's existing VGA display adapter and resides outside your computer. This is an excellent choice when you need video output from more than one computer.

An alternative product from the same company is the VIGA VGA+, an internal PC card that supplies both VGA monitor and video output. The hookup is essentially the same as for the PortaShow except that the video and VGA circuitry both reside inside your computer on a single card. Visionetics also offers a Genlock version of the board for high-end video applications such as video overlaying and chromakeying.

Visionetics International, 21311 Hawthorne Boulevard, Suite 300, Torrance, CA 90503, 310-316-7940.

TELEVEYES, TELEVEYES/PLUS AND TELEVEYES/PRO

This computer-to-TV converter group offers a variety of display conversion features through an external box. The standard model is appropriate for PowerPoint conversion or television monitor presentations. If you plan to move up to high-end desktop video applications, consider paying the premium for the Plus or Pro models (see Figure 7.30).

You can display both VGA and television video at the same time. These converters include audio input and output support to add audio to your PowerPoint presentations on the computer or to mix audio with your images on video tape. The Pro model includes Genlock and overlay features. All models output composite and S-Video signals through standard connectors and cables.

Digital Vision, Inc., 270 Bridge Street, Dedham, MA 02026, 617-329-5400.

Figure 7.30 *TelevEyes/Pro VGA-to-Video adapter.*

ViVA Basic and ViVA Basic/EX

The ViVA Basic/EX is an external converter box that translates computer VGA signals to S-Video, composite television, and RGB output simultaneously. Television and VGA outputs can be displayed at the same time. No software is required to make the conversion. However, utility software is included to control the positioning of the VGA data on the TV screen and to adjust such effects as overscan and underscan. The unit is supplied with the necessary cables.

The ViVA Basic provides essentially the same features as the ViVA Basic/EX model, but from an internal PC adapter card. The ViVA Basic card plugs into your PC's bus near the existing VGA adapter and connects to the VGA adapter through the feature connector on top of the card. Composite, S-Video, and RGB output are provided on the rear panel of the ViVA Basic card. As this book is written, the price for the two units is the same.

Omnicomp Graphics Corporation, 1734 W. Sam Houston Parkway North, Houston, TX 77043, 713-464-2900.

To Sum Up

It would be impossible to include information about all of the products and services available to support PowerPoint presentations. However, in this chapter I have shown you some of the major players in the service and hardware part of the marketplace to help you get more out of the presentations you prepare in PowerPoint. Remember that the multimedia business is among the fastest changing technologies. Contact the companies I've mentioned for the latest information on their products before trying to make a decision.

In the next chapter we'll look at how you can integrate PowerPoint with other components of the Microsoft Office suite and other applications.

CHAPTER 8

PowerPoint and the Microsoft Office Suite

Microsoft's PowerPoint is at the forefront of today's computer software development. It has an unusual marketing position brought about by its partnership with other members of the Microsoft Office suite. I think the new PowerPoint is a great program, and it is gaining popularity both among people who know up front they need it and among users who stumble across it in their Office package. But I have to say that by far the majority of users I polled as research for this book said something like, "Well, I know I have it on my system, but I haven't tried it."

That attitude is going to change, I predict, not only because version 7.0 is much easier to use and has more features than the previous release that most people have tried, but also because users are learning that "presentation" software is good for much more than just presentations. With the close link among the members of the Microsoft Office suite, more users are likely to begin experimenting with PowerPoint and other packages they just happen to have because they wanted Word or Excel and found they could get the whole package for just a little more.

In this chapter, I'll introduce you to some of the ways you can use PowerPoint with other software and other software with PowerPoint. (There is a slight difference!)

Microsoft Office Overview

Microsoft Office is among the leaders in a new software trend that bundles all of the major software applications most users are likely to need into a single package.

Why Microsoft Office?

WordPerfect Corporation is doing it, Lotus and Borland are doing it, and there likely will be others. The idea of such a bundle is threefold:

- Give the user all major applications at one time.
- Lock the user into the products of a single vendor.
- Make the marketing of some products easier.

Another possible benefit of this type of marketing is price maintenance. Software retail prices have fallen rapidly over the past few years. You can buy applications for $100 or less today that would have cost thousands of dollars not too long ago. While the mainstream products—word processors, spreadsheets, and databases from major manufacturers—still are offered for $300 to $500 each, even that price plateau is being eroded. By packaging a popular product such as Microsoft Word with one that many users may not immediately perceive as important, the manufacturer can maintain a higher price for the popular program while promoting the use of the less popular one.

Whatever the actual motivation for current marketing posture, product groupings such as Microsoft Office can only benefit the user. You, as a user or potential user of PowerPoint, reap the benefits of full-featured software, a variety of software, and low prices. In addition, by installing and using multiple software packages from a single vendor, you benefit from a common user interface. When you load Microsoft Word and Microsoft PowerPoint you will be struck immediately at the similarity of the opening screens. The colors, the menus, and the screen design are all very similar.

Besides, you have a single company from which to seek technical support. You become familiar with the procedure for getting technical support, and you learn what to expect. (See Chapter 9 for more information on technical support for PowerPoint.)

What is Microsoft Office?

Soon after the IBM PC was introduced and software developers began filling the applications gap, among the popular trends were integrated packages. There were a number of popular offerings early on, but they soon fell by the wayside as strong dedicated applications replaced them. The theory behind integrated applications was to provide users with all the software they were likely to need with a common user interface and from a single vendor. However, as vendors quickly found, users were more interested in features available within individual applications than they were in the integrated concept. Even users who bought integrated products frequently used only one or two of the integrated applications and bought additional third-party software to fill in the gaps.

The rule still holds. While a few integrated packages exist today, they are poor seconds, from a business standpoint, relative to single-application software. The suite movement in today's software business promises the benefits of both integrated and standalone packages. The concept is the same today as it was in the beginning: provide users with the major applications they need—word processing, spreadsheet, and database—within a common user interface and from the same vendor. However, today, instead of integrating all of these applications into one package, the trend is to provide separate applications that are closely linked. This allows vendors more freedom in designing applications. With today's Windows environment that supports object linking and embedding (OLE), these separate applications can operate together rather closely. Besides the "big three" applications, most vendors are offering additional applications such as presentation software (which wasn't available when the early integrated software was around), electronic mail, programming languages, and so on.

Microsoft Office 95 includes Microsoft Word 7.0, Excel 7.0, PowerPoint 7.0, and Mail. Microsoft Access 7.0 may be included as an additional database component. The Suite conglomerations offer other incentives as well. For example, the Microsoft offering includes support for Visual Basic for Applications and OLE 2.0. The Visual Basic component is part of a Microsoft strategy to unify applications through a common macro and development language designed for end user as well as developer use. OLE 2.0, the follow-on to Microsoft's earlier OLE technology, offers a sophisticated and capable way to link applications. With OLE 2.0, in-place editing across applications is possible. This provides users the ability to access external features from inside one application without actually launching the remote application in the conventional way.

The Microsoft Office concept lets you purchase the main application you need, learn to use it, become familiar with the user interface, and be able to access the power of other applications easily. A software scheme is evolving that lets you have a single interface into your computer system. This interface enables you to work with a number of computer features without having to learn a lot of different tools and screens. This single interface concept isn't flawless, but it does go beyond the common interface afforded by Windows alone.

In addition, even if you don't want to access a remote application from inside a current program, you can still launch and use other Office products easily with the Microsoft toolbar. Place the mouse pointer on any displayed toolbar and click the right mouse button. Choose **Microsoft** from the pop-up toolbar menu and you'll see the toolbar shown in Figure 8.1.

Figure 8.1 *Microsoft toolbar in PowerPoint.*

Each of the Office applications supports this toolbar, so you can launch any of the Office programs by simply clicking on the appropriate button.

Using Linked Objects

Whether you are using Microsoft Office products or other Windows-based applications, you can insert a class of objects in your PowerPoint presentations called *linked objects.* I have talked previously about inserting objects into PowerPoint using the Insert Object dialog box. These are embedded objects because you import an object from a foreign application into PowerPoint, where it becomes static.

When you link an object, you create a soft or live link with the external data. That means that if the data to which PowerPoint is linked changes—as when someone updates the spreadsheet or Word document, for example—then these changes show up in PowerPoint. A live link is an excellent tool when multiple users are working on a presentation or on the data that supports a presentation. It is a good choice when you want to get on with the process of creating a presentation in PowerPoint but you know the facts will change. When you create a live link to data outside PowerPoint, you can specify that you want the information to change automatically each time you load PowerPoint and the presentation that includes links. Or, you can set up the presentation to let you check the new data before updating it manually with a keystroke. You may not want to use live links, on the other hand, if you are not on a network, or if the presentation you are creating will be moved from your system or network to another system or network.

If your system and presentation configuration seem to support live links, there are a couple of ways to create them. If you've read my description earlier about using the Insert Object dialog box, you are 90% familiar with the linking process.

Make the slide on which you wish to place a linked object the current slide, then use **Insert: Object...** to display the Insert Object dialog box, shown in Figure 8.2.

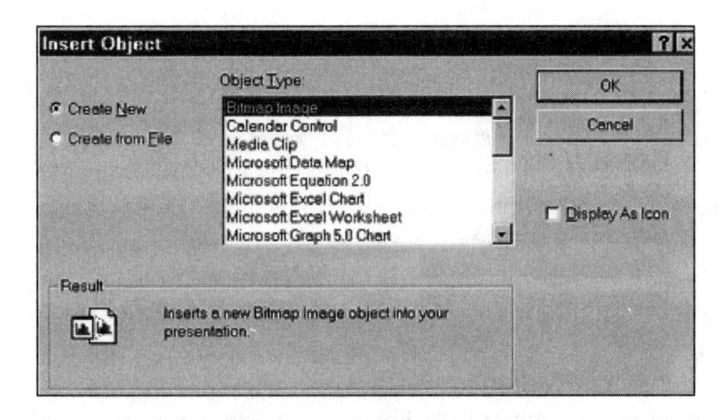

Figure 8.2 *Insert Object dialog box.*

Click on **Create from File** to open the File Selection window. Either type the path and file name in this field or use **Browse...** to locate the file you want to insert. Once the proper file name is in the File Selection window of this dialog box, click on **Link** to establish a link with the specified file. Notice that the Result window at the bottom of this dialog box changes to show the nature of the object relationship with PowerPoint. Click on **OK** to complete the process.

PowerPoint places the selected file or object into the current slide and establishes a link with that object. Now when you load this presentation, PowerPoint automatically checks the status of the selected object. If it has changed since you established the link, the new version of the object will be placed into the presentation.

You can check the status of the link at any time by using **Edit: Links...** to display the Links dialog box shown in Figure 8.3.

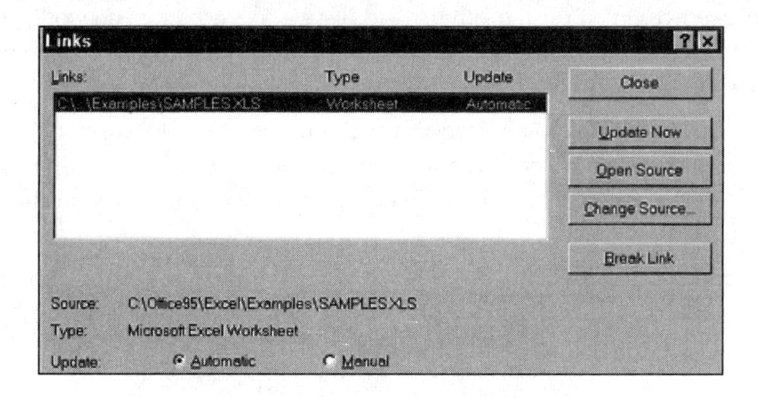

Figure 8.3 *Links dialog box in PowerPoint.*

Notice that this dialog box lists any current links, and it shows you the update setting (Automatic is the default). This dialog box provides facilities for updating the information, for launching the source application, or for breaking the link. You may want to use the **Update Now** button—even though Automatic Update is selected—to force an immediate update. You can wait and let the system update the linked information automatically, and the update shouldn't take too long. If you know it has changed (or you suspect it has), you can use the Links dialog box at any time to refresh the linked object or objects in your presentation. Simply select the name of the linked file as shown in the Links window of this dialog box, then click on **Update Now** to have the latest version inserted into your PowerPoint presentation.

There's another way to create a link in PowerPoint. You can shrink PowerPoint to an icon and launch the source application. Load the text or object you want to link and then use **Edit: Copy** to place a copy of it onto the Clipboard. Return to PowerPoint and make current the slide on which you want this object to appear. Now use **Edit: Paste Special...** to display the Paste Special dialog box shown in Figure 8.4.

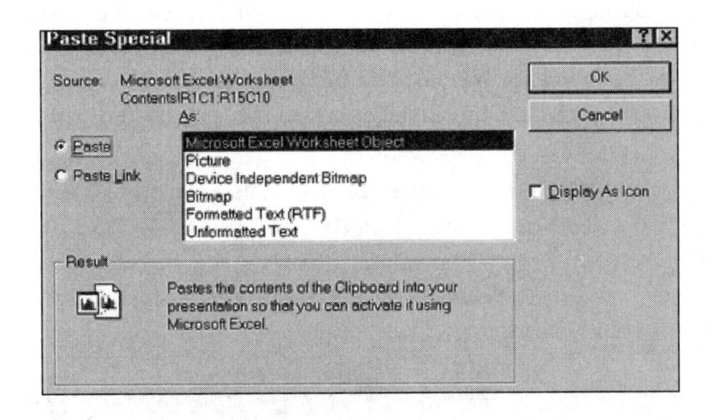

Figure 8.4 *Paste Special dialog box.*

The information displayed in the As window of this dialog changes with the type of object you have copied to the Clipboard. If PowerPoint knows about the source application, then you have the option of choosing either a straight Paste or a Paste Link by clicking on the appropriate button at the left of the dialog. If you are using older Windows software or a DOS application as the source, PowerPoint may not recognize the source. In this case, you will be given only the option of Paste; no link can be established through the Clipboard route.

If PowerPoint recognizes the source application (as with the sample in Figure 8.4), then you can choose **Paste Link** on this dialog box. When you do, the description in the Result area of the dialog box describes what happens when you insert an object in this way.

Whether you use **Insert: Object...** from the PowerPoint menu or use the **Copy** and **Paste Special...** technique, if the source application supports live links through OLE, then your PowerPoint presentation will be updated when the source object is modified.

I would like to discuss one more concept about PowerPoint objects, and then we'll go on to some specifics about using Microsoft Office products with PowerPoint. Suppose you have information on a slide that is embedded from another application. For example, you may have a WordPerfect document fragment that you want to edit. However, you don't have WordPerfect on your system—you only have Word.

You can use PowerPoint's conversion facility (actually a general Office facility) to convert the WordPerfect document to a Word document so that you can use Word to edit it. This same technique works with spreadsheet data and other embedded information, as long as the converter knows about both applications involved. If the embedded object comes from another user or another computer, for example, you may lack the facilities to edit it directly. PowerPoint may be able to convert it so that you can edit it.

Select the object and use **Edit: Linked Object** (the exact menu entry changes with the type of object selected). PowerPoint displays another menu level with a Convert... entry (the other entries on this menu will vary with the type of object you have selected). Click on **Convert...** to display the Convert dialog box shown in Figure 8.5.

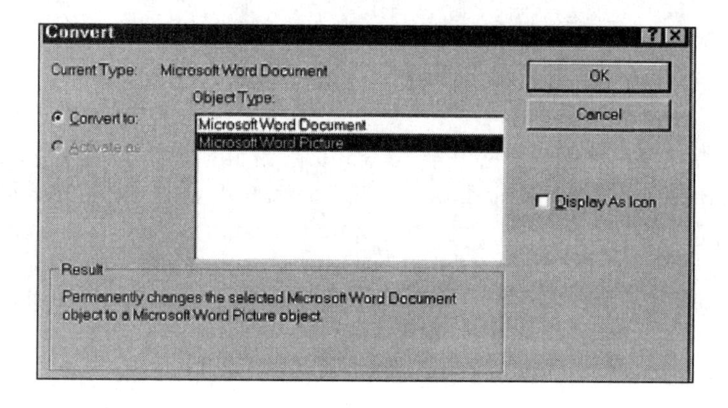

Figure 8.5 *Convert dialog box in PowerPoint.*

You will be given one or more options in the Object Type window of this dialog box. The exact choices you see depend on the source application for the selected object. Click on the application type which you want to convert the selected object to and click on **OK** to make the change. If the dialog box offers you the option of **Activate as**, then you can temporarily work with an object in the new format without changing it permanently.

You can use another technique to convert graphics objects into PowerPoint format so that you can use PowerPoint editing tools to manipulate the object.

Select the object you want to convert, and then use **Draw: Ungroup** to break the link with the source application and to separate the object into component parts. You will see the somewhat ominous message in Figure 8.6.

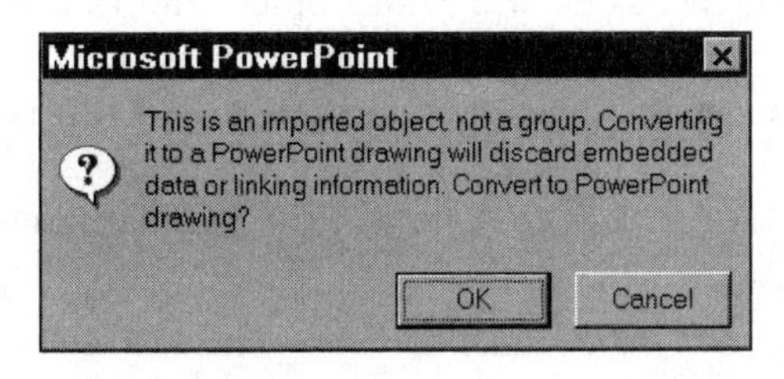

Figure 8.6 *Imported object warning from Draw: Ungroup.*

Click on **OK** to continue with the ungroup process. The display will change, showing many objects selected as individual components of the main image (if there are, indeed, multiple components in the imported object). If you want to work with individual components, you can click anywhere on the slide to deselect the individual objects. If, on the other hand, you want to work with the complete object in PowerPoint as a group, then use **Draw: Group** to regroup the object components as a PowerPoint group. The link with the source application is not reestablished. You only gather the object components together as a single object inside PowerPoint.

NOTE

If a complex object becomes ungrouped and you want to put it back together, don't try selecting each object sequentially. Use the mouse pointer to draw a box around the entire object. When you release the left mouse button all of the components of the object are selected. To select only some of the objects to assemble them as a group, hold down the **Shift** key and click on the objects you want to select.

If you want to edit the object, use standard PowerPoint editing procedures by selecting the object or one of its components and then making the changes you wish. If the object includes text, you can add or change text from the keyboard. Graphics objects can be moved, rotated, and so on by grabbing them with the mouse and by using the features of the Draw menu and Drawing toolbars.

Using PowerPoint with Excel

Microsoft Excel has been a popular spreadsheet for some time. It has been a strong contender against Lotus 1-2-3 and other competitors. In this chapter, when I talk about Excel, I mean Microsoft Excel version 7.0. It is the latest version of this venerable spreadsheet package and the one that is shipping with the latest version of the Office package. With the new features of version 7 and its inclusion in the Office package, look for Excel to gain even more user support.

If you aren't using a spreadsheet, then you likely won't see any immediate use for this part of your Office suite. However, in this section I'd like to introduce the concept of spreadsheets, show you about Excel specifically, and discuss how you might use the Excel/PowerPoint combination.

Why Spreadsheets?

As I showed you earlier in this book, PowerPoint includes a fairly competent graphing utility that is based on the Excel spreadsheet model. A full-fledged spreadsheet program, however, goes far beyond this simple graphing utility.

A spreadsheet program is based on a ledger concept where there are multiple rows and columns separated by thin lines. You can write text or numbers into any of the resulting cells defined by the crossing horizontal and vertical lines. On a paper ledger, you establish your own headings, enter the numbers, then use a calculator to add up the rows and columns.

With a spreadsheet program such as Excel, you establish your own headings and enter numbers. Then you use the built-in features of the software to add rows and columns, compute interest or payments, figure depreciation, predict income, and more. An electronic spreadsheet can serve the same functions as your familiar hand-kept ledger, except that it also has built-in intelligence to help with the math. A spreadsheet package is an excellent "what if" calculator, because once you set up the cell relationships, you can change one or more data entries and have all of the cells that depend on this data change automatically.

You can have Excel draw graphs and charts based on the data in your cells, and you can use Excel's fonts and other spreadsheet formatting features to make the most of the data you present. And, once you have an Excel spreadsheet designed the way you want it, you can import all or part of it into PowerPoint to illustrate a concept or make a point.

Why would you want to use Excel instead of PowerPoint's built-in graphing feature? You may already have the data and graphs you need in Excel, for one thing. Whenever you retype data you run the risk of introducing errors, and, if the data is complicated, it can take a long time to reenter it. There may be spreadsheet features you want to use in Excel that PowerPoint simply doesn't offer. That's the main reason for having multiple applications in the first place. You can use spreadsheet information from any Windows-compliant spreadsheet. You can even copy and paste or export and import spreadsheet information from a product that doesn't support object linking. Whatever the reason, there will likely be times when you will want to incorporate Excel information into a PowerPoint spreadsheet. I'll show you how to do that in this chapter.

Why Excel?

So why use Excel with PowerPoint? For one thing, Excel and PowerPoint are both Microsoft products. As such, they have a very similar appearance. The user interface for each will be familiar to you if you learn only one of the products well. This similar user interface lets you easily do in-place editing of Excel data while you are actually inside PowerPoint.

In addition, these two products work well together. Microsoft has implemented OLE 2.0 in Excel and PowerPoint, making the sharing of data between them particularly easy and reliable. Excel is relatively easy to learn and to use, but remember that when you launch an Excel editing window, you are working inside a full-featured, powerful application that is integrated with, but separate from, PowerPoint. Showing you how to use all the features of Excel is beyond the scope of this book, but I'll show you some of the more salient features in the next section of this chapter. As you gain experience and confidence with Excel, you will tap into more and more of its features.

Embedding an Excel Object

You can link or embed an Excel spreadsheet (or a portion of a spreadsheet) with a PowerPoint slide right from the PowerPoint Standard toolbar. (See the discussions on linking objects in PowerPoint earlier in this chapter and on how to link Excel objects in the next section.)

To embed an Excel spreadsheet, make the slide on which you want Excel data to appear the current slide. Then click on the **Insert Microsoft Excel Worksheet** icon on the Standard toolbar. PowerPoint pulls down a grid similar to a Microsoft Word table. (In fact, a Word table and an imported Excel spreadsheet can be very similar.) Specify the shape of the spreadsheet you want to insert by holding down the left mouse button and selecting as many cells (rows and columns) as you want to insert. This provides PowerPoint with the basic format you want to use. This is only a guide to help size the initial spreadsheet. You can change the number of rows and cells later if you wish.

When you release the mouse button, PowerPoint locates Excel and launches an editing window that lets you interact with Excel from inside PowerPoint. As you can see from Figure 8.7, the menu bars and toolbars also change. Although the main title bar still says Microsoft PowerPoint and your presentation slide is still on the screen, you are actually working in Excel at this moment. The Excel Forms toolbar is displayed right on the PowerPoint slide beside the Excel spreadsheet.

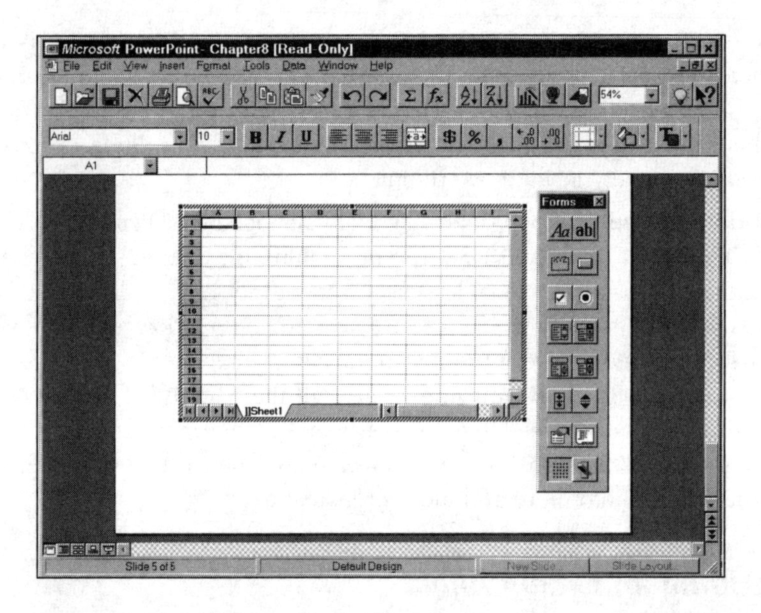

Figure 8.7 *Excel Editing window, menu, and toolbars in PowerPoint with labels.*

In addition, you can use the **Insert: Object...** menu sequence and specify a Microsoft Excel 7 object from the Insert Object dialog box. In this case, PowerPoint picks a default size for the spreadsheet and places it on the current slide for you. You can grab a sizing handle and adjust the size of the grid to fit your current application. These two procedures—the Toolbar icon and the Insert

Object dialog box—produce the same results. In both cases you are embedding an Excel spreadsheet into the current slide.

Note that even though you may have specified the shape of the spreadsheet segment to insert into your slide, you can grab one of the sizing handles on a spreadsheet border and drag the spreadsheet to any size and shape you want. Because you are working with Excel, this small window is actually a pane into a massive grid of cells, formulas, and other features that you have at your disposal.

However, there are some limitations inherent in this application link. Although the full Excel menu and toolbar are presented with the spreadsheet, some of these items don't function and some of the menu items actually belong to PowerPoint. For example, you can't load an existing spreadsheet into the spreadsheet form on your PowerPoint slide, nor can you save the spreadsheet you create on your PowerPoint slide as a separate Excel file. These are potentially confusing aspects of working through OLE 2.0 with embedded objects. Once you get the hang of how this works, however, it seems fairly natural.

Once the spreadsheet form is inserted onto your slide, you can begin to enter data, create formulas, format the cells, and so on. Suppose you want to create a spreadsheet that shows regional sales information. In this case you, want to show the actual numbers in a spreadsheet grid rather than a graphical representation such as a chart. A finished spreadsheet on a PowerPoint slide is shown in Figure 8.8.

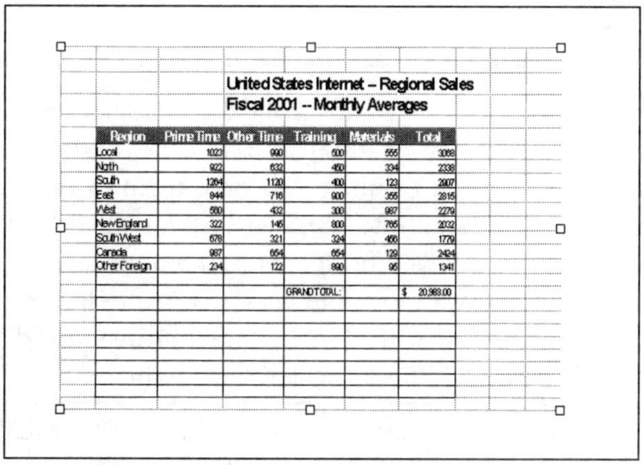

United States Internet – Regional Sales
Fiscal 2001 -- Monthly Averages

Region	Prime Time	Other Time	Training	Materials	Total
Local	1023	990	500	555	3068
North	922	632	450	334	2338
South	1264	1120	400	123	2907
East	844	716	900	355	2815
West	560	432	300	987	2279
New England	322	146	800	765	2032
South West	678	321	324	456	1779
Canada	987	654	654	129	2424
Other Foreign	234	122	890	95	1341
			GRAND TOTAL:		$ 20,983.00

Figure 8.8 *Finished Regional Sales spreadsheet.*

To create this sample sales spreadsheet, use the **Excel** icon on the Standard toolbar or the Insert Object dialog box to place a blank Excel spreadsheet onto the current slide.

Click in cell D3 (or anywhere near the center of the grid you have defined) to place the insertion point, then type the title of the spreadsheet:

United States Internet—Regional Sales

Depending on your screen configuration, the information you type can be quite small. However, the data you enter in a cell is duplicated at the top of the screen just under the Format bar. This lets you see what you type easily.

Press the down arrow or use the mouse to click in cell D4 to reset the insertion point, then enter the subtitle:

Fiscal 2001—Monthly Averages

Now enter the column titles. Start by moving the insertion point to Cell B6, then enter the column titles in adjacent cells:

Region/Prime Time/Other Time/Training/Materials/Total

These titles will occupy Cells B6 through G6 if you follow the guidelines I have suggested. Of course you can enter these column titles over any other set of columns you choose, in which case the cell addresses might be different.

You can either press the right arrow after entering data in each cell to move to the next column, or you can use the mouse to position the insertion point each time.

Notice that some of the titles seem not to fit the cells because the default cell width is too narrow to hold all of the text. You can use the mouse pointer to grab the vertical lines between columns and drag them to the width you want. Simply move the insertion point into the area of the spreadsheet that holds the alphabetic letter column labels (the left-most column is Column A, next is Column B, and so on). As you move the cursor over the line it changes from a broad cross to a narrow cross with double-ended arrows. Hold the left mouse button and drag any lines you want to widen the columns.

Some screen configurations (such as 640 x 480) make the spreadsheet extremely small. If you find you can't work with the small display, you could create the chart in Excel, then insert the finished sheet into a PowerPoint slide.

Next, you want to center the text in the columns for a more pleasing appearance. To do this, select all of the cells that hold column titles by placing the mouse pointer over the first cell, holding down the left mouse button, and dragging the highlight over the range of title cells. Now use **Format: Cells** to display the Format Cells dialog box shown in Figure 8.9.

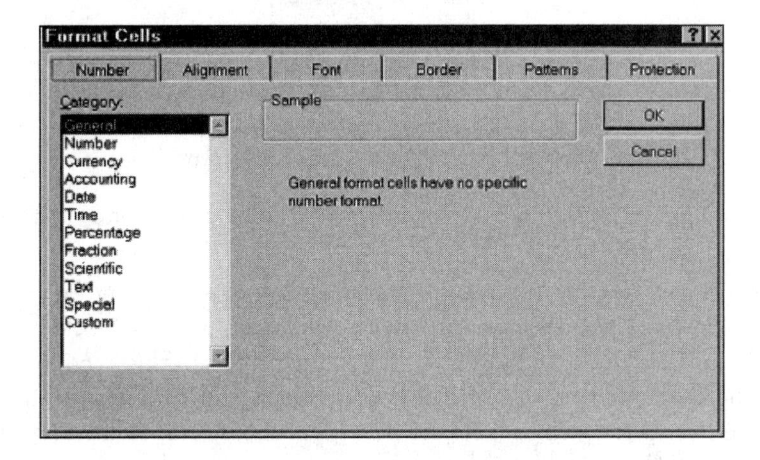

Figure 8.9 *Format Cells dialog box.*

Click on the **Alignment** tab to make the Alignment choices accessible. Click on **Center** under Horizontal alignment and then click on **OK**. This centers the text within each of the cells.

You can also use the Format bar **Center** button (similar to the Center button on the PowerPoint Format bar) to center the selected text.

While the text on the header line is still highlighted, let's enlarge the text and change its attributes. As you can see from the Format bar at the top of the screen, the default is Arial font at a 10-point size. Click on the down arrow beside the Point Size field and choose **14 points**. You may have to enlarge some of the cells once more to make the text fit.

Click on the **Bold** button on the Format bar to set the selected text in boldface. Now, while this text is still selected, let's color the background. Click on the down arrow beside the Fill Color icon on the toolbar (the tipping bucket icon) to display the Color Selection dialog box shown in Figure 8.10.

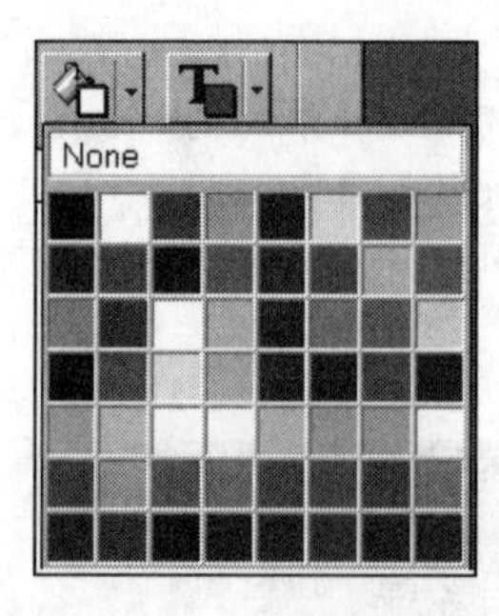

Figure 8.10 *Color Selection dialog box.*

Choose the light blue color on the top row of this dialog box (or any other color you like).

Next, pull down the Text Color Selection dialog by clicking on the down arrow beside the Text Color button (the large T with a color block beside it.) Choose **white** for the text. Now you have a light blue background with white text for the header bar on this spreadsheet segment. Select the text in the title at the top of the spreadsheet and make it 18-point bold. This will make the title stand out from the rest of the spreadsheet.

Now we'll add grids to the body of the spreadsheet and also enter sample data to match the figure. Use the mouse to select the section of the spreadsheet defined by the range B7..G25. To do this, place the insertion point in Cell B7, hold down the left button, and drag the highlight across the grid to Cell G25.

Use **Format: Cells** (**Ctrl-1**) to display the Format Cells dialog box shown in Figure 8.11.

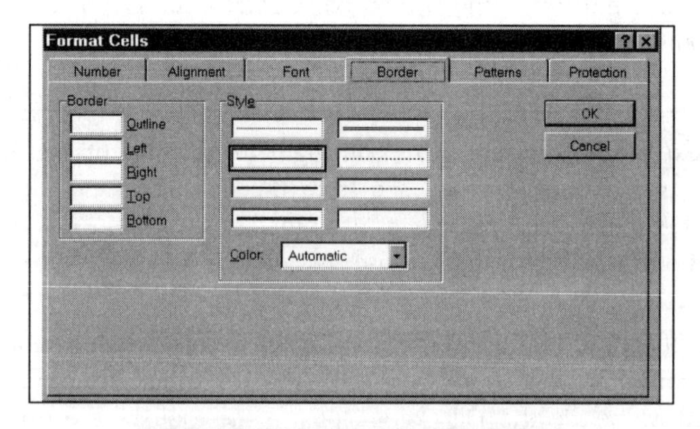

Figure 8.11 *Format Cells dialog box.*

Click on the **Border** tab to bring it to the front of the dialog box. Click on **Left**, **Right**, **Top**, and **Bottom** to place a border around every cell in the selected range. Click on **OK** to close the Format Cells dialog box.

Click in **Cell B7** to place the insertion point in that cell. Now let's enter data for the Region column of the spreadsheet. In Cell B7, type **Local**. Press the down arrow to move the cell pointer to Cell B8. In this cell, type **North**. Continue in this way, adding region names in this column as follows:

B7	Local
B8	North
B9	South
B10	East
B11	West
B12	New England
B13	South West
B14	Canada
B15	Other Foreign

Now select the cell range B7..B17 and use the pull-down Font Size list on the Format bar to enlarge the text to 12 points. Use the mouse pointer to enlarge the B column, if necessary, so that all of the text fits within the column.

Next, enter numerical data to represent dollar sales from each of these regions for each of the sales types listed at the head of the columns. You can enter the numbers I used, or make up your own. Of course, you can also use different column headings if you want to make this sample spreadsheet match a business or other application that is closer to something you might actually use. One of my businesses is indeed U.S. Internet, and we sell online time to Internet users. (The figures you see are strictly fictional, however.)

When you have numbers in every cell of the range C7..F15, insert a formula to add up totals by region in the Total column. Click in cell G7 to place the insertion point in that cell. Now type the following:

+SUM(C7..F7)

Press **Enter**. The sum of all the numbers in row 7 should appear in cell G7 (3068 in my example). The next step is to copy this formula down the G column so that all the rows will be added into totals. To do this, use **Edit: Copy** to place a copy of the formula in cell G7 onto the Clipboard.

Next, use the mouse to select the range of cells G8..G15. Use **Edit: Paste** to copy the formula to that range. Notice that Excel automatically adjusts the cell references so that the formula in each cell in column G refers to the cells in the row just to the left of the formula. The row totals should appear in the cells in column G, as shown in Figure 8.12.

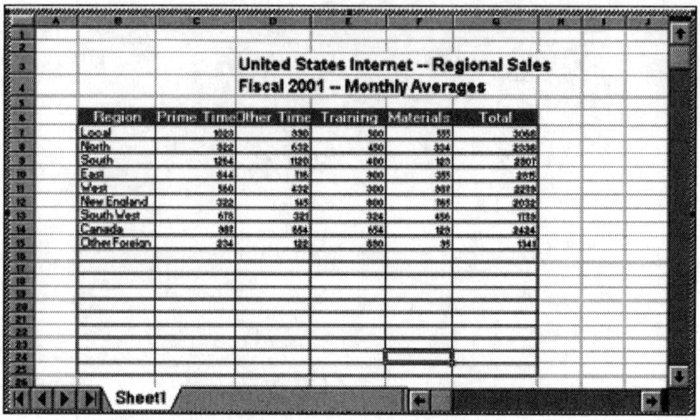

United States Internet -- Regional Sales
Fiscal 2001 -- Monthly Averages

Region	Prime Time	Other Time	Training	Materials	Total
Local	[illegible]	[illegible]	[illegible]	[illegible]	[illegible]
North	[illegible]	[illegible]	[illegible]	[illegible]	[illegible]
South	[illegible]	[illegible]	[illegible]	[illegible]	[illegible]
East	[illegible]	[illegible]	[illegible]	[illegible]	[illegible]
West	[illegible]	[illegible]	[illegible]	[illegible]	[illegible]
New England	[illegible]	[illegible]	[illegible]	[illegible]	[illegible]
South West	[illegible]	[illegible]	[illegible]	[illegible]	[illegible]
Canada	[illegible]	[illegible]	[illegible]	[illegible]	[illegible]
Other Foreign	[illegible]	[illegible]	[illegible]	[illegible]	[illegible]

Sheet1

Figure 8.12 *Spreadsheet with G column totals.*

Finally, we want to compute a grand total by adding up the totals for each row into a cell at the bottom of the G column. Click in cell E17 to place the insertion point in that cell, then type **GRAND TOTAL:** and press **Enter**. Click in cell G17, then click on the **SUM** button on the Excel toolbar. Excel suggests a formula in cell G17. Press **Enter** to accept the formula. The sum of the subtotals in column G is displayed in cell G17.

Format the Grand Total value for currency by clicking on the **dollar sign** on the Format bar. When the formatting changes, you may see a series of pound signs (#) in cell G17. This is because the resulting number, with its dollar sign and decimal places, is too long to fit inside the cell width. To correct the problem, simply grab the right column divider at the top of the column and drag the column width so it will accommodate the large number. Select cells E17..G17 and click on the **Bold** button on the Format bar to make the Grand Total title and numerical value bold.

Now you have the completed spreadsheet on a PowerPoint slide that I first showed you earlier in this section. Click anywhere outside the spreadsheet area of your slide to close Excel and leave the spreadsheet embedded in the current slide. You can double-click on the slide to reopen the Excel editor and make changes to the spreadsheet at any time, but this spreadsheet exists only inside your PowerPoint slide. You can't load it as a separate file in Excel. If you want to link an Excel spreadsheet to a PowerPoint slide, read the next section.

Linking an Excel Spreadsheet to PowerPoint

You can link an Excel spreadsheet to a PowerPoint slide in the same way you can link other external objects to PowerPoint. Make the slide you want to hold the Excel data the current slide, then use **Insert: Object...** and click on **Create from File** on the Insert Object dialog box. PowerPoint displays a File Name window. You can enter a path and Excel spreadsheet file name, or use **Browse...** to locate the spreadsheet you want to link to PowerPoint. For this example, let's use one of the sample files that came with Excel. Use **Browse...** or type the path and file name:

```
C:\Excel\examples\samples.xls
```

Now, click on the **Link** button to establish a link as opposed to an embedded relationship between PowerPoint and the Excel spreadsheet. Then click on **OK** to close this dialog box and insert the specified spreadsheet onto the PowerPoint slide.

NOTE

This operation requires ample RAM memory and plenty of hard disk storage. A link with a large spreadsheet can still be a slow process.

The spreadsheet specified is an interactive application that includes Excel macros that can respond to user input. The link to Excel is a live one, so if you or someone else changes the spreadsheet in Excel, these changes appear in PowerPoint. And, you can launch Excel and use the interactive aspects of the spreadsheet inside Excel. This technique adds another interactive level to your PowerPoint presentations. You can either display the Excel data as it is on the PowerPoint slide, or you can click on one of the interactive buttons to launch Excel and step through that program if you wish.

When you are through with Excel, use **File: Exit** to close Excel and return to the PowerPoint slide. You can also edit a spreadsheet at any time by double-clicking anywhere inside the linked spreadsheet on your PowerPoint slide. PowerPoint launches Excel with all of its features. Make the edits, be sure to use **File: Save** to store the changed version of the spreadsheet, then use **File: Exit** to return to PowerPoint.

You can do a lot more with Excel in PowerPoint, but you'll have to read your Excel user's guide to learn more about how to use Excel.

Using PowerPoint with Word 7

If Microsoft Word is your window into your computer, the transition to PowerPoint should be easy because the screens of the two applications are very similar. You can't use PowerPoint directly from inside Word, but the similarity of the two packages and the close integration between them will help you get the most from both of these members of your Office package. There are several ways to use Word directly with PowerPoint right from the PowerPoint toolbar.

Using PowerPoint Report It

Suppose you have prepared all or most of a presentation within PowerPoint, but you'd like to develop a more complete outline using the features of Microsoft Word. Simply click on the **Report It** button on the PowerPoint toolbar. (See Figure 8.13. The location of this and all toolbar buttons may be different depending on whether you have customized your copy of PowerPoint.)

Figure 8.13 *Report It button on PowerPoint toolbar.*

PowerPoint automatically launches Word and opens the current presentation outline. You can do this from within any view (except Slide Show) in PowerPoint. The current PowerPoint outline view of your presentation is inserted as a Word 7 document (see Figure 8.14).

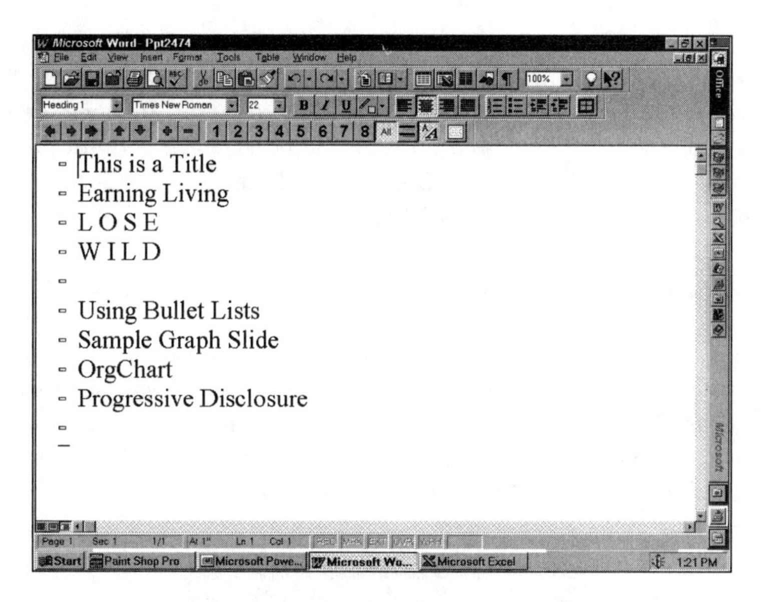

Figure 8.14 *PowerPoint outline in Word 7.*

NOTE

The PowerPoint outline view has one limitation: only text that is inserted on a slide in a preformatted title or as a bullet list will appear in the outline. When you get to Word you can create more outline text and levels. Word supports up to ten outline levels, whereas PowerPoint supports only six. Any outline entries beyond level six in Word are imported into PowerPoint as level six.

NOTE

If a particular slide doesn't have any title text or bullet text, you can still have something from the slide appear on a PowerPoint outline. Use **Format: Slide Layout** to display the Slide Layout dialog box. Choose a layout that includes a title by selecting the layout and clicking on **Apply** or by double-clicking on the layout. (The next-to-last layout has a title only and won't interfere with anything else on the current slide.) Click to add a title, then select the text and use **Format: Font** to specify a color that is the same as the slide background. The title won't appear on the slide but it will show up in the outline.

When you have finished editing the PowerPoint outline in Word, you can export it to PowerPoint by using **File: Save As...** and choosing **Rich Text Format** (RTF). This is the format PowerPoint uses to import Word outlines. When you restart PowerPoint, use **File: Open** and specify the .RTF file you just saved. You can also use the **Insert: Slides from Outline File** menu sequence to bring the Word-created outline into PowerPoint.

Creating Outlines in Word

If outlining is a familiar tool for you and you are accustomed to working in Word 7, you may find it easier to start your outline and begin slide show creation in Word 7. Launch Word and use **View: Outline** to turn on the outline view. Now use standard Word features to create an outline of a presentation. Figure 8.15 shows a sample Word slide show outline.

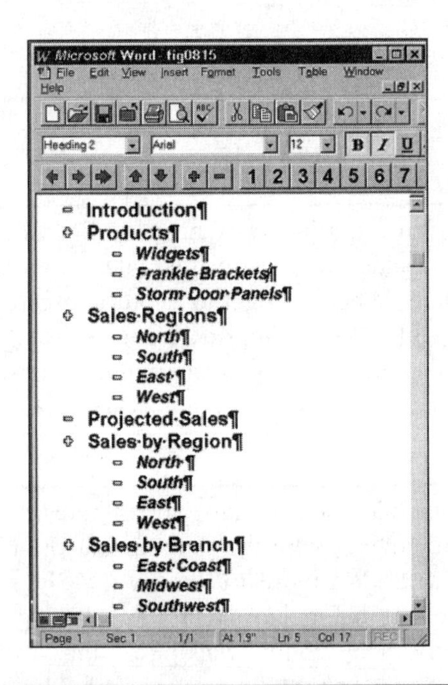

Figure 8.15 *Word sample slide show outline.*

For the outline to translate properly into PowerPoint, you should use Heading 1 style for the top level of the outline, Heading 2 style for the second level, and so on. Once you have the outline arranged the way you want it, you can export it to PowerPoint to serve as the basis of a new slide show by saving the Word outline in RTF, then opening the file in PowerPoint. You will have a basic set of slides with titles and bullet lists.

Once you have the basic slide show created, you can add templates, backgrounds, clip art, and more to enhance the basic presentation. To do this, first create the outline in Word. Use **File: Save as...** and choose **Rich Text Format** from the Save File as Type field. You can save this file in any directory you wish. It is a temporary file that you won't need once you get your presentation started in PowerPoint.

Close Word and open PowerPoint. Use **File: Open... (Ctrl-O)** in PowerPoint to display the Open dialog box (see Figure 8.16).

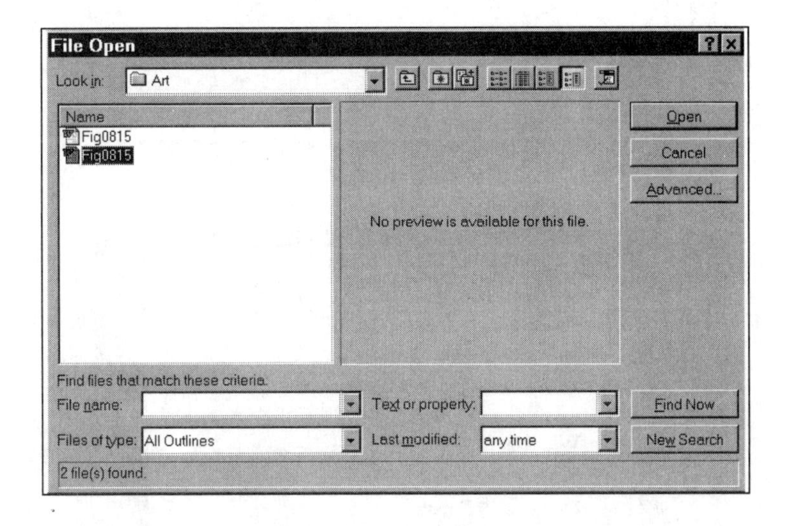

Figure 8.16 *PowerPoint Open dialog box.*

Pull down the Files of Type list and choose **Outlines**. Select the directory where you saved the Word outline in the Directories section of this dialog box. Choose the file you used to store your Word outline and click on **OK**. PowerPoint opens the file in Outline view, as shown in Figure 8.17.

Now use **View: Slides** to see how the Word outline is converted to a PowerPoint slide show. Figure 8.18 shows the outline in Slide view. As you can see, there is no special formatting, but the basic outline information is there and the beginnings of a slide show are complete.

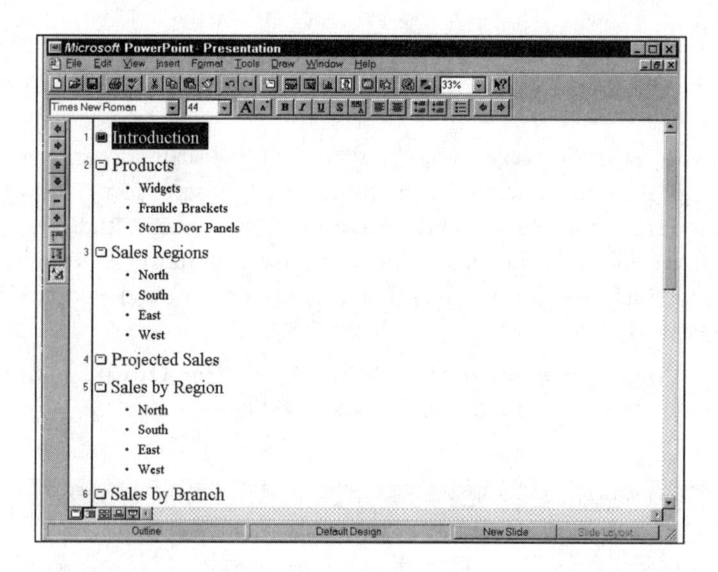

Figure 8.17 *Word outline in PowerPoint Outline view.*

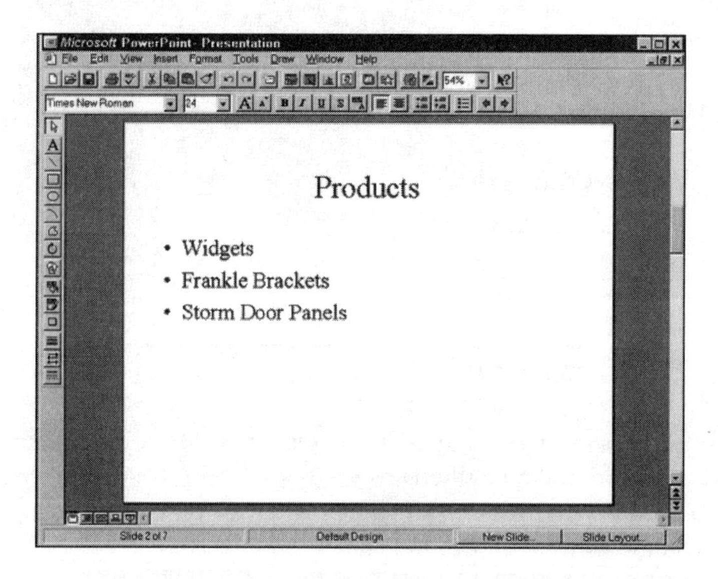

Figure 8.18 *Word outline in PowerPoint Slide view.*

Notice that the top level entries in the Word outline are used for the titles of the slides and the subordinate items are used as bullet lists. The basic slide format chosen automatically by PowerPoint is the one on top of the second column of the Slide Layout dialog box (title over a bullet list).

You can change this basic layout easily by using **Format: Slide Layout...** to display the Slide Layout dialog box. Choose a layout that includes a title and a bullet list, plus any other objects you want to include. PowerPoint places the title and bullet list from the outline into their proper position, and places other objects—such as room for clip art—onto the slide as well.

Add the new objects, choose a template or background, and otherwise enhance the basic slide design you created with the Word outline. Be sure to save the slide presentation as a PowerPoint file. Otherwise you lose the additional formatting.

Creating a Word Table

Microsoft Word has a strong table creating utility. PowerPoint can use this Word feature to insert a table onto a slide. To insert a Word table onto the current slide, click on the **Insert Word Table** icon (see Figure 8.19).

Figure 8.19 *Insert Word Table icon.*

PowerPoint pulls down a dummy table form, just like in Word, to let you select the number of rows and columns. Figure 8.20 shows this basic table form.

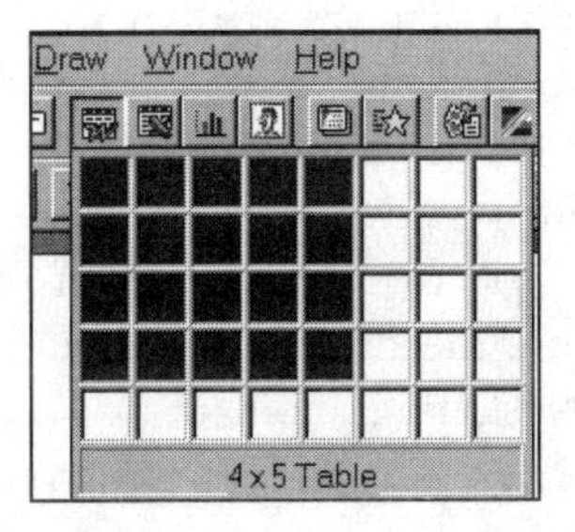

Figure 8.20 *Pull-down table form in PowerPoint.*

Place the mouse pointer inside the pull-down table and drag to define the type of table you want. When you have the number of rows and columns you want specified, release the mouse button. PowerPoint opens a Table Editing window on the current slide, as shown in Figure 8.21.

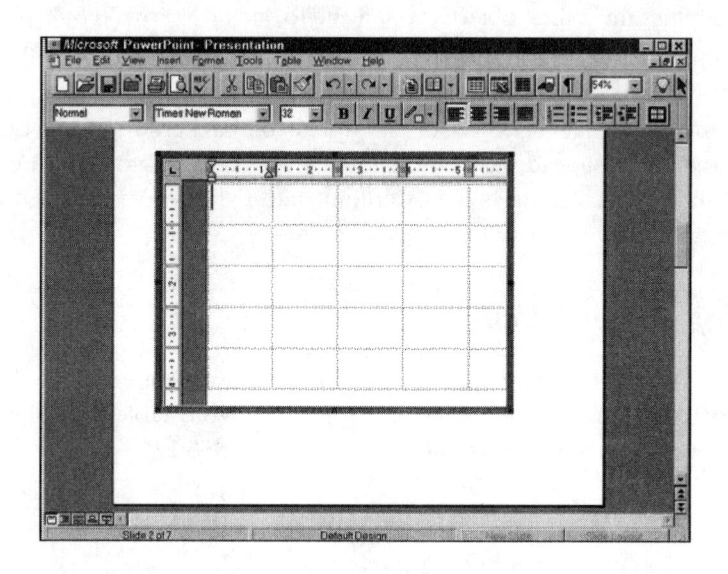

Figure 8.21 *Table Editing window on a PowerPoint slide.*

Although you are working inside PowerPoint, you actually are accessing the table features of Word through an OLE 2.0 link and a feature called in-place editing. Notice that the Format bar at the top of the slide screen changes to the Word toolbar. In addition, if Word is already open in Windows, you will see other toolbars and formatting that are current in the open version of Word. Some Word features may not function as you expect in this situation. If you are working with an outline in Word when you insert a table into PowerPoint, for example, the outline toolbar would be displayed. However, if you tried to use the outline toolbar features, you would get an error message such as "This command is not available because the document is being edited in another application." This is a potentially frustrating anomaly that comes with working with in-place editing through OLE 2.0.

Also, while you are working with Word through PowerPoint, the toolbar choices (when you click the right mouse button while pointing to any currently displayed toolbar) are different from those you find in PowerPoint. If the action you want to conduct is compatible with the PowerPoint environment, then the tools function just as they would in Word. When working with tables in PowerPoint, for example, you can insert borders or shading into a table cell with the Borders toolbar from Word. Just point to the Format bar, click the right mouse button, and click on **Borders** on the pull-down menu. This inserts the Borders toolbar into PowerPoint.

You can achieve the same effect with the **Insert: Microsoft Word Table...** command from the main PowerPoint menu. When you use this method, PowerPoint displays the Insert Word Table dialog box shown in Figure 8.22.

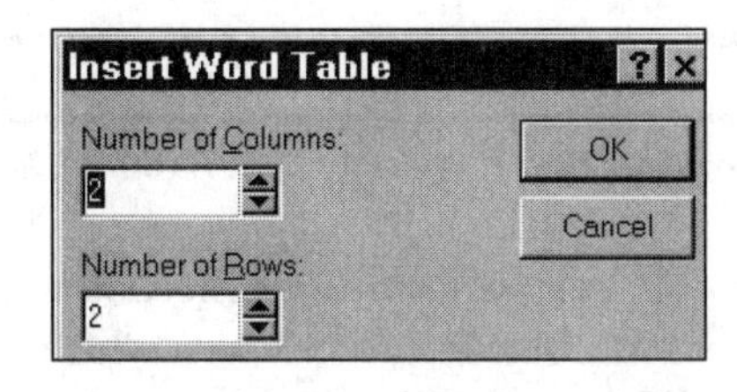

Figure 8.22 *Insert Word Table dialog box.*

If you have already inserted a Word table during the current session, PowerPoint's menu reads Insert/Repeat Insert Microsoft Word Table, and if you click it, it repeats the previous table size as a default.

Specify the number of columns and the number of rows you want for the table in this dialog box. This creates a table in the same way as using the pull-down table form from the PowerPoint Standard toolbar. When the table is specified as you want it, click on **OK** to close the dialog box and display the Table Editing window on the current slide.

In addition, you can choose a slide with a table placeholder from the Slide Layout dialog box. Click on the icon when PowerPoint prompts you to "Double-click to add table." The Insert Word Table dialog box shown in Figure 8.22 is displayed. Proceed as described above.

Enter the text you want into each cell of the table. You can use standard text formatting procedures for the table elements. This includes selecting the font, specifying font attributes (bold, underline, etc.), and choosing positioning (left, center, right). Figure 8.23 shows a sample table after the data has been entered.

Region	Widgets	Frankle Brackets	Storm Doors
North	9,600	19,200	57,600
East	1,200	2,400	4,800
South	300	600	1,200

Figure 8.23 *Completed PowerPoint table.*

You can also insert clip art images from the collection supplied with Microsoft Office. Position the insertion point in the cell into which you want to insert an image. Then use **Insert: Object** to display the Insert Object dialog box. Choose the **Create from File** tab. Choose the file name you want and click on **OK** (or double-click on the file name) to close the dialog box and insert the image into the current cell in the PowerPoint table editor.

NOTE

Once you have inserted a picture into a PowerPoint table, you can drag it to another cell if you wish. You can even drag it outside the table and place it onto the main body of the slide.

PowerPoint automatically selects a cell size for a new table, but you can change that if you wish. Simply move the mouse pointer into the leftmost column of the Table Editing window. Notice that as you move the pointer up and down this column, the pointer changes to a double-ended arrow as it moves across the boundaries between rows. Hold down the left mouse button when the pointer changes to an arrow, and drag the line that separates rows to change the height of any row. You can't make the row any narrower than the height of the current font, and in no case any narrower than about a 32-point font. But you can make the row much wider if you wish. You can also change the width of any table cell by dragging the line that separates columns to the width you want. You can't make the column any narrower than one character wide.

Although the Table Editing window shows a grid of lines around table cells, when you exit the Editing window (and leave Word) PowerPoint inserts the edited table into the current slide without the grid lines. If you want the table to appear on your slide with the grid lines, select the cell or cells that you want to have a border, and then click on the **Borders** tool on the Format bar. This will display the Borders toolbar.

From the icons on the Borders toolbar, choose the type of table border you want. This is the same process as choosing a paragraph border within Microsoft Word. You can also add shading with this same toolbar. The default is clear, but you can choose from a range all the way from solid (100%) shading to a light (5%) shading. Figure 8.24 shows the drop-down shading menu from the Borders toolbar. Notice that the type and pattern of shading is displayed in the small box to the left of each shading name on this pull-down list.

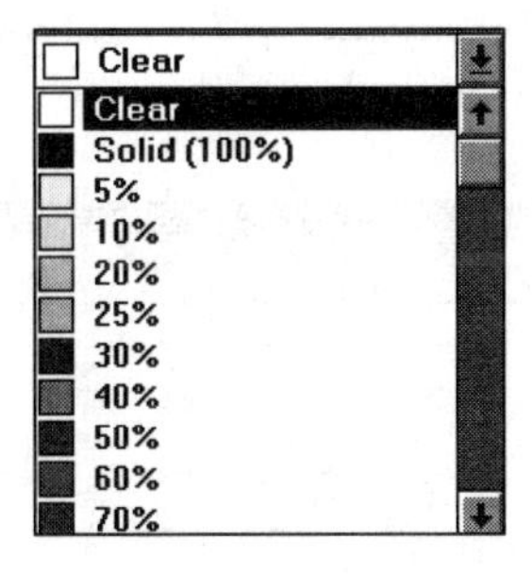

Figure 8.24 *Shading pull-down list from Borders toolbar.*

In addition, you can specify some unusual shading formats such as dark vertical or dark trellis. These choices add another level of pattern to the shading.

Because you are really working with features of Microsoft Word, the main menu changes to reflect Word features. So, to make additional changes to the table format, pull down the Table menu from the main menu bar, shown in Figure 8.25.

To design a custom table with shading, grid lines, and more, click on **Table AutoFormat...** to display the AutoFormat dialog box shown in Figure 8.26.

When you have the format of the table as you want it, click on **OK**, then click anywhere outside the Table Editing window to close the table editor and insert the finished table onto the current slide. When you close the Table Editing window, the Word menus and toolbars are removed and the standard PowerPoint screen appears.

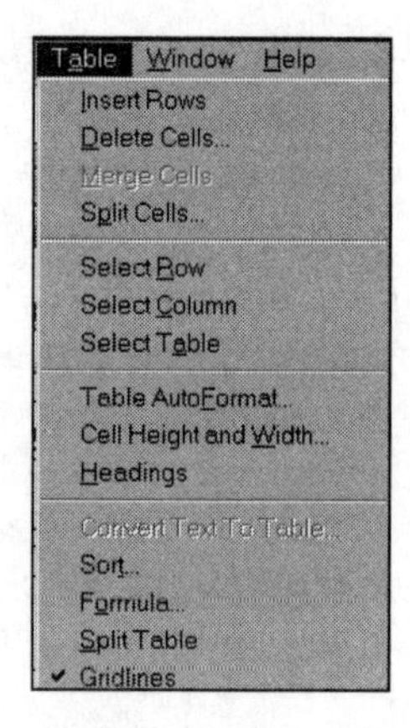

Figure 8.25 *Pull-down Table menu from menu bar.*

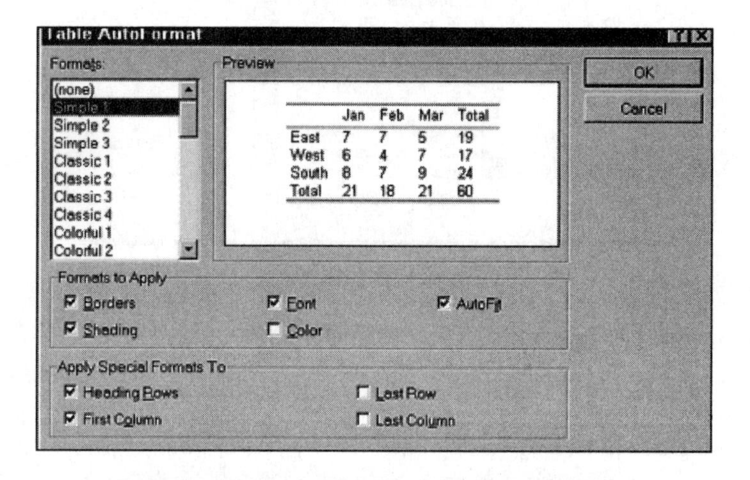

Figure 8.26 *Word Table AutoFormat dialog box.*

You can size the resulting table by selecting it and dragging a sizing handle. You can reposition the table by selecting it and dragging it to a new location on the current slide. If you change your mind and want to remove a table, select it by clicking once anywhere in the table area, then press the **Del** key.

Once a table is inserted onto a PowerPoint slide, you can edit it at any time by double-clicking on the table. PowerPoint automatically launches the Word table facility and opens a Table Editing window. Proceed as described above to make any changes or additions you wish to the selected table.

Creating Drill Down Documents

With linked applications such as those in the Microsoft Office group, you can use one program as the main interface into your computer, yet access the features and files from one or more other applications. A Drill Down document is one that lets you access additional layers of information from external applications. To create a Drill Down document in PowerPoint with Microsoft Word, make the slide on which you want to show additional information current. Next, use the **Insert: Object...** menu sequence to display the Insert Object dialog, shown in Figure 8.27.

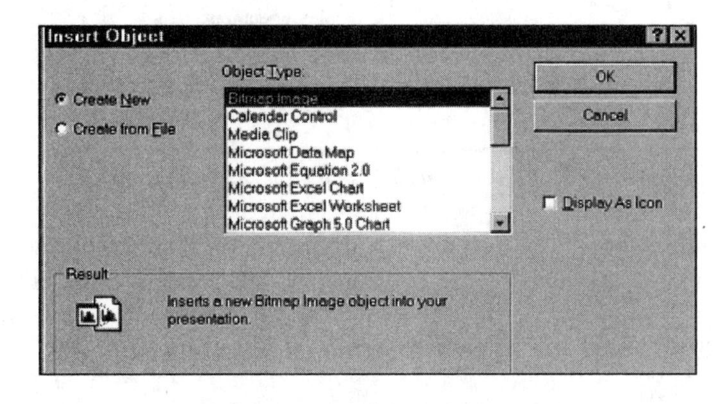

Figure 8.27 *Insert Object dialog box.*

Click on the **Create from File** button to open the File Selection window on this dialog box. Select the Word document you want to use as a Drill Down document on this slide.

NOTE

If you're not sure where the file you want is located, click on **Browse...** to open the Browse dialog box. This will make it easier to locate the directory and file you want to use.

Click on the **Display As Icon** button, then click on **OK** to return to the slide. PowerPoint inserts an icon onto your slide that represents the specified Word file. Figure 8.28 shows a slide that holds a Word document icon for use as a Drill Down document.

You can drag the document icon anywhere on the slide you wish. When you click on the slide outside the document icon, PowerPoint deselects the icon and makes it appear as an integral part of the slide.

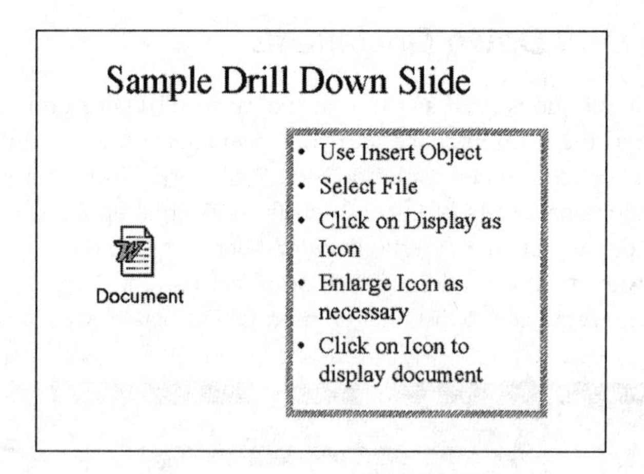

Figure 8.28 *PowerPoint slide with Drill Down document icon.*

During a presentation, the icon appears on the slide. When you want to display the additional information contained in the Word document represented by the icon, simply double-click on the icon to open the document, as shown in Figure 8.29.

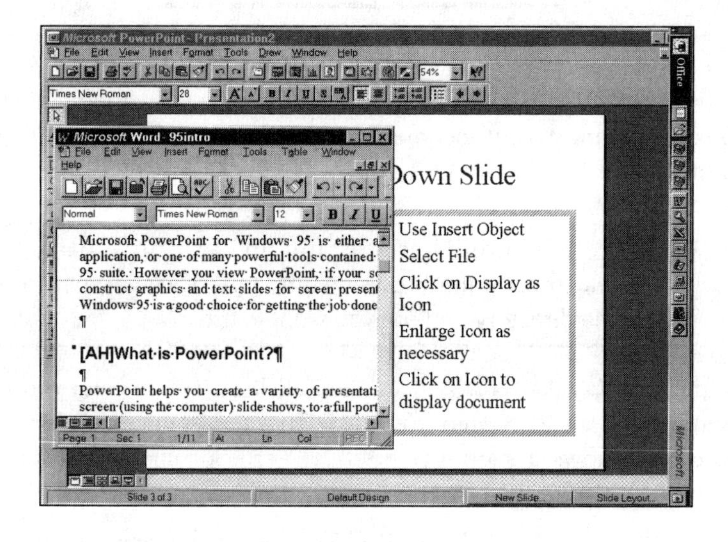

Figure 8.29 *PowerPoint slide with open Word document.*

NOTE

With some screen configurations, Word may launch in full-screen mode, covering up PowerPoint. Your presentation is still there. Grab the top of the Word window and drag it downward to reveal PowerPoint.

Notice that when you click on the icon, PowerPoint actually launches Word and opens a separate editing window on the slide. You have standard Word editing and menu features at your disposal while this window is open. To return to the slide, simply click outside the Word window to close it. If Word covers your PowerPoint application, see the note above.

NOTE

If you launch Microsoft Word and shrink it to an icon by clicking on the **Minimize** button at the upper right of the screen before starting your presentation, the Word document will appear on your slides more quickly. This is because you bypass the step of loading and opening Word before the specified document is displayed.

Word is opened in a window smaller than your slide display. You can enlarge the Word window by dragging one or more of its edges. When you close a Word window by clicking outside the window, PowerPoint doesn't actually close Word; it simply moves the Word window to the background. Word remains open and ready for rapid access as required. To close, choose **File: Close: Return to (PPT. File Presentation)**. This will close your drill-down file but not Word itself. Choose **File: Exit**.

NOTE

Although you can display any Word document in this window, it doesn't make sense to try to display a very long or complex document during a slide show. Keep the Word display as simple as possible, and it will serve as an excellent enhancement or a way to provide additional information on demand during a slide presentation.

If you have more than one Word document inserted into a slide show, each new document is inserted into Word as you call for it. As you move on to the next slide, Word is moved to the background with each new document kept in memory. You can check this by pulling down the Window menu inside Word to view the various documents you have opened. You can access these directly during a presentation by using the Window menu to select previous documents.

Using PowerPoint with Access

Microsoft Access is a database product that may or may not be part of your Office suite. There are two versions of the Office package. The professional version includes Access, but the regular package does not. Access is a useful tool for maintaining data records for sales contacts, inventory, accounting, customer lists, and more.

As a member of the Office group, Access also contains some of the features of Word and Excel. It is not as closely tied to the rest of the Office suite as these other applications, but you can still use information from your databases inside PowerPoint. You may want to use Access information as part of a PowerPoint presentation for the same reasons you would want to use Excel data.

You may have spent many hours compiling and editing database information in Access, so why spend time re-entering this information for a PowerPoint slide? In addition, if more than one user can modify the Access data, you may want to use information directly from Access to ensure that you have the latest information on your PowerPoint slide at all times.

Inserting an Access Package Object

You can insert an Access package onto a PowerPoint slide. This acts as a placeholder that represents database information that you can view or edit by launching Access. To do this, make current the PowerPoint slide on which you want to include an Access package. Use **Insert: Object...** to display the Insert Object dialog box, then click on **Create from File** to display the File Selection window.

Use **Browse...** to locate the Access directory and the sampapps subdirectory under the main Access directory. Now click on the **NWIND.MDB** file within this subdirectory. This is one of the sample applications that comes with Access. You can use any ***.MDB** file as the basis for the database package. Click on **OK** to return to the Insert Object dialog box.

Click on **OK** on the Insert Object dialog box to close this dialog box and return to the PowerPoint slide. An icon with the Access symbol and the name of the inserted file is placed on the PowerPoint slide, as shown in Figure 8.30.

NOTE

If you use a large access file, this display step could take a long time. A lot of memory (16MB or more) and a large swap file help. You can also run Access and then shrink it to an icon to bypass the loading step during your presentation.

Figure 8.30 *Access package with NWIND.MDB file.*

Usually these package icons are small when inserted. You can grab any sizing handle on the object to enlarge the package icon if you wish. You can insert additional clip art, text, and other PowerPoint objects to make a completed slide. The Access object becomes an interactive button that you can use during a presentation to open Access with the selected data file loaded. You can step through the database, viewing data as desired, then use **File: Exit** from the Access menu to return to PowerPoint and continue your presentation.

To open Access from inside PowerPoint, double-click on the package to display the screen shown in Figure 8.31.

This approach to using an external application with PowerPoint is more like linking an object than embedding one in that you must use Access in its native form to view or edit information. You can display an Access database directly on a PowerPoint slide. However, you can also use the full features of Access to view or change database information from inside Access, then exit Access to return to your PowerPoint presentation.

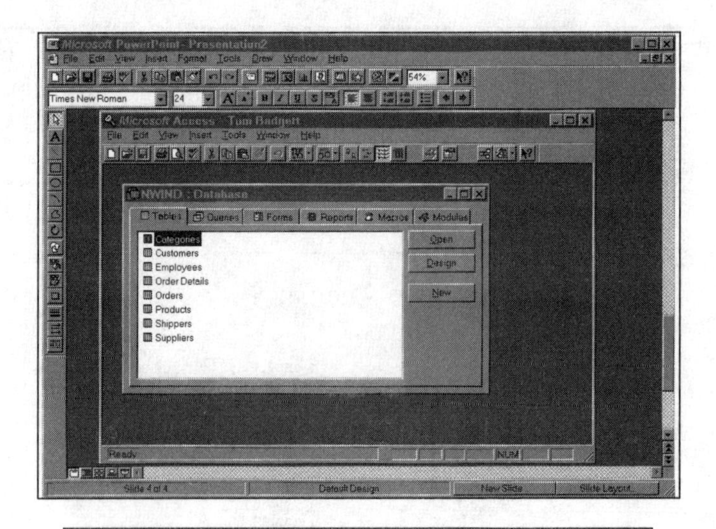

Figure 8.31 *Access screen with NWIND database loaded.*

Copying Access Information to PowerPoint

If you want to display Access information directly on a PowerPoint slide, you can copy database information from an Access screen to a PowerPoint slide. To do this, launch Access and display the database information you want to include in a PowerPoint slide. (Consult your Access user's guide if you need help in displaying database information from Access.)

Figure 8.32 shows a sample Access data file (NWIND) on the screen.

You can make it easier to switch between PowerPoint and other Microsoft applications by displaying the Microsoft toolbar. Move the mouse pointer to the main PowerPoint toolbar and press the right mouse button. Choose **Microsoft** from the list to display the Microsoft toolbar. Now you can launch Access by clicking on the **Access** icon (the icon with the key) on the toolbar.

Use the mouse to select the rows and columns on the database table that you want to include in a PowerPoint slide. Use **Edit: Copy** to place a copy of this information onto the Clipboard. Now you can shrink Access to an icon by clicking on the **Minimize** button at the top right of the Access window. Then open PowerPoint. If you have the Microsoft toolbar displayed in Access, you can jump directly to PowerPoint by clicking on the **PowerPoint** icon.

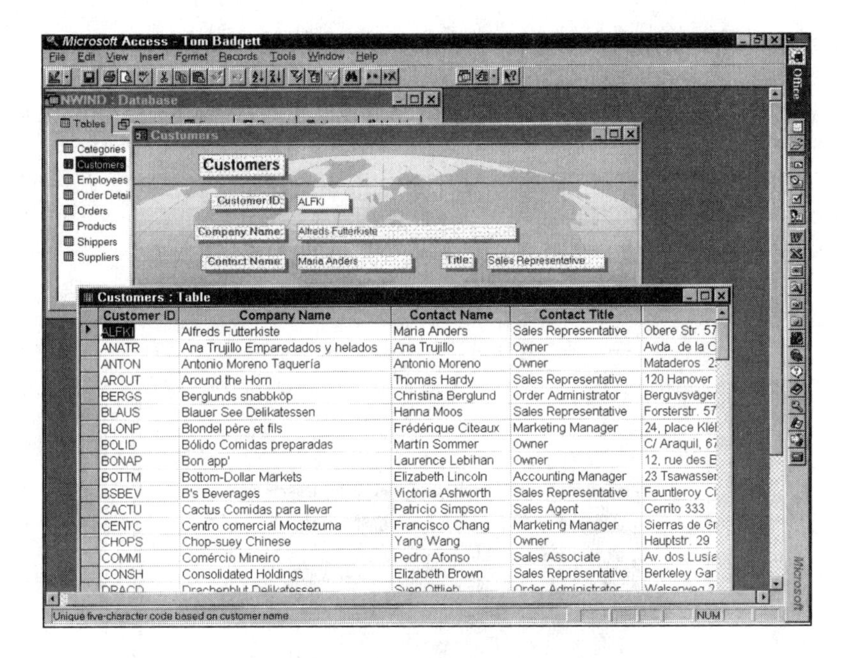

Figure 8.32 *Sample data from NWIND database.*

In PowerPoint, use **Edit: Paste** to place the information from the Clipboard onto the PowerPoint slide. This data will be inserted as text. You may find that you have to experiment with the amount of information you copy to make it fit the slide. You can also select this table, then the text, then use the Point Size pull-down list to shrink or enlarge the text to make it fit the area of the slide you want. PowerPoint inserts text from the clipboard as 24 point by default. If the amount of text you are inserting is relatively large, it may not fit onto the slide. Just make the point size of the text smaller to make it fit, or return to Access and select a smaller block of data to insert.

Using PowerPoint with Other Applications

Microsoft's Office products aren't the only applications that can offer you additional support when creating PowerPoint presentations. In fact, virtually any program you are using can supply data or graphics for a PowerPoint presentation.

PowerPoint and Screen Capture Utilities

One possible application for PowerPoint is as a training tool for computer users. If you need to demonstrate how a particular application screen looks and to show your audience how to select various aspects of the software, it might be helpful to include actual images of the screen on a PowerPoint slide. For example, the image in Figure 8.33, shows a screen from Kodak's CD Access Software in a PowerPoint slide.

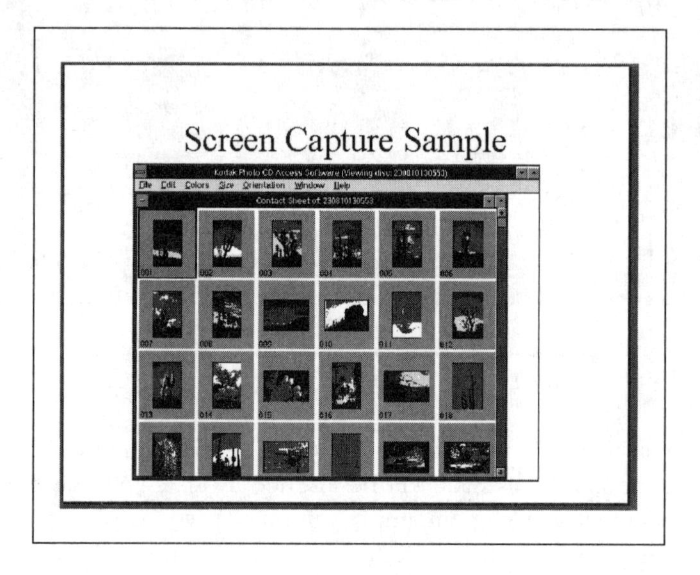

Figure 8.33 *Kodak CD Access Software screen.*
Photos by Tom DeMoss, Pictures & Words, Tucson, Arizona.

I used a utility called SnapPRO3 from Window Painters, Ltd. (9301 Bryant Avenue South, Suite 201C, Bloomington, MN 55420, 612-881-7576) to capture this screen. A utility such as this, or CaptureEze, a component of Pizazz Plus (Application Techniques, Inc., 10 Lomar Park Drive, Pepperell, MA 01463, 508-433-5201), can grab all or a portion of the computer display screen and save it into a graphics file. Most of these utilities support a wide range of file formats—TIF, PCX, BMP, GIF, and more. They grab the screen and save the graphics image to disk in the format you specify.

To use one of these images on a PowerPoint slide, use **Insert: Picture...** to display the Insert Picture dialog box shown in Figure 8.34.

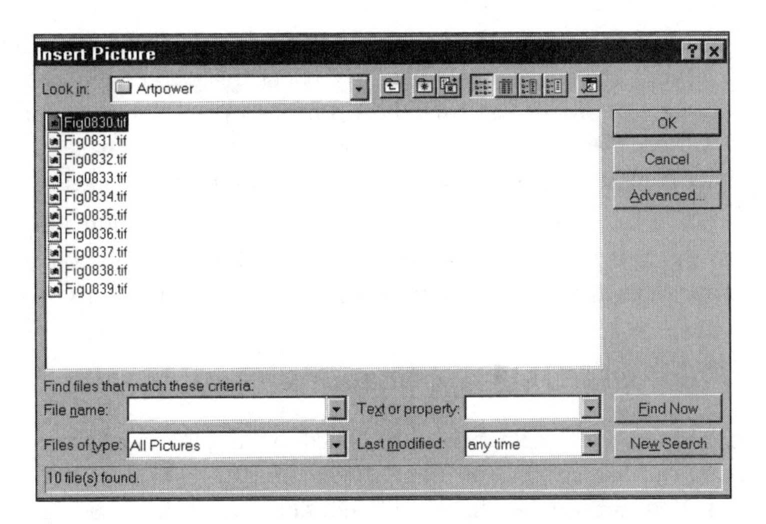

Figure 8.34 *Insert Picture dialog box.*

Select the directory where you stored the screen capture image from the Directories window, then choose the file you saved from the File name window. When you click on **OK** (or double-click on the file name), PowerPoint inserts the image into the center of the current slide. You can size the image or move it around on the slide just as you would any other PowerPoint object.

If you don't have a screen capture utility, you can still insert computer screen images into your PowerPoint presentations by using the Clipboard. First, shrink PowerPoint to an icon by clicking on the **Minimize** button at the upper-right corner of the screen.

Launch the application you want to show in the PowerPoint presentation. Manipulate the application to present the screen you want to use. Press the Print Screen key on the keyboard. (It may be labeled Print Scrn, Prnt Scrn, or something similar.) Shrink the second application to an icon by clicking on the Minimize button at the upper right corner of the screen.

Maximize PowerPoint by double-clicking on its icon on the Program Manager desktop. Make the slide that will hold the screen image current. Use **Edit: Paste** to copy the image from the Windows Clipboard onto the slide. Size or position the image as you would any other PowerPoint object.

The advantage to using a screen capture utility over the Clipboard is that screen capture utilities usually enable you to grab only a portion of the display screen if you wish. If you need only part of a screen on a PowerPoint slide and you don't have a screen capture utility, try using the Windows Paint utility to crop the image. Open Paint and use **Edit: Paste** to place the image into Paint. Now you can use the Paint eraser to remove portions of the image, or you can use the other Paint tools to color, crop, and otherwise edit the image.

Once you have the Paint image edited as you want it, use **File Save As...** to store it as a graphics image. Then relaunch PowerPoint and import the file as described above as if it had been created by a screen capture utility.

PowerPoint and DOS Applications

DOS-based applications can't share data directly with a Windows-based application, but you can use information from a DOS program in PowerPoint in a number of ways. You can use the Clipboard in the same way I described earlier in this chapter, but you have to remember one simple trick to make this work with DOS.

First, shrink PowerPoint to an icon by clicking on the **Minimize** button at the top right of the screen. Now, launch the DOS-based program you want to incorporate into PowerPoint. If the program is running in full-screen mode, reduce the DOS application to a window by pressing **Alt-Enter**. Now you can use Windows facilities on the DOS program because the less-than-full-screen window is incorporated into the Windows desktop.

Press **Print Screen** to copy the current screen to the Clipboard. Use Paint to edit the image, if you wish. Then launch PowerPoint and use **Edit: Paste** to copy the screen from the Clipboard onto a PowerPoint slide.

Another way to use data from a DOS application in PowerPoint is to print the information to a disk file. Then either import it into Word for editing or import it directly into a PowerPoint slide.

PowerPoint and Microsoft Mail

The **Send...** command on the File menu (see Figure 8.35) lets you use Microsoft Mail to transmit PowerPoint files via email.

This interface to Microsoft Mail lets you send your PowerPoint presentation to one or several other people who are also on your network and have access to Mail.

To send a presentation via Microsoft Mail, make the presentation you want to mail the current one. Then use the **File: Send...** command sequence. You may see a Microsoft Exchange dialog box, then the Send Mail dialog box integrated with a Word editor and Mail toolbar (see Figure 8.36).

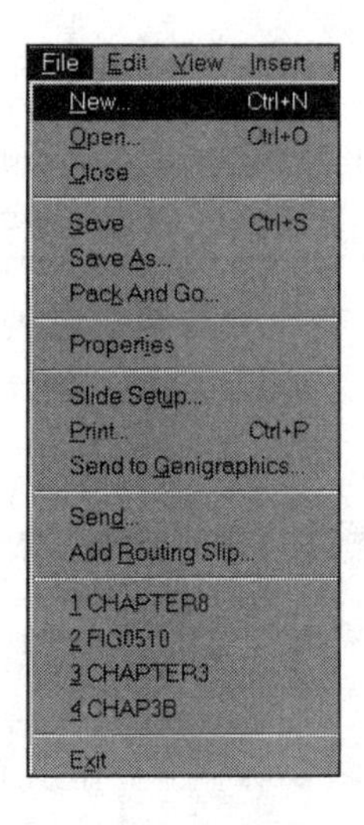

Figure 8.35 *PowerPoint File menu with Send... command.*

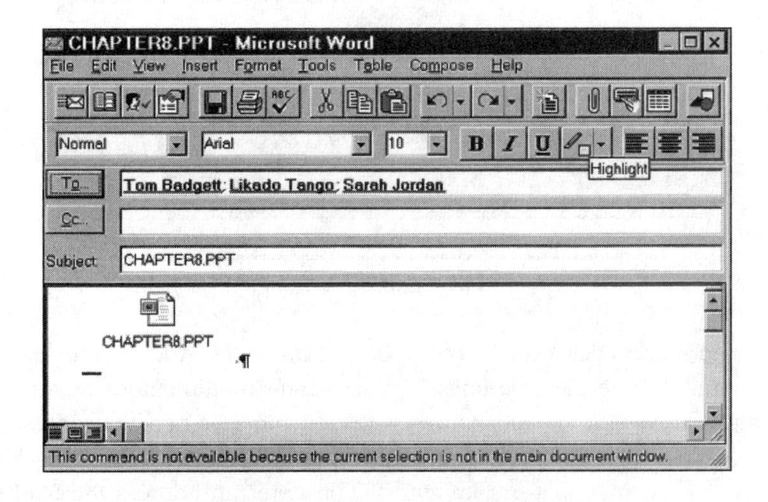

Figure 8.36 *Send Mail dialog box.*

The name of the current presentation appears on the title bar of this dialog box and in the Subject field of the Mail address.

Enter the address of the person to receive your presentation in the To field of this dialog box. If you want to send a copy to another person, enter that address in the Cc field.

NOTE

You can enter the first few characters of a user name in the To or Cc field, then press **Alt-K** to have the mailer fill in the rest of the name from the internal database of Mail users on your network.

If you're not sure of the names or addresses of recipients, click on the **Address** button on the Mail toolbar. This displays the Address dialog box shown in Figure 8.37.

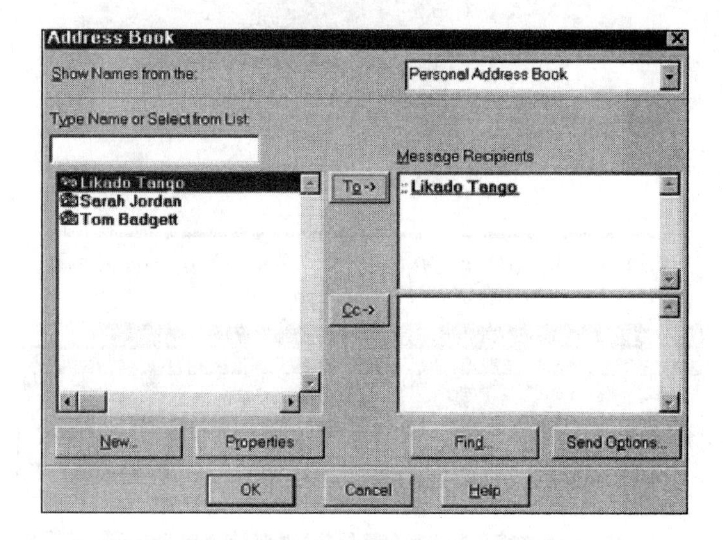

Figure 8.37 *Address dialog box from Microsoft Mail.*

Select a name and click on the **To** or **Cc** button at the Add prompt to add the selected name to one of these lines. You can enter multiple addresses on the To or Cc lines by separating the names with a comma. When you enter a name from the keyboard or specify a name from the Address dialog box, the Mail system underlines names that are known. If you enter an address the Mail system doesn't recognize, then Mail displays the error message shown in Figure 8.38.

Notice that an icon representing the current presentation appears in the message area of the Send Mail dialog box. You can add text to go with the presentation, if you wish. Simply click in the message area beneath the presentation icon and type any message you want to mail along with the PowerPoint file (see Figure 8.39).

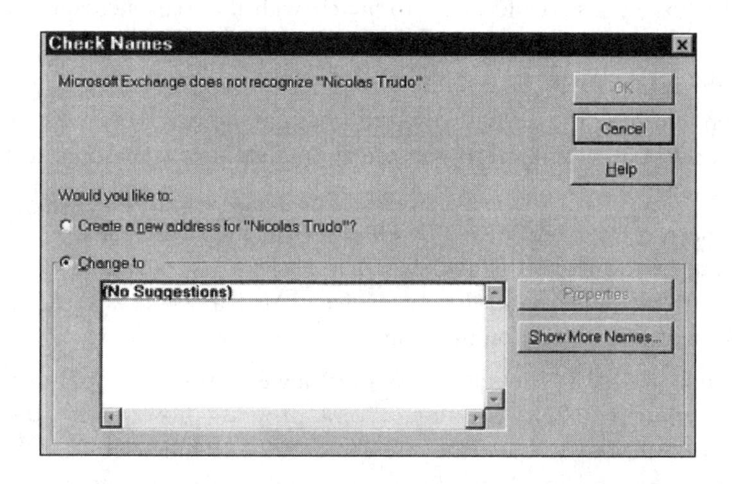

Figure 8.38 *Mail Error message: Addressee Unknown.*

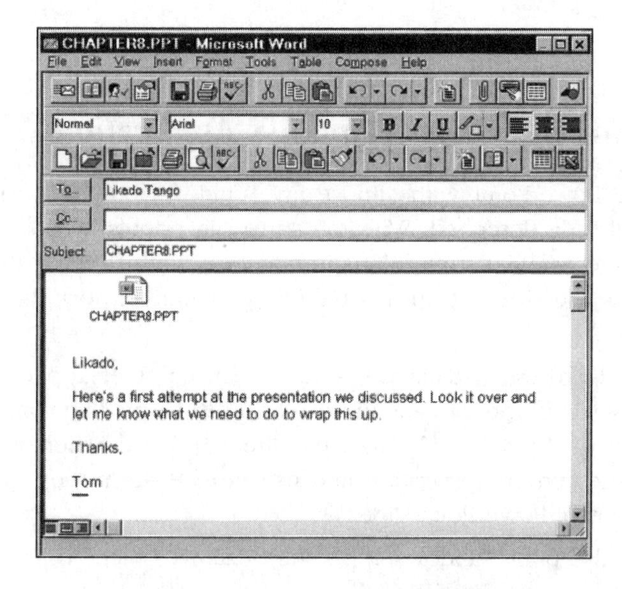

Figure 8.39 *Send Mail dialog box with typed message.*

If you want to send another file along with the presentation and any typed message, click on the **Attach** button. Mail opens a directory and file name dialog box to let you choose a file name to attach with the Mail message. You might want to do this if you have a separate word processor file of notes or ideas that go with the presentation, for example.

When you have the address and the message the way you want them, click on the **Send** button. Mail clears the screen and sends the message to the users you specified.

On the receiving end of a PowerPoint Mail message, you'll need to have PowerPoint or the PowerPoint Viewer installed to look at a slide presentation sent to you over a network. If you receive a Mail message with a PowerPoint icon, you can double-click on the icon to open the presentation.

If you don't have PowerPoint or the Viewer installed, you'll get an error message telling you that the PowerPoint program is required to view the attached file. If you do have the Viewer or PowerPoint itself installed, when you double-click on the PowerPoint presentation icon on your Mail screen, the link is made automatically. You can view the slide show in full-screen Slide Show mode. In addition, you can forward the message to others if you wish. You can add more text, such as your comments or suggestions, to the next recipient.

PowerPoint and Other Windows Applications

You can use PowerPoint with almost any Windows program using the techniques I've already described. With the spread in popularity of OLE links, you can use links to external applications in many cases. But even if the application you want to use doesn't support OLE, you can export data for use in PowerPoint.

In a word processor, database, spreadsheet, or other application, you frequently can select blocks of data and use an **Edit: Copy** command sequence to place a copy of the selected data onto the Clipboard. Then you can make PowerPoint the current application and use **Edit: Paste** to copy the Clipboard information onto a PowerPoint slide.

You can also print Windows application data to a file and import that information into Word, into another application, or directly into PowerPoint.

Using PowerPoint with Other Applications

I've talked a lot in this chapter about how to integrate files or data from external applications into PowerPoint presentations. There may be times when you want to include slides you have created in PowerPoint with other applications.

Suppose you want to use a slide you have designed in PowerPoint in a Word document, for example. You can capture the PowerPoint screen with the Clipboard or a screen capture utility, of course, and then use **Edit: Paste** in Word. An alternative to that is to save a slide you want to use in an external application as a Windows Metafile. To do this, manipulate your PowerPoint presentation so that the slide you want to use is current. Then use the **File: Save As...** command to display the Save As dialog box. In the Save File As Type field of this dialog box, choose **Windows Metafile**. Pick a directory and file name, then click on **OK** to save the file and exit the Save As dialog box.

Now, open the application with which you want to use the slide you just saved. Use **Insert: Picture** (or an equivalent command) and choose the file you saved. If the external application supports Windows Metafiles, you should be able to import the slide you saved directly into the other application. (This works well with Microsoft Word, for example.)

You can also print a PowerPoint presentation, or a portion of a PowerPoint presentation, to disk instead of to a printer. (See Chapter 6 if you need help in doing this.) Then import the print file into an external application. This won't work with all printer types, nor can all applications import printer files, but you may find that it works with the program that matters to you.

To Sum Up

Few software applications stand alone today. Thankfully, the newest designs enable applications to exchange data and to provide a common user interface. This makes the transition from one application to another much easier than it was a few years ago. Although PowerPoint, as part of the Microsoft Office package, is more closely related to Word, Access, and Excel than to other applications, you can use any product that supports OLE to share inserted or linked applications directly.

In addition, any product that generates graphics or text images that you might want to incorporate into a PowerPoint presentation can serve as a resource for you. This is because most applications have the ability to save their output in a format that PowerPoint can use. Sometimes this is a direct transfer, where PowerPoint can import another application's files directly. Sometimes it is an indirect transfer, where the foreign application exports its files into a format that PowerPoint can use. Either way, don't ignore the possibility of using the features of another software package with which you are familiar or that offers special features you want. This will help you produce imaginative presentations that have the maximum impact and effectiveness.

In the next chapter, I'll show you how to get the most out of the PowerPoint online Help system. Like a growing number of current software applications, PowerPoint depends heavily on its Help system to provide you with in-depth information about using the product.

CHAPTER 9

Using PowerPoint Help

The trend in modern software is to make user interfaces as similar to each other as possible. This makes the transition from one program to another easier. In addition, because an increasing number of software packages follow the Microsoft Windows format, software suppliers tend to put more and more information into the online Help facility and less information into the printed manual.

In general, if you are comfortable with the online Help system of any other Windows-based product, you should have no problem finding your way around PowerPoint Help. However, because there is a lot of information in Help, and because it isn't always where you might expect to find it, I'll give you a brief tour of the PowerPoint Help system in this chapter.

Context-Sensitive Help

The concept of *context-sensitive help*—help that directly addresses the current task—has been around for some time, but only with the latest Windows products have we seen it applied consistently and effectively. You can get context-sensitive help in PowerPoint with the toolbar **Help** button or by choosing **Help** on any PowerPoint dialog box.

Using the Toolbar Help Button

Probably the quickest way to get direct help with something on the PowerPoint screen is to use the context-sensitive **Help** button from the Standard toolbar (see Figure 9.1).

Figure 9.1 *Context-Sensitive Help button.*

When you click on this button, the PowerPoint mouse cursor changes to a question mark beside an arrow, indicating that you have activated the Help pointer. Now move the pointer to the PowerPoint menu, button, dialog box, or other object about which you'd like more information, then click the left mouse button. PowerPoint opens a Help file that describes that object.

For example, if you click on the Help button, then click on the check mark icon on the Standard toolbar, the Help window shown in Figure 9.2 is displayed.

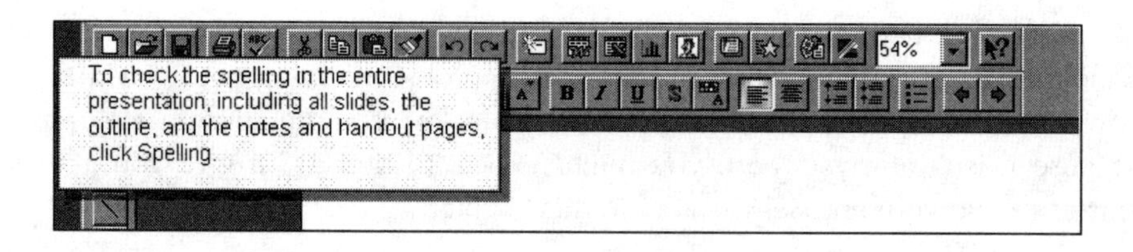

Figure 9.2 *Spell Check Help window.*

Notice that this is a pop-up, quick-reference window of the type you get inside the hypertext Help system when you want to display the definition of a word or phrase. Use the Help button for this type of quick-reference help. Close the pop-up Help display by clicking the left mouse button anywhere on the PowerPoint screen. To view information about another symbol or on-screen object, click the Help button again, move the mouse pointer over the object you want to know more about, and click the left mouse button. Repeat this process as often as you like to learn about PowerPoint objects.

Using Dialog Box Help

Another way to get context-sensitive help is to choose a **Help** button on an open PowerPoint dialog box. The Help window you get may contain very specific information about the task you are attempting, or it may be a more general Help window that also addresses the current task. This depends on the operation. For example, if you use **Insert: Clip Art...** to display the ClipArt Gallery dialog box, and then click on the **Help** button, you'll get the very detailed Help window shown in Figure 9.3.

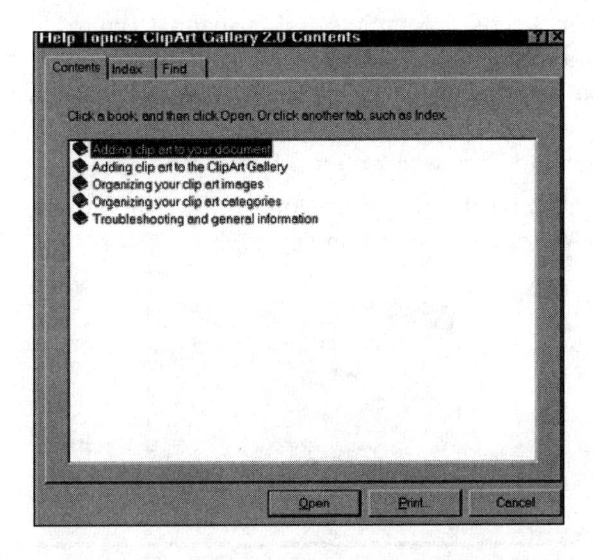

Figure 9.3 *Insert Clip Art.... Help window.*

On the other hand, if you use **Insert: Picture...** to display the Insert Picture dialog box, you have access only to the question mark Help button at the top of the dialog box. This produces the short, pop-up Help windows of the type you saw in Figure 9.2.

Figure 9.3 is the same Help window you get from the Insert Slides from File... and the Insert Slides from Outline... dialog boxes because it is the same File Manager dialog box in all cases. For general operations this is a step forward from the older systems in which the full Help system was displayed whenever you clicked on a Help button. This way you have quick reference help without having to step through the much slower, complete Help system.

If you want more detail on any topic, then it is time to delve into the main-menu Help system, discussed in the next section.

Help from the Menu

I've already shown you a little bit about accessing Help from the main PowerPoint menu. In this section we'll look deeper into what's available from the Help menu. As with an increasing number of Windows-based software packages, PowerPoint keeps a complete user's manual online for quick access. Because the information is in electronic form, you can search for the specific information you need when you need it. When you don't have a context for Help in mind, you can start with the Help menu selection and work your way through the system to learn what you need to learn.

When you click on the Help selection on the main PowerPoint menu bar, you get the pull-down menu shown in Figure 9.4.

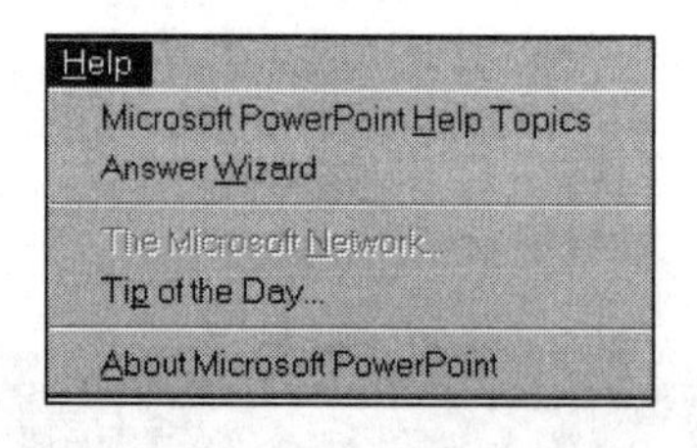

Figure 9.4 *Main PowerPoint Help pull-down menu.*

PowerPoint Help Topics

The basic Help window is the Microsoft PowerPoint Help Topics dialog box, which is the first selection on the Main PowerPoint Help menu (see Figure 9.5).

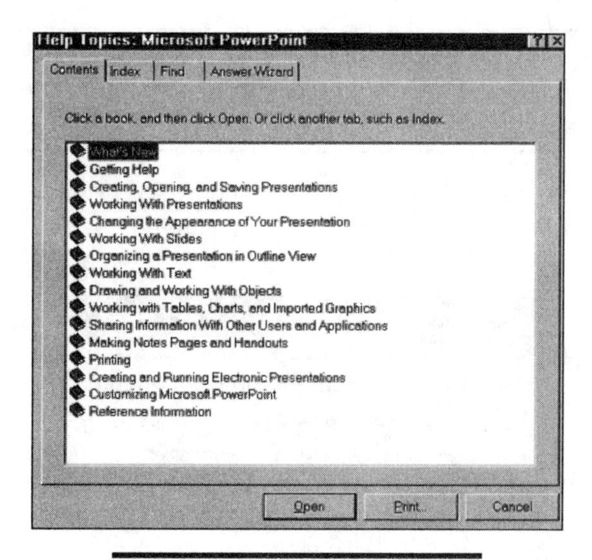

Figure 9.5 *Help Topics dialog box.*

CONTENTS TAB

The Help Topics dialog box has four tabbed choices. The default selection is the Contents tab, shown in Figure 9.5. This part of PowerPoint Help is arranged in "books"; you can click on a topic to open up subtopics, like the display in Figure 9.6.

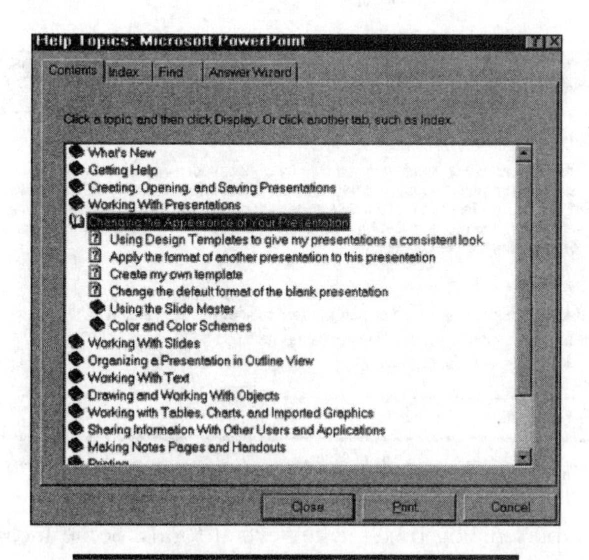

Figure 9.6 *Contents tab with Subtopic list.*

NOTE

To learn more about this version of PowerPoint, click on the **What's New** book and choose one or more subtopics to view. You'll learn about new features available in PowerPoint 7.

To read about one of the subtopics in the pull-down list, simply double-click on a topic of interest to display a dialog box like Figure 9.7.

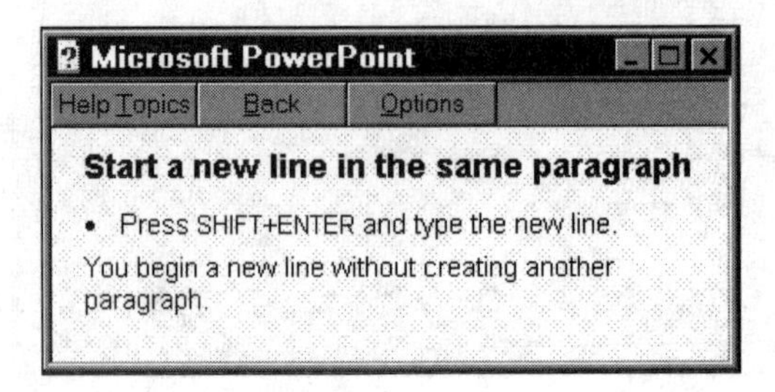

Figure 9.7 *Simple, self-contained Help Subtopic dialog box from Contents tab.*

The actual makeup of these informational dialog boxes changes with the topic. Sometimes the dialog boxes are simple and self-contained, like Figure 9.7. At other times, the topics are more complex and include hypertext links to related topics, such as the sample in Figure 9.8.

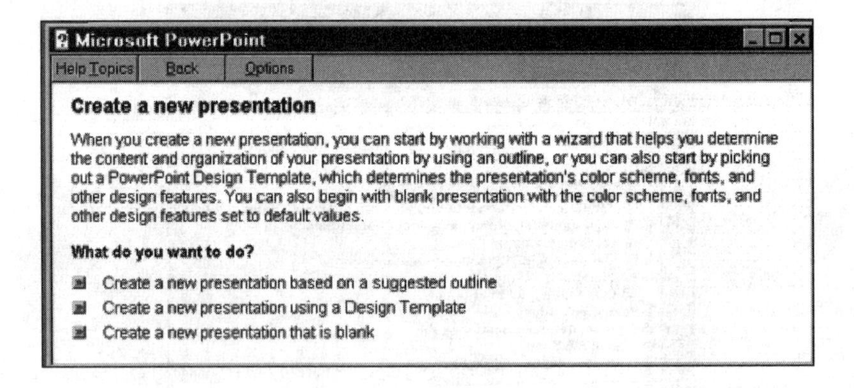

Figure 9.8 *Hypertext Help Subtopic dialog box from Contents tab.*

These more complex dialog boxes take several forms. Some include green text that is a hyperlink to additional information. Others contain buttons to click to bring up additional information. Notice, too, that when you have stepped through one or more hyperlinks, the menu bar at the top of the dialog box changes. The Back button is enabled to let you step back through these related topics. The left-most button is Help Topics, which brings you back to the main Help dialog box shown in Figure 9.6.

The Index Tab

The Index tab provides another way of viewing and searching available PowerPoint Help topics, as you can see from Figure 9.9.

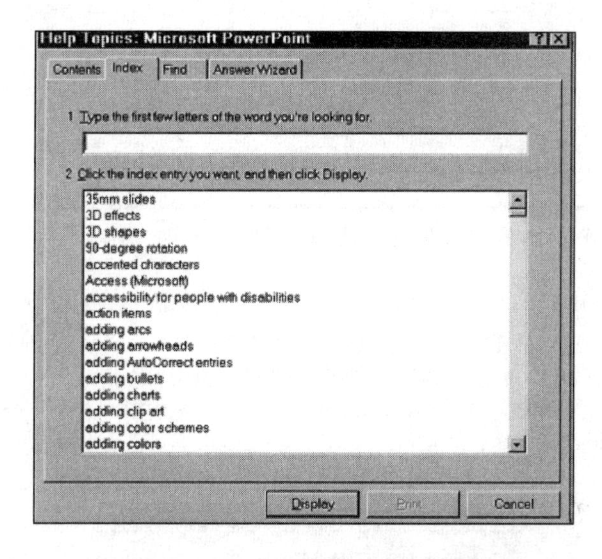

Figure 9.9 *Index tab from Main PowerPoint Help Topics dialog box.*

This tab provides a list of topics that you can search by entering a word or phrase under the **Type the first few letters of the word you're looking for** prompt. As you type, PowerPoint searches the topic list and tries to match a topic with the word or words you are entering in the search field. As soon as you enter one letter, the display jumps to the first word that begins with that letter. The more letters you type, the more refined the search.

For example, if you enter the letter *p*, the display jumps to *pace of movies*, the first entry in the topic list that begins with the letter *p*. Now add the letter r after the p. The display jumps to Preferences (Defaults). Continue typing until you have entered the word print. The display looks like the one in Figure 9.10.

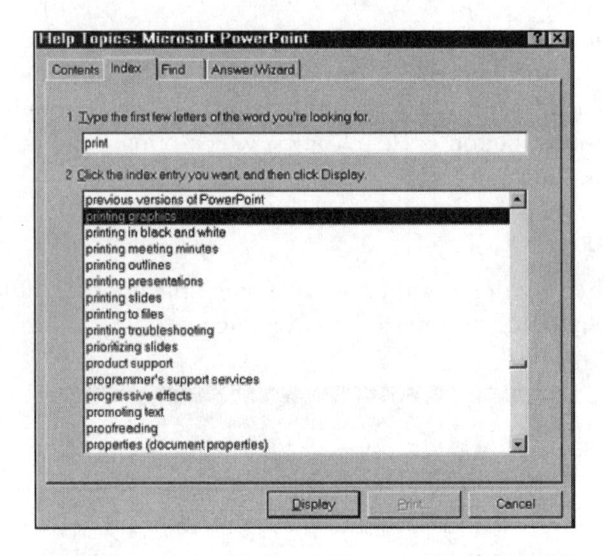

Figure 9.10 *Index Help with Print in the Search field.*

Notice that there are several topics that relate to printing. You can either select one from the list or type another word to narrow the search. When you have found a topic you want to read, double-click on the topic (or click once and then click on **Display**). If there are multiple topics under this index entry, you will see a Topics Found dialog box like Figure 9.11.

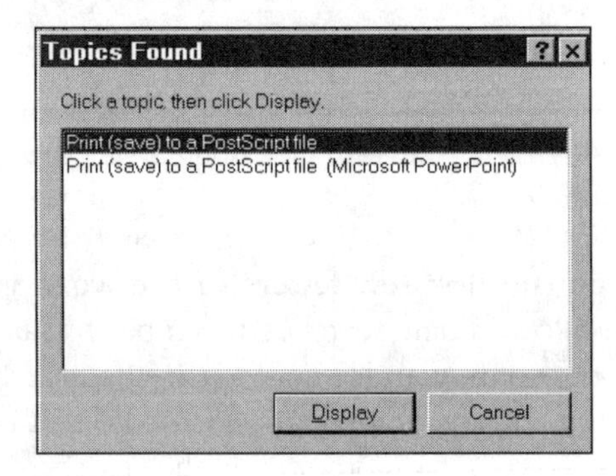

Figure 9.11 *Topics Found dialog box from Help Index dialog box.*

To step to the next level of information, double-click on one of these topics to display a dialog box similar to Figure 9.7.

In addition, some of these topics include dynamic links to the Answer Wizard, which can provide detailed, step-by-step information on completing the task discussed in the topic. (Additional information on the Answer Wizard is provided later in this chapter.)

THE FIND TAB

The Find tab from the main PowerPoint Help Topics dialog box provides still another way of finding and displaying Help information. The first screen from the Find tab is shown in Figure 9.12. As you can see, this is really a Wizard that will help you locate a particular Help topic that is mentioned within the Help text. This lets you drill deeper into the Help information than you can do by just searching the topics. With the Find tab you are searching for individual words within the Help text under the main headings.

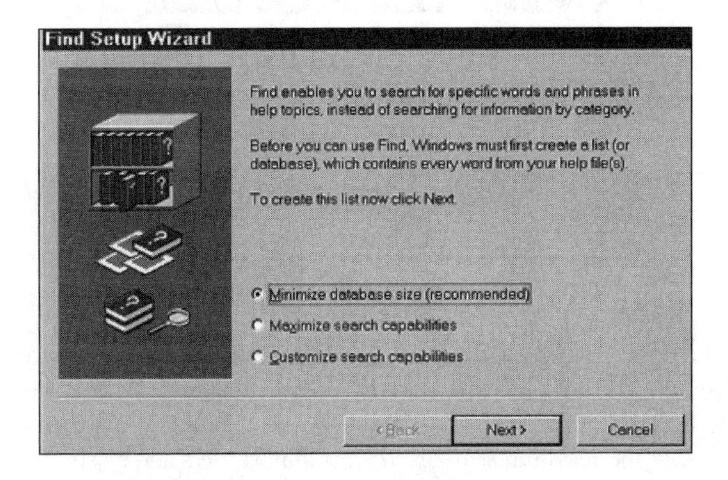

Figure 9.12 *Opening dialog box from Find Help tab.*

As is common in Microsoft Wizards, you are asked to click on the **Next** button to display the next screen. Which screen is displayed and exactly how this feature functions depends on which of the three buttons you select on this first dialog box. The default button is the first one, **Minimize database size**. This provides the quickest search, narrowing the topics to the most common ones. However if you've tried this and you want to see if you can find a more obscure topic, choose the second button, **Maximize search capabilities**. And, to provide some custom input to the search, choose the third button, **Customize search capabilities**.

Once you have created the index, you can use the Find tab without waiting to build the list the next time, unless you want to change the way the list is built. If you accept the default on the first run, for example, PowerPoint searches all Help text, building a key word list, and then displays the dialog box in Figure 9.13.

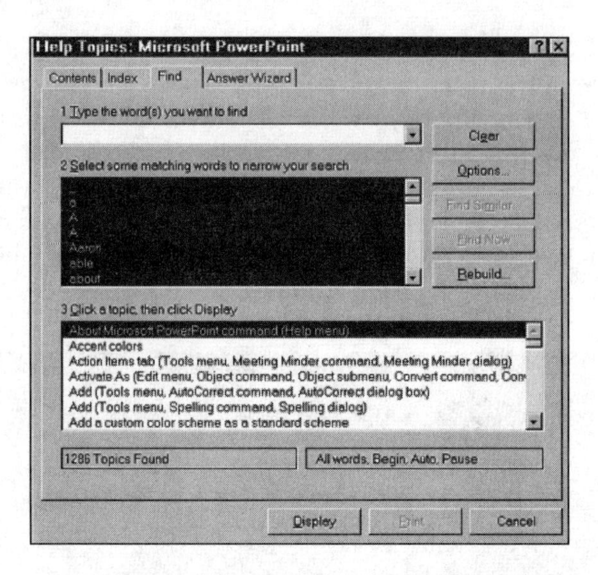

Figure 9.13 *Find dialog box after word list built.*

You can change the word list by clicking on the **Rebuild...** button on this dialog box, presenting the first Wizard screen shown in Figure 9.12. If you choose **Maximize** from this first dialog box, the process of building a word list takes a little longer, but the resulting search screen is almost the same as shown in Figure 9.13. When you expand the number of topics (you can see how many topics were found during the list build at the lower left-hand corner of the dialog box) check boxes are added to the topics in the third window of the dialog box.

You can choose to customize the search by stepping through a series of screens and selecting various criteria, including:

- Choose the text files to search. PowerPoint Help and PowerPoint Quicktips are the defaults.
- Include/Ignore untitled topics.
- Include/Don't Include phrase searching.

▼ Display/Don't Display matching phrases.

▼ Support/Don't Support similarity searches.

After you have selected from these options, the PowerPoint Help system once again sets to work building the final group from which the Help topics will be taken. After the word or word and phrase group is built, the searching is the same as for the other options. You'll use the screen shown in Figure 9.13, with check boxes beside the topics in the third window of the dialog box.

To conduct a search, you can scroll through the topics in the third window at the bottom of the dialog box, look for short one- or two-word topics in the middle window, or type in a word or phrase to look for in the top window. When you have narrowed down the topic, double-click the topic in the bottom window or click on **Display** to present the complete Help topic.

The resulting Help dialog box will be one of the types already described: a simple standalone dialog box; a dialog box that includes hyperlinks to additional topics; or a dialog box that also presents an Answer Wizard display to take you step-by-step through the process of completing the selected task.

THE ANSWER WIZARD TAB

The Answer Wizard replaces the earlier PowerPoint Cue Cards. Whereas the Cue Cards displayed on-screen Help continuously while you conducted a PowerPoint task, the Answer Wizard actually emulates the keystrokes you will use to complete the task yourself. As I mentioned earlier, some Help topics automatically launch an Answer Wizard. But you also can choose the Answer Wizard tab from the Help Topics dialog box or from the main Help pull-down menu.

NOTE

The second main entry on the PowerPoint Help pull-down menu is the Answer Wizard. This choice displays the same dialog box as is discussed here under the Answer Wizard tab of the Help Topics dialog box.

When you click on the **Answer Wizard** tab, the dialog box in Figure 9.14 is displayed.

To use the Answer Wizard, finish the unstated question "How do I..." in the top list box of this dialog box. "How do I...print to a file," is an example. After you type a question and press **Enter** or click **Search**, the Answer Wizard searches its list of topics and displays a list of questions for which it has answers that seem to match your request. If you type **print to a file**, as I have suggested, and then press **Enter** or click on the **Search** button, the suggested questions shown in Figure 9.15 are displayed.

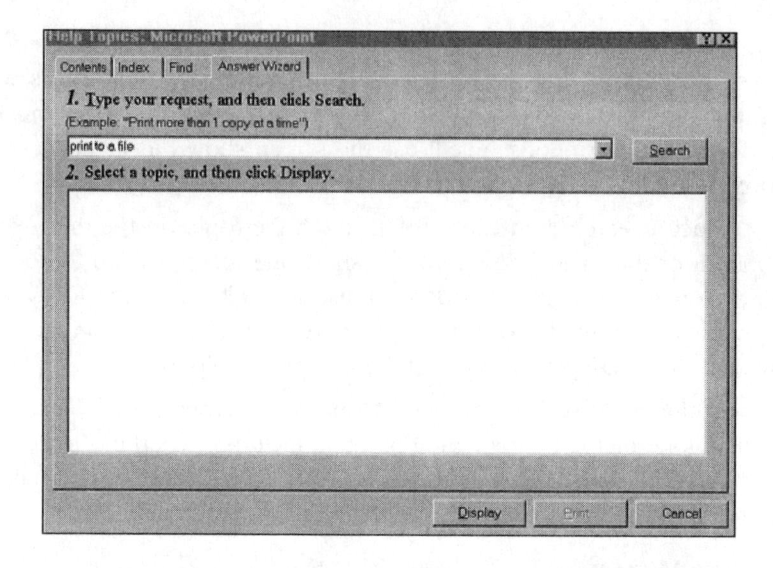

Figure 9.14 *Answer Wizard tab from Help Topics dialog box.*

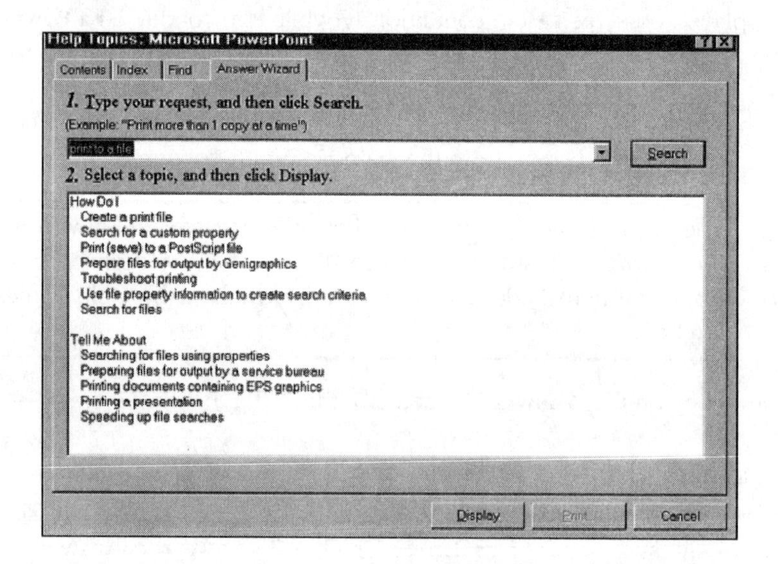

Figure 9.15 *Suggested Answer Wizard questions: print to a file.*

You can display details about one of these topics by double-clicking on it, or by selecting it and then clicking on **Display**. The resulting dialog box is one of PowerPoint's standard Help dialog boxes. Once you have read the information in the displayed dialog box, you can close the Help dialog box by clicking on the Close icon at the upper right corner, or you can click on the **Help Topics** button to return to the Answer Wizard to search for more topics.

Tip of the Day

The Tip of the Day is a random display of Help topics that pops up when you choose the topic from the Help menu (as well as when you open the program). A typical Tip of the Day display is shown in Figure 9.16.

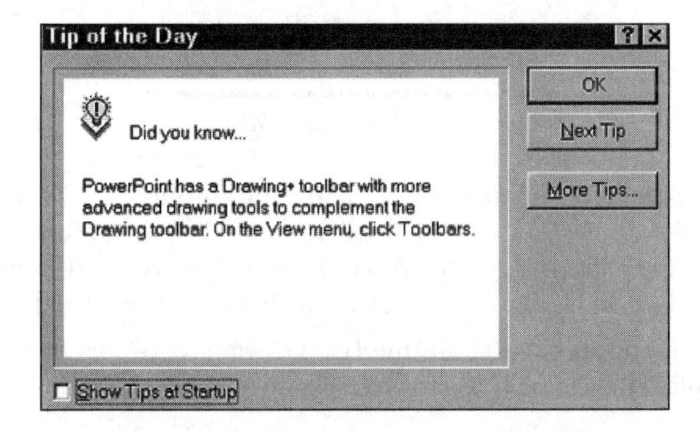

Figure 9.16 *Typical Tip of the Day dialog box.*

PowerPoint displays a new Help topic automatically each time PowerPoint launches. you can change this default by unclicking the **Show Tips at Startup** button in the lower left corner of the Tip dialog box.

You have three choices once the Tip of the Day is displayed. You can click on **OK** to close the Tip dialog box and return to what you were doing, you can click on the **Next Tip** button to display the next topic, or you can click on **More Tips** to display the dialog box shown in Figure 9.17.

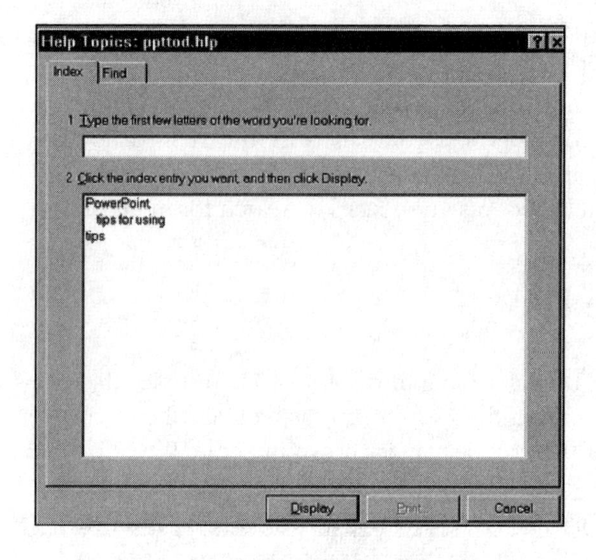

Figure 9.17 *More Tips dialog box.*

From this screen you can search for Help topics using the Tip system as a launching point for the study of any topic in the Help system. Just type a word in the first field of this dialog box to see if the topic is covered in the Tip system. This works like the Find and Index dialog boxes described earlier.

When you click on a topic in the bottom window of this dialog box and choose **Display**, the dialog box shown in Figure 9.18 is displayed.

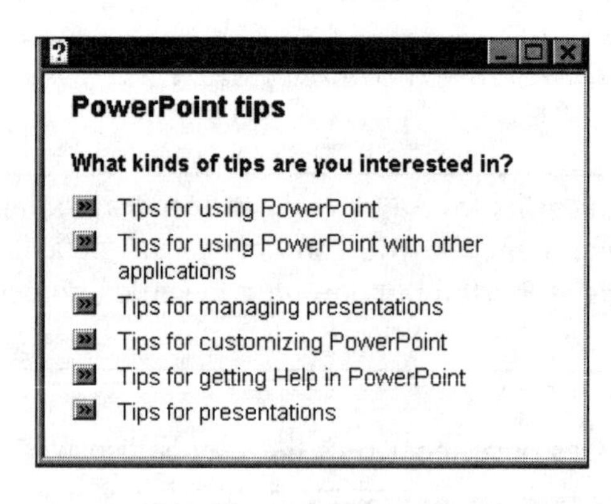

Figure 9.18 *Topics dialog box from Tips.*

You can browse through this summary list of Help topics until you find the information you need.

Getting Continuous Help

Between the Index/Find features and the Answer Wizard, PowerPoint offers a lot of online Help. But here's a technique that is sometimes more useful than the prompted Answer Wizard.

To get continuous help on a task, shrink PowerPoint so that it takes up less than a full screen by clicking on the **Shrink Document** button at the far right of the title bar. Now you can open a Help window and, by adjusting the size of the Help and PowerPoint windows, produce a side-by-side display like the one in Figure 9.19. This provides easy access to Help while you work with PowerPoint.

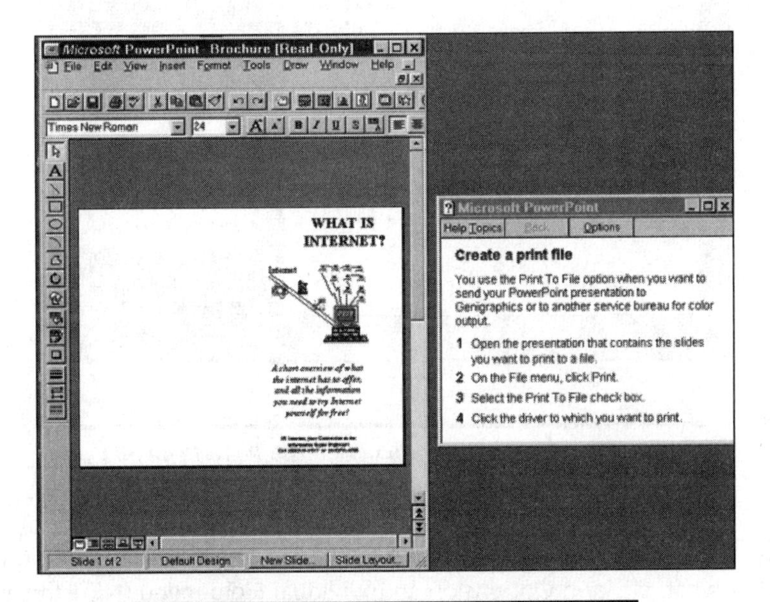

Figure 9.19 *Side-By-Side Help with PowerPoint.*

Notice that I have shown the display with a rather narrow Help window and a wider PowerPoint window. You can adjust either of these as needed by grabbing any of the edges of a window and dragging the window to a new size. Obviously while working with PowerPoint, you need the PowerPoint window to be as large as possible and still let you see Help.

Another way to do this is to make the PowerPoint window almost fill the screen and leave just enough room to display a small segment of the Help window. Then, when you want Help, you can click anywhere in the Help window. PowerPoint will bring the Help window to the front of the display, covering PowerPoint. When you're ready to return to PowerPoint, just click anywhere inside the PowerPoint window to send Help to the background and bring PowerPoint to the foreground. Figure 9.20 shows a screen with PowerPoint on top of Help. Figure 9.21 shows a screen with Help on top. You can switch between Help and PowerPoint whenever you need.

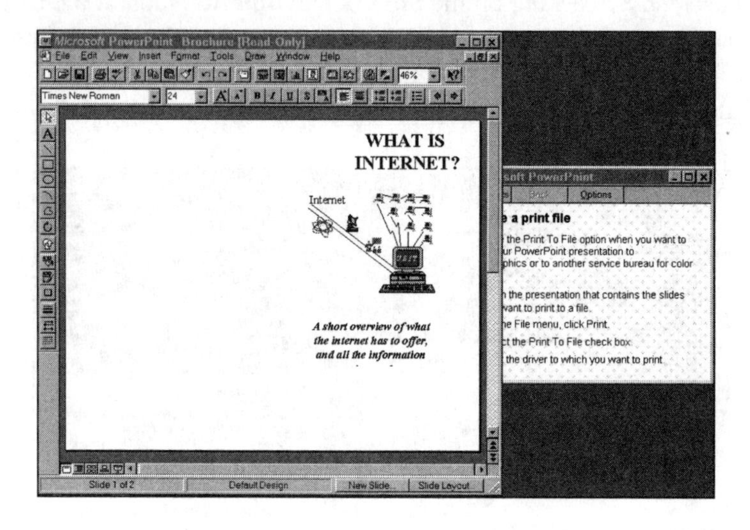

Figure 9.20 *PowerPoint/Help screen with PowerPoint on top.*

NOTE

If you want the Help window to stay on top of PowerPoint no matter what, click on **Options** on an individual Help menu (NOT the general PowerPoint menu) and choose **Keep Help on Top**. Then choose **On Top** from the additional pop-up menu. This forces the Help window to be always visible, but it causes the Help window to obscure part of the PowerPoint window. While you learn how to conduct certain tasks, however, having Help always visible may be useful.

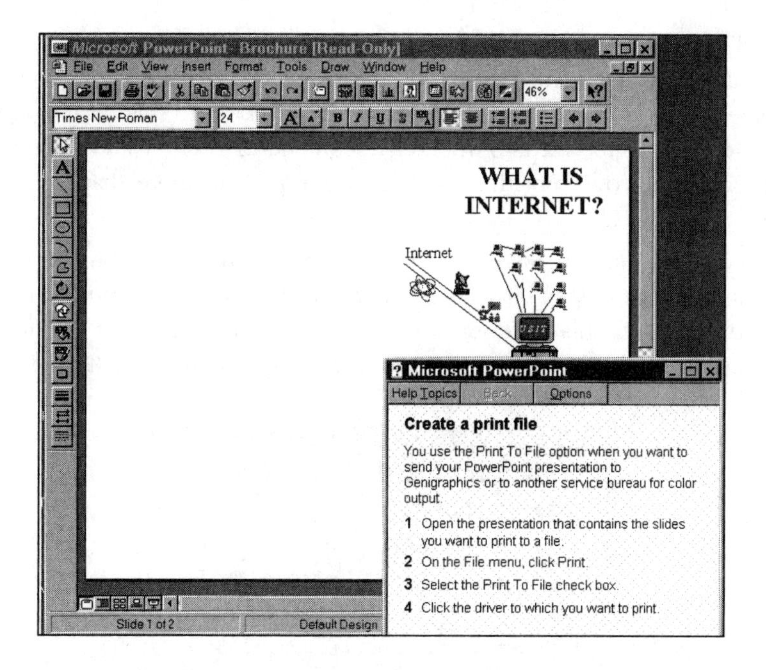

Figure 9.21 *PowerPoint/Help screen with Help on top.*

The Help Options Menu

When you display a Help dialog box, you can choose several options from the Help menu. If you click on **Help Topics**, PowerPoint displays the dialog box from which you launched the current Help window.

Click on **Back** to return to the previous Help topic displayed during this Help session. If the Back button is unavailable (grayed out), it means you are looking at the first screen of the current Help topic.

Click on the **Options** button to display the Options pull-down menu shown in Figure 9.22.

The Annotate Option

Use the **Annotate** option to pop up a small editor window that you can use to type additional help information or notes to supplement the current topic. When you have the annotation as you want it, click on **Save** to place the text and any included graphics onto the current Help window. Notice that this dialog box also includes a Copy button. When you click on this button, PowerPoint copies the contents of the Annotation window to the Clipboard. This lets you incorporate this custom Help text into another document, or paste it into another annotation window if you want the same text to appear in more than one location within PowerPoint Help.

When you click on **Save** on the Help Annotate dialog box, PowerPoint places a hypertext paper clip on the current Help window, indicating that an annotation exists for this window. You can display the contents of this annotation by clicking on the paper clip, or by choosing **Annotate** from the Options menu.

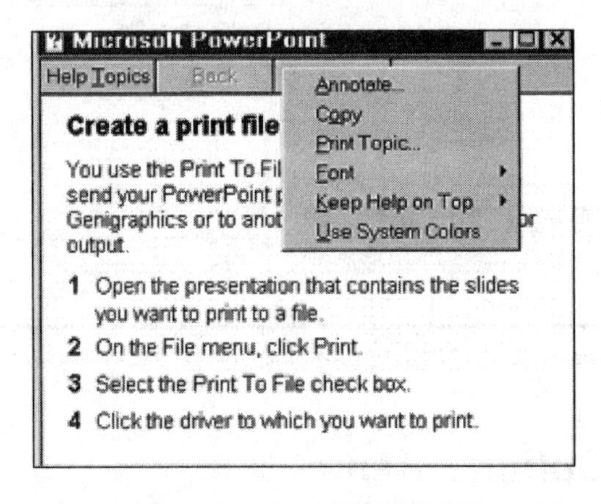

Figure 9.22 *Help Options pull-down menu.*

The Copy Option

Use the **Copy** option to copy portions of a Help topic to the Clipboard. Hold down the left mouse button to select the text you want to copy, then click on **Options** and choose **Copy**. The selected text is copied to the Clipboard. Now you can paste the information into other Windows applications that accept text from the Clipboard. In this way you could build your own file of help and print it out or display it.

The Print Topic Option

Choose the **Print Topic** option from this menu when you want to create a printout of the displayed Help topic. The printout includes all of the information on the main Help dialog box and shows hypertext links as underlined text. The text associated with any hyperlinks on this dialog box is not printed, however. To print these related topics, click on the hyperlink text, then choose **Print Topic** again. Unfortunately, each time you do, a few sentences (typically) will appear at the top of a new sheet (see "The Copy Option" for a way to avoid this).

The Font Option

Use the **Font** option to change the size of the font in the displayed Help dialog box. The choices on this dialog box are Small, Normal, and Large, with Normal as the default.

The Keep Help on Top Option

Choose **Keep Help on Top** to keep the Help windows on top of the PowerPoint display, even as you choose other PowerPoint operations. Normally, when you click outside the displayed Help window, it is moved into the background and focus is given to the selected PowerPoint screen. If you choose to keep Help on top, however, the current Help dialog box will stay visible.

There are three choices on this submenu: Default lets the Help system decide whether or not to keep a topic on top; On Top forces the Help dialog box to stay on top; and Not on top forces the Help dialog box to move to the background when you deselect the displayed Help dialog box.

The Use System Colors Option

The Help system normally displays Help topics with a light yellow background, black text, and green hypertext links. You can force the Help dialog boxes to use the same color scheme you have selected for the rest of the Windows 95 system by choosing this option. You must close the Help dialog box and re-open it for the color change to take effect.

This is a toggle. The first time you select it, a check mark appears beside the selection; the second time, the check mark is removed.

To Sum Up

Online PowerPoint Help is a useful and important part of your PowerPoint package. It is a standard Windows-compliant Help system that gives you several ways to access the information it contains. Whether you use the main Help menu, search for Help, or use the context-sensitive features of Help, you can view detailed information about all aspects of using PowerPoint. In addition, by adding annotations, you can create a custom Help system that can help you or other users become familiar with PowerPoint in general or learn how to conduct specific tasks within the system.

The remainder of this book details some of the hardware and software issues with which you should be familiar and provides you with a menu and command reference.

APPENDIX A

Hardware and Software Issues

In this appendix, I'll give specific hardware and software requirements and suggestions that can help you get the most out of PowerPoint.

Required Hardware and Software

This book is about Microsoft PowerPoint 7, the version that ships with Office 95. The entire package is designed to run with Windows 95; if you aren't yet running Windows 95, you can't successfully run PowerPoint 7.

If you have configured your system for optimum performance with Windows 95, then you will get along well with PowerPoint 7. While you can run Windows 95 with a minimal hardware configuration, your system will perform much better if you upgrade at least a little. You need 16 Mb of RAM, for example, to get reasonable performance from Windows 95 and associated applications.

To take advantage of the features offered by PowerPoint 7, you need a relatively high-end PC. A machine that uses the 80486 DX processor running at 50 MHz or higher should be considered the minimum power for any serious Windows 95–based application. It is true that Windows 95 will load and run on a less powerful machine, but you won't be happy with it for very long. Windows 95 and the applications that use it offer many improvements in user interface, online Help, graphics, and more, but these features require a lot of memory, a lot of storage (disk space), and a powerful processor (CPU). Anything less than a 486DX/50 with 8 to 16 MB of memory runs painfully slow.

In fact, if you are outfitting for PowerPoint and have to buy a new machine, look carefully at your budget and at what is available from suppliers. Then consider a machine that uses a Pentium CPU.

You will need at least one floppy disk drive, of course, to copy the distribution floppy disks to your hard drive. This should be a 1.44 MB high density, 3.5-inch drive. Your hard disk needs about 25 MB of free space, *not* counting space for swap/temp files. You can install PowerPoint for a laptop or minimal installation with less storage space than that. However, to get a full installation with all the templates, drivers, and Help files, and still have room for presentations, you should free up at least 25 MB. And, since PowerPoint and Office are available on CD-ROM, consider adding a CD-ROM drive to your system if you don't already have one. This makes installation and updates much easier and faster than with floppy disks.

Your display adapter should be SVGA-compatible, and the monitor should be a high-resolution color device. Part of the power of PowerPoint is in its handling of color and graphics. You'll be able to design better presentations and get more out of PowerPoint itself with a high-quality monitor. I recommend setting up Windows for 1,024 x 768 resolution. This gives you a full screen of information that should be reasonably easy to read if your monitor is of good quality. When you use the standard VGA 640 x 480 display, the screen is crowded and you can't display as many Windows applications or objects as you might like. And, with the price of hardware coming down, consider at least a 15-inch monitor; a 17-inch screen is better.

You'll need a laser printer for PowerPoint. With a quality laser printer you can print directly to overhead projection foils, and you can produce high quality black and white pages for reports or audience handouts. Today's printer standard is 600 dots per inch resolution, compared to the 300 dots per inch of just a couple of years ago. If you're buying a new printer, don't settle for less than 600 dpi. The cost difference is slight, but the quality difference between 300 dpi and

600 dpi is very noticeable. And, for the price of a standard 300 dpi laser printer of a few years ago you can buy 1200 dpi resolution today.

In fact, with prices the way they are today, you also should consider a color printer, especially if overhead projection is a large part of your presentation output. For anywhere from $600 to $2,000 you can have quality color output that can make a real difference in how the audience receives your presentation.

Tuning for Top Performance

Even if you have the basic hardware and software I recommend to run PowerPoint, you may find that performance isn't what it should be. There are a few things you can do if you find PowerPoint—and Windows in general—running a little slow.

First, look at your memory. If you have only 4 MB of RAM, double it, at least. Again, while you can run Windows 95 and its applications in 8 Mb of RAM, I believe that a 16 MB system is the minimum for running modern Windows applications. If you can afford 32 MB, that's better still. More memory enables Windows to run more in RAM instead of swapping information to the hard drive, which is a much slower device than solid-state RAM.

Next, check out your hard drive. If it is nearly full, that could slow things down. Use the Windows Explorer to find out what is on your disk and whether there are any files you can eliminate. With additional free space, some applications become more efficient and may run faster. In addition, you should run SCANDISK or another optimizing utility to eliminate disk fragmenting. Files that are scattered across the surface of your hard disk load and save a lot slower than files that reside in contiguous disk space. SCANDISK or another utility will remove fragmentation and place files in side-by-side disk locations.

Beyond the Basic PC

I've already mentioned in Chapter 7 that you can enhance your basic PC setup by including screen cameras and other tools for presentation. In this section I'll summarize some of this hardware that you can add to your PC for more creative presentations.

Screen Capture Cameras

If you need an occasional color slide, the best choice is to use a slide service such as Genigraphics, the company that designed the templates and slide views for PowerPoint. If you regularly produce slide-based presentations, on the other hand, you should consider investing in a screen capture camera. These devices generally attach to your PC's video display to present a parallel screen image. A 35mm camera body takes pictures from this display to produce a high-resolution color slide of the computer screen.

Multimedia Hardware and Software

PowerPoint supports many enhanced presentation features, including the ability to embed sound files and motion video. I showed you how to use these features in Chapter 7. However, to produce your own sound and video files, you'll need additional hardware beyond the basic out-of-the-box PC.

VIDEO HARDWARE

I described in Chapter 7 how you can connect a converter to change your computer's VGA output to standard television signals that you can display on a TV monitor or record on a video tape recorder. That's just one aspect of using video with your PowerPoint presentations. Because PowerPoint has the ability to link with the Windows Media Player, you can play motion video from inside PowerPoint.

You can purchase video clips from stock agencies, but these generally serve only as concept footage. When you want to convey something specific, you'll want to insert your own video within your PowerPoint presentation. To do this you'll need hardware to interface a standard video source to your computer. Some of the hardware I mentioned in Chapter 7 is two-way. It can be used to convert VGA video information to standard NTSC television video, and it can also take input from NTSC (television) sources and convert it to computer files.

Below, I've listed sources for hardware that you can use for video conversion. Some of these devices aren't inexpensive. They can cost $2,000 to $3,000. However, prices are falling all the time and inexpensive units are hitting the market. Contact several of the vendors listed here to find out the current state of the art and pricing information.

Creative Labs Inc.

1901 McCarthy Boulevard
Milpitas, CA 95035
408-428-6600
800-647-9933

Fast Electronics U.S., Inc.

5 Commonwealth Road
Natick, MA 01760
508-655-3278

IBM Corporation

4111 Northside Parkway
Atlanta, GA 30327
404-238-1282
800-426-9402

Jovian Logic Corporation

47929 Fremont Boulevard
Fremont, CA 94538
510-651-4823

New Media Graphics Corporation

780 Boston Road
Billerica, MA 01821-5925
508-663-0666
800-288-2207

TrueVision

7340 Shadeland Station
Indianapolis, IN 46256
317-841-0332
800-344-8783

With a board that lets you connect a video camera or recorder to your computer, you can capture live video such as a short statement from a company owner, engineering director, or sales manager. This can give a personal and believable quality to your presentation. Or, you can dub portions of an existing company or personal video into the computer so you can attach them to a PowerPoint slide.

AUDIO HARDWARE

I showed you in Chapter 7 how to attach audio clips to a PowerPoint slide, and I listed sources for prerecorded digital music and sounds. The audio information in PowerPoint is presented on the slide as an icon that you can click to play music, sound effects, or narration. Windows and other applications ship with sound files, and you can purchase presentation audio. However, the key to successful sound integration with PowerPoint presentations is to have available the sounds or narration you need and to have the proper hardware to output sound. In most cases a single sound board is all that you need to accomplish both tasks.

A number of companies supply sound adapters that plug into your PC bus much like a video display adapter card or a hard disk controller. Connectors on the rear of the board let you attach the sound output to an external amplifier, directly to a set of low-power speakers, and to a microphone or other audio input device. Software that ships with your board lets you digitize sound presented to the input connector, usually in stereo. Sound you digitize in this way—or sounds you purchase or obtain from another source—can be sent out from the sound card. Most cards include internal amplifiers so that you can attach speakers directly to the card for low-level sound output. A sound level of one to four watts is usually provided with these cards. If this level of sound is not enough, you can plug the output of your sound card into the input connector of an external amplifier and a set of speakers that can handle the output. This lets you produce sound levels appropriate for a small room or an auditorium.

I can't possibly list all the suppliers of PC sound cards here, but the following list will get you started.

Ad Lib, Inc.

50 Staniford Street
Suite 800
Boston, MA 02144
800-463-2686

Advanced Strategies Corporation

60 Cutter Mill Road
Great Neck, NY 11021
516-482-0088

Alpha Systems Lab

2361 McGaw Avenue
Irvine, CA 92714
714-252-0117

Antex Electronics

16100 South Figueroa Street
Gardena, CA 90248
310-532-3092

ATI Technologies, Inc.

3761 Victoria Park Avenue
Scarborough, Ontario, Canada M1W 3S2
416-756-0718

Aztech Labs, Inc.

46707 Fremont Boulevard
Fremont, CA 94538
510-623-8988

Computer Peripherals

667 Rancho Conejo
Newberry Park, CA 91320
805-499-5751
800-854-7600

Covox, Inc.

675 Conger
Eugene, OR 97402
503-342-1271

Creative Labs, Inc.

1901 McCarthy Boulevard
Milpitas, CA 95035
408-428-6600
800-647-9933

Digispeech, Inc.

550 Main Street, Suite J
Placerville, CA 95667
916-621-1787

Kurzweil Music Systems

Young Chaing Research and Development Institute
1432 Main Street
Waltham, MA 02154
617-890-2929

Media Vision

3185 Laurel View Court
Fremont, Ca 94538
510-770-8600

Microsoft Corporation

One Microsoft Way
Redmond, WA 98052-6322
206-882-8080

Roland Corporation, USA

7200 Dominion
Los Angeles, CA 90040
213-685-5141

Turtle Beach Systems

PO Box 5074
York, PA 17405
717-843-6916

Yamaha of America

6600 Orangethorpe
Buena Park, CA 90620
714-522-9240

Before you purchase a sound card, check with the manufacturer to make sure it will function properly with the software and hardware you have or plan to use. Also, different cards ship with different kinds of support and utility software.

The Sound Blaster series from Creative Labs, Inc., is probably the most popular of the sound card offerings. It is this standard to which most software is written. You can see that this is true as you read the specifications of the offerings of other companies. Most claim to be "Sound Blaster compatible." Some are, others are not. If Sound Blaster compatibility is important to you, the safest route is to buy Sound Blaster. The Sound Blaster card and any truly Sound Blaster–compatible cards work fine with PowerPoint.

Appendix B

Menu and Command Reference

I've shown you the majority of PowerPoint menu commands throughout this book, within the context of a particular task. This appendix is designed to provide a succinct reference to all the menu commands and to help you relate the main menu entries to the tasks performed under these main headings.

The File Menu

The PowerPoint File menu is similar to the File menus in all Windows-compliant products. This series of commands lets you start a new presentation, open an existing one, save the current presentation, print it, or send it. The main File menu is shown in Figure B.1. If your Windows installation does not include networking capability, your menu may not be exactly like this one. Also, you need to have a file open to see all of these options.

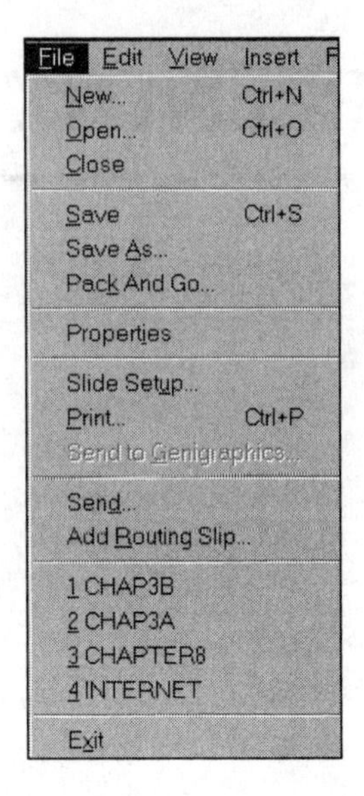

Figure B.1 *PowerPoint File menu.*

New... Ctrl+N

Use **New...** to start designing a new presentation. PowerPoint lets you choose how you want to create a new presentation (a Wizard, template, and so on), and then what slide layout to use for the initial slide. The **File: New** command presents the New Presentation dialog box, from which you choose a template or preformatted presentation to use for the new file.

If you choose a template (Presentation Design), PowerPoint presents the New Slide dialog box so you can choose the slide layout. If you choose one of the folders on the Presentation tab, then a preformatted presentation is opened so you can fill in the slides with the information you want.

NOTE

You can open a new presentation by clicking on the **New Presentation** icon on the Standard toolbar. In this case, PowerPoint offers only the New Slide dialog box to let you choose the slide layout. No templates, Presentations, or Wizards are offered. The new presentation is opened with a blank background.

You can use **File: New** from a blank PowerPoint screen or with other presentations displayed. Either way, PowerPoint opens a new file and a new screen, placing existing material in the background.

Open... Ctrl+O

Use **Open...** to load from disk an existing presentation. PowerPoint displays a typical Windows file and directory list, showing files that end in the ***.ppt** extension. Double-click on the file you want to open, or select the file name and click on **OK** to open the presentation.

The File Open dialog box, shown in Figure B.2, offers a screen rich in features and tools. From this screen you can open a file in the conventional way, control the appearance of the file list, and search for a file.

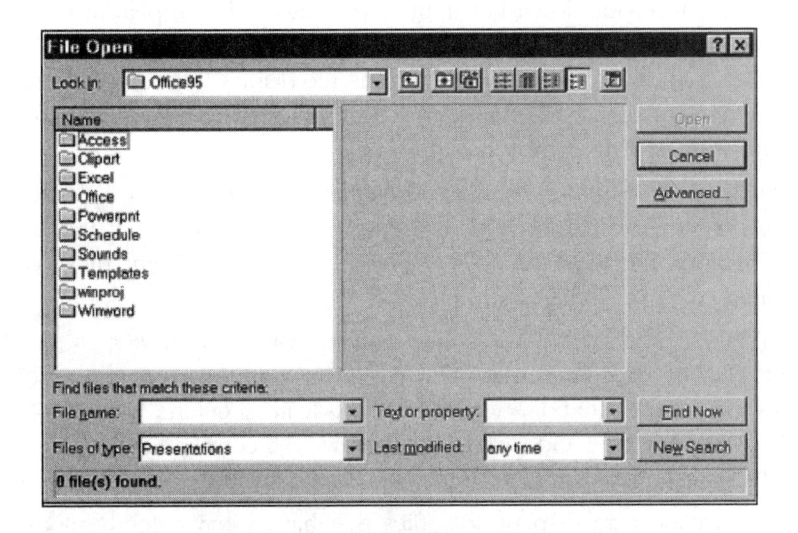

Figure B.2 *File Open dialog box main screen.*

Controlling the Open Dialog Display

You can display the file list in the Open dialog box in a number of ways. I find that the most useful setting displays the file name without the extension and other file statistics, and previews the file contents in a pop-up window as each file is selected. Change the file display by clicking on the icons at the upper right corner of the dialog box. The three yellow icons to the right of the Look in field of this dialog box let you move the file display up one directory, look in your favorites folder, or add to the favorites folder.

The next four icons change the way the files are displayed. The first icon presents a simple file name list, and the second icon offers file details such as the creation date, size and type. The third icon selects file properties, a pop-up box that appears beside the list of file names to provide such information as who saved the current version of the file, which revision it is, and so on. Finally, choose the **Preview** icon to display the first slide in each file as you select the name with your mouse.

FIND FILE...

Earlier versions of Windows included a functional Find facility. With Windows 95 this basic find facility is enhanced in several ways.

Notice the four pull-down fields and two buttons that appear at the bottom of the Open dialog box in Figure B.2. The File name field displays the file name search criteria you want to use in filtering the file display. If you have a series of presentations with similar file names, for example, you could enter the root file name with wild cards to display the full list.

The Files of type pull-down field filters the list according to the type of file you want to see. The default type is Presentation, of course, but you can pull down selections for Presentation Templates, early PowerPoint files (versions 2–4), Outline files, or All Files.

The Text or property pull-down field is blank when you first open this dialog box, but you can enter information that you want the Open program to locate in the files within the selected directory. To use this feature, enter a word or phrase in the Text or property field and click on **Find Now**. The current directory is searched and the files that contain the entered text will be displayed in the Name window.

You can choose to display only files that have been recently modified or those that are older than a certain date, by choosing a time frame from the pull-down list in the Last modified field. Choose from Anytime (the default), today, last week, this week, last month, this month.

Click on the **New Search** button to clear the current search criteria—file name, files of type, text or property, and last modified—and start a new search.

Beyond this simple filter type of search, you can click on the **Advanced...** button to display the Advanced Find dialog box shown in Figure B.3. Notice that the previously entered search criteria—file name filter, modified date, and so on—are displayed in the Find files that match these criteria window of this dialog box.

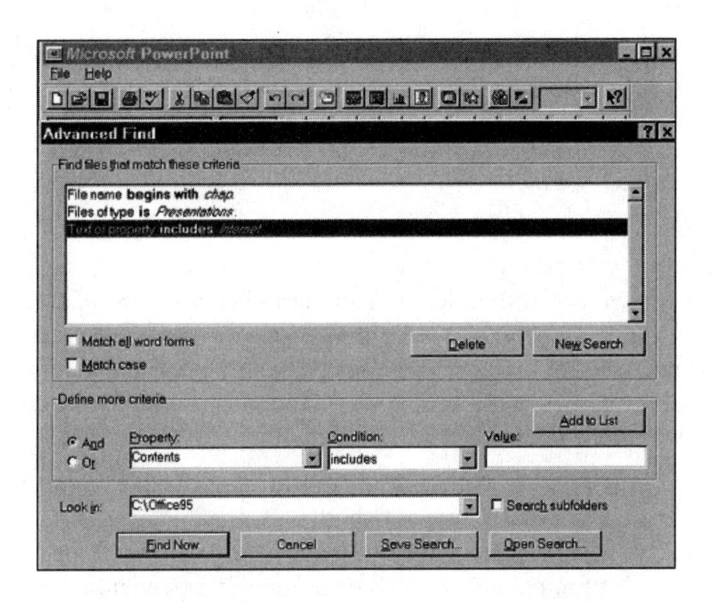

Figure B.3 *File Open Advanced Find dialog box.*

You can keep these search criteria, delete one or more entries, or start a new search from scratch. Click on **Match case** or **Match all word forms** to modify the search routine.

The section in the middle of the dialog box, titled Define more criteria, lets you specify additional search criteria to logically AND or OR with the previously entered criteria. Three drop-down fields in this section let you specify Properties, Condition, and Value information. Drop down separate lists to add an author search to the criteria, for example, or to tell the search routine to search document comments.

The Condition drop-down field specifies how the information will be searched: includes, includes phrase, begins with, ends with, includes near each other. The final field lets you type in the value you want the search engine to look for. Click on **Add to List** to have the new criteria added to the list of search criteria at the top of the dialog box. You can repeat this process as often as you like to narrow the search criteria.

The section at the bottom of the dialog box lets you specify the search path. Enter the directory where you want the search to begin, then click on **Search subfolders** if you want to include directories under the specified parent in the search.

Click on the **Save Search** button to store the criteria under a name that you can recall later. This is an excellent way to build repetitive search criteria that you can use over and over. Click on **Find Now** to start the search.

Close

Close removes the current presentation from memory and from the PowerPoint screen. If you have saved the file since the last changes were made, no further message will appear. PowerPoint will simply close the file and switch to the previous open file or to the blank PowerPoint screen. If you have made changes to the presentation since saving it last, PowerPoint will ask you if you want to save the changed file prior to closing it.

You may want to say **No** at this prompt if you have made temporary changes that you don't want to save. Otherwise, answer **Yes** so that PowerPoint will save the changed presentation to disk. If you have changed the presentation and say No at this prompt, any changes since the last save will be discarded.

Save Ctrl+S

As you work on presentations, you should save them every few minutes. The File Save command stores to disk the current presentation. If you have not previously saved the file, PowerPoint displays a typical Windows Save As dialog box. Otherwise the version of your presentation that is in memory is copied to disk, replacing the previously saved version.

Save As...

Use **Save As...** the first time you store a presentation (or use **Save**, in which case PowerPoint displays the Save As dialog box automatically). This gives the presentation a name, establishes the directory where you want to store it, and sets up the system so that the **File: Save** command knows where to put the current file.

You can also use **File: Save As...** to store a changed version of a presentation to a new location. Suppose you have a completed presentation that you want to modify or experiment with. Load the presentation from disk, then immediately use **File: Save As...** to store it under a new name. Now as you work with the file, use **File: Save** to store the new version, leaving the original unchanged.

Pack And Go...

The Pack And Go Wizard helps you package a specified presentation with the PowerPoint Viewer onto a floppy disk or other storage device. Use this Wizard to create a compact package to carry to another computer for a presentation. The Wizard also helps you store a lengthy presentation on more than one disk.

As with all PowerPoint Wizards, Pack And Go provides good on-screen prompts and interactive screens; using the facility is a matter of issuing the menu command sequence and following instructions.

Properties

The Properties selection displays the dialog box shown in Figure B.4. The specific makeup of this reporting dialog box changes with the type of presentation that is current, but the general information is the same.

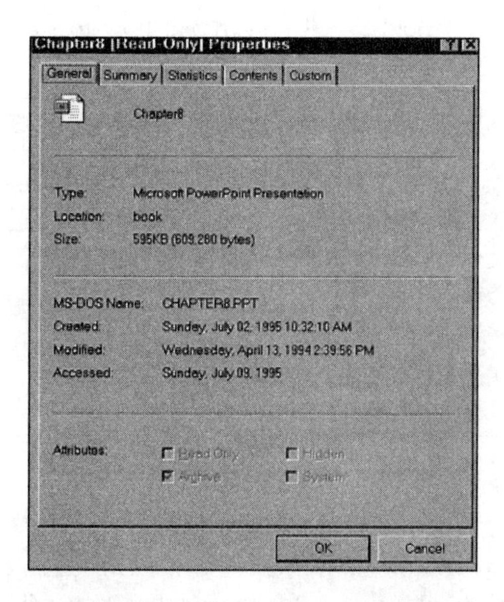

Figure B.4 *File Properties dialog box.*

This is a tabbed dialog box that lets you display different groupings of information by selecting a different tab. You can learn about the file title, the size of the file, the contents of the file, and more from the Properties dialog box.

Slide Setup...

The **Slide Setup...** command displays the dialog box shown in Figure B.5.

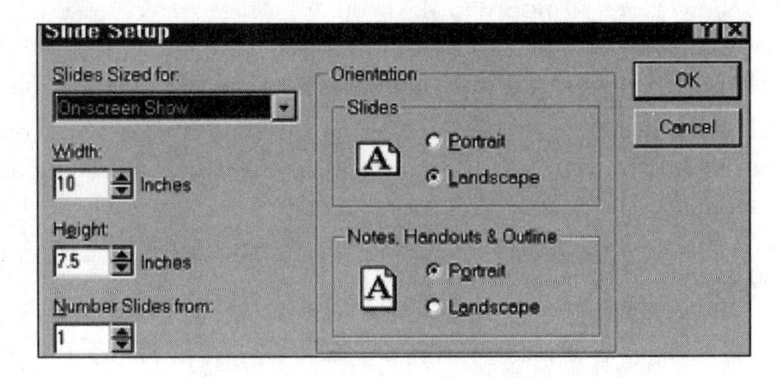

Figure B.5 *Slide Setup dialog box.*

Use the Slides Sized for field to tell PowerPoint how to size the slides in your presentation (see Figure B.6).

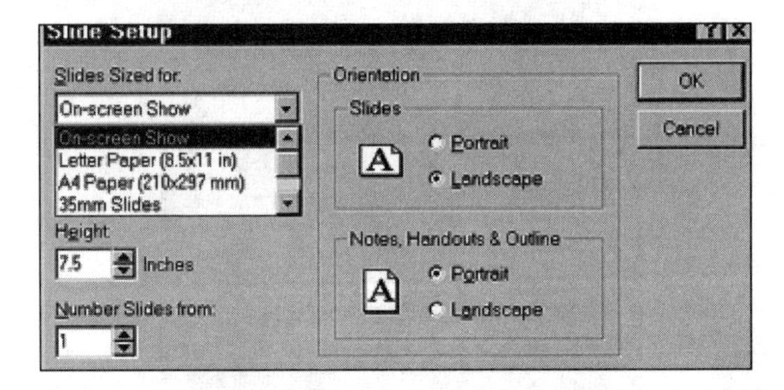

Figure B.6 *Slides Sized for pull-down list.*

For most applications you probably will use either On-screen or Letter Paper sizing. The On-screen show sizing is for times when you will present the show from your computer, whether you actually show it on the computer screen or project it for a larger audience. The Letter Paper sizing will probably produce overhead projection foils of the proper size and orientation.

When you select one of these preformatted sizes, PowerPoint automatically sets the Width and Height values. When you choose **Custom** from the size list, you can change these values. If you attempt to change the Width or Height values with anything other than Custom selected in the Slides Sized for field, PowerPoint automatically selects Custom sizing.

You can also choose orientation for the slides and for the notes, handout, and outline material from this dialog box.

Print... Ctrl+P

The Print dialog box, shown in Figure B.7, lets you specify what you will print and how it will be printed.

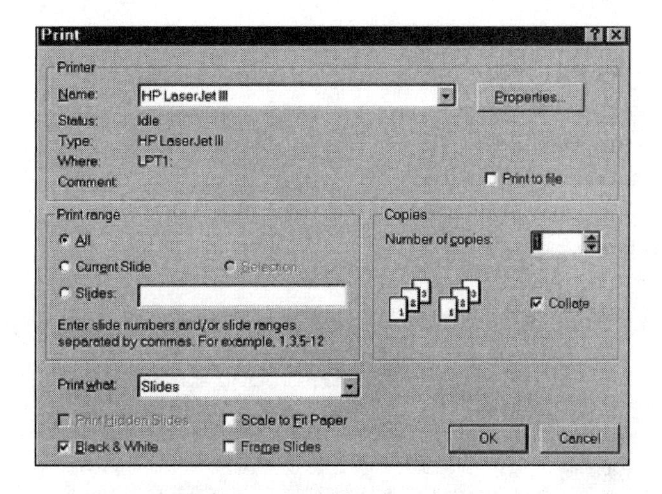

Figure B.7 *Print dialog box.*

I provide details on printing PowerPoint presentations in Chapter 6. Refer to this material for more information on using the **File: Print...** command.

Send to Genigraphics

One of your options in presenting PowerPoint material is to convert the computer images to 35mm slides or overhead foils. You may be able to do that yourself, depending on the facilities you have at your disposal. But you certainly can send data files to Genigraphics or another of the many available service bureaus whose focus is providing just that kind of service.

PowerPoint includes utilities to make it easy for you to send your PowerPoint presentations to Genigraphics. If you choose to work with another service bureau, that company will likely provide you with custom software to help you prepare your material for mailing or transmission to the company.

To prepare the current presentation for transmission to Genigraphics, make the presentation you want to convert to slides the current presentation, then choose **Send to Genigraphics** from the File menu. On-screen prompts and interactive dialog boxes will step you through the process. You can also call Genigraphics for additional information about preparing your material.

Send...

Use the **File: Send...** command to access Microsoft Mail and send the current presentation file to one or more users across your network. If your computer is not part of a network, then this option is not available. When you use the **Send...** command for the first time during the current session, and if you haven't used Mail from another application previously, then you must sign in to the mail system. Then the standard Mail dialog box shown in Figure B.8 is displayed.

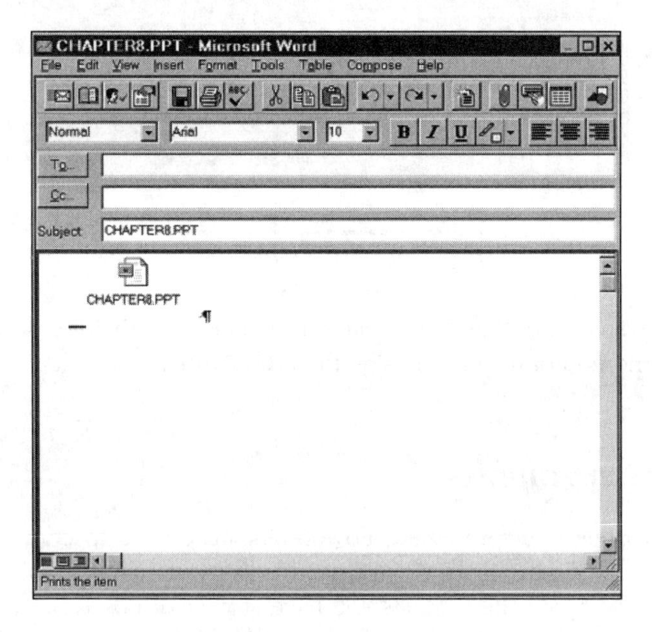

Figure B.8 *Microsoft Mail dialog box.*

Windows 95 also includes built-in support for the Microsoft Network and for TCP/IP communications. You can use the **Send** command to load a presentation into the Microsoft Exchange utility so that you can access the Microsoft Network and other mail facilities.

Add Routing Slip...

If you are sending the current presentation to a single recipient via Microsoft Mail, you probably don't need the Routing Slip option. However, if you want to send the presentation to several people and you want to control the sequence in which they receive it, use the **Add Routing Slip...** command to display the Add Routing Slip dialog box shown in Figure B.9.

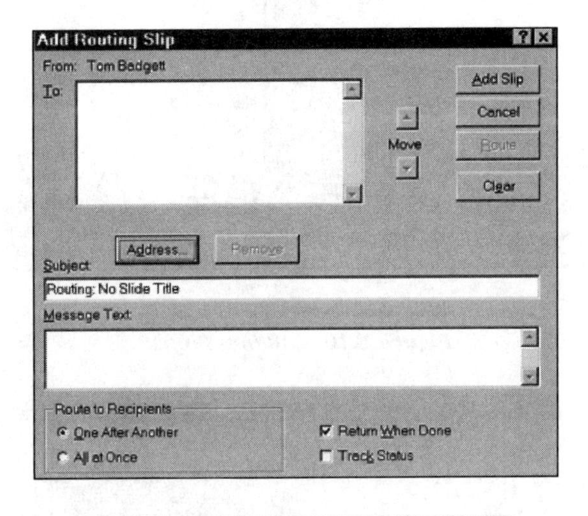

Figure B.9 *Add Routing Slip dialog box.*

The To window of this dialog box lists the recipients you want to receive the file. Use the **Address...** button to access Mail's Address dialog box, where you can choose recipients (see Figure B.10).

Once you have built a list of recipients, you can select individual names and move them up or down in the list by clicking on the up or down **Move** arrows on the Add Routing Slip dialog box. The position of the names in this list determines the order of receipt if you specify a serial routing by clicking on **One After Another** in the Route to Recipients area of this dialog box. Specify serial routing (the PowerPoint default) if you want each person on the list to see the comments offered by everyone before them on the list. If you choose parallel routing (**All at Once** from the Route to Recipients area), then the order of the To list doesn't matter. Choose parallel routing when you simply want everyone on the list to get the message and perhaps make individual comments. Figure B.11 shows the Routing Slip dialog box with an address list inserted.

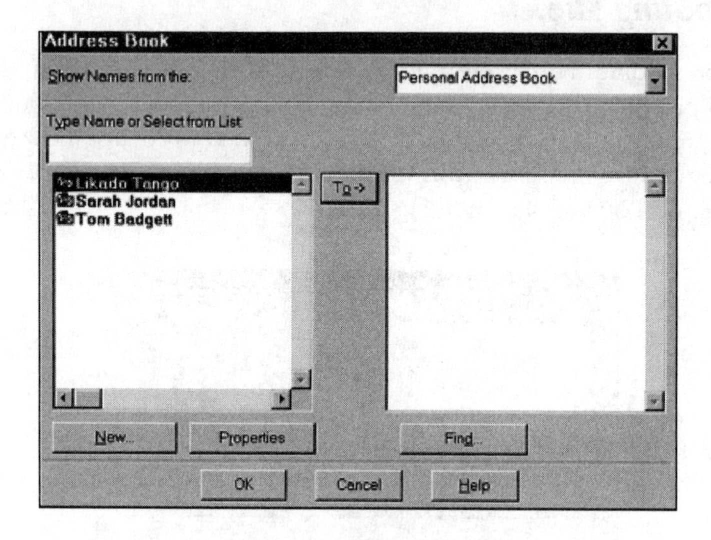

Figure B.10 *Address Profile.*

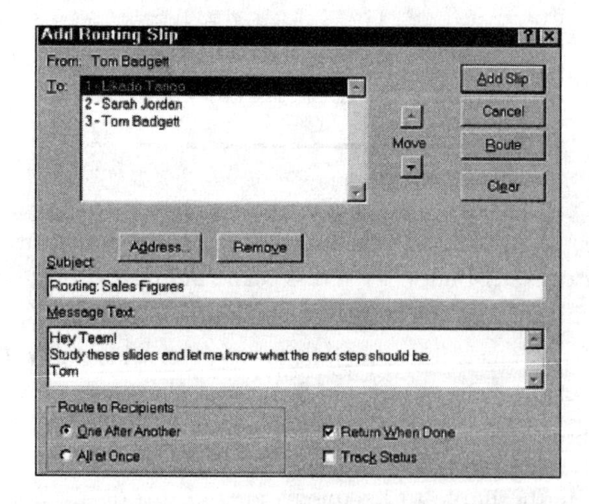

Figure B.11 *Routing Slip dialog box with address list.*

Once you have built a To list, you can remove a selected addressee by clicking on the **Remove** button beneath the To list. Add new recipients to the list at any time by displaying the Address list again and choosing new names.

PowerPoint automatically adds text to the Subject field of this dialog box, but you can type anything you want there. The text in this field appears on the Subject line of the received mail at the other end of the connection. You can also type a message in the Message Text box. This text will appear with the icon that represents the presentation file at the receiving end of the mail message.

If you enable **Return When Done** (the default), the message will be routed back to you when everyone on the list has seen it. The Track Status option (also a default) keeps track of where the message is along a serial route. If you specify All at Once, this option is not available.

You have two final options for completing the routing information. If you click on **Add Slip** at the top of the dialog box, then the routing information you have just specified is attached to the file and the dialog box is closed, but the mail isn't actually sent. Note that the routing option on the File menu changes when a routing slip has been added. The new command is **Edit Routing Slip** instead of Add Routing Slip. Also, you must save the file (**File: Save** or **File: Save As...**) to retain the routing slip information.

If you want to add the routing slip to the file and also send the mail, click on **Route**. In this case, the routing slip is added to the file and the mail system is launched to send the message according to the routing information you have just specified. Again, if you want to retain the routing information, you must save the file after specifying Route.

The Edit Menu

Like the File menu, the PowerPoint Edit menu shares many characteristics common to all Windows-compliant applications. It also has a few commands of its own. When you click on **Edit** from the main PowerPoint menu, the pull-down menu shown in Figure B.12 is displayed. Note that many Edit menu choices are frequently grayed-out, meaning they are unavailable. The available options change depending on what previous commands you have executed, what portions of a presentation are selected, and so on.

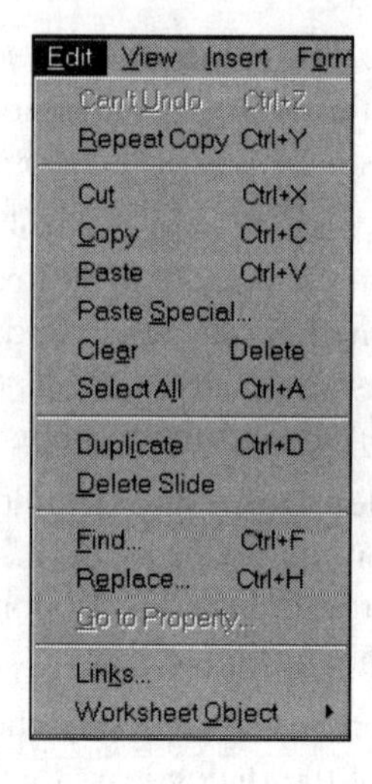

Figure B.12 *PowerPoint Edit menu.*

Undo Ctrl+Z

The **Undo** command lets you change your mind about the most recent PowerPoint operation. Suppose you delete a slide, then decide you'd like it back, or you remove some text and want to replace it. Just use **Edit: Undo (Ctrl+Z)** or click on the **Undo** button on the Standard toolbar. You can also remove new text or a new slide you've added with the **Undo** command.

After you use **Undo**, and before you do anything else, the **Undo** command functions like **Undo: Undo**. Suppose you remove a slide, then click on **Undo** to replace it. If you use **Undo** again, the slide is removed. If you type any characters, remove objects, or do anything else after using **Undo**, then **Undo** reverses that most recent operation.

If **Undo** can't reverse the previous actions, probably because there are no actions to reverse, then this menu item becomes **Can't Undo** and is grayed out so you can't access it.

Repeat Routing Slip Ctrl+Y

Use this menu item to display directly the Add Routing Slip dialog box. You can then edit the recipient list and send the presentation through one of the configured services.

Cut Ctrl+X

The **Cut** (**Ctrl+X**) command is a standard Windows command. It removes a selected object or text and places it on the Clipboard. You can copy it from the Clipboard back to PowerPoint or to another Windows application with **Edit: Paste**.

Copy Ctrl+C

Copy (**Ctrl+C**) works like **Cut** except that it leaves the original text or object and places a copy of it on the Clipboard.

Paste Ctrl+V

Use **Paste** (**Ctrl+V**) to copy information stored on the Clipboard to the current slide.

Paste Special

The **Paste Special...** command lets you control how information from the Clipboard is stored in your PowerPoint presentation. The command presents the Paste Special dialog box shown in Figure B.13.

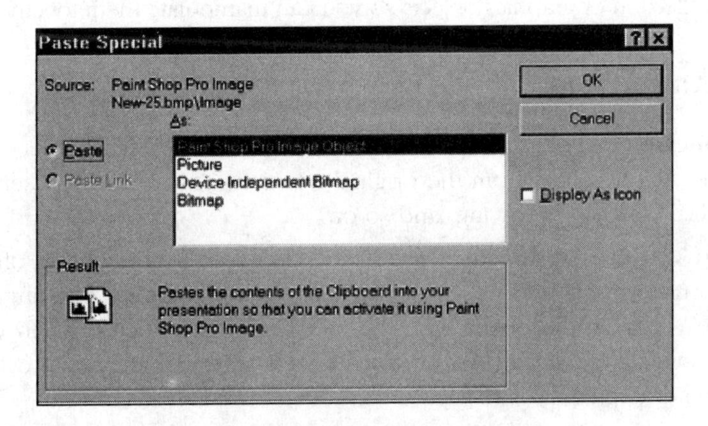

Figure B.13 *Paste Special dialog box.*

What you see on this dialog box varies slightly, depending on the type of information you have stored on the Clipboard. If PowerPoint recognizes the type of information, then a source is listed. You may be able to specify a Paste Link, which creates a live relationship between PowerPoint and the source application. This lets you update your PowerPoint slide automatically when the source data changes. (See Chapter 8 for more information on using **Paste Special**.)

Clear Del

Clear is the equivalent of **Delete**. When you use **Clear**, any selected text or objects are removed from the slide. The difference between **Cut** and **Clear** is that **Cut** places the removed object or text on the Clipboard, whereas **Clear** simply removes it without storing it on the Clipboard. You can, however, restore deleted objects with the **Undo** command if you haven't done anything else in between.

Select All Ctrl+A

The precise operation of **Select All (Ctrl+A)** varies depending on what you have displayed on the screen and what portion of that displayed data is selected already. If you have a text window on a slide with other text windows and graphics, for example, and one of those text windows is selected, the **Select All** command selects all of the text inside the current text box. If nothing on the slide is selected, however, then **Select All** selects all the individual graphics objects on the slide. You may want to use this command to delete all of the text within a text box, or to group a collection of graphics objects so you can manipulate them together.

Duplicate Ctrl+D

Use **Duplicate (Ctrl+D)** to make a copy of a selected object and place it on the same slide slightly offset from the original position. This feature is useful in creating special effects, shadowing, and so on.

When you use **Duplicate**, PowerPoint chooses the amount of offset. You can also create your own offset by selecting an object, then pressing the **Ctrl** key while you drag the object with the mouse. Use **Duplicate** when you want to show several objects stacked on top of each other, for example, or to create the illusion of depth.

Delete Slide

Delete Slide removes the current slide. Unlike **Cut**, **Delete Slide** does not place a copy of the slide onto the Clipboard. You can restore a deleted slide with the

Undo command if you have not conducted additional PowerPoint operations in the meantime.

Find Ctrl+F

The **Find** (**Ctrl+F**) command displays the Find dialog box shown in Figure B.14.

Figure B.14 *Find dialog box.*

Enter any text you want to locate within the current presentation into the Find What field of this dialog box. You can refine the search by specifying **Match Case** or **Find Whole Words Only**. Click on **Find Next** to locate the next occurrence of the text you specified.

NOTE

The **Find** command locates only text on the body of PowerPoint slides. If the text you seek is part of a graphic—such as text on an organizational chart—the **Find** command won't locate it.

You can use this same dialog box to change a string of text throughout a presentation by specifying the text you want to find and then clicking on **Replace...** to add the Replace With field shown in Figure B.15.

Figure B.15 *Replace dialog box.*

Enter the new text into the Replace With field. If you click again on **Replace**, PowerPoint replaces the next occurrence of the Find What text with the Replace With text. If the Replace button is grayed out, use **Find Next** to locate the next occurrence of the Find What text; then you can use **Replace** to change it. If you want to replace all occurrences of the Find What text in the presentation with the Replace With text, click on **Replace All**. Unlike some word processors, which display the last occurrence of the found and replaced text, PowerPoint keeps the current slide on the screen (all of the specified text has been replaced, however).

Replace... Ctrl+H

The **Replace** command (**Ctrl+H**) is a variation of the **Find** command. Instead of displaying the Find dialog box shown in Figure B.14 as the initial dialog box, the **Replace** command displays the Replace dialog box shown in Figure B.15. Simply enter the Find What and Replace With text and use the **Find Next**, **Replace**, and **Replace All** buttons as described in the Find section.

Links...

The **Links...** command may not be available. If it is grayed out, that simply means that you do not have any active links as part of the current presentation. If the **Links...** command is available, you can use it to display the Links dialog box shown in Figure B.16.

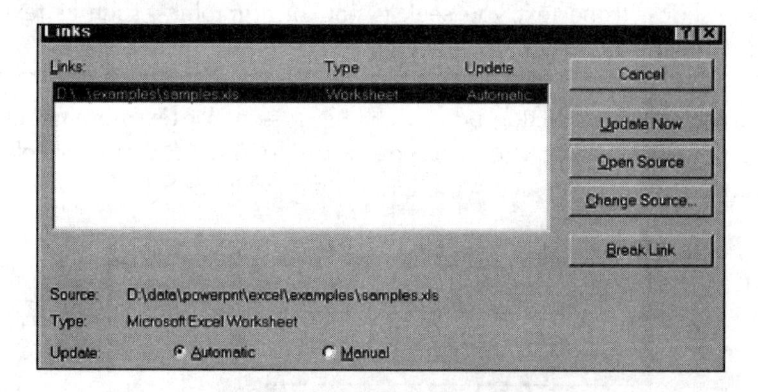

Figure B.16 *Links dialog box.*

You can use this dialog box to manipulate any links between the current presentation and external files. Refer to Chapter 8 for more information on using the Links dialog box.

Object

The **Object** command (or the **Edit: Object** command if you have selected an object prior to using this menu) is a variable menu item. It changes according to the type of objects you have within the current presentation or on the current slide. When you select an object inserted from an external application, the Object menu entry changes to reflect the type of object. If you select a Media Clip object, for example, the menu entry becomes **Media Clip Object**. If you select a linked spreadsheet object, this menu item becomes **Linked Spreadsheet Object**, and so on.

When you click on this menu item, another menu is displayed, such as the one in Figure B.17.

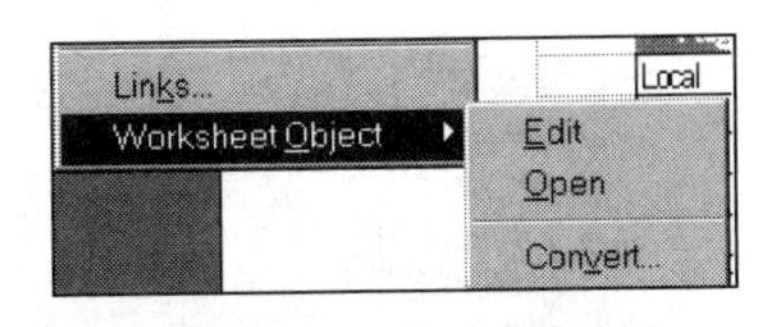

Figure B.17 Object pull-down menu.

The selections available on this menu also vary depending on the type of object you have selected. In Figure B.17, for example, one of the choices is **Play**. If this were a spreadsheet object, Play would not be an appropriate choice.

Regardless of the type of object selected, the final selection on this pull-down menu is **Convert...**. If you choose this entry, the dialog box shown in Figure B.18 is displayed.

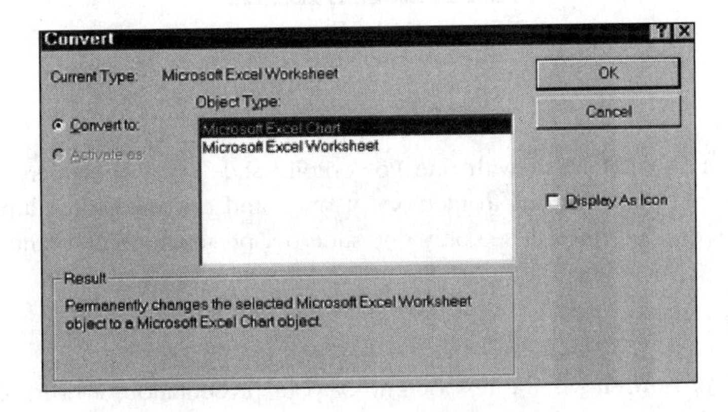

Figure B.18 *Object Convert dialog box.*

Some objects cannot be converted. Others can be changed from one file format to another. For more information about using the conversion feature of this dialog box, refer to Chapter 8.

The View Menu

The View menu changes how you see the components of your presentation. The default view is Slides, with one slide per screen. You can choose other views as required to work with or print different components of the presentation. Figure B.19 shows the View menu.

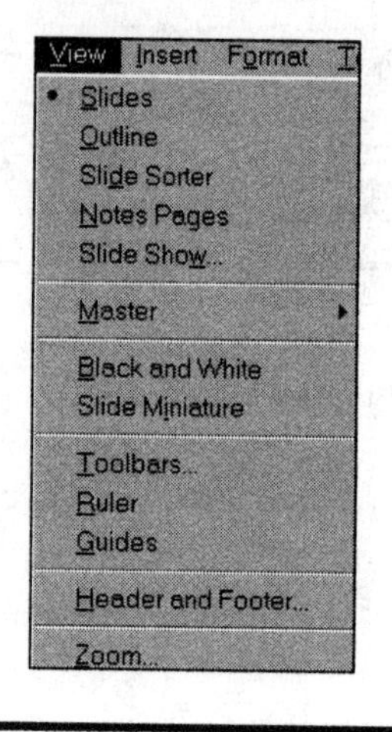

Figure B.19 *View menu.*

Slides

Slides is the default view, with one PowerPoint slide on each screen. You can have multiple presentations in memory at once and can display multiple slides on the screen, but you will see only one slide per presentation at a time.

Outline

The Outline view shows the text outline of your presentation. PowerPoint automatically builds the outline based on the major text components of your slides. If you have created a presentation from blank slides (which do not have title or bullet list templates from the AutoLayout dialog box), then the outline will be blank. You can create an outline without displaying unwanted title or bullet list information on the screen by editing the outline in the Outline view to add the topics you want. These topics will appear on your slides, but you can use the **Text Color** button to make the text the same color as the background so that unwanted text won't be visible.

Slide Sorter

The Slide Sorter view lets you look at a screen full of slides at once. This is an excellent way to get an overview of your presentation or to move individual slides to new locations if you need to. Figure B.20 shows a typical Slide Sorter view.

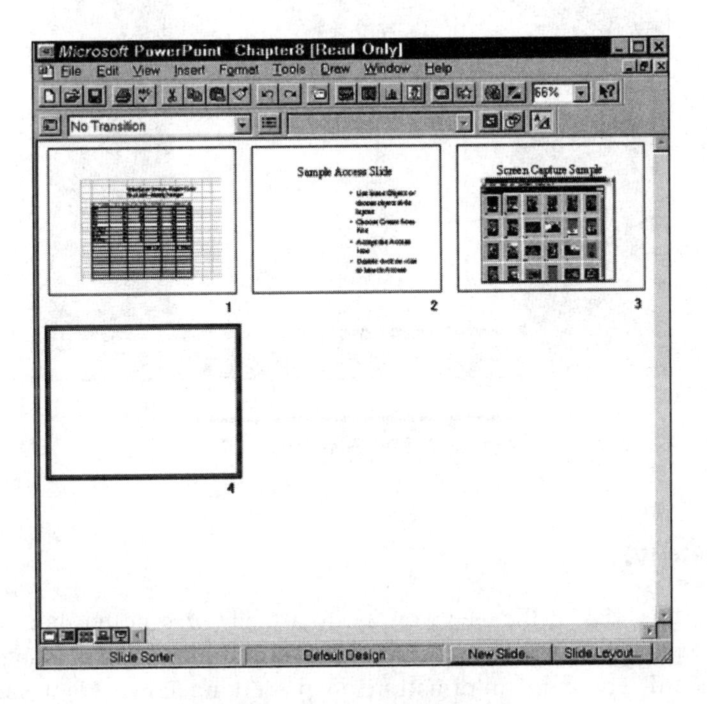

Figure B.20 *Slide Sorter view.*

Notes Pages

Choose **Notes Pages** to view your slides with a notes area beneath them. You can type whatever text you want to accompany this notes version of each slide.

Use these slides as speaker's notes, as an aid to presentation planning, or as part of your handout package. Figure B.21 shows a Notes Pages view of a slide shown in Figure B.20.

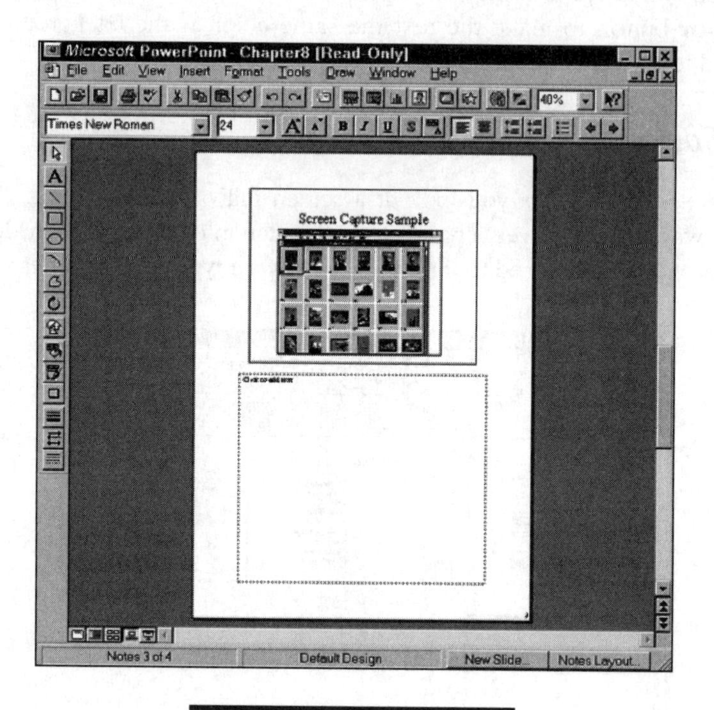

Figure B.21 *Notes Pages view.*

Slide Show...

The Slide Show view is the view you use to actually present the slide show. It is a full-screen view that is advanced by clicking the mouse or pressing keys on the keyboard. For more information on presenting PowerPoint shows, see Chapter 5.

Master

The Master menu choice presents an additional list of menu items, shown in Figure B.22. A dot appears in front of the selected view on the screen.

Figure B.22 *Master pull-down menu.*

The master sheets for Slide, Title, Handout, and Notes let you set parameters for the display of each of these slide show components. Figure B.23 shows the Notes Master page. Other Masters are similar.

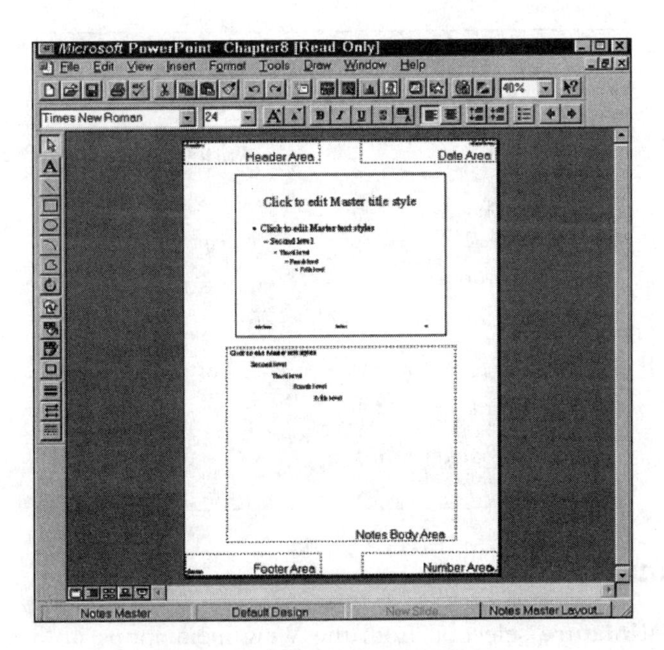

Figure B.23 *Notes Master view.*

See Chapter 5 for additional information about using master sheets.

Black and White

Working in PowerPoint is a colorful experience. You can use the power of your high-resolution color display to enjoy creating presentations in full color. However, if you need to print a slide or an entire presentation on a laser printer, for example, you may want to view the presentation in black and white. This will help you understand how the presentation will appear when printed on a black and white printer.

To view a presentation in black and white view, simply select **Black and White** from the View menu. A small version of the current slide pops up in color while the body of the slide is displayed in black and white.

You can change how an object prints (and how it appears on the screen). First, point to the object you want to change, and then select one of the options on the shortcut menu that appears when you click the right mouse button and point to Black and White.

In general, here's how objects appear in Black and White view:

Text	Black
Text shadows	Hidden
Embossing	Hidden
Fills	Grayscale
Frame	1-point frame
Pattern fills	Grayscale
Lines	Black
Object shadows	Gray
Bitmaps	Grayscale
Slide backgrounds	White

Slide Miniature

The **Slide Miniature** selection from the View menu pops up a small, black and white copy of the current slide. To view all slides in the presentation as miniatures, choose the Organizer view by clicking on the icon at the lower left of the PowerPoint screen, or by choosing **Slide Miniature** from the View menu. This view of your slide show is useful in organizing slides, getting an overall view of the presentation, adding slides, and so on.

Toolbars...

The **Toolbars** menu choice displays the Toolbars dialog box shown in Figure B.24.

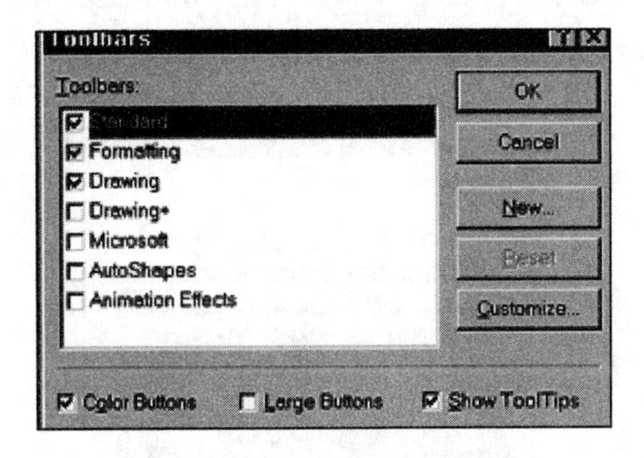

Figure B.24 *Toolbars dialog box.*

The choices on this dialog box are toggles. If there is a check mark inside the box beside one of these entries, that toolbar is displayed. If you click on this box, the check mark is removed and the toolbar is removed from the display. If you click on a blank box, a check mark is added and the selected toolbar is added to your screen display.

You can conduct the same tasks by pointing to one of the active toolbars and pressing the right mouse button to display the pop-up Toolbars menu shown in Figure B.25.

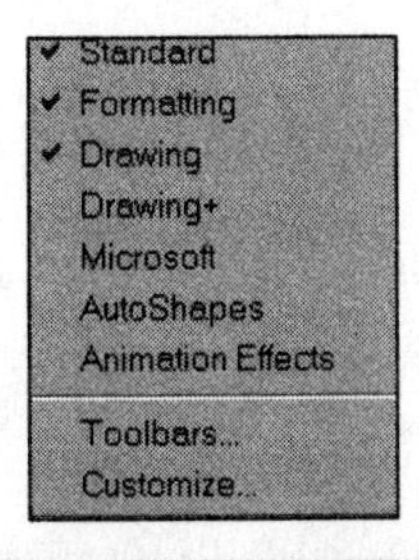

Figure B.25 *Pop-up Toolbars menu.*

Ruler

Use the Ruler display to show precise screen positioning as you place objects or text on a PowerPoint slide. With the Rulers enabled, you will see a vertical and a horizontal grid beside your slides, as shown in Figure B.26.

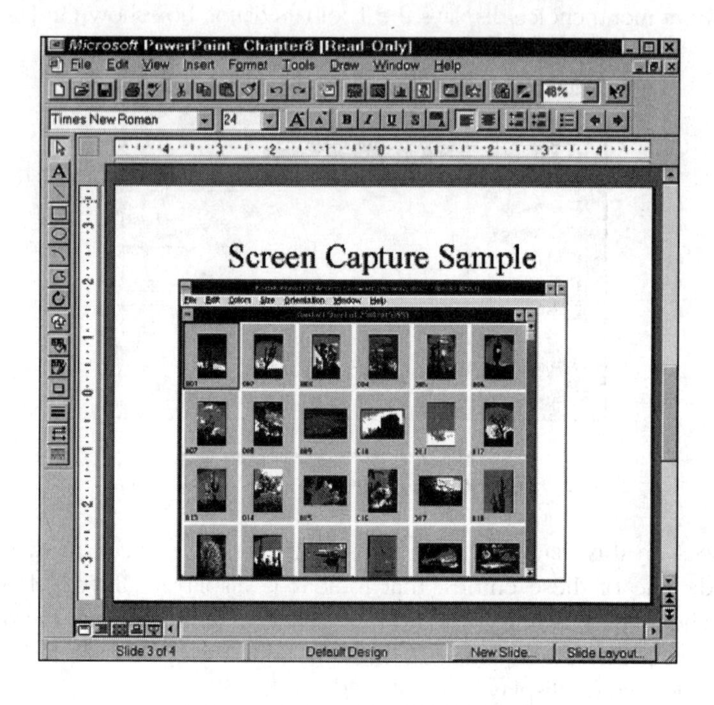

Figure B.26 *Ruler Slide display.*

The size of the ruler changes with the type of object displayed on the PowerPoint slide.

Guides

Like the Ruler display, Guides help you position objects precisely on a PowerPoint slide. When you turn on the Guides display, a dotted-line cross is inserted on top of the current slide. When the guide lines are first displayed, they cross in the middle of the screen. This is designated as point 0,0. As you move one of the lines by grabbing it with the mouse pointer, PowerPoint shows the relative position from the center 0,0 position. You can display the Guides in conjunction with the Rulers to make it easier to tell where an object is located, or you can use the Guides alone.

The guides help you to automatically position objects by causing them to snap to the guide, either as you move the center point of the guides near an object or as you move an object near the center point of the guides. Either the center of the object or the edge of the object—whichever is nearest the guide intersection—will snap to the guide.

NOTE

The snap to guide action takes place while you are dragging the object, not when you release it. Move an object back and forth across a guide line and you can see it snap to the guide.

Header and Footer...

Use the **Header and Footer** menu item to display the dialog box shown in Figure B.27. From this dialog box you can design how the header and footer information on each slide in your presentation will appear. This dialog box also lets you specify a separate header and footer for the notes and handout pages in your presentation.

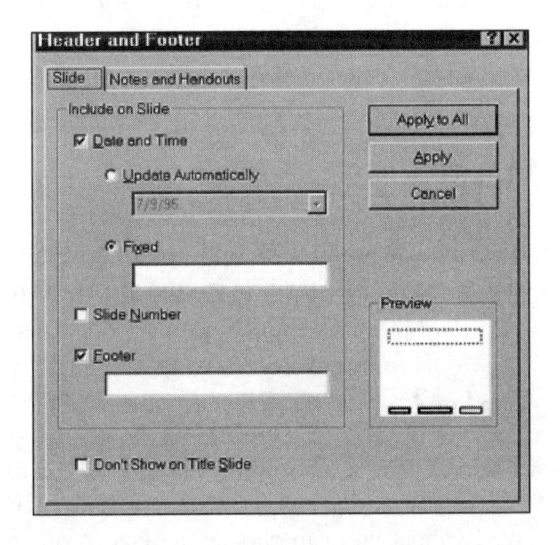

Figure B.27 *Header and Footer dialog box.*

You can specify an automatically updating date in a format of your choice, enter fixed text, and display a slide number as part of the header and footer information.

Zoom...

Use the **Zoom** command to display the Zoom dialog box shown in Figure B.28.

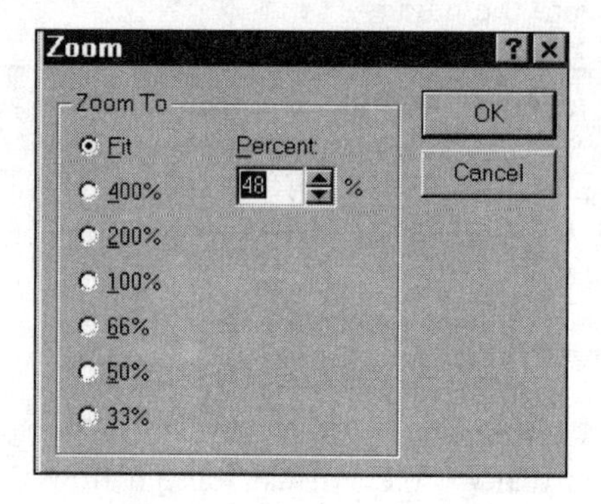

Figure B.28 *Zoom dialog box.*

If you click on **100%**, the current slide fills up the slide space on the screen. Anything less than that reduces the display. You can enlarge a slide up to 400% if you want to study details or position objects precisely.

The Insert Menu

The Insert menu gives you a number of options for inserting information or objects onto a PowerPoint slide. The main Insert menu is shown in Figure B.29.

You can access many of the Insert menu options from the Standard toolbar.

New Slide... Ctrl+M

Choosing the **New Slide...** command from the Insert menu is the same as clicking on the **New Slide** button at the bottom of the slide display. The New Slide dialog box is displayed so that you can choose the layout you want for the new slide. PowerPoint inserts a new slide after the current slide in the presentation.

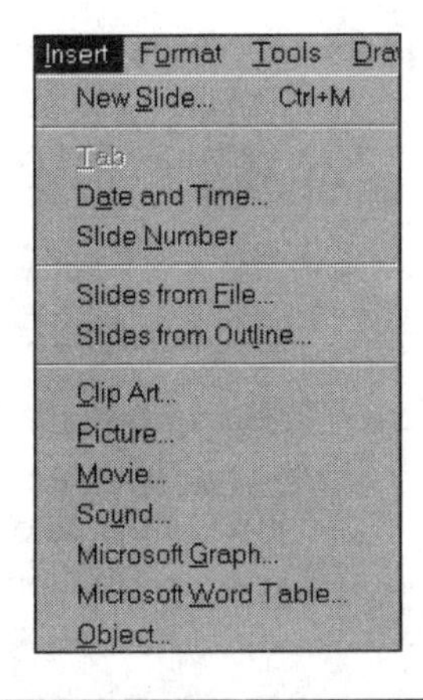

Figure B.29 *Insert menu.*

Tab

This is the equivalent to pressing the **tab** key on the keyboard when the insertion point is inside a text object.

Date and Time...

The **Date and Time** option lets you format an entire presentation by inserting the current date or time on the Master pages or insert the date and time into a single slide. When you choose this menu option, the dialog box shown in Figure B.30 is displayed. If you try to use **Insert: Date and Time** without a text box selected, you will see an error dialog box.

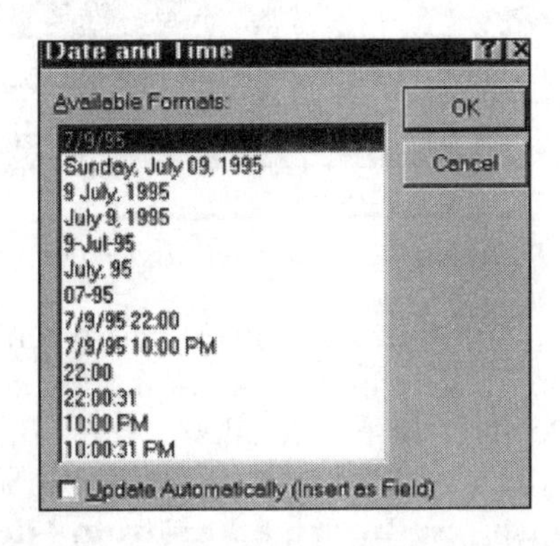

Figure B.30 *Date and Time dialog box.*

If you are looking at a Master view, then the **Insert: Date and Time** command sequence places a // object on the Master view. You can select this object like any other object and place it wherever you want PowerPoint to display the current date on all slides.

Slide Number

You can insert a Slide Number code on a Master view or anywhere on an individual slide. The slide number is inserted into any text field on a slide. If it is moved into position on the Master, it will appear on all slides. If you insert the code on an active slide, the number appears only on that slide.

Slides from File...

When you use the **Slides from File...** command, PowerPoint displays the Insert File dialog box, shown in Figure B.31.

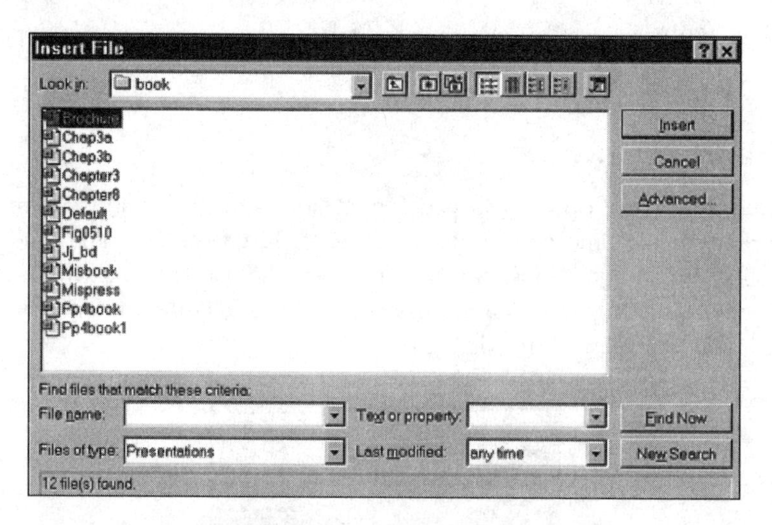

Figure B.31 *Insert File dialog box.*

You can choose a file from the list. PowerPoint inserts the slides from the selected file after the current slide in the current presentation. This is one way to use modules to build PowerPoint presentations. You can create short presentation files with slides that can be used in many presentations. Then, as you build new presentations, you can use **Insert: Slides from File...** to place the modules where you want.

Slides from Outline...

Like **Slides from File**, **Slides from Outline** lets you merge an existing presentation or presentation module with the current file. The Insert Outline dialog box shown in Figure B.32 is displayed.

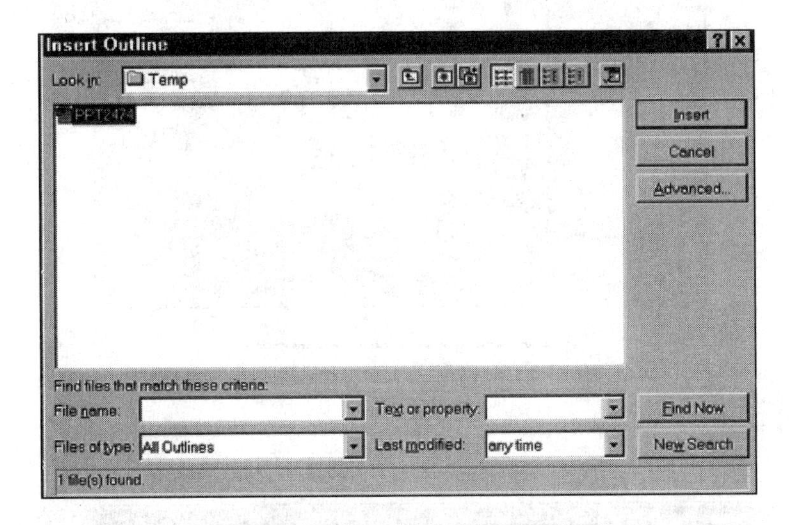

Figure B.32 *Insert Outline dialog box.*

Choose a file name, and PowerPoint will insert the outline after the current slide.

Clip Art...

When you use **Insert: Clip Art...**, PowerPoint displays the ClipArt Gallery, shown in Figure B.33.

You can select from among the many clip art categories and images to insert a picture onto the current slide. For more information about using clip art, refer to Chapter 4.

Picture...

Use **Insert Picture...** to place a graphics image (.TIFF, .PCX, or other file) onto a PowerPoint slide. The Insert Picture dialog box, shown in Figure B.34, is displayed.

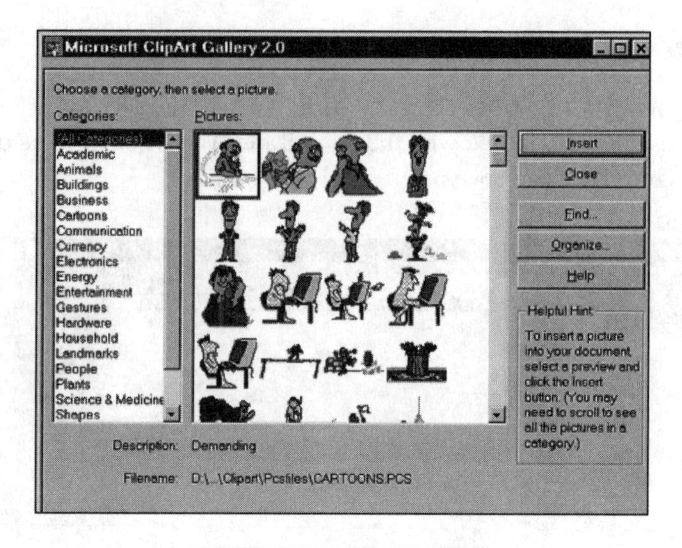

Figure B.33 *ClipArt Gallery.*

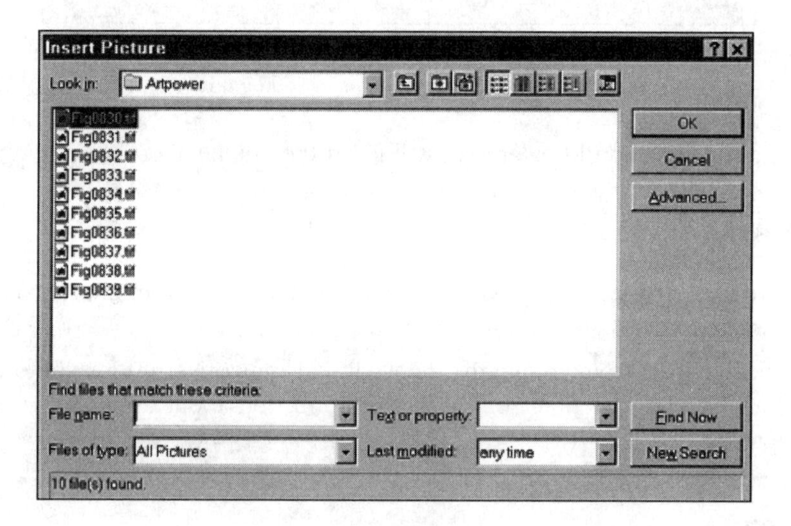

Figure B.34 *Insert Picture dialog box.*

I've included more information about using graphics images in Chapter 5.

Movie...

A movie clip is just another object to PowerPoint. When you choose this option from the Insert menu, PowerPoint displays movie files so that you can choose one to insert. You can display movie objects either as a poster, where the first frame of the movie appears on the slide, or as an icon, where only a generic icon is shown on the slide. You can play the movie by double-clicking on the icon or the poster.

Sound...

Like movies, sounds are objects you can insert onto your PowerPoint slides. Choose **Sounds...** from the Insert menu; you will see the familiar Insert Object dialog box from which you can choose the sound file you want to place on the current presentation.

Microsoft Graph...

The Graph facility is like an Excel spreadsheet except that it is confined to row and column data that will be charted. When you choose this command, PowerPoint displays the Graph dialog box shown in Figure B.35.

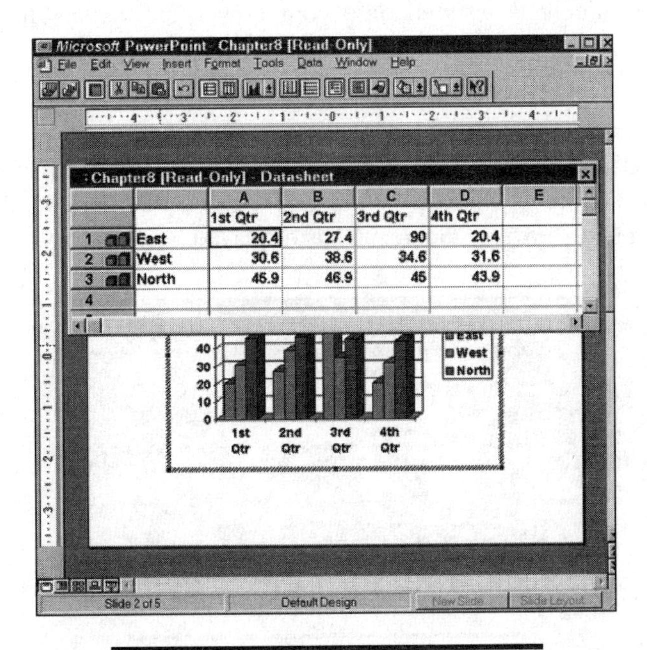

Figure B.35 *Microsoft Graph dialog box.*

You can enter row and column information on the spreadsheet grid to construct a custom graph.

Microsoft Word Table...

The Word Table facility lets you insert a Microsoft Word table into a PowerPoint slide. When you choose this option, PowerPoint displays the Insert Word Table dialog box, shown in Figure B.36.

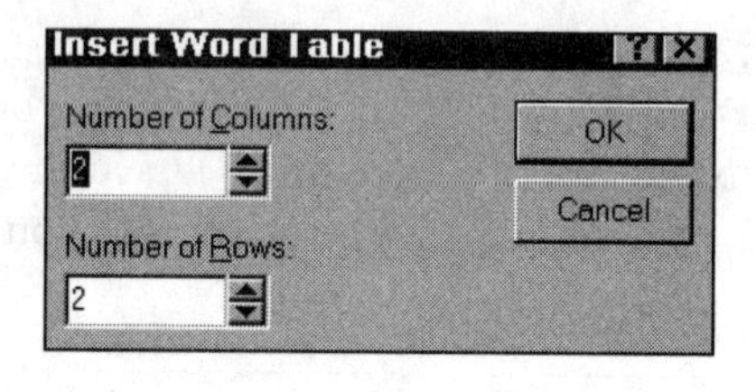

Figure B.36 *Insert Word Table dialog box.*

The default table has two rows and two columns. You can change the table configuration by entering new values into these fields. You can also edit the table configuration after it is inserted onto your PowerPoint slide. Click on **OK** to insert the table form you have defined onto the current slide.

Object...

Use **Insert: Object...** when you want to insert something not covered by one of the other Insert menu choices. When you choose this command, the Insert Object dialog box shown in Figure B.37 is displayed.

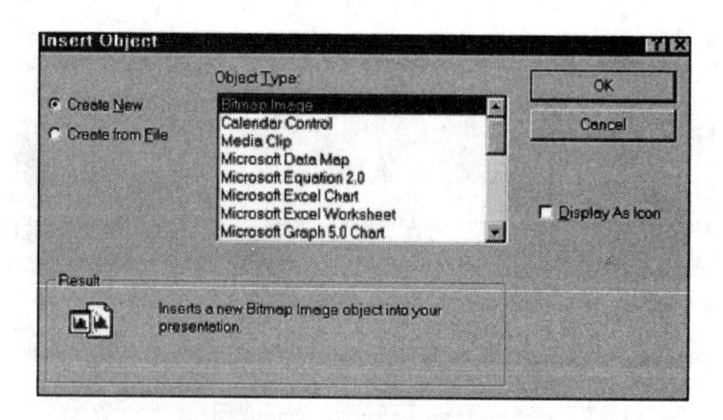

Figure B.37 *Insert Object dialog box.*

For more information about inserting objects into PowerPoint presentations, refer to Chapter 8.

The Format Menu

The Format menu lets you choose fonts and apply attributes to text and other objects. The Format menu is shown in Figure B.38. Notice that many of the choices on the Format menu apply to text. If you don't have text selected, many of the Format choices will be grayed out.

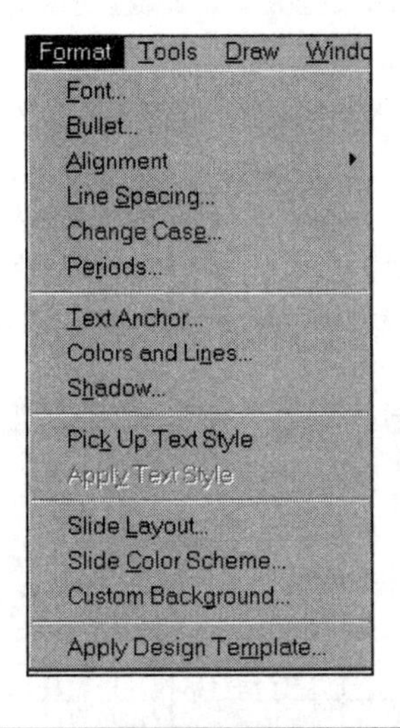

Figure B.38 *Format menu.*

Font...

The **Font** command applies to text inserted on a PowerPoint slide. When you use this menu choice, PowerPoint displays the Font dialog box shown in Figure B.39.

From this dialog box you can choose the font, the font style (bold, italic, and so on), and the font size. In addition, you can specify other text attributes such as underline and color.

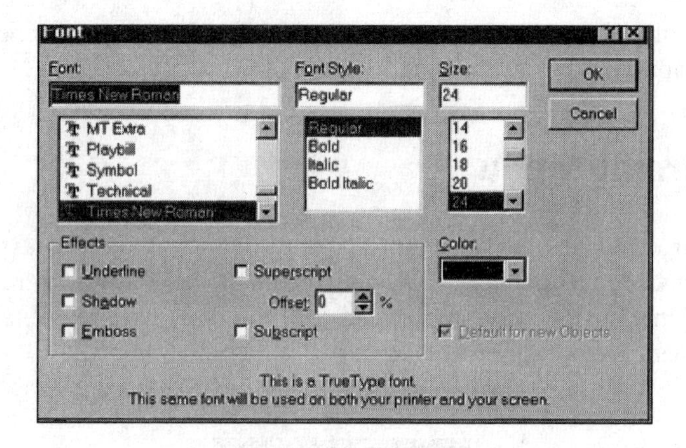

Figure B.39 *Font dialog box.*

Bullet...

The **Bullet** menu choice displays the Bullet dialog box shown in Figure B.40.

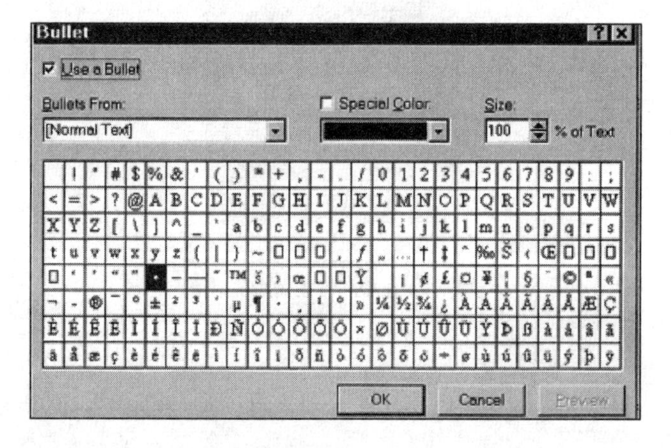

Figure B.40 *Bullet dialog box.*

The default bullet list is from the Normal Text set of fonts, but you can select from a number of additional font groups to specify what characters will be used for bullet lists. First choose the font group, then choose a specific character from the Bullet dialog box.

Alignment

The **Alignment** menu choice specifies how selected text will be aligned: Left, Center, Right, or Justify. **Left alignment** is the PowerPoint default. Choose **Center** to center the text on each line. Right justification makes the right side of text lines flush, but the left side ragged. Justified text is aligned so that both the left and right edges are smooth.

Line Spacing...

The **Line Spacing** menu choice displays the Line Spacing dialog box shown in Figure B.41.

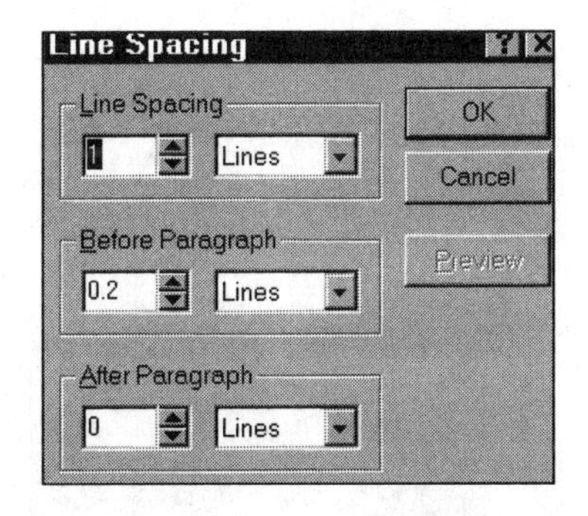

Figure B.41 *Line Spacing dialog box.*

This is typical Windows text formatting in which you set the line spacing and the amount of additional spacing before and after a paragraph. Once you change the PowerPoint defaults, the **Preview** button becomes active so that you can look at the results of your changes.

Change Case...

This command displays the Change Case dialog box shown in Figure B.42.

This dialog box provides five choices for setting the case of selected text. Sentence case is the default and it capitalizes the first character in a sentence. The **lowercase** option makes all of the selected text lowercase, while the **UPPERCASE** option makes all of the selected text uppercase. **Title Case** capitalizes each important word in a sentence. The **tOGGLE cASE** option reverses the case of selected text: capital letters are changed to lowercase, and lowercase characters are changed to uppercase. Click on **OK** when you have selected the option you want.

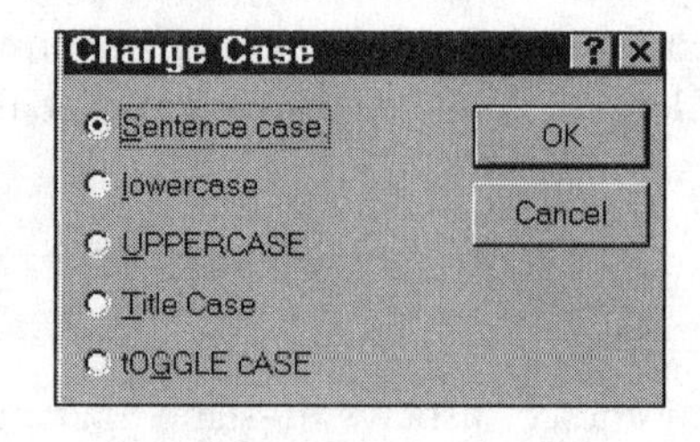

Figure B.42 *Change Case dialog box.*

Periods...

The **Periods...** menu choice displays the Periods dialog box shown in Figure B.43.

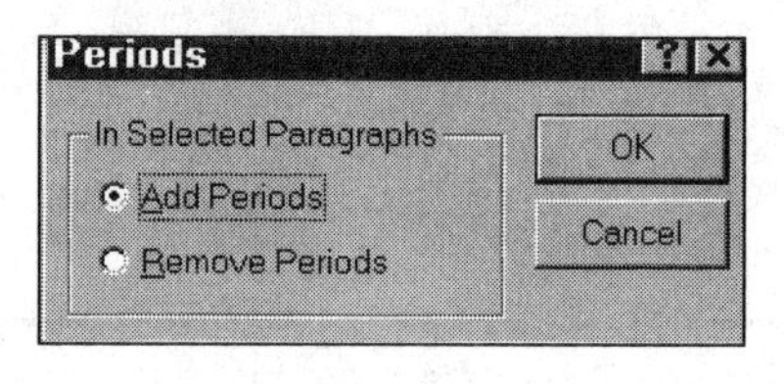

Figure B.43 *Periods dialog box.*

The **Add Periods** selection on this dialog box adds periods to the ends of selected paragraphs, while **Remove Periods** removes periods.

Text Anchor...

The Text Anchor dialog box, shown in Figure B.44, lets you specify how selected text will be anchored to the current slide.

Use this dialog box to adjust the shape of a text object to the shape of the graphics object that contains it. The Anchor Point can be any one of six choices: Top, Middle, Bottom, Top Centered, Middle Centered, or Bottom Centered. The *anchor point* is the point on the text rectangle (text box) from which the text grows or to which it shrinks when edited. If you anchor the text in the middle center, for example, the text remains centered in the object's text area as the amount of text shrinks or grows.

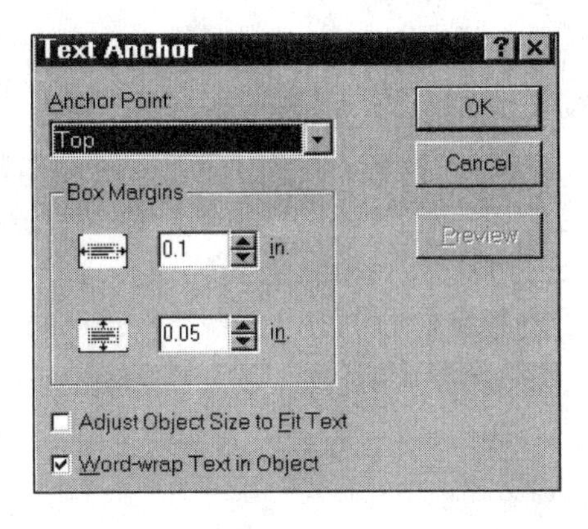

Figure B.44 *Text Anchor dialog box.*

As you adjust the Box Margins, you change the amount of space between the text and the graphics object that contains it. You can also force the object to adjust to the size of the text by clicking on the **Adjust Object Size to Fit Text** button. By default, PowerPoint wraps text in the object. You can disable this function by clicking on the **Word-wrap Text in Object** button to remove the check mark in this box.

Colors and Lines...

The **Colors and Lines** menu choice displays the Colors and Lines dialog box shown in Figure B.45.

The Line Style area of this dialog box lets you select from several line styles (various levels of thickness and types of compound lines). If you choose **Dashed lines**, you can specify a dashed line format from among several formats available. The **Arrows** selection lets you specify left-facing arrowheads, right-facing arrowheads, or arrowheads that face in both directions. In addition, you can pull down Fill and Line menus to specify fill and line colors.

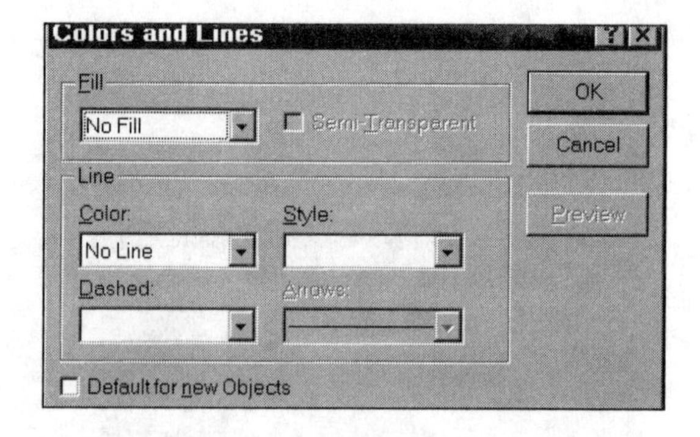

Figure B.45 *Colors and Lines dialog box.*

Shadow...

The **Shadow** menu choice displays the Shadow dialog box shown in Figure B.46.

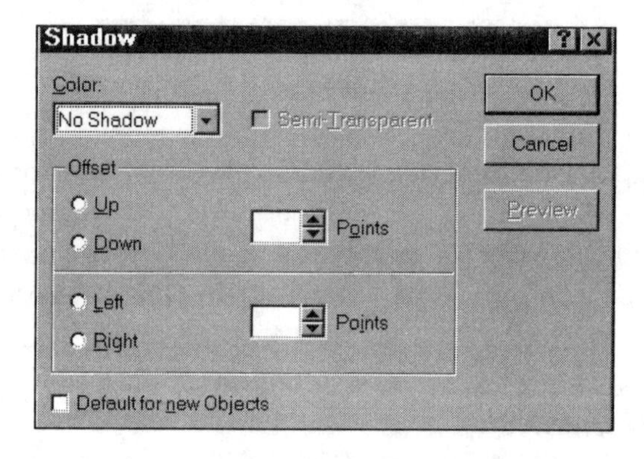

Figure B.46 *Shadow dialog box.*

As with other PowerPoint and Windows-compliant dialog boxes, you can change the format of text with the pull-down menus available on this dialog box. If you pull down the Color menu, you get three choices: **No Shadow** (the default), **Embossed**, and **Other Color**. The **No Shadow** choice formats text without any shadow. You can produce an Embossed effect by choosing **Embossed** from the Color menu.

Once you have chosen the color scheme, you can specify an offset for the shadow effect in points up and down, left and right. The best advice is to experiment with various settings to find the combination you want for the selected text. Click on **Preview** to see how the text will appear before you make a change. Click on **OK** to make the change and return to your PowerPoint slide.

Pick Up Object Style

The **Pick Up Object Style** command lets you copy the style of one object to another. This is the same as using the **Format Painter** from the Standard toolbar. The precise menu wording changes with the type of available objects you have.

Use **Pick Up Object Style** to copy attributes such as color, shadow, pattern, and so on. As with the Format Painter, you must first select the text or object whose style you want to pick up. Then choose the **Pick Up Object Style** command. This copies the style to a temporary memory area.

Apply Object Style

This menu command is only available after you have copied an object style using **Pick Up Object Style**. With a style picked up, or copied, you can then apply this copied style by selecting the new text and issuing the **Apply Object Style** command. As with the **Pick Up Object** command, you don't see a dialog box when the command is used. Rather, you see the results of the command on the screen.

Slide Layout...

The Slide Layout dialog box, shown in Figure B.47, is the same dialog box you see when you start a new presentation in PowerPoint.

You can add one of these Slide Layout formats to a PowerPoint slide at any time.

Slide Color Scheme...

When you choose the **Slide Color Scheme...** command, PowerPoint displays the tabbed Slide Color Scheme dialog box shown in Figure B.48.

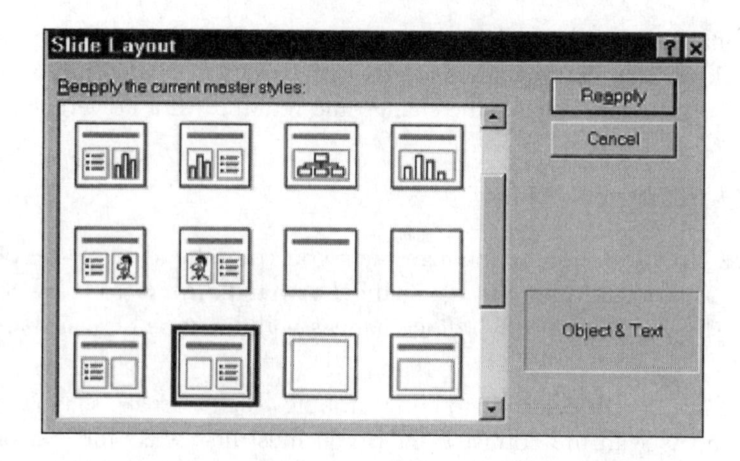

Figure B.47 *PowerPoint Slide Layout dialog box.*

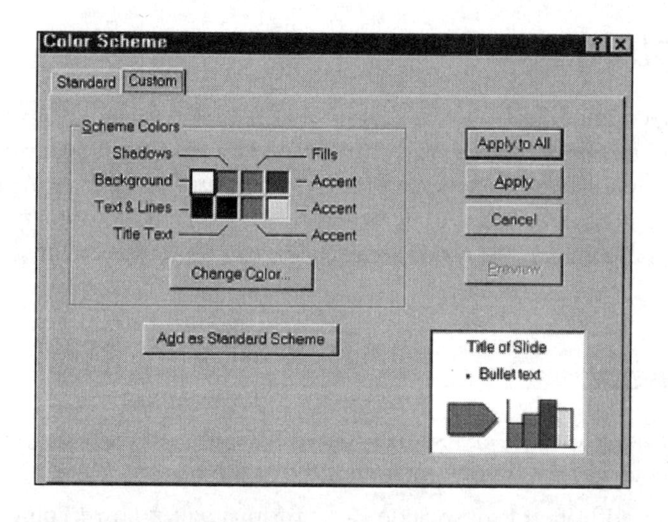

Figure B.48 *Slide Color Scheme dialog box with Custom tab.*

Two tabs are available: Standard and Custom. Notice from the Custom tab that you can specify individual colors for shadows, background, fills, and more. When you double-click on one of these color boxes, you can change the defaults by selecting a new color from the Color dialog box. Figure B.49 shows the choices for the Standard tab, which gives you a choice among several standard color schemes for common screen objects.

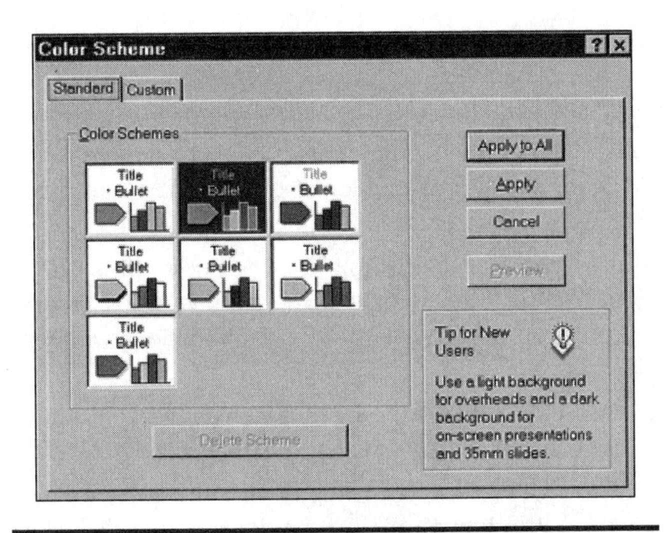

Figure B.49 *Slide Color Scheme dialog box with Standard tab.*

If you choose **Apply** from the Slide Color Scheme dialog box, the new color scheme is applied to the current slide. If you select **Apply to All**, then the new color scheme is applied to all slides in the presentation.

Custom Background...

The default PowerPoint slide background is white. However, you can choose a new background at any time by displaying the Custom Background dialog box, shown in Figure B.50.

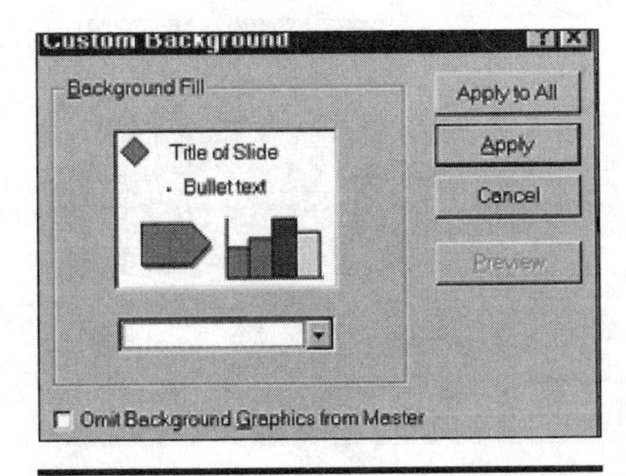

Figure B.50 *Custom Background dialog box.*

The check box at the lower-left corner of this dialog box determines whether or not objects from the Master view will be displayed on the slides. If you disable this feature, then date and time data, for example, won't be displayed on your slide.

Use the pull-down list below the sample screen to present a display of available color backgrounds. Click on a color box to select the background color you want and to change the display in the sample window.

You can also specify shading from this pull-down list. Click on different shade styles and patterns to view the variants on this dialog box. Separate pop-up dialog boxes let you choose from the available options within each category on this pull-down list.

You can adjust the relative intensity of the shading by clicking on the **Dark** or **Light** buttons. You can display a dialog box of available colors by clicking on the **Other Color...** button on this dialog box.

Finally, click on **Preview** on the Custom Background dialog box to look at the changes you have made. Choose **Apply** to place the chosen background and other formatting onto the current slide. Choose **Apply to All** to apply the changes you made on this dialog box to all slides in the presentation.

Apply Design Template...

The **Apply Design Template** command displays the Apply Design Template dialog box shown in Figure B.51.

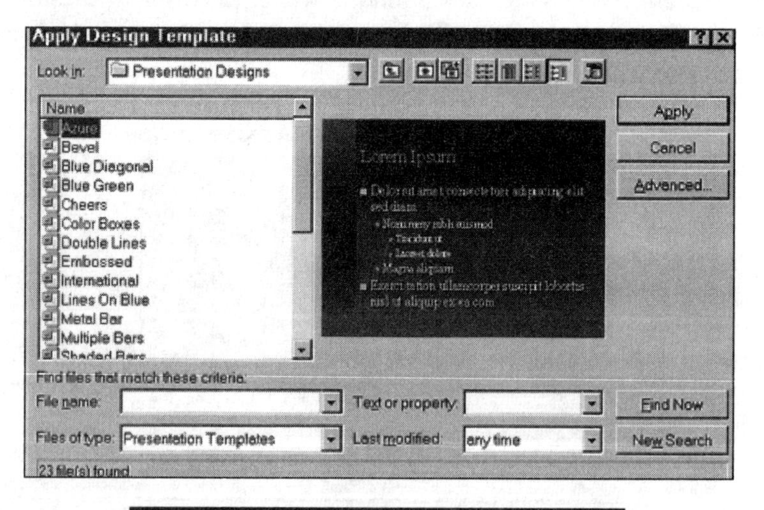

Figure B.51 *Apply Design Template dialog box.*

As I described in Chapter 4, you can choose from among a number of PowerPoint templates to set the mood and color scheme of your presentations. Template files are stored with the **.pot** extension and by default are placed in the `\msoffice\templates\presentation designs` directory. Select the template you want for the current presentation from the list on this dialog box.

The Tools Menu

The Tools menu presents a number of utility features that help you fine-tune, format, or spell check your PowerPoint presentations. The basic Tools choices are shown in Figure B.52.

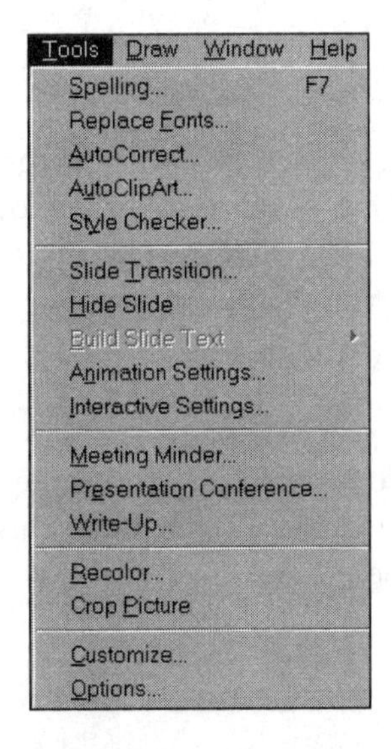

Figure B.52 *Tools menu.*

Spelling... F7

The **Spelling...** selection displays the PowerPoint Spelling dialog box, shown in Figure B.53.

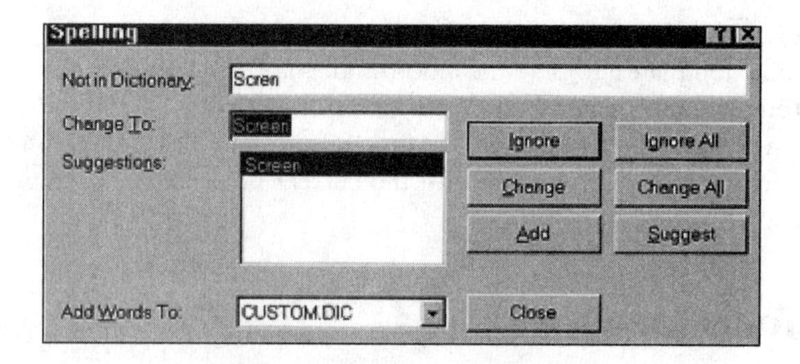

Figure B.53 *Spelling dialog box.*

When you launch the Spelling routine, PowerPoint starts scanning your presentation with the current slide, looking for any misspelled words. When a word that isn't in the PowerPoint dictionary is found, the speller notes this and suggests other words or asks for input from you.

If you click on **Ignore**, the selected word is ignored once. If you click on **Ignore All**, then that spelling is ignored throughout the document. You can accept PowerPoint's suggested spelling by clicking on **Change**, or you can add the selected word to your own custom dictionary by clicking on **Add**.

Replace Fonts...

The Replace Fonts dialog box lets you search the current presentation for a specified font and replace it with another one. This way you can change the overall look of a presentation.

AutoCorrect...

The AutoCorrect feature is a utility that first showed up in Microsoft Word 6, and it has now moved to other Office products. It lets you anticipate how you might make mistakes during typing so that the program can correct errors for you automatically, on the fly. When you select the **AutoCorrect** menu item from the Tools menu, the dialog box in Figure B.54 is displayed.

From this screen you can add or edit the AutoCorrect entries. As you can see, you simply specify how you want PowerPoint to handle each occurrence of a specific string of characters. Some terms are already in the list; you can change them or add to them as you wish. This feature is useful not only to help you correct typing mistakes (*teh* instead of *the*, for example), but it also helps you insert special characters, symbols, and so on.

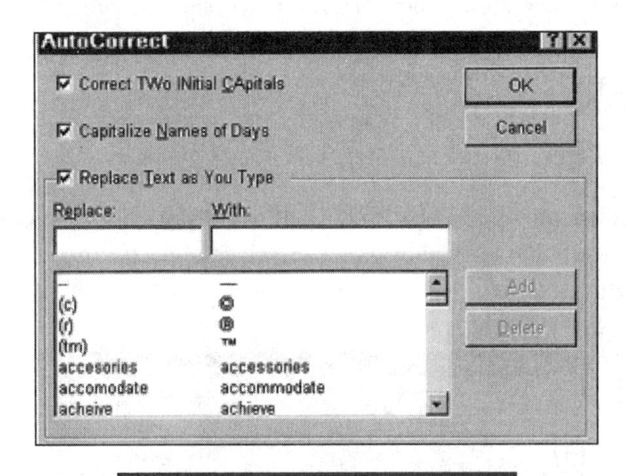

Figure B.54 *AutoCorrect dialog box.*

AutoClipArt...

AutoClipArt is another of PowerPoint's Wizards. It can scan your presentation and suggest clip art from the ClipArt Gallery based on the content of the slides. This program searches for key terms, looks for corresponding information in the Gallery, and suggests art for each slide.

To use this facility, open the presentation for which you want to choose clip art, then issue the command. You are presented with the dialog box shown in Figure B.55.

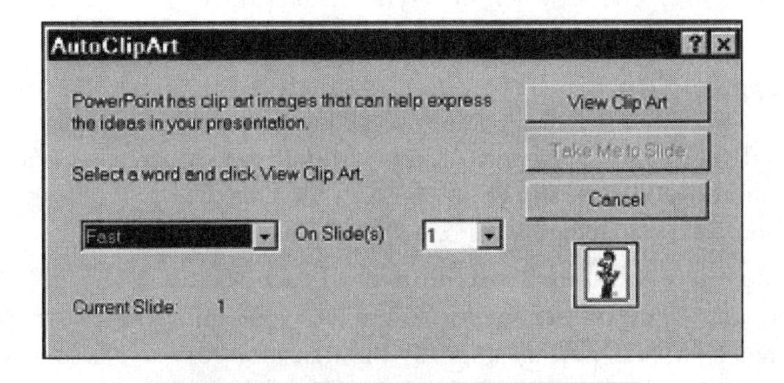

Figure B.55 *Initial AutoClipArt dialog box.*

Specify the word or phrase from the first slide for which you want to choose art. When you click on **View Clip Art**, the Wizard opens the ClipArt Gallery and presents the suggested slide. Click on **Insert** to place the image onto the current slide near the word with which it is associated. Click on **Take Me to Slide** to change which slide is being reviewed.

Style Checker...

The Style Checker utility is a way to have PowerPoint check for common design or implementation flaws: spelling, visual clarity, case, and end punctuation errors (see Figure B.56).

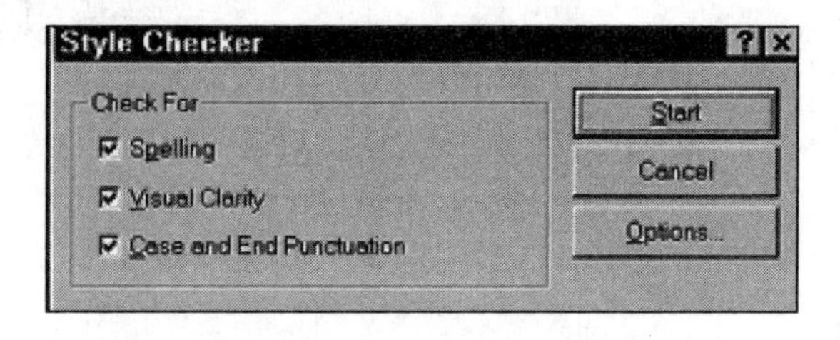

Figure B.56 *Style Checker Opening dialog box.*

Select one or more of the options on the initial Style Checker dialog box and click on **OK**. PowerPoint scans the current application, reports any errors, and suggests changes.

Use **Options...** from this first dialog box to display the Options dialog box, shown in Figure B.57. From this screen you can tell PowerPoint how to handle the various items it checks when the Style Checker runs.

Slide Transition...

I discussed transitions in Chapter 5. The **Slide Transition** command displays the Transition dialog box, shown in Figure B.58. This dialog box lets you decide how PowerPoint will change from one slide to the next.

If you specify **Random Transition**, then each slide will change with a different pattern. If you pull down the Effect list, you can specify how each slide will change. Note that you must specify the transition for each slide in your presentation. By default, PowerPoint changes slides with a straight cut.

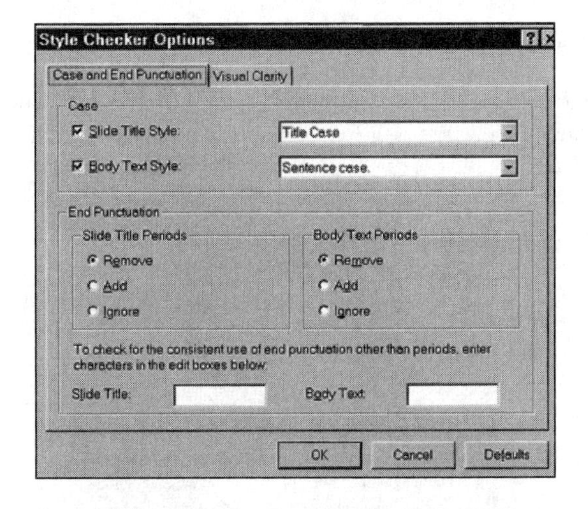

Figure B.57 *Options dialog box from Style Checker.*

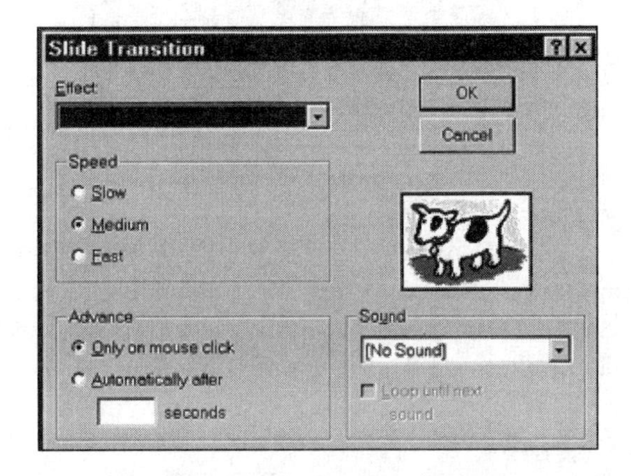

Figure B.58 *Transition dialog box.*

Hide Slide

Use **Hide Slide** to suppress the display of the current slide during a slide show presentation. If you click on this choice, a check mark appears beside the menu choice but you won't see any change on the Slide display. When you start a slide show (**View: Slide Show**), any slide for which **Hide Slide** is specified won't be displayed. You can reverse this setting at any time by clicking on **Hide Slide** again.

Build Slide Text

Build slides, or *Progressive Disclosure slides*, display text one line at a time. You have some control over the build process through the Build menu, shown in Figure B.59.

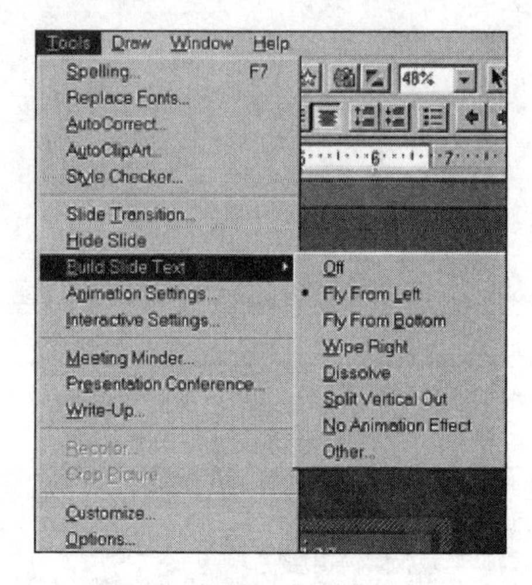

Figure B.59 *Build menu.*

Choose the type of build from this menu to tell PowerPoint how to display each body text element. If you click on **Other**, the animation effects dialog box is displayed. From here, you can choose the build level, specify reverse order, and specify other build options.

Animation Settings...

The Animation Settings dialog box helps you create Build (Progressive Disclosure) slides. First select the text on the slide you want to display progressively; then issue the **Tools: Animation Settings...** command to display the dialog box shown in Figure B.60.

The default on this dialog box is **Build** (or choose **Other** from the Build Slide Text... menu). Use the pull-down list to the right of the Build Options field to view a list of options. The makeup of this list changes with the type of text you have selected on the current slide. For the sample shown in Figure B.61, the slide consists of a title and a five-item bullet list.

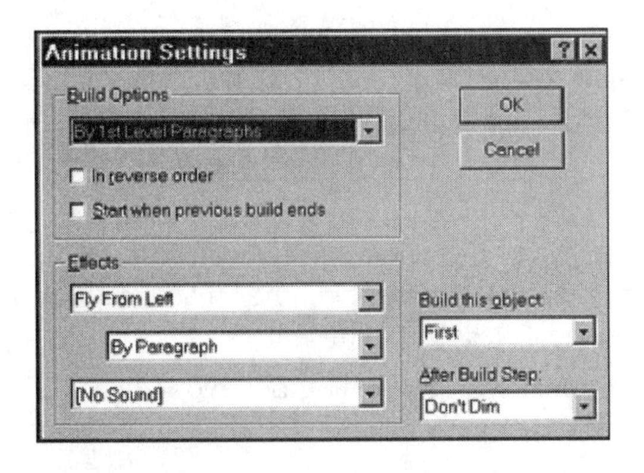

Figure B.60 *Initial Animation Settings dialog box.*

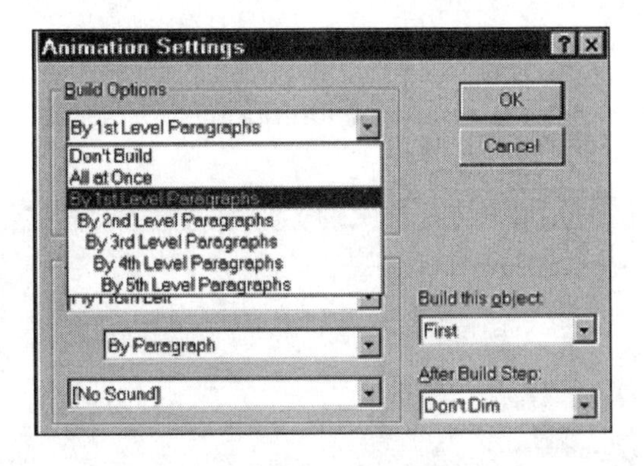

Figure B.61 *Animation Settings dialog box with pull-down list.*

If you choose **All at Once**, all of the selected text will move onto the slide (build) at one time. Use this choice to move blocks of text onto the screen. If you choose one of the other options, such as **By 1st Level Paragraphs**, you can create a slide that builds step by step, moving new data onto the screen with each click of the mouse. Suppose each main bullet has two subtopics under it. If you specify **By 1st Level Paragraphs**, then three lines of text come onto the slide at once. If you specify **By 2nd Level Paragraphs**, then the second and third lines come on together, and the first level comes next. If you choose **By 3rd Level Paragraphs**, then it will take three movements to get all three lines onto the screen, and so on.

At the bottom of the dialog box are options for the way the information will be presented. You can choose **Fly from Left**, **Fly from Right**, etc., from the pull-down list. In addition, you can specify whether the data will enter the slide a paragraph at a time, a word at a time, or a character at a time. In combination, these settings give you a lot of flexibility in how progressive information will be presented.

You can select what kind of sound will accompany each new block of text as it appears on the slide, and what will happen to previous text. It usually is good practice to dim previous text to help the audience focus on the new material while still having the older data to review.

The changes you make on this dialog box won't become effective until you switch to Slide Show view.

Interactive Settings...

The Interactive Settings dialog box, shown in Figure B.62, lets you specify what happens when you click the mouse button during a presentation.

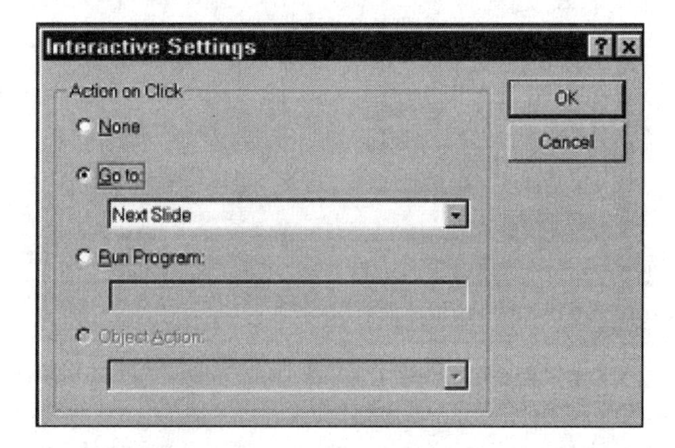

Figure B.62 *Interactive Settings dialog box.*

Normally, when you are in Slide Show view and you click the left mouse button, the next slide is displayed. With this dialog box you can change this default and force a jump to any slide in the presentation; you can even have PowerPoint launch another program. By programming individual slides for special behavior with this dialog box, you can highly customize a presentation. Figure B.63 shows this same dialog box with the pull-down action list.

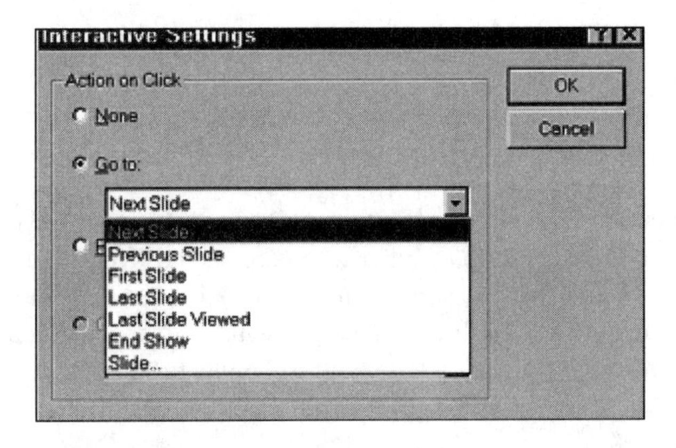

Figure B.63 *Interactive Settings dialog box with pull-down list.*

Meeting Minder...

The Meeting Minder lets you add comments, reminders, or other information to a slide during a presentation. You can select the dialog box shown in Figure B.64 from the pull-down list that is displayed when you press the right mouse button during a presentation. Or, you can use this menu item to type information about a slide prior to a presentation or after it is over.

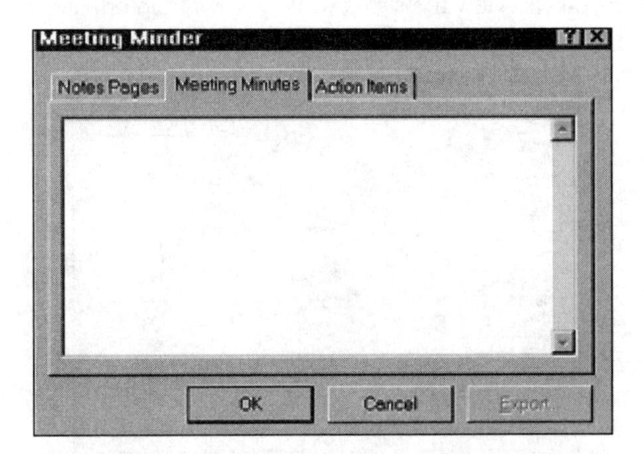

Figure B.64 *Meeting Minder dialog box.*

This is a three-tabbed dialog box that lets you enter notes, minutes of a meeting, or action items (a to do list) associated with each slide. Minutes and action items, particularly, can be enhanced when you have the slide to help you remember precisely what was decided at a meeting or what you are supposed to do later.

Presentation Conference...

This menu item launches another PowerPoint Wizard. It will help you participate in a presentation with a group of other users connected over a network. Answer the questions on the Wizard screens to choose the PowerPoint presentation tools you will use, to establish a connection with one or more remote sites, to load the presentation you want to use, and to conduct the show.

Write-Up...

The Write-Up facility helps you configure a PowerPoint document for insertion into Microsoft Word so that you can work on outlines, notes, and audience handouts in Word instead of PowerPoint. As long as your notes and other write-ups are fairly simple, you might as well use PowerPoint. If you want to get more involved and use special fonts and other text formatting, then Word is a better choice.

Use the dialog box shown in Figure B.65 to configure the Write-Up, then click on **OK** to launch Word with the preliminary information from PowerPoint already inserted. Copies of the slides in the current presentation are inserted into a new Word document where you can view the slides while you write information about them.

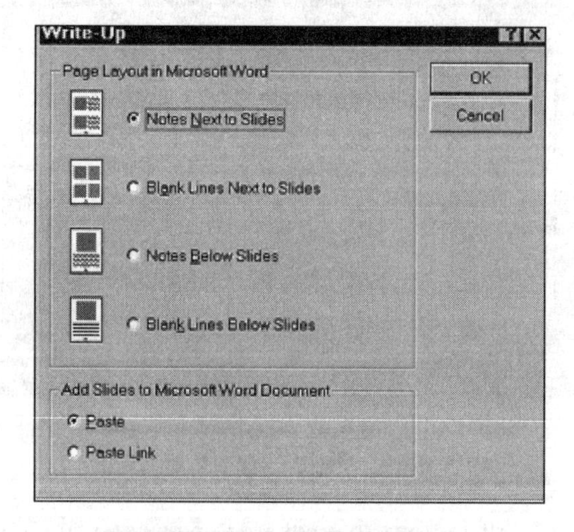

Figure B.65 *Write-Up dialog box.*

Recolor...

Use the **Recolor...** command to change colors for existing PowerPoint objects. This command displays different Recolor dialog boxes depending on the type of object (see Figure B.66 for an example).

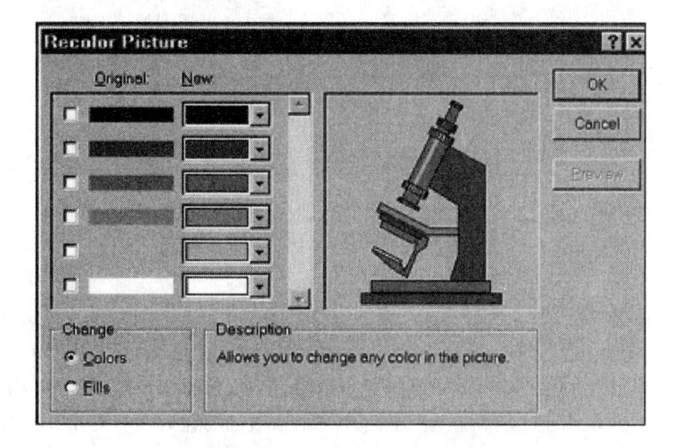

Figure B.66 *Recolor dialog box.*

The colors that make up the selected object are shown in the Original area of the dialog box. You can specify different colors for each of the original colors by pulling down a color list for each New color. If the range of colors you get with the pull-down list isn't enough, click on **Other Color** to display the Other Color dialog box, which offers a number of new colors for each shade in the selected object.

Crop Picture

To use this command, select a picture on a PowerPoint slide, then issue the **Crop Picture** command. The PowerPoint mouse pointer changes to a small square. Move the square onto one of the sizing handles on the selected picture. Hold down the left mouse button and drag the picture border to the new size you want.

Customize...

The Customize Toolbars dialog box, shown in Figure B.67, lets you add new icons to any displayed toolbar, remove existing icons, or move any icons to new locations.

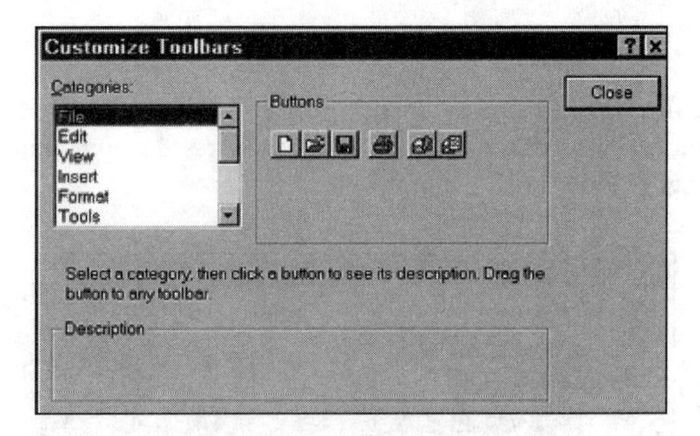

Figure B.67 *Customize Toolbars dialog box.*

Use this dialog box by first selecting the category of commands or macros you want to add, then choosing an icon from the Buttons area of the dialog box. You can drag a button to a toolbar. While the Customize Toolbars dialog box is displayed, you can drag any icon already on a toolbar to a new location, or you can drag an icon completely off of a toolbar.

Options...

The Options dialog box, shown in Figure B.68, lets you specify a number of operational options for PowerPoint.

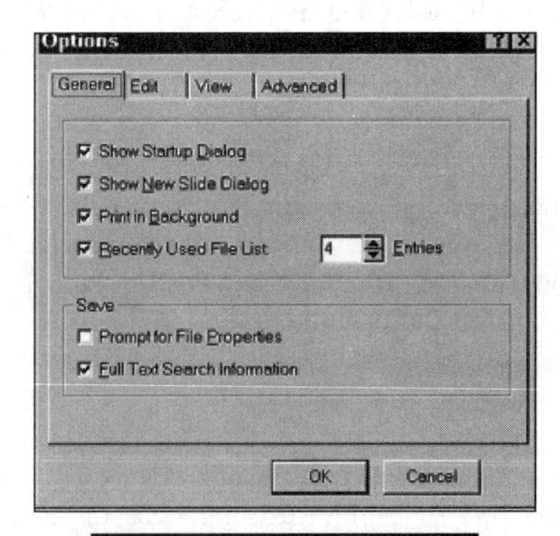

Figure B.68 *Options dialog box.*

Each of the choices on this dialog box is a toggle. If a check mark appears in the box beside an entry, then that entry is enabled. Remove the check mark by clicking on it. Click on a disabled option to place a check mark in the box and enable that option.

The Draw Menu

Use the Draw menu to manipulate various aspects of drawing objects within your PowerPoint presentation. As you can see from the menu in Figure B.69, some Draw menu items will not be available at times, depending on what types of objects are on your presentation slides and whether or not you have selected one of these objects.

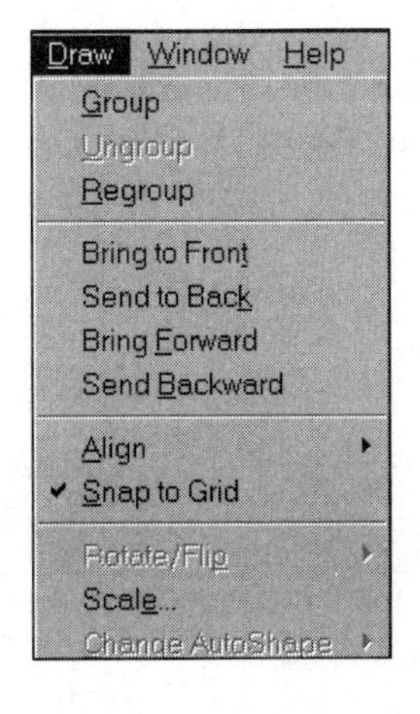

Figure B.69 *Draw menu.*

Group

You can group separate PowerPoint objects into a single graphic that you can move or edit as one. Hold down the **Shift** key as you click on individual components to select objects in a series. Then use **Draw: Group** to put them together.

Ungroup

Many PowerPoint graphics objects are made up of collections of smaller objects that are grouped together into one. After you select a graphic on a PowerPoint slide, you can ungroup the object to separate it into individual components. This lets you edit these components separately.

Regroup

Use **Regroup** to reverse an **Ungroup** command. Simply select one of the objects that formed part of the original group and use the **Regroup** command to put the individual components back together.

Bring to Front

Many PowerPoint objects consist of several objects, some layered on top of others. You can use the **Bring to Front** command to control which object is most prominent. The **Bring to Front** command moves a selected object to the top of a stack of objects.

Send to Back

This is the reverse of the **Bring to Front** command. When you choose **Send to Back**, the selected object is sent to the bottom of a stack of objects.

Bring Forward

This command, along with the **Send Backward** command, moves objects in a stack one layer or level at a time. This is different from the **Bring to Front** command in that the selected object is moved only one level at a time instead of being moved to the front or top of the stack.

Send Backward

The **Send Backward** command is the opposite of the **Bring Forward** command. It sends the selected object back in the stack one level.

Align

The **Align** command helps you line up a group of objects along certain borders, such as the left, right, or top borders. To align objects, first select the objects you want to align, then choose the **Draw: Align** command. This displays the Align pop-up menu shown in Figure B.70.

Figure B.70 *Draw Align pop-up menu.*

Choose the type of alignment you want from the pop-up menu.

Snap to Grid

Each PowerPoint slide is crisscrossed by an invisible grid of lines that can help you keep individual objects aligned. By default, PowerPoint is set up to snap objects to the invisible grid. You can't see the grid, but you can see the effects of it as you move graphics objects around the screen. When you drop an object you are moving, it will snap to the nearest grid line.

If you want to have more precise control over the placement of PowerPoint objects, use the **Draw: Snap to Grid** command to turn off the automatic Snap to Grid feature. You can tell whether this feature is enabled by a check mark beside the menu entry. A check mark means it is enabled; no check mark means it has been disabled.

Rotate/Flip

Select a PowerPoint object, then use **Draw: Rotate/Flip** to display the additional menu shown in Figure B.71.

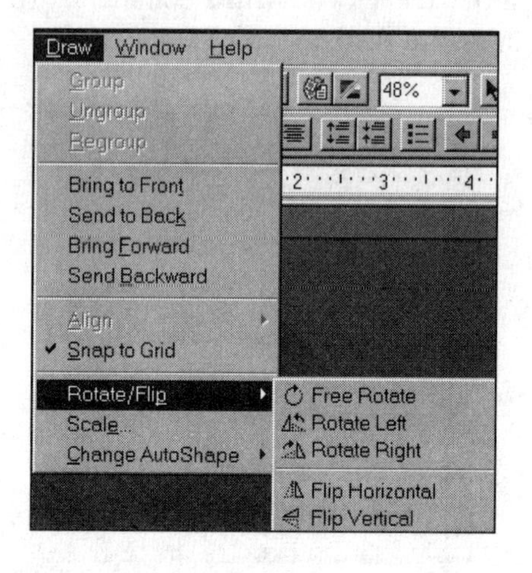

Figure B.71 *Rotate/Flip pull-down menu.*

In addition to left, right, horizontal, and vertical rotation, you can choose **Free Rotate** to display the selected object with rotation handles. Grab a handle to move the object around a center axis and rotate the object to the angle you want. Let go of the mouse button when the object is at the desired angle.

Scale...

After you select an object, you can choose **Scale** to display the Scale dialog box shown in Figure B.72.

The default scaling is 100% of the original object, as shown in the Scale To field of this dialog box Change the scaling by clicking on the up or down arrows to the right of this field or by selecting the field contents and typing a new value.

You can click on **Preview** to see how the new scaling will look without actually making the change. You can specify that the size changes be made relative to the original picture size or that the best scale for the slide show be chosen. When the values on this dialog box are set the way you want them, click on **OK** to close the dialog box and return to the slide display.

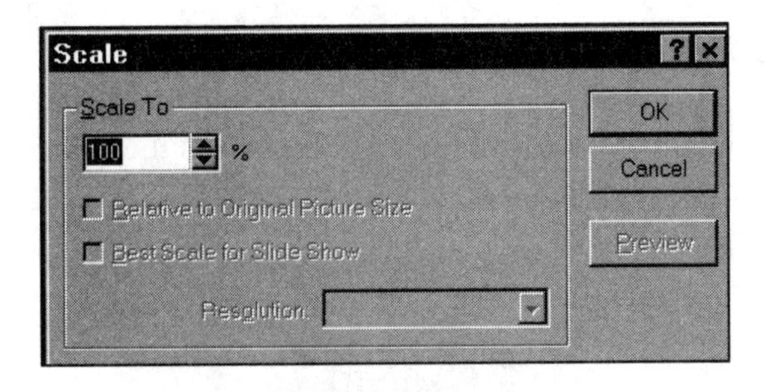

Figure B.72 Scale dialog box.

Change AutoShape

PowerPoint includes a facility that makes it easy to draw a number of geometric shapes. The AutoShapes feature is accessible from the Draw toolbar. Once you have drawn one or more AutoShapes, you may decide that you want to change the basic shape. You can do this with the **Change AutoShape** selection from the Draw menu.

To use this feature, first select an AutoShape object. Then use **Draw: Change AutoShape** to display the Change AutoShape dialog box shown in Figure B.73.

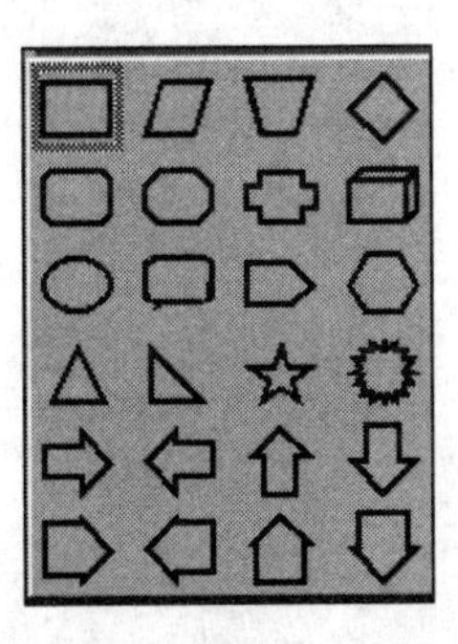

Figure B.73 Change AutoShape dialog box.

When you choose a shape, PowerPoint immediately changes the selected AutoShape to the new one.

The Window Menu

The PowerPoint Window menu is virtually the same as the Window menus of all Microsoft Windows applications (see Figure B.74).

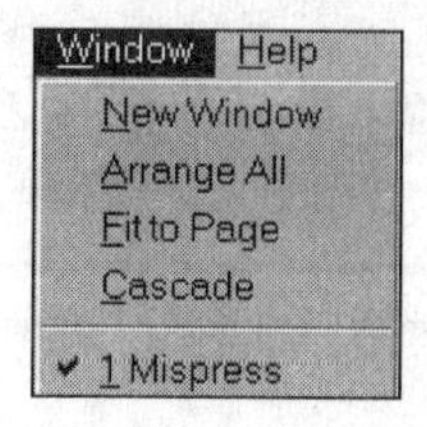

Figure B.74 *PowerPoint Window menu.*

This menu has four main components: Arrange All, Fit to Page, Cascade, and the open file list.

The **Arrange All** command displays all of the open files in memory like the sample display in Figure B.75.

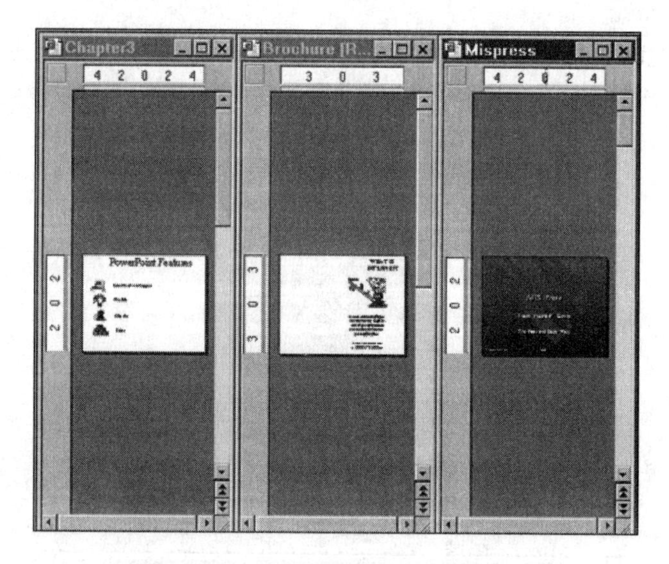

Figure B.75 *Sample Arrange All display.*

Use the **Fit to Page** selection from the Window menu to properly size the current presentation to the specified page size (determined by **File: Slide Setup...**).

The **Cascade** selection shrinks all of the open presentations and displays them like a stack of cards, as shown in Figure B.76.

Figure B.76 *Cascade format.*

You can select and enlarge any of the presentations on the Cascade display by clicking on the title bar of the presentation you want to enlarge and make it current.

The Help Menu

When you click on **Help**, PowerPoint displays the menu shown in Figure B.77.

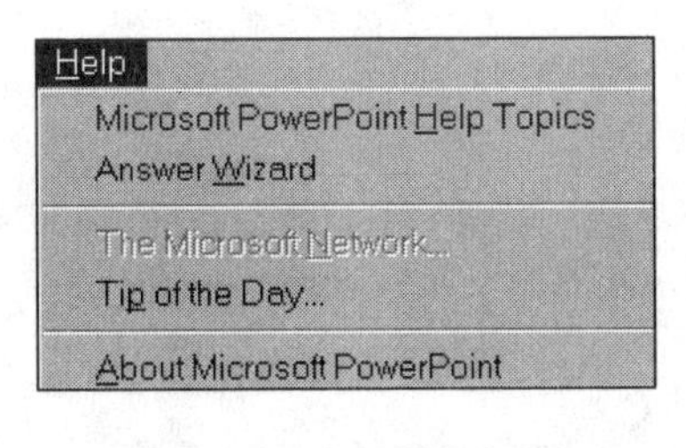

Figure B.77 *Main Help menu.*

For detailed information on using PowerPoint Help, refer to Chapter 9.

The About Microsoft PowerPoint window shows you what version of PowerPoint you are using and displays your product number (see Figure B.78).

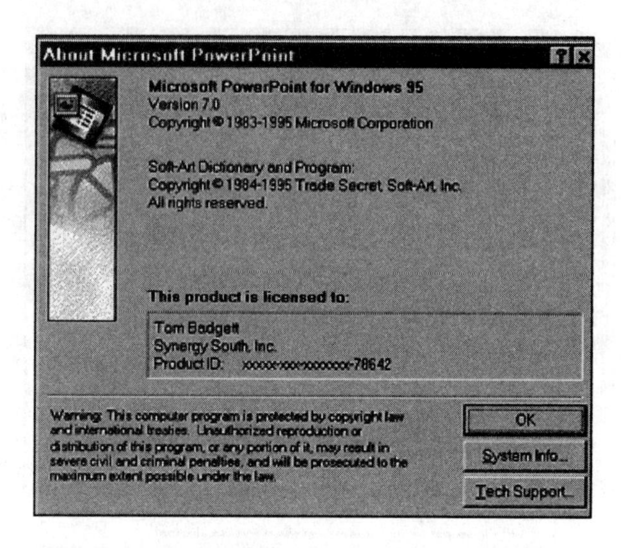

Figure B.78 *About Microsoft PowerPoint Window.*

Click on **System Info** to have PowerPoint display a summary of your computer configuration.

Glossary

1-2-3 — A popular spreadsheet software application from Lotus Development Corporation.

applets — Utility programs that are shipped with main software packages such as PowerPoint and other Microsoft products. Many applets, such as WordArt, are common to several Microsoft products and are installed only once, when the first package that includes the applet is installed.

application window — In Microsoft Windows, a separate window object that contains a running program. Also, a window object that contains icons that represent other software applications. These applications can be launched into their own application windows by choosing the icon.

aspect ratio — The relationship between an object's width and height. Different aspect ratios are common for different applications. A 35mm slide has a different ratio for pleasing appearance and fit than does an overhead projector foil, for example. You can restore a PowerPoint object's aspect ratio with the **Draw: Scale...** command.

AutoLayout A feature of Microsoft PowerPoint and other Office products that lets you choose table and slide layout automatically from predefined screens. To use AutoLayouts, click on the **New Slide** button, or use **Format: Slide Layout...**.

AutoShape A PowerPoint utility that lets you insert a number of predefined shapes such as arrow points, squares, and rectangles onto a slide. AutoShape tools are accessed through the AutoShapes toolbar. Point to an existing toolbar and click the right mouse button to display the toolbar menu, and then select **AutoShapes**.

backtab Backtab or reverse tab moves the insertion point to the left a standard tab width. This is the reverse of the standard tab key. Insert a backtab by pressing **Shift+Tab**.

brainstorming A creative process that can be used for planning and designing PowerPoint presentations. Brainstorming consists of stream-of-consciousness planning through repetitive lists in which a broad topic is narrowed to topics of smaller scope.

branching In computer programming or PowerPoint presentations, the ability of a program to go directly from one program module or slide to another, based on some decision process. Presenters frequently design PowerPoint presentations with built-in branching to allow for different audience skill levels or reactions to the standard material.

bullet list A succinct list of information set off by relatively large dots or other symbols called bullets. A bullet list is useful in summarizing data for an audience.

cascade A computer screen design that stacks several programs or program components one on top of the other with slight offsets, like a deck of cards fanned out. A cascade arrangement usually lets you see a title line or other distinguishing feature of each screen object so you can access any object you wish.

click — In using a computer mouse, the process of pointing to or selecting a specific screen object. A click is a single, rapid depression of one of the mouse buttons (usually the left one unless specified otherwise). See also **double-click**.

clip art — Relatively simple drawings that can be inserted into a PowerPoint presentation. PowerPoint is supplied with hundreds of clip art images. Third-party companies also sell clip art collections in a variety of file formats that you can use with PowerPoint and other applications.

ClipArt Gallery — A PowerPoint utility that makes finding and choosing clip art images fast and easy.

Clipboard — A section of temporary memory in Windows-compliant applications where objects can be stored during copy and paste operations.

context-sensitive help — An electronic Help system that provides information about specific software operations. Context-sensitive help displays specific Help messages that relate to the current software operation, rather than displaying a general Help message or requiring you to step through menus or search for specific information.

Control menu — In Microsoft Windows, a menu common to all window objects that lets you close the current window, move the window, size it, or switch to another running application. The control menu is represented by a short horizontal bar at the upper left corner of all window objects.

Control Panel — In Microsoft Windows, a system utility that lets you set up the operation of various Windows components, including the printer, screen colors, and networking. The Control Panel icon is located in the Main application window or off the **Start: Settings** flyout.

copy — The process of making a duplicate of an object within PowerPoint or another application. In Windows-compliant applications, the copy process usually involves placing a duplicate image onto the

Clipboard, then copying it from the Clipboard to the new location.

cross-hair
A graphics tool designed to help with object design or placement. In PowerPoint, cross-hairs are used for precise placement or alignment of objects. The **View: Guides** command displays a large cross-hair, for example.

cut
The process of removing a selected object from a document or display. A cut is frequently used in Windows-compliant applications to move the object to a new location. The selected object is removed from its present location and placed onto the Clipboard. Then it is copied from the Clipboard into a new location.

desktop
In Windows applications, the basic user interface in which most operations are conducted. The desktop generally consists of an editing area, a set of menus, toolbars, and so on. Individual documents or objects can be loaded onto the desktop for manipulation.

dialog box
In Windows, a pop-up object that either presents information to the user or asks the user for information.

directory
A logical disk structure used to associate or group information on a computer. Sometimes called subdirectory when it is subordinate to another directory.

dissolve
The process of changing from one display to another by fading out the first display and fading in the second. Dissolves can be used as transitions between PowerPoint slides during a presentation.

DOS
Disk Operating System. Each computer design has its own disk operating system. Most operating systems have a name, such as UNIX, VMS, and so on. In Windows 95, the original PC DOS is emulated to provide a command-line interface.

DOS prompt
The disk operating system prompt, a character or characters that tells the user that the operating system is waiting for input.

double-click The process of choosing a Windows object by pointing to the object and then pressing the left mouse button twice in quick succession. A single click usually selects an object, and a double-click chooses it or causes it to carry out its intended operation.

drag The process of moving an on-screen object by grabbing it with the mouse pointer and dragging it from one location to another.

driver A software program that enables a specific piece of hardware or sometimes another software application to function properly. The most common types of drivers are printer drivers, which help an application send the proper codes and formatting instructions to a specific printer.

drop shadow A graphics device for offsetting a portion of an object and making it appear that it is casting a shadow. Useful with lettering, borders, and other objects to provide the illusion of depth.

equation editor An applet within other applications that lets you enter mathematical equations and, in some cases, calculate them. An equation editor usually serves as an adjunct to other mainstream applications such as a word processor or presentation products such as PowerPoint.

Excel Microsoft Excel is a spreadsheet application that is popular for conducting "what if," bookkeeping, and financial projection operations.

fade A process for removing an on-screen object by causing it to get progressively darker until it disappears. Fades can be used as a transition between PowerPoint slides during a presentation.

flow chart A series of boxes connected by lines that shows the progression of an activity or that shows relationships among various people or projects within a company.

font A collection of typefaces in a certain style.

Format bar A specialized toolbar in PowerPoint and other Microsoft applications that displays current font information as well as details about other text formatting. The Format bar also can be used to set font attributes through drop-down list boxes and buttons.

FORTRAN A high-level computer programming language, rarely used with microcomputers but once very popular in the development of engineering or other technical applications on minicomputers and mainframes.

graphical user interface (GUI) A computer interface, such as Microsoft Windows, that shows the user graphically how to conduct applications and system-level operations.

handles Protrusions around the perimeter of graphics objects that can be used to move or size the object. Handles make it easier to grab an object's border for sizing or moving.

handouts In PowerPoint, printed sheets based on a presentation that are designed to be handed out to the audience during or after a presentation. Handout sheets contain one or more of the presentation's slides and perhaps some descriptive text.

hot key A key or keystroke combination designed to invoke a software application, applet, or utility. A hot key bypasses the usual menu or mouse access methods to make utility or feature access faster and easier for experienced users.

I-beam The insertion point in Windows-based applications. Usually used to indicate where text will be typed.

icon A simple picture used to represent an application, applet, or utility in a Windows environment.

interactive presentation A presentation that can take input from a user and change the direction of the presentation based on user input.

landscape Page or screen orientation in which the longest part of an image or text is oriented left to right, instead of top to bottom like a standard business letter. See also **portrait**.

layout The process of designing a screen, slide, or printed page. Layout includes margin descriptions, object placement, attributes, and other display or print characteristics.

live links — A process for creating a continuous relationship between a PowerPoint object and the application that created it. When an object that is part of a live link is modified within its host application, the copy of it on a PowerPoint slide changes automatically to reflect that modification.

LPT1 — Shorthand for the main printer port on an MS-DOS computer.

Menu bar — A colored, (usually) horizontal bar that holds the main menu items for a computer program. In PowerPoint, the main menu bar is located beneath the title bar and above the Standard toolbar.

Microsoft Graph — A Microsoft applet that is used in PowerPoint and other applications to create graphs from rows and columns of numbers.

Microsoft Office — A collection of Microsoft software applications that includes PowerPoint, Word, Excel, Mail, and Access.

mouse — A data input and pointing device used to select screen objects within a graphical user interface such as Microsoft Windows.

mouse pointer — The small graphics character—usually an arrow—that represents the current position on the graphics screen of the mouse input device. The pointer is used to select objects in conjunction with the left mouse button.

MSAPPS — The subdirectory where Microsoft stores its common applets such as WordArt, Chart, and so on. This subdirectory usually is located within the Windows directory.

object — Anything displayed on a graphical user interface screen. Objects can consist of text, graphics, pictures, clip art, or a combination of items.

Object Linking and Embedding — Microsoft's term for the ability to embed or link objects from one application into the files of another application.

OLE — See **Object Linking and Embedding**.

OLE 2.0 — Microsoft's second version of Object Linking and Embedding. OLE 2.0 includes the ability to do in-place editing, in which the source application is launched in the background but you edit its objects from within the target application.

OrgChart — A Microsoft applet that helps you create organization chart objects for inclusion in PowerPoint or other applications.

Outline toolbar — A special toolbar with buttons and icons that is displayed when you enter an Outline view.

paste — The process of copying information stored on the Clipboard into a new file or document or to a new location in the same file or document.

point — The process of moving the mouse pointer over or near an on-screen object prior to selecting or choosing it.

port — A physical or logical doorway to attach a computer system to another computer, a printer, an input device, or a software application.

portrait — A page or screen orientation that places the longest portion of the page or screen in an up-and-down orientation like a standard business letter. See also **landscape**.

PostScript — A printer control language frequently used for printing complex graphics or text. To use PostScript output, your printer must be designed with a PostScript language interpreter.

Print Manager — In Microsoft Windows, a software utility that manages the printer output from one or more software applications. The Print Manager queues information designated for the printer, manages conflicts, and spools output to disk to free up printing applications more quickly. See also **print spooler**.

print spooler — A software or hardware device that accepts software output intended for a printer and stores it temporarily on disk or in RAM memory. A print spooler frees up the printing application more quickly than printing directly to a printer, because memory and the hard disk work more quickly than the printer. Most print spoolers also manage output from more than one printing application at a time. See also **Print Manager**.

Program Manager In Microsoft Windows 3.1 and below, the main user interface software that contains application windows and icons. The Program Manager launches programs, displays program icons, and otherwise provides the user a graphical interface into the computer system.

Report It In PowerPoint, a facility for automatically launching Microsoft Word and inserting the current presentation outline. The outline can be edited or enhanced before sending it back to PowerPoint.

resizing The process of reshaping or changing the size of on-screen objects. Resizing usually is done by grabbing a sizing handle and dragging an object border to a new size.

Restore button In Microsoft Windows 3.1, an icon at the upper-right corner of most window objects that enlarges the window after it has been reduced.

Rich Text Format A document format frequently used to transfer text files among different word processing or text editing programs. The RTF format can transfer many text attributes such us bold and italics, even among incompatible programs.

routing slip In Microsoft Mail, a software attachment that tells the mail program where to send the current document and in what order. The **File: Add Routing Slip...** command lets you add a routing slip attachment to a PowerPoint document.

RTF See **Rich Text Format**.

sans serif Type without serifs (the accenting protrusions on some characters). Sans serif type is plain and clean, and is good for titles and headings. However, serif type is better for body text. See also **serif**.

scroll bars In Windows, horizontal and vertical objects with arrows that let you move the contents of a display screen up and down or left and right.

serif The small accenting protrusions on some typefaces, designed to add emphasis and make text easier to read. See also **sans serif**.

shadowed text Text that is formatted with a background or side shadow.

slide shows In PowerPoint, a method of displaying a presentation as sequential on-screen slides or as graphics slides converted to 35mm film.

Slide Sorter In PowerPoint, a view that displays several slides from the current presentation on the same screen. Use **View: Slide Sorter** to access this view.

slides Graphics in PowerPoint used as individual elements of a presentation.

Speaker's Notes view In PowerPoint, a view that includes a slide and room beneath it to type notes about the slide or the topics it covers. These notes can be used to help you remember major topics you want to mention in conjunction with each slide.

spreadsheet A software application designed to make projections, mathematical analysis, and "what if" computations easy. See also **Excel**.

storyboard In PowerPoint or other graphics-oriented applications, small sequential drawings of a presentation that show how the presentation will be designed. Storyboards usually are temporary devices used during the design of a slide show or other visual presentation, including motion pictures.

straight cuts In PowerPoint, a straight transition between two slides that does not include any special effects such as fades or dissolves.

subdirectory See **directory**.

submenu A menu subordinate to a main menu entry. A submenu is displayed when you choose a main menu item that has additional choices under it.

template A computer file that is used as a guide or form for designing additional files. In PowerPoint, template files are provided to give your slides creative and colorful backgrounds and graphics characters. You can start with a template and design your own presentation to produce professional results.

Text tool In a graphics program such as PowerPoint, an icon that represents a character or text application. To use a text tool you usually select it from a toolbar or icon. Then you place it within a graphics object where you want to apply text, and you type text from the keyboard.

Tip of the Day In PowerPoint and other Microsoft Office applications, a random pop-up Help dialog box that presents tips on how to conduct various software applications.

title bar In Microsoft Windows, the topmost horizontal bar of a window object that carries the name of the object or application.

toolbar buttons Small icons that reside together on a toolbar and that represent software utilities or applets. You launch the feature represented by the button by clicking on the button. Toolbar buttons frequently represent commands or features that are also available from a standard menu.

toolbars Collections of icons that represent software utilities or features.

ToolTips In Microsoft Office applications, a feature that displays the function of an on-screen object when the mouse pointer is moved over the object. This feature helps users understand the function of software buttons and icons.

transition A technique for switching between two PowerPoint slides by placing a special effect on the screen between the slides. See also **Fade**, **Dissolve**, **Wipe**.

TrueType A Microsoft Windows scalable font technology that maximizes the probability that on-screen text will appear precisely as printed text. TrueType is an outline font technology used by Apple and Microsoft. It does not necessarily produce WYSIWYG (What You See Is What You Get) displays, but that is the goal, and it is close to WYSIWYG.

user interface A method of communication between a computer and computer user that enables the user to respond to an application's request for data. Microsoft Windows is a graphical user interface. Other interfaces use straight menus or command prompts (like MS-DOS, for example).

Windows for Workgroups An implementation of Microsoft Windows that includes networking and mail components. It is a system of computers, each running Windows for Workgroups and connected by standard Ethernet cable, that can function as a local area network.

wipe A transition technique for advancing from one PowerPoint slide to another.

Wizard A series of interactive screens in Microsoft applications that helps the user conduct a specific task.

WordArt A Microsoft applet that helps you format text as a graphics image. WordArt is used to build creative text titles for PowerPoint slides, word processing letterhead, and so on.

INDEX

C

D

E

F

G

H

I

P

T

U